AN INTRODUCTION TO LANDSCAPE ARCHITECTURE

SECOND EDITION

AN INTRODUCTION TO LANDSCAPE ARCHITECTURE

SECOND EDITION

MICHAEL LAURIE
Department of Landscape Architecture
University of California, Berkeley

Elsevier
New York • Amsterdam • Oxford

Elsevier Science Publishing Co., Inc.
52 Vanderbilt Avenue, New York, New York 10017

Sole distributors outside the United States and Canada:

Elsevier Applied Science Publishers Ltd.
Crown House, Linton Road, Barking, Essex IG11 8JU, England

Library of Congress Cataloging in Publication Data

Laurie, Michael.
An introduction to landscape architecture.

Bibliography: p.
Includes index.
1. Landscape architecture. I. Title.
SB472.L38 1986 712 85-7023
ISBN 0-444-00970-1

Current printing (last digit):
10 9 8 7 6 5 4 3 2 1

Manufactured in the United States of America

CONTENTS

PREFACE TO THE SECOND EDITION

This second edition retains its original format and objectives, but includes material, especially in the Garden History chapter, which was blatantly missing in the first edition. Secondly, I have attempted to include more on the subject of urban design, which has always been, and continues to be, a major activity of landscape architecture. Other additions reflect new concerns such as design for energy and resource conservation, community participation in the design process, and landscape evaluation for purposes of environmental impact assessment. These topics were only beginning to be major issues ten years ago but now are increasingly involved in professional practice. Further inserts and deletions are intended to clarify or modify in some way the original text. The modifications reflect changes in my thinking and particularly the fact that the text has found a large readership in the developing countries. Although I am flattered by this, I sense a responsibility not only to make clear the essential principles and concepts, but also to emphasize the fact that forms and solutions to design and environmental problems should and must respond to local conditions and not imitate those found elsewhere.

For North America, changes in the nature of practice have been predicted.[1] These are expected to result from a set of new factors including changes in the population structure (new major user groups such as the elderly and minorities) and diminishing resources (placing emphasis on coal extraction, with associated reclamation and environmental protection programs). Other likely new areas of involvement include waste management, urban forestry (as an interim solution to air pollution), and enhancement of wildlife habitat. Economic and political trends may create other new design problems such as higher density, energy efficient housing with smaller units, infilling of existing suburbs, rehabilitation and adaptation of outmoded urban structures, joint ventures between the public and private sectors in urban open space, historic preservation, new zoning ordinances to allow mixed use development, citizen involvement in planning and design, renewal of existing parks and concentration of new park and recreational facilities at the neighborhood level, and so on. To be effective in the electronic age, it is suggested that the landscape architect must be literate in computer applications, energy and resource conservation, politics, and business.

The key issues and trends for other societies will differ according to time and place. The mode of practice and the respective roles of the private and public sector in defining and carrying out plans and projects will depend on the political system adopted by any society. But the framework of landscape architecture, its concerns and potential, remain the same. Advances in technology and methodology improve the product, but without a clear sense of purpose and expression of values the work will lack authenticity. Values are a reflection of society and are not always easy to define. They are demonstrated through attitudes toward such issues as conservation and economy, social responsibility, aesthetics, history and, as Jellicoe has put it, "universal realities and a sense of human purpose in place and time."[2]

---

1. Marshall, Lane (ed.), *Landscape Architecture into the 21st Century*. A special task force report (Washington: American Society of Landscape Architects, 1982).

2. Jellicoe, Geoffrey, and Susan Jellicoe, *The Landscape of Man* (London: Thames and Hudson, 1975).

With an unpredictable future, professional definition is much less important than value informed problem solving skills within the broad realm of land and people. Environmental design is a concept in which buildings and land are seen as integrated elements. Their interface is neither architecture nor landscape architecture as traditionally defined. Urban design is a concept that also links the two disciplines, resulting in an approach which amounts to more than the sum of the two. In these ideas lie the seeds of change in traditional professional skills and responsibilities, with a much needed widening of project boundaries and the development of a synoptic view for designers and planners.

It is with this in mind that readers are cautioned to regard this text as a framework for action and problem solving, and not as an answer book.

Michael Laurie

PREFACE TO THE FIRST EDITION

This book consists of a series of essays on various aspects of landscape architecture as it has developed in recent years. We are now faced with new and challenging environmental problems of land use, conservation, landscape design, and planning. A rational approach to the solution of such problems draws upon the earth and biological sciences and the principles of conservation as well as the behavioral and social sciences. The health of the ecosystem and of the people is the basis on which concepts are developed.

The theoretical base I seek to establish is broad and applies at the scale of the region as well as that of the garden or courtyard and everything between. The central idea is a process which synthesizes ecological and social data relevant to the particular situation or task, resulting in either land use policy or detailed design form as the case may be. The interrelationship of the products is fundamental. Policies regarding the use of land at a regional level depend on a detailed understanding of criteria for various land uses and their impact on the land. Conversely, regional characteristics become determinants of form in house and garden design.

The "what" and the "why" as well as the "how" are integral parts of the theory. That is to say, program formulation is as important as the technology of construction and implementation. We cannot stand aside from value judgments nor can we ignore certain aspects of the problem because they are not specified in the client's brief or program. Our role in society must be positive, constructive, and informative, an advocacy for quality and long-term values. This book addresses itself to the fulfillment of that role.

The essays are short statements on different subjects and are introductions rather than comprehensive reviews. They draw on my personal knowledge and experience so that the examples or case studies are random but, I hope, meaningful. They also draw extensively on the varied but limited literature in landscape architecture and related fields. I have included an historical review because I believe it is helpful to see what we are doing today in the context of the past. It also helps us to appreciate the origins of forms and concepts and the development of ideas and attitudes which are part of our present consciousness. Many of the historical sketches are based on several sources in an attempt to portray the concepts. They are thus often combinations of the way the place looks today, the way it appeared in early prints and illustrations, and the way I think the designer intended it to look. I have not included a discussion of basic design principles, aesthetics, or graphic communication. That is not to suggest that they are unimportant, but rather that they are to some extent separate from a deterministic theory of form.

Inasmuch as the book is a general overview of the field of landscape architecture and its component disciplines, it is suitable as a text for an introductory course for students of landscape architecture and others in related fields with an interest in environmental design and planning.

ACKNOWLEDGMENTS

It is clearly impossible to acknowledge all the people who have contributed to the content and ideas set out in the book. The Bibliography represents most of them. I have been fortunate in the past 30 years in meeting or having the opportunity to listen to most of the distinguished landscape architects and many architects, planners, and environmentalists primarily in the United Kingdom and in North America, but including visitors from elsewhere. Others I have met while traveling in Europe, South America, and Asia. It is inevitable that they will find thoughts here which originated with them.

I wish to recognize specifically six people who have been very influential in the development of my concept of landscape architecture: my father, Ian M. Laurie, who introduced me at an early age to plants and planting, the nub of landscape architecture; Frank Clark, who taught me the importance of the interrelationship between disciplines and how the study of history made the present meaningful; Dame Sylvia Crowe, in whose office I had my first job and from whom I learned how to link design to philosophy and, among other values, what dedication was. My graduate studies in 1960–1962 were made possible by a generous Thouron Scholarship to the University of Pennsylvania. There, two great teachers, Professors Ian McHarg and Karl Linn, directed me toward the theory of this text. From Professor H. L. Vaughan at Berkeley, I learned much, including how to decide what was important and what was not, and then how to say it clearly.

In addition to these must be added my students at Berkeley, who in the last twenty years in more ways than they will ever know have challenged and inspired me. This is appropriate company with which to express my indebtedness to Lawrence J. Fricker, longstanding friend and critic, who read the manuscript for the first edition at an early stage and advised me on improvements. I take this opportunity also to acknowledge the encouragement of my colleagues in the Department of Landscape Architecture and the College of Environmental Design at Berkeley, who have helped me to come to grips with many of the issues in the book. My special thanks to Russell Beatty, who read the entire original draft and helped me considerably with the chapter on planting design, to Clare Cooper Marcus, to whom I am indebted for several ideas included in the chapter on social and psychological factors, and to Tom Brown, who provided film and literature references for Chapter 2. I also wish to thank Roger Osbaldeston for the additional musical notes he prepared for the same chapter.

I have received considerable assistance with photographs to illustrate the text. Specific acknowledgments are given for pictures that are not my own, but I particularly wish to thank William Garnett for kindly allowing me to use several of his fine aerial photographs, R. Burton Litton for several magnificent landscapes, Peter Kostrikin for taking, developing, and printing photographs specially for the book, Robert Sabbattini for permission to use his photographs published earlier in *Landmark '72*, Trinidad Juarez for specially taken photos, photographic work, and graphics, and Willfred Hoover for printing many of my photographs.

Further thanks are due to Professor Jot Carpenter, who read the manuscript and gave me helpful criticism and guidance, and especially to Robert Goodman who originated the idea of the book. I am also indebted to Ava Lydecker who typed early drafts of the manuscript, to Yee Sen Lee who prepared the original bibliography and to the many other individuals in agencies, libraries, universities, and private offices who are unfortunately too numerous to mention, but whose assistance is not forgotten.

In the preparation of the second edition, I am particularly indebted to Kim Wilkie for his careful reading of the text, subsequent criticism, recommendations, and bibliographic research. In addition, the comments received from students and teachers were most helpful.

I am also indebted to Professor Tadashi Kubo and faculty members at Osaka University for introducing me to the gardens of Kyoto and helping me to understand them. Thanks are also due to Professor Chen Congzhou of Tong ji University and to Dr. William Wu for their help in my understanding of the Chinese garden. And, once again, I must thank my colleague, Professor R. B. Litton, Jr., for his generous assistance in the area of landscape evaluation. Thanks also to an old friend, Joe Karr, for his contribution of the Oak Park case study in Chapter 7.

For technical assistance in preparing the revised manuscript, thanks are due to Martha Bergmann, who typed new sections and Robin Anderson, who helped to put it together.

A special debt of gratitude is due Regina Dahir for her outstanding work on the design of this edition and to Kathryn Silverio and Louise Gruendel of Elsevier for their editorial and production work.

My thanks to all who have helped in the production of the first and second editions of this book.

Michael Laurie

AN INTRODUCTION TO LANDSCAPE ARCHITECTURE

SECOND EDITION

THE HUMAN ENVIRONMENT: LANDSCAPE ARCHITECTURE

1

Since land is one of the basic commodities of the world, its planning for use and conservation is a central political and social issue. Land becomes landscape when it is described or seen in terms of its physiographic and environmental characteristics. Landscape varies according to these characteristics and according to the historical impact of man on it. Thus landscape is a reflection of dynamic, natural, and social systems. Landscape architecture is concerned with the planning and design of land and water for use by society on the basis of an understanding of these systems. "Planning" implies a futuristic approach to land: land is regarded as a resource to be viewed in relation to the demands and predicted needs of society and its values. "Design" refers to the qualitative and functional arrangement of parcels of land set aside in the planning process for some specific social purpose such as housing, education, or recreation.

ENVIRONMENTAL FRAMEWORK

Clearly, these are not recent human preoccupations, indeed the conscious planning and arrangement of land for agricultural and social purposes has been going on since the earliest civilizations of China, Egypt, and the Middle East. The rice terraces of the Orient (Fig. 1.1) and the earliest recorded domestic garden at Thebes (Fig. 2.2) are both very clear examples of conscious landscape design. Our approach to land use and design today is inevitably conditioned by this backlog of experience, tradition, and practice, and our perception of landscape and attitude toward nature are influenced by the cultural context from which each one of us has grown and the society in which we presently exist.

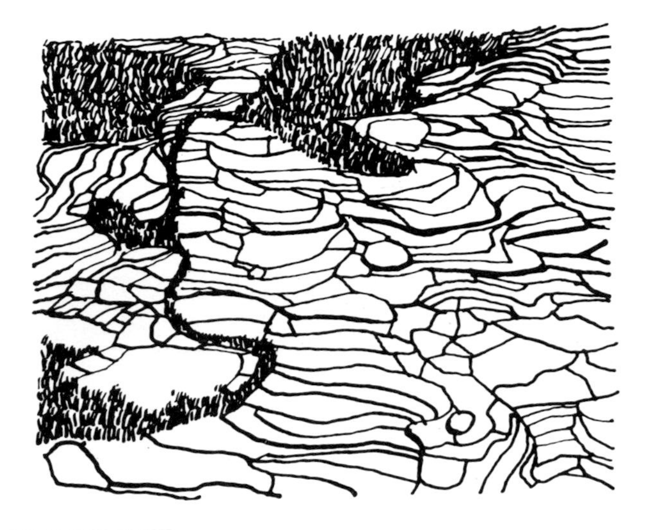

FIGURE 1.1
Pattern of rice fields in China illustrates the I-thou relationship between man and nature.

FIGURE 1.2
The criteria for modern highway construction frequently results in drastic changes to the landscape. As technology has increased, so has the degree to which we can change the face of the earth and the speed at which it can be accomplished.

The words planning, design, and use suggest human intervention. By definition, however, there is no such thing as an entirely man-made landscape. Rather, there are degrees of human adaptation of natural systems. For example, the California Indians changed or modified very little the landscape in which they lived, whereas the physical impact of the state's Department of Highways is clearly great (Fig. 1.2). Yet in both cases the landscapes can be said to have been modified and used. Moreover, there are two types of adaptation. Adaptation may be related to our use of the land for growing crops, raising stock, or supplying resources, or it can take the form of "impressions" made on the land as an expression of philosophical and artistic urges, the needs of the soul. This second type is represented by the great gardens of the world such as the Villa Lante, a product of the sixteenth-century Renaissance in Italy (Fig. 2.27). Throughout the history of civilization there is ample evidence of both forms of adaptation.

As technology has increased, so has the degree to which we can change the face of the earth and the speed at which this change can be accomplished. The primitive digging stick and the modern excavator are used for basically the same purpose but have clearly different potential. These two tools may be associated with two basic relationships between man and nature, the I-thou and the I-it, which are defined by E. A. Gutkind.[1] The I-thou represents a mutual adaptation between man and nature, whereas the I-it reflects an estrangement.

Gutkind identifies four stages in man's changing attitude to his environment over the known period of civilization. The first stage in the I-thou tradition is characterized by fear—fear of the unpredictable forces of nature with an accompanying desire for security. This is the general pattern of primitive societies who form hunting and self-sustaining agricultural groups in which the individual recognizes the need for the cooperation of other individuals to survive. These

[1] E. A. Gutkind, *Our World from the Air* (New York: Doubleday, 1952).

primitive societies have a very direct relationship with the landscape which they work and in which they live, and the relationship of the people to the external world is imbued with symbolism. In terms of physical form, Gutkind regards the organic interdependency of primitive villages and fields and the layout of tribal settlements as reflections of this stage (Fig. 1.3).

The second stage is one of growing self-confidence leading to a more rational adaptation of the environment for different needs. Nonetheless, man accepts the challenge of nature as a discipline and the I-thou relationship persists. In this stage people work with nature on the basis of understanding its processes and knowing man's limitations in terms of manipulating them. Landscape is regarded as a resource and it is recognized that the continuation of crop yield year by year depends on refertilization of fields and careful management and husbandry. The rice terraces and fields of China and the Orient, the regulation of rivers for the irrigation of crops as in the ancient civilizations of the Middle East, and the pyramids and temples of Egypt are physical manifestations of this stage (Figs.1.1 and 1.4). So too is the Medieval town with its church and castle and organic winding street pattern closely related to physiographic features (Fig. 2.20).

The third stage has led to our present situation and is the one advanced technological societies are still in; this is the stage of aggression and conquest. The adjustments to the environment of the second stage are replaced by exploitation and waste of natural resources. This I-it relationship may be symbolized by the contemporary automobile-oriented, spreading urban region with its hinterland of felled forests, worked-out mineral deposits, and polluted rivers (Figs. 1.5 to 1.7). Gutkind argues that it is the result of the depersonalization of nature through scientific specialization in the nineteenth century which weakened the awareness of the total relationship between man and nature.

The fourth stage lies, according to Gutkind, in the future. He describes it as an age of responsibility and unification. The I-it attitude is seen transformed into renewed understanding and insight into the workings of nature resulting in social awareness and more sensitive adjustments to environmental conditions. This new attitude depends on the science of ecology and conservation of nonrenewable resources. There is already some evidence of this fourth phase. The Tennessee Valley Authority project of the 1930s (Fig. 3.6) and more recent river basin planning studies for the Delaware and Potomac recognize the implications of ecological relationships and the hydrologic cycle in land use planning and management. The work of the

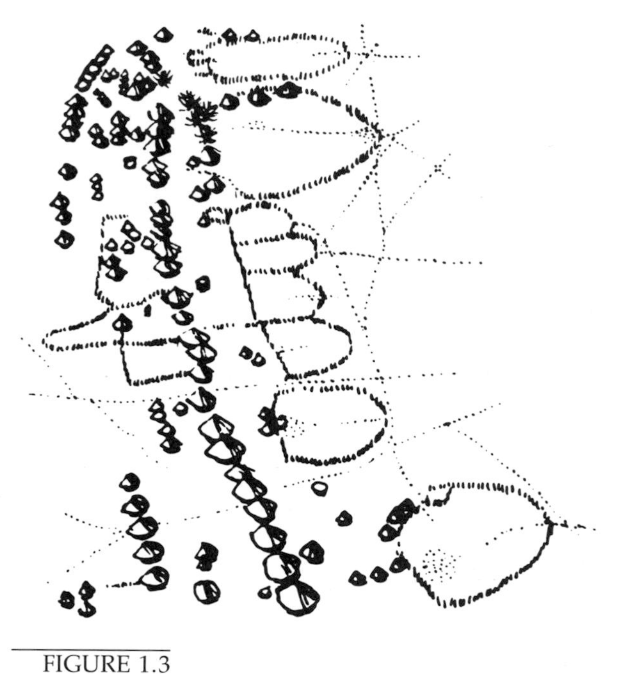

FIGURE 1.3
The I-thou relationship between man and nature is manifested in the layout of an African tribal village.

FIGURE 1.4
The pyramids of Egypt, a reflection of increasing self-confidence of man in nature.

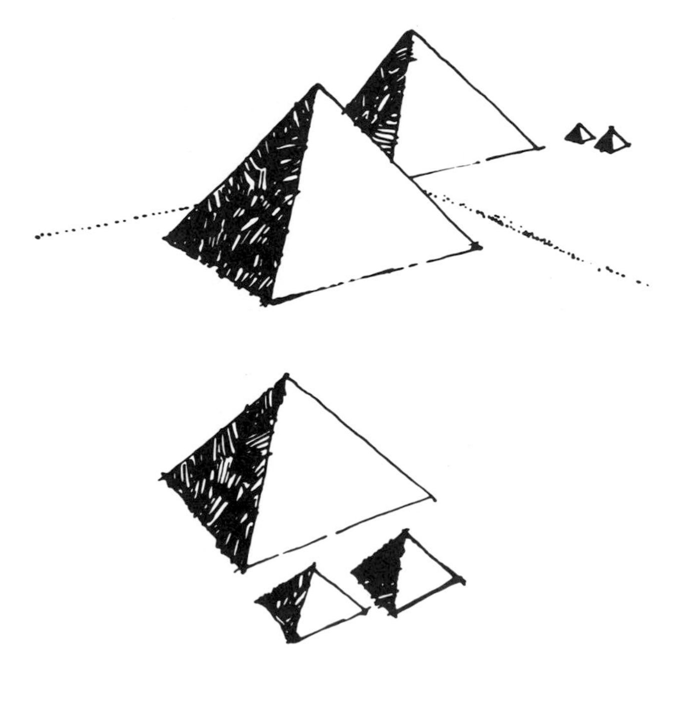

FIGURE 1.5
Los Angeles, an automobile oriented spreading urban region symbolic of in I-it relationship between man and nature (early 1950's). Photograph by William A. Garnett.

FIGURE 1.7
Strip mine right near Farmington, Illinois (1965)(on facing page). The scale of operation is characteristic of the I-it phase of the man—nature relationship. The mechanical shovel is higher than a five—story building. The intended restoration of the land to agriculture reflects the fourth stage of understanding and responsibility. Photograph by William A. Garnett.

FIGURE 1.6
As early as 1949, smog in Los Angeles (Hollywood) reached intolerable levels, the result of a neglected relationship between the physio graphic form of the landscape, the climatic pattern, and the dependence on the individual automobile for transportation. Photograph by William A. Garnett.

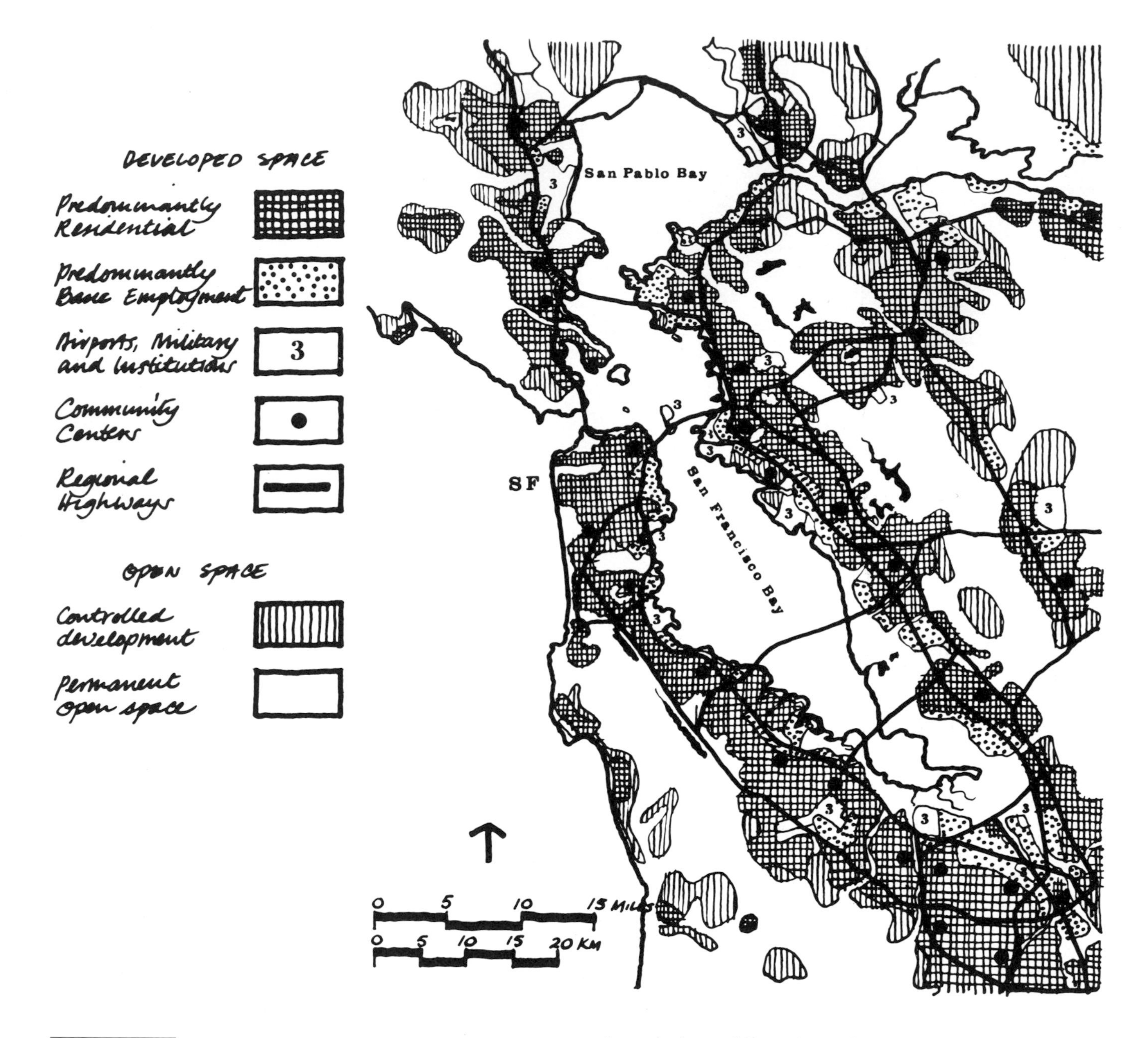

FIGURE 1.8
Regional plan, 1970–1990. This plan prepared by the Association of Bay Area Governments in 1970 includes nine counties and attempts an overview of major land uses and transportation. Metropolitan rapid transit (*not shown*) presently connects eleven of the community centers and is projected to connect all of the centers shown on the plan.

Association of Bay Area Governments and the Bay Conservation and Development Commission in California also is symptomatic of the new attitude toward land use that is slowly gaining acceptance world wide (Fig. 1.8).

More specifically, the energy crisis of the 1970s brought home the need for resource conserving houses and the possibilities of solar and wind power. Housing layouts such as Village Homes, Davis, California, responding to these issues have set precedent and are models on which the fourth stage will be based (Fig. 1.9). Strong conservation groups, such as the

FIGURE 1.9
Village Homes, Davis California (1972).

Sierra Club and Friends of the Earth, are also central to the development of responsible and innovative approaches to the essential next phase involving a simpler life-style and embracing Schumacher's "small is beautiful" philosophy. Ernest Callenbach's *Ecotopia* gives a glimpse of life as it might be in the year 2000 if we follow this direction.

In his imaginary nation of Ecotopia, consisting of Northern California, Oregon and Washington, society is run on the principles of conservation. Many suburbs have been ploughed under. The population is in steady state. Trees and gardens take over the freeways and much of the streets. Electric trains and buses replace the automobile; recycling of all waste is part of the daily routine. Plastics are made from wood so that they are biodegradable. Forests are managed by selective cutting and regeneration. Minicities of 40-to 50,000 inhabitants are surrounded by green belts and connected by rapid transit.

Major social and political changes are implied by this vision of the future and it is not easy for Third World countries to move directly into a conservation position having been denied the fruits of colonial exploitation.

In many ways Gutkind's statement or belief is similar to the hope expressed by Kenneth Boulding.[2] Boulding suggests that we are in the process of a great transition as a result of changes in science and technology, in the physical machinery of society and in the utilization of physical energy. His theme is simply that if we can avoid the entropy trap: the wasteful consumption of energy, and the war trap, which we seem to have difficulty in doing, and *if* we can learn to use the enormous potential of the great transition for good rather than for evil, then we may indeed be able to achieve Gutkind's fourth phase. Although this seems difficult, the option is open and one of the responsibilities of the environmental professions, including landscape architecture, must be to demonstrate and advocate this alternative to their clients and to the public in every possible way and at every possible moment since it is the only reasonable alternative for survival.

According to the optimists there is evidence that we are emerging (or at least can emerge) from the third stage, characterized by short-term goals and destructive practices and are approaching a new age of enlightenment in which the reshaping of the environment is seen in terms of land and landscape as a resource, to be planned and designed first according to the principles of the natural sciences and ecology and second to meet people's basic needs for physical and mental health and happiness according to the principles of the social and behavioral sciences.

Thus in a theory of landscape architecture responsive to these values we must understand the natural processes that constitute and have formed the landscape and the social processes that result in, or represent, the use of the landscape or environment and the way in which it is perceived. Next we need a methodology for analysis, evaluation, synthesis, and problem solving. And finally we need a technology to match the solution so that it may be implemented. Planning techniques involve political and economic procedures; design involves construction, planting, and management.

THE PROFESSION OF LANDSCAPE ARCHITECTURE

Before proceeding further with this theoretical framework it is perhaps useful to discuss earlier and other interpretations of the term landscape architecture. It is a difficult title, for the words seem to contradict one another: landscape and architecture, the one dynamic and ever changing, the other static and finite. Professionals frequently find it frustrating that their role in society has been consistently misunderstood. Landscape gardening is the usual interpretation, but the terms site planning, urban design, and environmental planning are frequently added to the names of landscape architectural firms as a means of expressing their broader concerns and capabilities.

[2] Kenneth Boulding, *The Meaning of the 20th Century: The Great Transition* (New York: Harper and Row, 1964).

FIGURE 1.10 (a, b, and c)
The impact of time is clearly seen in photographs of the same garden taken from the same spot ten years apart. The ability to project such change is the key to landscape architecture. See also Figs. 1.11 (a, b, and c), 7.9, 7.10, 7.11, and 11.18 (a and b).

Frederick Law Olmsted, designer of New York City's Central Park, coined the term *landscape architect* in 1858. And in case any of us think it is a difficult name to live with we should know that he apparently chose it in preference to his alternative, "rural embellisher." Olmsted was a prolific man and in addition to city parks he also planned complete urban open space systems, city and traffic patterns, subdivisions, university campuses, and private estates. In addition, he was active in the conservation movement and in 1865 was largely responsible for the first area of scenic landscape, Yosemite Valley in California, being set aside for public use and enjoyment. All this he called "landscape architecture," so it is not surprising that there has been some confusion about what landscape architects do. Olmsted had no training in the profession which he established at the age of 40. His previous experience in farming and engineering, his ability in writing and management, and his romantic disposition fitted him for the role he adopted. Others, such as Horace Cleveland and Charles Eliot, followed in his footsteps and in 1901 the first complete program in landscape architecture was established at Harvard University. The American Society of Landscape Architects was founded in 1899 by five practitioners, four men and one woman.

After these auspicious beginnings, the prestige of the profession waxed and waned. Landscape architects found themselves in competition with other environmentalists of the nineteenth century: architects, engineers, surveyors, foresters, park superintendents, and city planners. In fact, the city planning profession emerged out of landscape architecture in 1907.

Thus from being responsible for some very large and important work in the nineteenth century, the landscape profession entered a somewhat less ambitious phase in the early 1900s with greater emphasis on large estates, gardens, and small scale site planning. However, during the depression years of the 1930s, landscape architects became involved again in larger scale projects, playing a significant role in the various public works programs, particularly those of the U.S. National Parks Service. Since World War II, the work of landscape architects, often operating as members of a team, has changed to include the restoration of derelict land, regional landscape analysis and planning, urban design and site planning for housing, schools, and large scale industrial plants. These now form a major portion of the landscape architecture carried on in public agencies and private practice. In spite of this, the contribution of the landscape architect to the overall development and maintenance of a stimulating, agreeable, and viable environment may not appear to be very great. People of landscape sensitivity and expertise do not occupy all the positions from which decisions affecting landscape are made.

Much of the environment is ill-planned, inefficient, unattractive, and poorly managed. The landscape profession is small and perhaps overly protective of the field. With notable exceptions, few practitioners have aggressively entered the political arena where projects are often defined and professionals selected. However, changes in professional strategy and successful demonstration of the economic and social benefits of sound landscape design, may in the years ahead result in a more central role for Landscape Architecture.

It should also be remembered that landscape work, unlike architecture, does not always have an immediately perceptible impact and the effectiveness of planting and land use decisions or policies may not be appreciable for twenty to thirty years. For example, the landscape of the first new towns in England is just beginning to achieve the effect and visual qualities that were in the minds of the designers twenty-five years ago, and war housing built in the United States has often been demolished, leaving mature trees for a replacement project. This fourth dimension, time, is an important aspect of landscape architecture (Fig. 1.10). Olmsted understood it when he talked of the far-reaching conception that the designer must have in developing "a picture so great that nature shall be employed upon it for generations, before the work he has arranged for her shall realize his intentions" (Fig. 1.11).

FIGURE 1.11
(**a**) Sproul Plaza, University of California, August 1964; (**b**) Sproul Plaza, June 1980; (**c**) Sproul Plaza, April 1984.

CONCEPTUAL DEFINITION OF LANDSCAPE ARCHITECTURE

To bring us closer to a meaningful definition of landscape architecture for today let us look briefly at some earlier concepts. Hubbard and Kimball refer to landscape architecture as primarily a fine art whose

> most important function is to create and preserve beauty in the surroundings of human habitations and in the broader natural scenery of the country; but it is also concerned with promoting the comfort, convenience and health of urban populations, which have scanty access to rural scenery, and urgently need to have their hurrying workaday lives refreshed and calmed by the beautiful and reposeful sights and sounds which nature, aided by the landscape art, can abundantly provide.[3]

[3] H. V. Hubbard and Theodora Kimball, *An Introduction to the Study of Landscape Design* (New York: Macmillan, 1917).

This definition reflects Olmsted's belief that contact with natural landscape was essential for human morality, health, and happiness.

Garrett Eckbo defines landscape architecture as covering

> that portion of the landscape which is developed or shaped by man, beyond buildings, roads, or utilities and up to wild nature, designed primarily as space for human living (not including agriculture, forestry). It is the establishment of relations between building, surfacing, and other outdoor construction, earth, rock forms, bodies of water, plants and open space, and the general form and character of the landscape; but with primary emphasis on the human content, the relationship between people and landscape, between human beings and three-dimensional outdoor space quantitatively and qualitatively.[4]

This definition is essentially concerned with site planning and the relations between people and design in that context. Thus it is more limited in scope than that of Hubbard and Kimball.

Eckbo's definition is related to the concept expressed by others that landscape architecture is an extension of architecture by other means. They are regarded as the same job. It is argued that until about the end of the eighteenth century no architect would have considered himself incapable of designing the space between buildings or the space around buildings, that is, gardens and landscape. The people we think of as the great landscapists of the eighteenth century thought of themselves as architects as much as gardeners; for example, in England Lancelot Brown, called Capability Brown, renowned for his landscape gardens also designed houses, although the quality of the houses is not thought to be too high. Conversely, some of the people we think of as great architects of eighteenth-century England, like William Kent, were also great landscape architects, and Kent saw no incompatibility between the two pursuits. Chiswick House and Garden, which Kent designed, illustrate his skill at both. Joseph Paxton is another famous gardener who practiced architecture. His design for Crystal Palace, a landmark in the evolution of modern architecture, was the result of his work in greenhouse construction at Chatsworth where he made a great garden for the Duke of Devonshire. Paxton was also to become a leader in the design of public urban parks in nineteenth-century England. According to this theory the differences between architecture and landscape architecture occur in the means, techniques, and materials, not in the basic objectives.

Herein lies a parallel with Urban Design. As an architect, Brown had a greater control over the siting and form of buildings in his landscapes. The urban designer is concerned with the space between buildings in an urban context and also needs to know about both architecture and landscape.

However true this may be, Brian Hackett points to another essential difference between landscape architecture and other design professions. This is the medium in which we work, the landscape, subject to change and growth, which has existed for millions of years and will doubtless continue to exist. "All that we can and should do is to modify or adapt the landscape to fit the new program." Thus the constraints inherent in the ecological cycles and environmental processes of a landscape limit the opportunities for an individualistic approach to design which is more possible in engineering, architecture, or industry.[5]

More recently Elizabeth Kassler points out that the oldest gardens of China and Japan were the works of poets, painters, and philosophers whereas in the West, landscape design has frequently been considered as a form of architecture. She continues,

> As it becomes obvious that we have applied ourselves with more whim than wisdom to the critical problem of how best to live on this earth, or rather with this earth, we begin to realize that the work of fitting people to the land and fitting the land to people must be undertaken with much the same care for action and interaction that a forester might apply to his far simpler problem of ecology. And since a measure of beauty seems to be the happy by-product of any ecological approach to land use, it is unlikely that our physical environment will be ugly if it is planned to respect both the nature of man and the nature of nature.[6]

Kassler challenges the concept that landscape is a form of architecture and suggests that landscape architecture would do better to draw its determinants of form from scientific knowledge and research in ecology and behavioral studies as well as from painting, sculpture, and architecture. She thus identifies broader responsibilities for the landscape architect to see beyond the boundaries of his design project and to become involved with and understand the larger region in which his project lies, where the impact of numerous projects and developments represents another level of concern for him.

It can be seen that the definition of the profession has varied over the years in an attempt to match its

---

[4] Garrett Eckbo, *Landscape for Living* (New York: Architectural Record, 1950).

[5] Brian Hackett, "Landscape Student and Teacher," *Institute of Landscape Architects Journal*, 81 (February 1968).

[6] Elizabeth Kassler, *Modern Gardens and the Landscape* (New York: Doubleday, 1964).

goals with the problems and needs of society. Recently the American Society of Landscape Architects amended its official definition to include "stewardship of the land" as one of its commitments.

The point becomes clear, however, that no one philosophical position is appropriate for a profession whose work occurs in both the countryside and the city. Neither art, ecology, sociology, architecture, nor horticulture alone can provide an adequate basis for responsible landscape design. The relevance that each might have in any situation depends on the nature of the project and the context.

THE PRACTICE OF LANDSCAPE ARCHITECTURE

Over the years and especially since World War II, the realm of landscape architecture has diversified and classified its activities in response to the needs of a changing world. There now appear to be four clearly definable and related types of practice.

First, there is landscape evaluation and planning. It is concerned with the systematic study of large areas of land and has a strong ecological and natural science base in addition to a concern for visual quality. The history of human use and current demands represents a third subject area for analysis. In addition to the landscape architect, the process usually involves a team of specialists such as soil scientists, geologists, and economists. The result is a land use plan or policy recommending the distribution and type of development, for example, housing, industry, agriculture, highway alignment, and recreation within a framework of resource and amenity conservation. The study area ideally coincides with a natural physiographic region, such as the watershed of a major river or some other logical unit of land, but unfortunately these seldom coincide with county and state boundaries. In other cases, the planning function may be less comprehensive and focus on the impact on the environment of single major proposals. The identification of land suitable for one major use, such as recreation, is another function of landscape evaluation and planning.

The second activity of landscape architects is site planning. This represents the more conventional kind of landscape architecture and within this realm lies landscape design. Site planning is the process in which the characteristics of the site and the requirements of the program for its use are brought together in creative synthesis. Elements and facilities are located on the land in functional and aesthetic relationships and in a manner fully responsive to program, site, and regional context.

FIGURE 1.12
Copley Square, Boston. Design by Frank A. Bourne in 1924. The square has undergone two redesigns since then by landscape architects.

Third, there is detailed landscape design. This is the process through which specific quality is given to the diagrammatic spaces and areas of the site plan. It involves the selection of components, materials, and plants and their combination in three dimensions as solutions to limited and well-defined problems such as entrance, terrace, amphitheater, parking area, and so on.

The fourth form of landscape architecture is urban design. Although this may seem a recent activity on account of well publicized postwar urban renewal and the construction of new towns, it was, in fact, a central portion of the practices of Olmsted, Cleveland, and other pioneers of the profession (Fig. 1.12). Urban design defies precise definition. Two things are sure, however; the setting is the city and several properties are involved. An agency of government may be responsible for assembling the parcels and organizing the program. The location, not the design, of buildings and the organization of the space between them for circulation and public use are major concerns. Typically, but not always, hard surfaces predominate. Streets and malls, river front developments, government and commercial centers, rehabilitation of neighborhoods, and recycling of groups of industrial buildings may be classed as urban design projects. Complicated as they are, with multiple ownership, political, legal, and economic considerations, such projects are rarely in the hands of one planner or designer. They are team efforts sponsored by a major developer or government agency. Planners are involved with the project's viability and infrastructure, architects with buildings. But it is the organization and design of the space between buildings (site planning and landscape design) that is central to its overall success. It is essential to have an understanding of microclimate, sun and shadow patterns, proportion and scale, human needs and behavior, and the potential of space division and differences in level to facilitate and enhance them. In addition, urban horticulture is a specialization that recognizes the extreme and often difficult growing conditions created by glare, drafts, and limited root area for trees. Together, open space design and urban horticulture, although not the most costly elements of a comprehensive urban design project, are critical to its unity (see page 149).

There is clearly an interrelationship among these four types of landscape architecture: landscape planning, site planning, urban design, and detailed landscape design. The wider landscape, urban or rural, is the context for the site, which in turn is the framework within which lies the details. But just as it is reasonable to expect that small scale projects, such as a garden or a park, should be influenced by and respond to the larger environment, so it is true that criteria for certain large scale land planning decisions or urban design depend on an understanding of the details of design and technology in siting buildings, roads, and facilities. Landscape architects have to understand both scales to do the projects with responsibility and sensitivity.

A THEORY OF LANDSCAPE ARCHITECTURE

Five major components of a theory have been mentioned. They are natural process, human factors, methodology, technology, and values. Whatever the scale or emphasis of operation, these five components are consistently relevant. Social and natural factors clearly permeate every facet of a profession that is concerned with people and land. Problem solving, planning, and design methods apply at all scales. Good judgment is consistently required.

Consider how natural factors data are relevant to both planning and design. At the regional scale, in a responsible society, the impact of development or change in use on a landscape must be known and evaluated before a policy to allow such action is set. An inventory of the natural factors, including geology, soils, hydrology, topography, climate, vegetation and wildlife, and the ecological relationships between them is fundamental to an understanding of the ecosystem to which change is contemplated. Equally important is an analysis of visual quality which is the sum of the components. Land use policy can thus be made on the basis of the known vulnerability or resistance of the landscape. In other circumstances the natural processes which add up to a given landscape at a given moment in its evolution may, as at Grand Canyon and other unique places, be considered a resource to be preserved, protected, and managed as a public trust (Fig. 1.13). On a smaller scale, soil and geological conditions may be critical in the determination of the cost and the form of building foundations: where it is most suitable to build and where it is not. Sun, wind, and rain are important factors of design where the development of comfort zones for human activity or the growth of plants is a primary objective. Thus, natural factors influence land use, site planning, and detailed design.

Similarly, human factors apply equally at all scales. In site planning and landscape design, cultural variation in the use and appreciation of open space and parks and the physical and social needs of the young and old are some of the many variables to be considered in a design process that aims to be responsive to social values and human needs. In decisions related to appropriation of landscape for recreation and aesthetic value people's perception of the environment and the behavioral patterns and tendencies of people in the out-of-doors are clearly relevant. It is also important that designers understand the impact of environment on behavior and also appreciate the basic human need to manipulate and control the environment. The value of community participation in urban planning and design is now widely recognized.

Technology is the means by which a design is implemented or on which a policy depends. Some of it changes year by year as new materials, machinery, and techniques are developed. Its role in the three types of landscape architecture is clear. Specific areas of technology include plants, planting and ecological succession, soil science, hydrology and sewage treatment, microclimate control, surface drainage, erosion control, hard surfaces, and maintenance. Other techniques of importance in landscape architecture relate to communications, community participation, development economics, and political process.

Design and planning methodology involve systems whereby landscape problems are defined, all relevant factors and variables are assembled, given values and

FIGURE 1.13
The form of natural landscapes is a direct reflection of the processes of nature. Ideally, man-made form should be equally responsive to social processes and equally dynamic.

incorporated in the solution. Computer graphics, analytical techniques, and notation systems aid in this process. As a device to modify the bias of planners in the creative process, Halprin suggests scoring techniques, as in music or choreography. These open up the design process, allowing more people to participate in decision making and facilitate the generation of more humanistic ways to plan and design large scale complex environments.[7]

Finally, landscape architecture must be based on a set of values. This is perhaps the most difficult part of the theory to deal with. Natural and social science, methodology, and technique can be learned; values have to be lived and felt. Experience and good sense tell us that we need to develop a set of priorities and subscribe to a land ethic related to our belief in the "alternative for survival," in which short term profit at the expense of long term regeneration and conservation of resources would be unthinkable. Environmental impact must be seen in a regional context. Quantity must be equated with quality. We must learn to make judgments in terms of what is considered best for the common good and the future of mankind. Even Third World countries, who have experienced exploitation without much benefit, must see the importance of this. The professional must present such considered judgments to the investment banker, government agency chiefs, and others in whose hands lie the ultimate decisions—even though his recommendations may be at variance with their programs.

The objective of combining these components is the development of a basis from which landscape planning and detailed design can be made responsive to human behavioral patterns (people) and specific situation characteristics (the setting). Since both will vary in

[7] Lawrence Halprin, *R.S.V.P. Cycles* (New York: Braziller, 1970).

terms of culture, region, and neighborhood there can be no panaceas and no preconceived solutions.

Little has been said so far about aesthetics or visual quality. This is because it is possible, and in my opinion misleading, to stress these aspects of landscape architecture with a resulting lack of attention to the other sources of form already mentioned. But of course how things look is important and proportion and relative size are particularly critical where new work is fitted into an existing framework. Color and form influence human comfort and often have symbolic meaning. It can be seen, then, that aesthetic principles are essentially techniques associated with human factors in the production of meaningful form. Thus, a design which fully satisfies all criteria is likely to be aesthetically pleasing. It has been said also that a landscape in ecological repose will be beautiful (Darling). When all is said and done, responsible, effective, and pleasing landscape design results from clear and objective thinking and a synoptic view from start to finish.

The process of design, the aim of which is the evolution of forms and relationships suited to the needs of people, may be compared to the fundamental form-giving processes which have created the geomorphology of the great natural landscapes of the world. Here the visual form of the land's surface—valleys and ridges, water-filled basins, and jagged peaks—represents an evolutionary stage in the interaction between the geological structure and the agents of erosion. The forms we see result from the response of inorganic material to a set of imposed conditions of weathering (Fig. 1.13). The variations in vegetative cover from north to south slopes, from meadow to subarctic plateau, from river valley to rocky talus constitute exact responses to the range of environmental conditions created by the physiographic differentiation of the landscape. In turn, the wildlife distribution is dictated by the type and extent of the vegetation. No one aspect of the pattern is without cause or consequence. All merge irrevocably into a self-sustaining and evolving ecological system, representing the resolution of the natural forces and processes up to a specific moment in time.

This model for the creation of form is similar to the one of the design process which also produces form(s) representing the resolution of forces with a built-in capacity for adaptation. Such forms are the goal of the landscape planner and designer.

SUGGESTED READINGS

Landscape Architecture

Colvin, Brenda, *Land and Landscape.*

Crowe, Sylvia, *Garden Design.*

Eckbo, Garrett, *Landscape for Living*, Ch. 2.

Eckbo, Garrett, *Urban Landscape Design.*

Newton, Norman T., *Design on the Land*, Ch. XXVI, "Founding of the American Society of Landscape Architects."

Simonds, John O., *Landscape Architecture.*

Environmental Problems

Blake, Peter, *God's Own Junkyard.*

Callenbach, Ernest, *Ecotopia.*

Darling, F. Fraser, *Wilderness and Plenty.*

Dasmann, Raymond F., *The Destruction of California.*

Gutkind, Erwin A., *Our World From the Air.*

Kahn, Herman, *The Year 2000.*

McHarg, Ian, *Design with Nature*, "The Plight," pp. 19–29.
Scientific American, Cities.

Spirn, Ann Whiston, *The Granite Garden.*

Tunnard, Christopher and Boris Pushkarev, *Man-Made America—Chaos or Control.*

The film "Multiply and Subdue the Earth" (McHarg).

THE GARDEN IN HISTORY

2

LEGACY OF THE PAST

A review of the history of landscape design begins with emerging and developing societies based on agricultural productivity and a symbolic approach to the universe. The gardens and urban environments, which were created, reflected both the relationship of society to nature and the structure of the society itself. The role of plants and gardens in the city and the surrounding agricultural countryside varied according to climate and attitude. In time, essentially two systems of landscape design evolved, one based on geometry, and the other on nature, although the rationale and meaning has varied with time and place.

In spite of the fact that many gardens and urban spaces were products of dictatorship, power, and personal wealth, it is of value to trace the connection between the form, the underlying concept, and the geographic setting. If we can make a clear connection between form and concept in the great gardens of the world, be it an idealized paradise garden, a protected shaded retreat, a vast expression of geometry and mathematical proportions, an expression of nature, or a botanical collection, it will help us to understand why they look the way they do and, as a result, help in the development of forms and design suited to our own time and location. Perhaps the most difficult aspect of design today is finding concepts as simple and strong as those underlying the gardens of the past. Thus, as we examine briefly the forms in response to climate and context, the expression of attitudes and ideas, we must think about the way in which our own particular social and environmental conditions should be reflected in contemporary landscape design and consider how it might differ.

To give some focus to the history of landscape design in gardens and parks, it is convenient to deal in prototypes. Divided into two major categories, the architectural and the natural, more specific investigation reveals further differences in organization, use, symbolism, and setting which, together, add up to significant varieties. The prototypes are basically ideal forms (rarely achieved) based on three sources: (1) literature; (2) illustrations; and (3) visible remains. Literature may be proscriptive or descriptive, the former tending to be contemporary whereas the latter may be of any time. Proscriptive literature consists of advice on laying out a garden, written for contemporary use. Descriptive literature usually comprises accounts by travelers and others who visited the gardens and parks at the time of their construction, height of maturity, or decay. In either case, the components, details, planting, and objectives are evident and can be synthesized into an imaginary prototype. To make this easier, we can consult old prints and illustrations and, in some cases, photographs made at the time of, or subsequent to, the moment of creation. Final evidence is obtained from remains of the gardens where they existed and where they have not been altered too much with time and remodeling. The remains of gardens, however well preserved, have usually, except in recent prototypes, undergone change, but the experience of the setting, scale, and certain unchanged details and spaces is invaluable and highly recommended for students. Together, these sources and methods build up to an understanding of the gardens, their context and organization, illustrating the application of design principles imbued with symbolism and aesthetic qualities.

In my attempt to portray the concepts of landscape architecture many of the historical sketches in this chapter are based on several sources. They are thus often combinations of the way the place looks today, the way it appeared in early prints and illustrations, and the way I think the designer intended it to look.

Although it is perhaps more interesting and often more convenient to illustrate and describe specific examples in developing prototypes, it must be remembered that each specific garden is different in detail as a reflection of the site, the client, and the designer. Together, the examples and prototypes constitute the vocabulary of landscape architecture from which current practice has grown.

In addition to the role of historical studies in illustrating design principles and helping us to understand our own time, the increasing concern for heritage landscapes and the restoration of significant gardens and parks, which have fallen into disrepair, requires landscape architects to have understanding of the originals.

LANDSCAPE DESIGN AND AGRICULTURE

If we define landscape according to its original Dutch meaning, as an organization of fields and villages, an expression of community use and impact, then it is legitimate to link it with *Design* implying the marking out or designation of land or objects for some social purpose. With these definitions there is no distinction as to whether landscape design is an artistic or a functional endeavor. Many of the agricultural landscapes of the world, organized on purely functional principles, are considered attractive. Much can be learned from the purposefulness of design that is to be found in primitive systems of intensive cultivation and habitation where the basic needs of shelter and privacy are provided with the simplest of materials and in the most convenient ways. Beauty or aesthetics as we understand these terms today were not uppermost in the minds of the people who created these landscapes. Yet, in most cases, where they understood the land and the environment, the organization of fields, terraces, buildings, roads, and shelter belts which the people produced, often over generations and constantly subject to change, had a sense of fit and appropriateness that gives to the landscape a quality satisfying to the artist and the farmer alike. Even in more artificial situations where design was linked with aesthetics as in gardens, architecture and urban design, the best examples frequently exhibit a sense of logic, inevitability and a relationship to context equal to that of a well-organized and productive farm.

ORIGINS OF THE GARDEN CONCEPT

The meaning of the word garden can be traced to the Hebrew *gan*, to protect or defend, implying a fence or enclosure, and *oden* or *eden*, meaning pleasure or delight. Thus in the contemporary English word garden we have a combination of the two, meaning the enclosure of land for pleasure and delight.

The concept of the pleasure garden perhaps originates in mythology, whereas its layout and organization seem to derive from ancient cultivation and irrigation practices. Most of the major religious faiths describe gardens or paradise at the beginning of time or the end of life on earth. The promised garden of Mohammed was said to be filled with groves of trees and fountains. Here enjoyments which lasted for mere moments on earth were prolonged for a thousand years. There are also legends of the Garden of Eden in which God placed Adam and Eve. This is described in Genesis I and II as a park created by God in which there were all kinds of trees, delightful to see and bearing good fruit to eat and, of course, the tree in the center that yielded knowledge of good and evil. There was also a river which branched into four streams on leaving the park. The image is vivid and persistent even in modern times. Everyone knows what is meant by Eden. This universal knowledge gives meaning to book titles such as *East of Eden* or *Eden in Jeopardy*. Similarly, a nightclub called The Garden of Eden needs no further explanation.

In addition to the symbolism attached to the garden, early civilizations attributed special meaning and significance to certain trees and plants such as the olive, the thorn, the fig, and the vine. In times when starvation was a recurring phenomenon, it is not unnatural that trees, the longest living things known to man, should be revered for the fertility, life, and nourishment they represented.

Thus in our deepest ancestry there are strong myths and legends whose meaning may now be obscure but which, nonetheless, were influential in early thought and civilization. They are still part of our cultural heritage and partly responsible for the attitudes and emotions we hold today and, no doubt, for our unquenchable interest in plants, gardens, and gardening.

BABYLON, EGYPT, AND PERSIA

If the origins of garden layout and form also lie in agricultural practices, we may regard the fenced vegetable patch as the original prototype. As leisured segments of society could be supported by the productivity of settled civilizations, such as those of the Euphrates Valley around 3500 BC, so gardens were made for pleasure and as representations of paradise. True to their origins, the dimensions and shape of planting beds were those of the fields. Irrigation channels and ponds were incorporated for functional reasons, as well as for the sensuous enjoyment of water in a hot climate. Shade was provided by forest trees planted in regular groves, and the garden was protected with a wall to keep out animals and intruders. The heads of state and the ruling classes lived in palace complexes of sun-baked brick with gardens of this type. The Hanging Gardens of Babylon were unique. This great monument is said to have occupied four acres and to have risen in a series of planted and irrigated roof

FIGURE 2.1
Hanging Gardens of Babylon, 3500 BC.

terraces to a height of 300 feet from which views of the valley and the surrounding desert were obtained (Fig. 2.1).

The Nile Valley was another center of early civilization. Egypt's long period of preeminence lasted from 3500 to 500 BC. The religious and symbolic significance of certain trees and flowers such as the lotus, the papyrus, and the date palm gave rise to the use of plants for ornamental purposes. The rich built residences and walled gardens in the agricultural countryside. The officials' garden at Thebes, of which there are good records, is probably typical. It consists of a rectangular and axial arrangement of flower beds, ponds, enclosures, and a vine trellis under which one walked from the gate to the house. Fruit trees were planted for shade. There were irrigation channels and garden pavilions and the garden was surrounded by a high wall (Fig. 2.2).

Much later, about 500 BC, the kings of Persia created lavish formal gardens for delight, consecrated to joy, love, health, and luxury. A Persian palace garden of this era would have irrigation channels running through it as though it were a field of some economic crop. Here, guarded by high lookout towers and walls, fruit trees and scented flowers were cultivated between rills of water. The Persian garden has been described by Sorensen as a stylization of the agricultural landscape employing water for irrigation and air cooling and imbued with symbolism.[1]

FIGURE 2.2
The house and garden of an Egyptian government official at Thebes, 2000 BC.

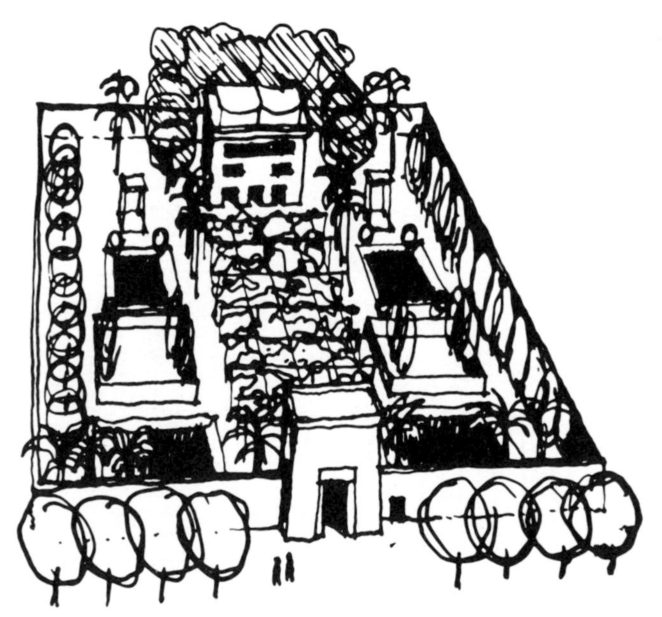

These early attempts at garden design in the ancient civilizations of the fertile crescent led through different cultural sieves and over a considerable period of time to two major prototypes—the Italian garden and the Islamic garden.

CHINA

A second major cradle of civilization and source of garden design was the Orient. As a center of civilization, China had reached a climax in its development around 600 BC. The effects of deforestation were recognized and there was an established system of controlling tree cutting and forest management. The tradition of roadside tree planting dates back to this time. Cities were planned on a grid system with wide tree-planted streets oriented north–south and east–west. The hierarchical, axial, and symmetrical organization of rectangular enclosures represented the cosmos and reflected the teachings of Confucius on which that society was structured. Confucianism provided a code of rules for social behavior and relationships. The places of daily routine, e.g., house, palace, temple, were thus organized around the rules, conventions, and rituals of social and political institutions dealing with the relationships between the emperor and the high government officials, parent, wife, children, friends, strangers, and so forth. The Palace of the Forbidden City in Peking was designed as a series of spaces or enclosures (representing purifications) aligned along a major axis rising up gradually from one level to a higher one before finally reaching the inner sanctuary of the emperor. The ordinary house, although rarely reaching such extremes, was laid out by similar principles.

As though to modify the stifling effect of Confucian order, obsessed with interpersonal relationships, the Chinese adopted Taoism as a counterforce, concerned with the relationship of the individual to nature. In time, Buddhism made strong inroads into Chinese philosophy. Its central reverence of nature and meditation added strength to the Chinese interest for natural landscape and the laws of nature.

Landscape gardening (whose origins can be traced back to the eleventh century BC), in the seventh and eighth centuries BC, attempted to recreate idyllic scenes of the artist and applied the rules of painting and poetry to the garden. The Chinese word for landscape, shanshui, means mountains and water. These opposites were regarded as contrasts, not opposing forces

[1] Carl T. Sorensen, *The Origin of Garden Art* (Kobenhavn: Danish Architectural Press, 1963).

(as Taoism was a contrast and therefore complementary to Confucianism). The view of the universe was that it represented a dynamic equilibrium between active and passive forces constantly changing and in motion (it was not regarded as wild). The yin–yang is a harmony between contrasting forces and forms such as rivers and mountains and woman and man. Within the harmonious balance of nature, man was seen as an integral part, no more or less important than any other element. Harmony resulted from a continuous series of balanced contrasts in the environment. This became the underlying concept of the designed gardens which attempted to recreate the essence of natural landscape.

There is considerable variety in Chinese gardens depending on the date and the place, but for our purposes (in search of prototypes), oversimplification leads to two main forms. First, imperial gardens, built as settings for the summer palaces of the imperial families, were large estates. Consisting of mountains, forests, streams, lakes, and islands, often stocked with exotic plants and animals from distant countries, they were frequently furnished with bright pavilions and bridges for the amusement of the royal party, removed temporarily, as they were, from social and political life. The pavilions in the large gardens were often built for special purposes, e.g., viewing the moon or lotus flowers. The second major form derives from the smaller private gardens attached to town dwellings and suburban villas. These belonged to landlords, rich merchants and bureaucrats. But, regardless of whether it was a large estate or a small town garden, the objectives were the same: to create a symbolic landscape in which the contrasting forces of nature were harmoniously arranged as a setting for the individual in contemplation or for a release from the conformity of social life.

The summer palace near Beijing is representative of the large royal landscape parks created specially for imperial indulgence in the beauties of nature (Fig. 2.3). Its history as a special place goes back over a thousand years. In the twelfth and thirteenth centuries a lake was dredged and a productive landscape of well tended field created. The scenery was considered so beautiful that it inspired poetic description and a favorite pleasure for the aristocracy was to stroll along the lake shore taking in the perfume of lotus flowers which grew profusely. It was not surprising that this idyllic

FIGURE 2.3
The summer palace near Beijing. Construction started in 1749.

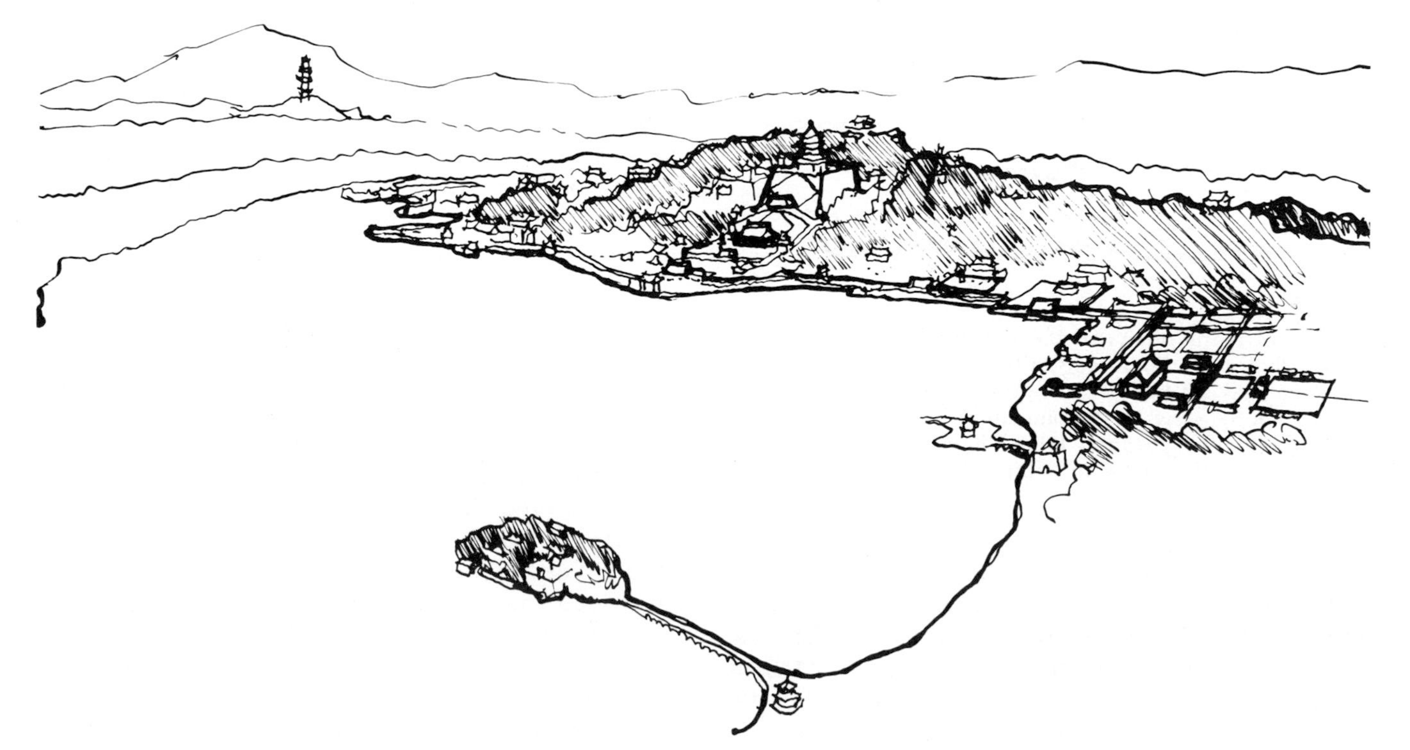

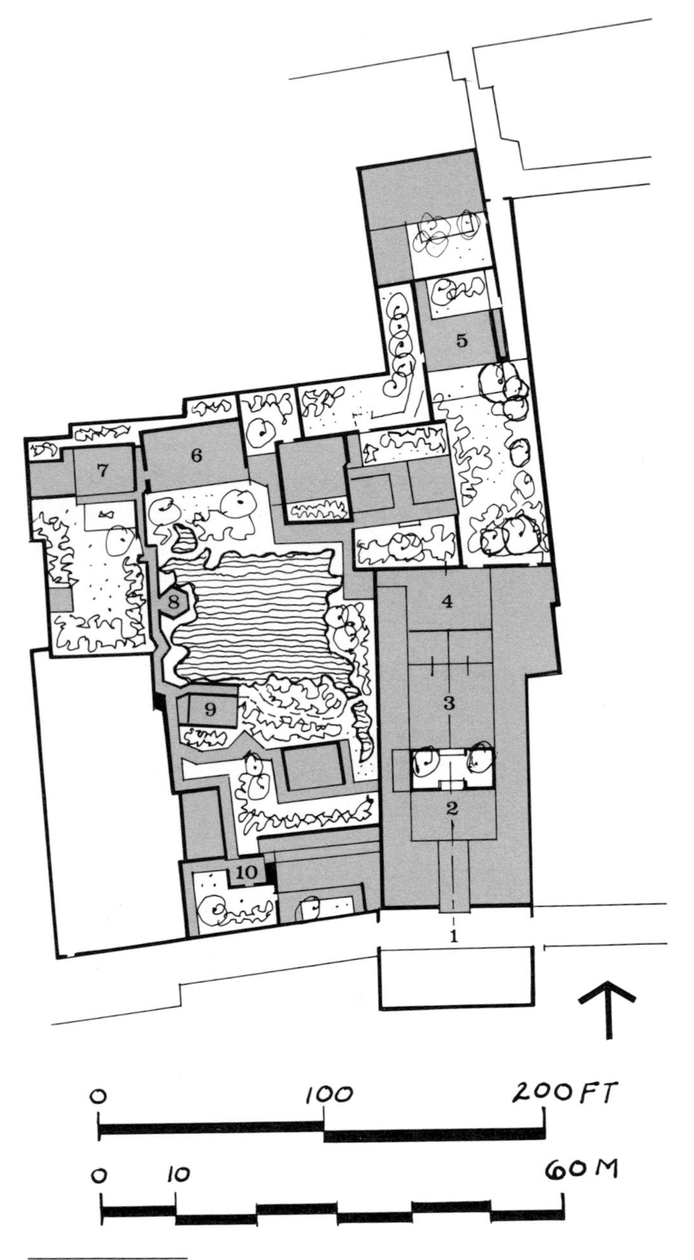

FIGURE 2.4
Plan of Wang Shi Yuan at Suchow. **(1)** Front gate, **(2)** chair hall, **(3)** reception hall, **(4)** hall of gathering elegance, **(5)** hall of ascending to the clouds, **(6)** hall for viewing the pine and seeing a painting, **(7)** Late Spring Studio, **(8)** pavilion overlooking pond, **(9)** Washing Cap strings, **(10)** lute room.

site was selected as the location for a summer palace by Emperor Qianlong (1736–1795), fourth emperor of the Qing dynasty. Work on the project began in 1749. The lake was enlarged and artificial hills built. As it began to take shape, it was given the name "Garden of the Clear Ripples" and the hill to the north of the lake was called "Longevity Hill." The landscape was then furnished with a series of pavilions, spacious studios, majestic halls, and towers or pagodas which added to the charm of the scenery and provided places from which to enjoy it. In addition to residential quarters, the buildings served other specialized functions such as holding court, celebration of birthdays, recitation of poetry, feasting, and so on. In all, over 100 structures were carefully located on the slopes of Longevity Hill. The complex took 15 years to complete and covers 290 hectares (823 acres). As with so many historical artifacts, what we see today is the result of two rebuildings of the original layout which was destroyed in 1864 and again in 1900 by foreign powers. Nonetheless, the scale and concept of an imperial landscape park can be experienced.

Wang Shi Yuan (the garden of the master of the fishing nets) is an interesting example of a private town garden (Figs. 2.4 and 2.5). First built in the twelfth century by a bureaucrat, it was given its name by the owner who longed for the simpler life of a fisherman. Over the years, the house and garden changed owners, fell into disrepair and were rebuilt several times. The garden which we see today is largely the conception of Qu Yuancun who acquired it in the late eighteenth century. It was not unusual for a scholar trained in classics and literature to design his own house and garden and this is what Qu did. As with all gardens, it has been embellished and altered subsequently but it illustrates the essential characteristics of the type.

The house, oriented north–south consists of a series of axially related formal reception rooms and a courtyard on the ground floor, with living quarters on the second floor. The subdued interiors contrast with the fanciful main garden reached through a side door. The pond is the main focus as well as the physical center of the garden. The full extent of the water is hidden and two stream-like extensions crossed with stone bridges give the impression that it continues into other parts of the garden. Three buildings overhang the pond offering different views and cooling proximity to the water. Other buildings and walls further back virtually enclose the area, but they are low in height and masked by rocks and trees increasing the illusion of space. Paths and corridors connect the pavilions which have allegorical or symbolic titles. To the west, entered through a gate in a wall, lies a small courtyard that contains a room called "Late Spring Studio" and a moon viewing terrace. Against the south wall is an arrangement of rocks with a spring fed pool. Half seen through fretted windows in the south wall is a plant nursery. To the east is another enclosed garden in front of the "Hall of Ascending to the Clouds" and another building, the "Lute Room" is almost hidden to the south of the pond by a rock construction. It faces

FIGURE 2.5
Wang Shi Yuan. View from pavilion overlooking the pond.

a narrow garden with bamboo and rocks. This is a set piece to be viewed from within.

The entire garden takes up a mere 1⅓ acres but its complexity, division of space, and control of sight-lines, views, and circulation gives the impression of a much larger space in spite of its many buildings and walls. The effect is not overwhelmingly architectural due to the pervading sense of naturalism and the avoidance of evident order. Buildings do not face each other and the interpenetration of trees and shrubs, rocks and water mask but do not conceal them.

Therefore, in ancient China, we find a rigid, rectangular and axial city, palace and house forms contrasted with the natural appearance of public parks, burial grounds, landscape gardens, and hunting parks. Both were the product of symbolism, the city plan reflecting the ancient conception of the universe and the role of the emperor as intermediary between heaven and earth. The love of nature, evident in the pleasure gardens, reflects the original symbolic meaning attributed to landscape elements, mountains and lakes (shan and shui) and the contrasts of natural form. The religious philosophies of Taoism, Confucius, and Buddha relied upon nature to induce spirituality and reveal the inner harmonies of humans.

The ideal Chinese house had an enclosed garden. The garden was used for a variety of purposes: recreation, rest, study, meditation, and appreciation of the processes and aesthetics of nature. Privacy and quiet were essential. Symbolism was prevalent in every feature and in the arrangement. Water, as a balance to land, was essential for perfect harmony; its constantly changing appearance a reminder of the continual motion of the cosmos. Rocks contained all the creative forces of the Tao and were symbolic of wilderness and mountains. Plants symbolized man's life in the universe and each one held traditional meaning for the viewer. The entire garden was a symbol of the universe.

JAPAN

The island nation of Japan, lying close to the northern shores of China, fell inevitably within its cultural sphere of influence. By 550 AD, Buddhism with its concept of an earthly paradise which had intensified the Taoist's interest in nature and contributed to the typical garden forms in China, was introduced into Japan, where already the Shinto religion had evolved. The latter, with its rudimentary emphasis on the processes and forms of nature, was receptive to the more sophisticated Chinese philosophy and garden design. A very strong religious doctrine took hold in Japan and dominated that society for the ensuing 13 centuries.

The historical development of the Japanese garden is exceedingly complicated and the early garden forms which were adopted by nobles, were heavily influenced by religious beliefs, symbolism, and Chinese influence in varying proportions. Meditation was the garden's chief purpose, through which the meaning and purpose of life was revealed. Gardens of the Nara period (645–784), often built by craftsmen from Korea and China, included lakes and rocks arranged to resemble nature based on the Chinese model. Subsequent periods, especially those associated with the location of the capital at Kyoto, saw the refinement of this garden type as a pleasure ground representing paradise and within which imperial courtiers amused themselves, boating on the lakes, writing poetry, and discussing aesthetics. The gardens, too, contained symbols of longevity and purity, as well as allusions to specific places in Japan. To the initiated, then, the garden could be read and enjoyed like a book. The

FIGURE 2.6
Ryoan-ji. A Zen dry garden dating back to 1500.

importance of Zen Buddhism in the Kamakura period (1185–1392) brought new concepts to life. Zen contrasted to the more formal Buddhist symbol-laden and elaborate doctrine. The garden was seen more strictly as an aid to meditation. For this purpose it was enclosed with a wall, and the relationship of the viewer to the garden was fixed. Later, during the Muromachi period (1393–1568), the dry garden, of which Ryoan-ji is a prime example, was produced in a time of nostalgia for the eleventh and twelfth centuries. The dry garden was the ultimate Zen aesthetic. Temples contained dry gardens as places to find spiritual peace in turbulent times.

Ryoan-ji is a small, enclosed, inward looking garden made of simple materials conducive to meditation, viewed from a veranda of a temple building (Fig. 2.6). It contrasted to the more lavish gardens of previous periods and ideals. This garden forms part of a Zen temple (formerly a nobleman's estate). Over time buildings have been destroyed and rebuilt, but the garden has existed since approximately 1500 BC. The enclosure measures 75 feet by 30 feet wide and is approached and viewed from a wooden veranda raised above the ground along one side in front of the Abbot's rooms. The enclosing wall of clay with a tile roof is approximately 7 feet high and the surrounding forest can be seen beyond. The sky is above. The rectangle contains 15 stones in 5 uneven groups set in coarse sand which is raked in circular pattern around the stones and in straight lines elsewhere. The only vegetation within the enclosure is some moss around the stones. The composition is framed by a border of stones, more complex under the veranda and building eaves, and quite simple on the wall sides. The Zen priests prefer that the arrangement of stones be given no specific meaning. Their value is in improving meditation leading to images originating in the observer.

> Within the space of the garden, framed by the wall, images are compressed that extend from a view of landscape that is cosmic, to a pinpoint focus on matter which is microscopic. You can refer immediately to the native landscape that is reflected—the rocks stand like the rugged islands in the waves of an ocean, an image so familiar after the native coastline; or they rise with the thrusting volcanic rhythm of the mountains, the sand swirling around their base like cloud lingering on the lower slopes. The garden encompasses the depth of vision, the sense of space and the grandeur of scale that was explored by the painters, but by virtue of its abstract form, it offers further experience. As the eye closed in from the panorama and the illusory horizon is reduced, the wavelike patterns of the sand flow with the force of the current rushing against the stepping-stones of a river. When you concentrate further on this wave-like motion, the raw image itself is revealed. The ripples of the sand flow as patterns of energy, as lines of force on some molecular scale, polarized around the stones. The wave motion is itself the fundamental image, rising and falling, but never actually moving, only appearing to move.[2]

The Zen dry garden is a perfect reflection of the monk's life, imbued with simplicity and austerity, leading to spiritual enlightenment.

In the Edo period (1620–1645) political power moved to Tokyo (Edo). The Emperor, whose power was merely symbolic, remained in Kyoto and spent time embellishing court and family life with the arts. Many of the earlier garden concepts were reexamined and brought together in what is usually called the stroll garden. This is the second type of garden most commonly associated with Japan. Several good examples exist in Kyoto.

The idea of the stroll garden was the creation of a series of views and experiences in the garden. In this sense it resembled the gardens of China, although the route to be followed was more clearly prescribed. Ideally it followed a clockwise route around an irregularly shaped lake and was laid out with bends and turns in relation to planting and topography such that the whole garden could not be seen at any one time. Each view was carefully composed and framed. Buildings, the villa, the teahouse, the temple, and bridges and other garden structures featured unobtrusively in these views as did rocks, pebble beaches, and planting. The path, itself, would consist of various materials and forms: gravel, cobbles, stepping stones. Symbolism and allusion pervaded the elements and their composition: rock, streams, and plants that were carefully pruned to emphasize their essence.

The illusion of space and landscape continuity was a major goal of the Japanese garden. The concept of borrowed landscape, i.e., opening up a view of a distant valley or mountain while concealing the garden boundary, was frequently applied. To aid the illusion, the trees inside the garden were the same species as those in the distant view. Other techniques such as planting large trees in the foreground and smaller ones in the background, or placing a large hill in front of a smaller one, also contributed to a sense of distance and space within the garden. It is not often discussed, but these gardens were also often seen by the emperor and his courtiers from a boat, revealing the same elements and views from another angle.

---

[2] Holborn, Mark, *The Ocean in the Sand* (Boulder, Colorado: Shambhala Publications, 1978).

At the Katsura Imperial Villa near Kyoto we find all of these features and concepts combined into a magnificent stroll garden (Figs. 2.7 and 2.8). The villa, which also remains intact, is a fine example of Japanese architecture. Together they illustrate the idea of integration which typifies the national Japanese house and garden. It also demonstrates the adaptable architectural form. Built in the Edo period over several years starting in 1620, it is thought to be the conception of Prince Toshihito, a brother of Emperor Goyozei. Many of the views are based on an eleventh century novel and the garden is imbued with literary allusions to the initiated.

The villa would be approached through a series of gates and along paths following an indirect route to

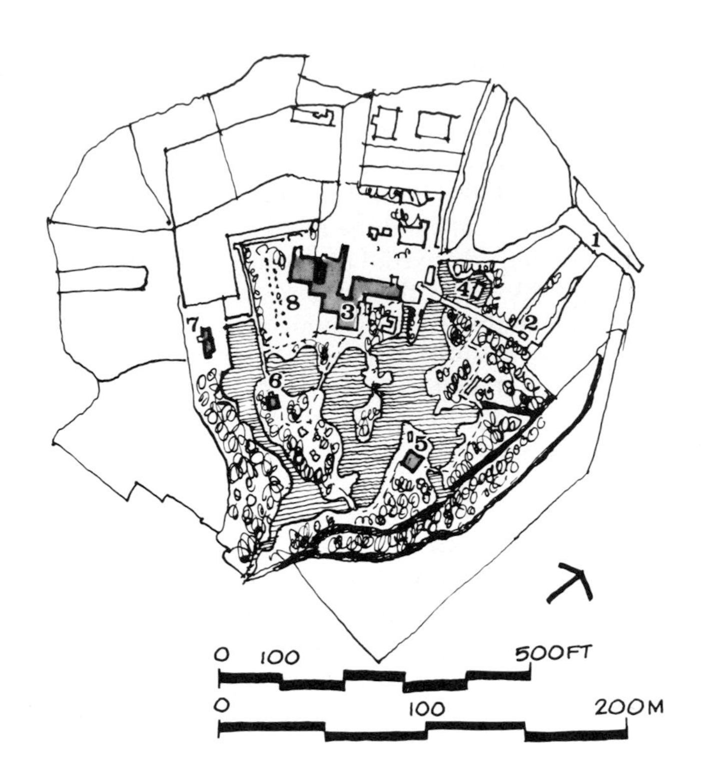

FIGURE 2.7
Plan of Katsura Imperial Villa garden at Kyoto, started in 1620 (at right). **(1)** Front gate, **(2)** Imperial gate, **(3)** villa, **(4)** boathouse, **(5)** Shokin-Tei (tea house), **(6)** Onrin-Do (Buddhist temple), **(7)** Shoi-Ken (a large pavilion), **(8)** riding ground.

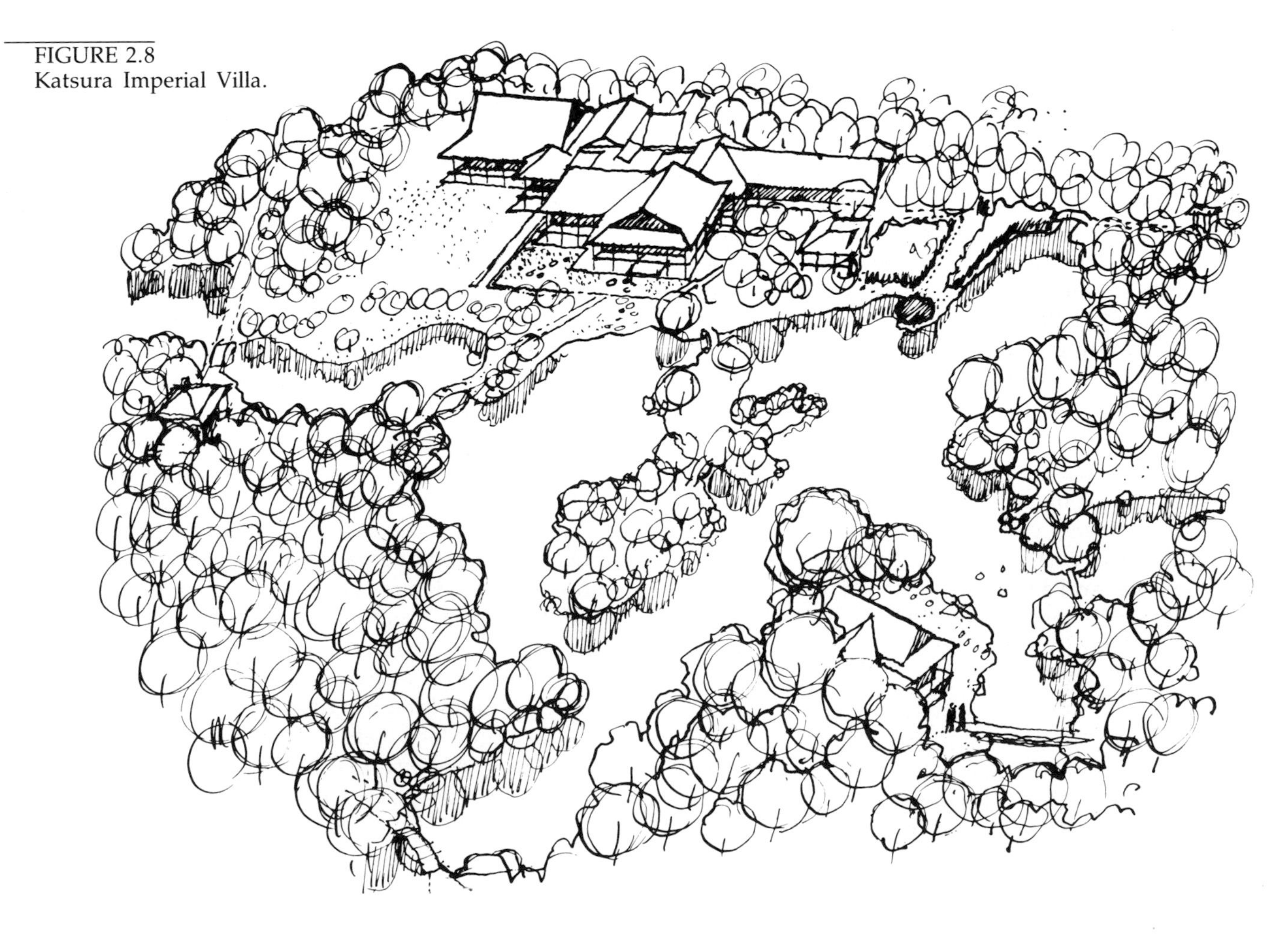

FIGURE 2.8
Katsura Imperial Villa.

the main door at the side of the villa. The door itself is not seen until the last moment. From the building, raised for protection from floods and for ventilation, specific views of the garden can be controlled by sliding screens or the entire front can be opened up to the garden which lies to the south. The villa consists of a series of units, built on the tatami mat module, added together and forming an informal edge on the garden side. The orientation and design of the buildings permits winter sunshine to enter but summer sun is shaded. (The building also faces the fall moon in autumn.) The central feature of the garden is a lake with five islands.

Along the pathway, the lake is always present. The stroller encounters landscape views composed with trees, shrubs, rocks, a roofed bench or stone basin, lanterns, stone and wooden bridges, a waterfall and a pebble beach reminiscent of a famous scenic coastline in Japan. A rustic pavilion on top of a hill provides a place to view the moon reflected in the lake. There are several tea pavilions and a temple. This complicated landscape and its revealed views is filled with aesthetic experience and opportunities for meditation. In this we have the essence of a prototype.

Ideally, the Japanese house, like a palace, would be elevated off the ground and situated in the middle of a garden surrounded by a high fence of wood or bamboo for seclusion. A household would probably consist of several interrelated buildings forming courtyards, but the main room would ideally have a southern view. The buildings were simple, of unpainted wood and based on the 3-by-6-foot module of the rice straw tatami mat. Semitransparent movable paper screens divided the interior space. The architecture itself, responding to a wide range of climatic conditions, was highly adaptable. Free flow of air to combat summer humidity was permitted by the incorporation of large doors and window openings and a flexible interior. Shelter from heavy and high rainfall and from the penetration of the summer sun was provided by wide overhanging eaves. Such a design provided frequent views of the garden from inside the house and the veranda, and a physical link between indoor and outdoor. Steps led to the gardens.

Ideally the main garden lay in front of the principle rooms on the south side of the house. Typically it would be a hill and water garden, the most complete form. Other smaller courtyards and entrance spaces would be flat gardens. The view from the main rooms was of prime importance, but other important viewpoints were located within the garden itself. Traditionally, the garden was considered a work of art and the monks and scholars who laid them out, artists. The gardens were intended to stimulate a flow of meditation and provide a serene, refreshing, and quiet setting for it. The garden was a symbol of nature and a suggestive representation of landscape.

ANCIENT GREECE AND ROME

In contrast to the Orient, there is little concern with gardens in early Greek history. The private house seems to have been a very modest affair in comparison with the important social places such as the agora and gymnasium, theater, and sacred groves. The living rooms of the house faced onto an inner court which was often paved and decorated with statues and plants in pots (Fig. 2.9). Distant palaces of the Greek empire, particularly in the time of Alexander the Great, are said to have had elaborate gardens inspired by those of Persia and Egypt.

The Roman house basically followed the Greek pattern. Houses were built flush to the street with inward-facing rooms connected by colonnades and opening onto an open square or atrium. The gardens were essentially social sanctuaries, enclosed shelters from the fierce sun, wind, dust, and noise of the streets. Since shade was provided by the surrounding portico, there was little need for trees. Planting, if any, was chiefly in pots or raised beds, and stone water

FIGURE 2.9
Greek house, at Prienne (300 BC).

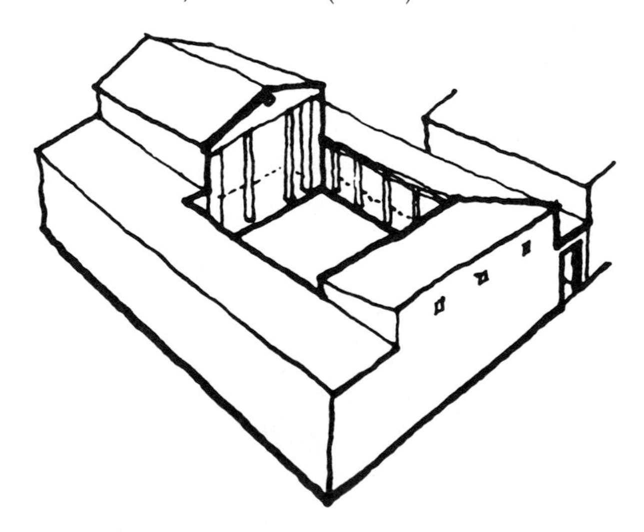

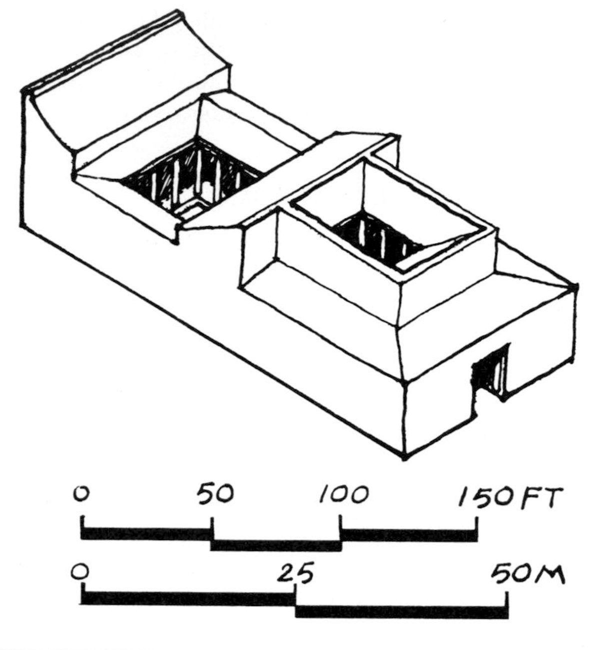

FIGURE 2.10
Roman house at Pompeii (50 BC).

basins, marble tables, and small statues were frequently used to embellish the courts (Fig. 2.10).

Since much of the original wealth of Rome came from the surrounding agricultural landscape, many aristocrats built villas outside Rome. Cicero is said to have owned about eighteen such country homes. In AD 100 Pliny the Younger built a villa seventeen miles from Rome at Laurentinum, where the garden was chiefly planted with fig and mulberry trees. The formal layout included a well-stocked kitchen garden, cloisters, a summer house, and a terrace with fragrant flowers. The villa, situated on water for a cooler climate, is basically a farm house set in fields (Fig. 2.11). Pliny's Tuscan garden was set on a hillside and incorporated water features and fountains, topiary and colonnades. Hadrian's villa at Tivoli, built between AD 117 and 138, was much more elaborate and extensive, since it was used for many years as a government center. It was in fact a large estate containing many buildings, pools and water basins, terraces and statues. Although the garden units which make up the complex are architectural, there was no overall design concept within which to fit later additions (Fig. 2.12). The layout included a wooded park area, called the Valley of the Tempe, representative of a legendary forest said to have stood at the foot of Mount Olympus. This wooded park area substantiated the claim of advocates of the eighteenth century landscape garden in England that the ancient Romans appreciated nature and deliberately included a symbol of wilderness within their estates.

ISLAM

The great unifying force of the Prophet Mohammed and Islam underlay the establishment of the powerful and expansive Islamic empire in the seventh century centered in Damascus and Baghdad. With extensions to northern India, north Africa, Sicily and southern Spain, the world of Islam dominated a large part of the known world for eight centuries.

FIGURE 2.11
Pliny's villa at Laurentinum (100 AD).

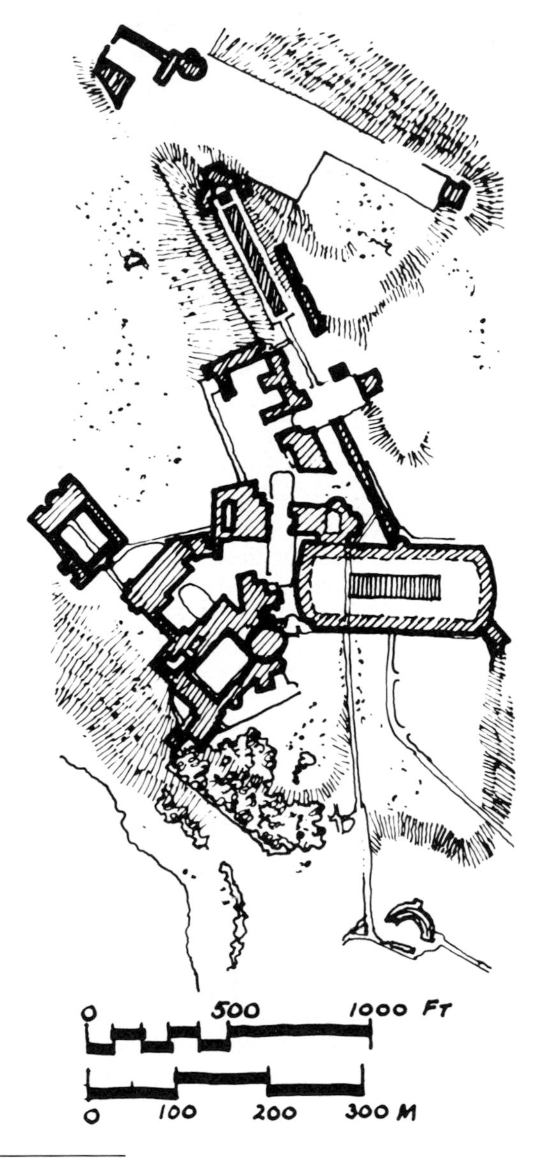

FIGURE 2.12
Hadrian's villa at Tivoli (117–138 AD). A series of buildings and courts built over a long period of time without any coordinating plan. The Valley of the Tempe is in the lower left.

The origin of the basic form in Persia and the Middle East has been discussed. The strength of the Islamic prototype lay in its religious connotations and traditions combined with the development of art and the definition of pleasure and uses of a garden which immense wealth and power made possible. But first and foremost, the concept of the Islamic garden was based on an image of paradise, the well-watered land of milk and honey described in the Koran.

Water was the essential ingredient of the garden for practical and symbolic purposes. In Persia, it was brought to the garden by quanat from aquifers located at the base of snow-covered mountain ranges. Water flowed by gravity in underground pipes and flooded the channels and tanks around which the garden was organized and served as the irrigation system for the trees and plants in the spaces between. The water would then flow out of the garden and supply the agricultural and domestic needs of the community or village. The system was entirely gravity fed and the gardens, ideally and conceptually flat, were, in fact, made on a slight slope. The water channels were contrived to quarter the garden into four major rectangular portions, symbolizing the cosmos and the four rivers of life (Fig. 2.13).

The organization was axial and geometric, but the growth of plants was profuse and natural, providing an attractive contrast. Trees were planted in rows parallel to the water channels. Many were fruit trees including those of local origin such as pomegranates, dates, and plums, and other imports such as peaches and oranges from China. Certain plants were included for symbolism—the cypress, symbol of death contrasting with the almond, for life and hope. Flowers abound-

FIGURE 2.13
The plan of the tomb garden of Humayun, Delhi, illustrates the features of a prototypical Islamic garden.

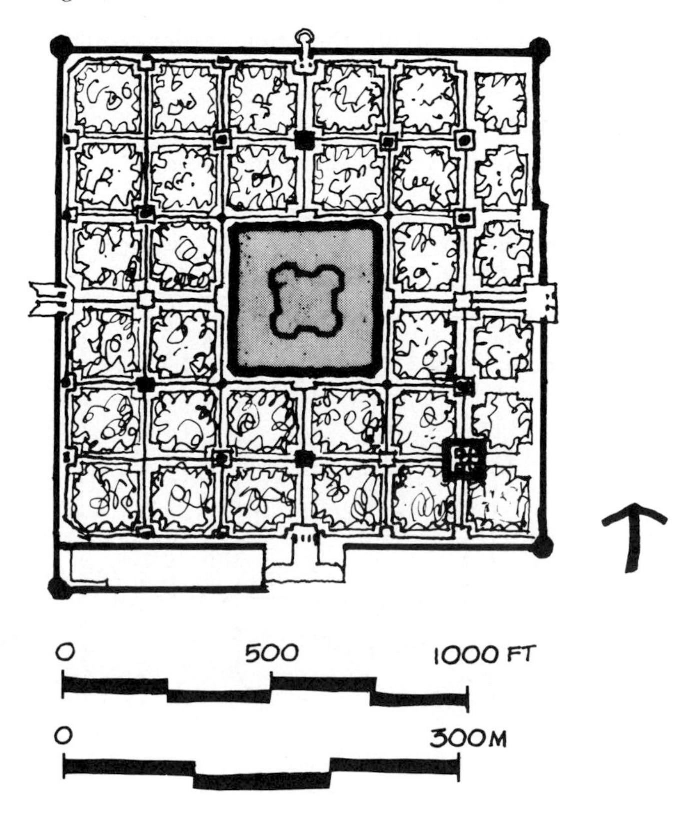

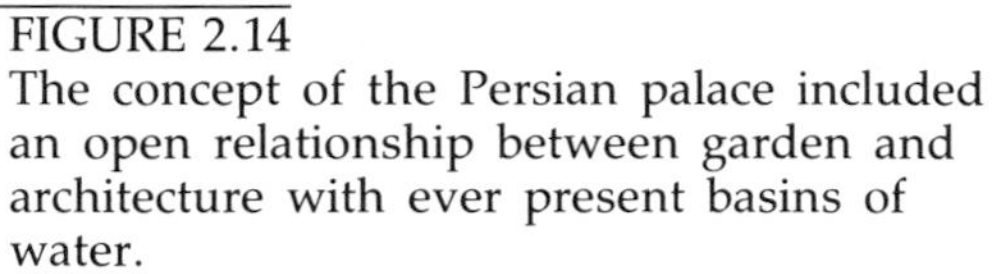

FIGURE 2.14
The concept of the Persian palace included an open relationship between garden and architecture with ever present basins of water.

ed, especially roses (an indigenous plant). Roaming in the garden we would find animals such as gazelles and exotic birds. At the center of the garden, associated with the meeting of the water channels and a large geometric pool, there would typically be a raised pavilion, house, or even a palace (depending on the scale) with an open form of architecture providing a free flow of air and an intimate relationship between indoors and out (Fig. 2.14). Finally, the whole garden would be surrounded by a protective wall with small towers or pavilions at the corners and gates located in each side.

FIGURE 2.15
The Court of the Lyons, Alhambra, Spain.

The paradise garden of Islam was essentially an oasis, a secluded retreat protected from the desert winds and dust. Trees provided fruit and shade from the hot sun. Flowers provided color and scent. Water helped to cool the air. The whole was pervaded with supportive symbolism of the religious and philosophical basis of life. These pleasure gardens were favorite resorts of the ruling classes and royal families who used them as settings for indulgence in poetry and music, horticultural pursuits, and for festivals and receptions.

SPAIN

The Moslem expansion into Egypt and north Africa reached southern Spain by the eighth century AD where an independent colonial settlement lasted until ousted by the Christians at the end of the fifteenth century. Known as the Moors, they introduced irrigation practices and improved agriculture. Remnants of the Roman Empire inspired the adoption of the internal courtyard as a typical form for gardens within the fortified palaces of the rulers. The Spanish version of the Islamic garden is, therefore, a combination of the small Roman courtyard and the Islamic concept of space division and symbolism. The intent was undoubtedly to create gardens like those of Damascus. A comparison of Persian palaces and the Court of the Lyons at Granada illustrates the similarities in architecture, and the use of water (Fig. 2.15). Similar open

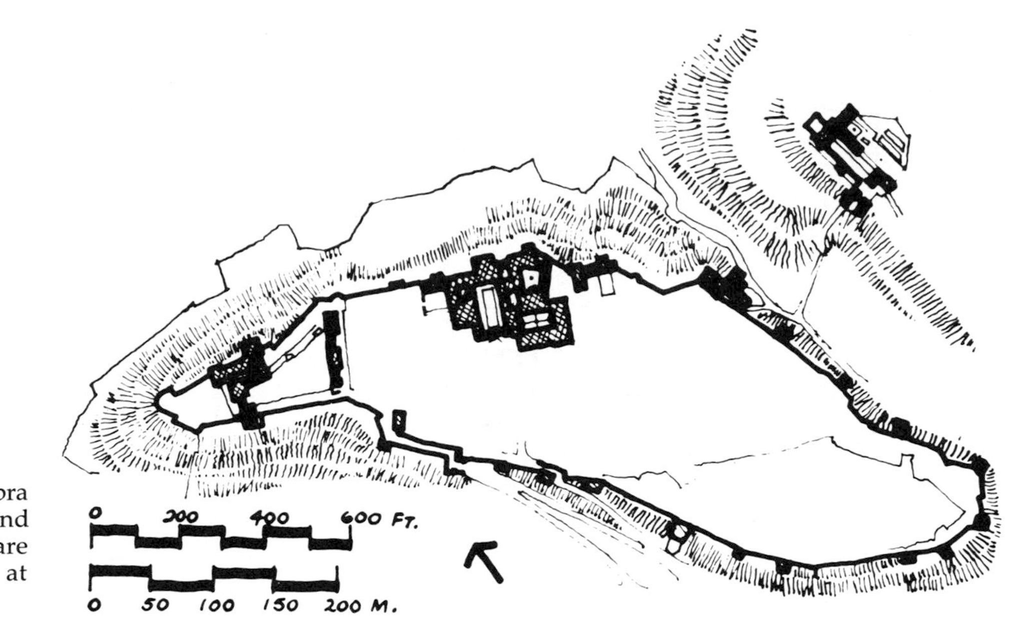

FIGURE 2.16
Probable plan of the Alhambra at some point between 1238 and 1358 (more recent additions are omitted). The Generalife is at the upper right.

pavilions permit the free flow of air. Water is used symbolically and as a cooling agent.

The Alhambra was a fortified palace built on high ground. It developed in stages between 1350 and 1500, and, as a result, its series of chambers and enclosed courtyards is without any connecting organization (Fig. 2.16). The form of the complex is a response to the climate. The outside is hostile, hot, and dusty. The inside is shaded, cool, and protected by thick walls. Since the entire structure is perched on high ground, the windows which provide views out over the landscape also permit breezes to blow in. Rooms associated with pools of water thus provide a primitive but successful air conditioning system (Fig. 2.17). Channels of water ran not only in the courtyards but sometimes also actually into and through the buildings, lowering temperatures and providing the cooling sound of running water.

Despite similarities, the Spanish version of the Islamic garden differs from the Persian in that the former encloses the garden in courtyards surrounded by buildings whereas the latter is a walled garden within which the palace is located.

THE MOGHUL GARDEN

The Islamic garden in India is commonly referred to as the Moghul garden after the Moghul emperors of Turkish origin. Attracted by the riches and wealth of the Hindu temples, the Moslems followed the Mongols, to whom they were related, in creating a military presence in India, sacking the cities and temples and removing everything of value to Persia. But, in 1526 the Moghuls, in the form of a prince named Babur, came to stay and began a dynasty which persisted and controlled more than half of India through six successive emperors until 1750, lingering on less influentially thereafter. They settled in the great northern plain,

FIGURE 2.17
The Court of the Myrtles, Alhambra, Spain. Breezes blowing from outside across the water basin act as an air conditional system for the palace.

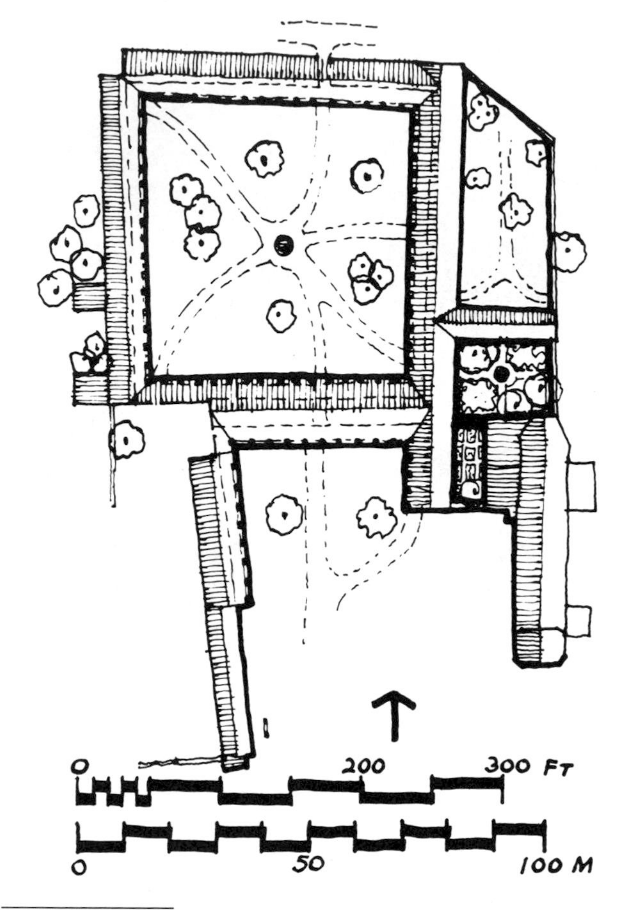

FIGURE 2.18
Plan of Mission San Juan Capistrano (1776). The missions of California introduced the architectural forms of Spain—arcades and enclosed courtyards.

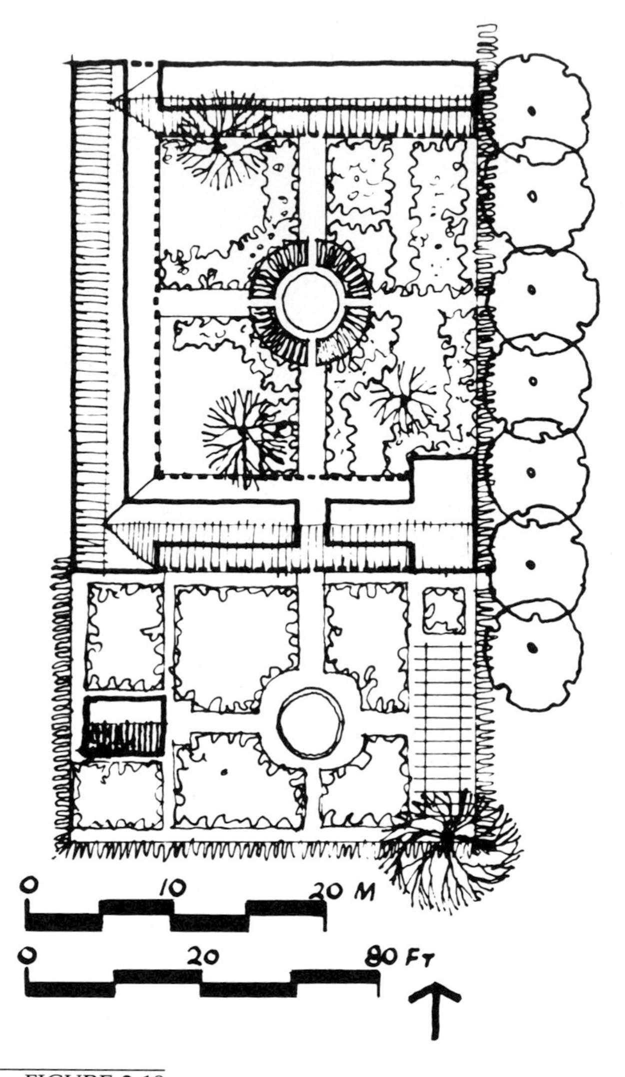

FIGURE 2.19
Plan of an early California homestead (1858). The central source of water and the architectural enclosure are Spanish in origin.

subject to heat, humidity, and winds, but they also discovered Kashmir, where summer palaces were built. In addition to the Hindu traditions, the Moghuls found established irrigation practices in agriculture and gardens associated with the temples. These were largely devoted to growing flowers which played an important role in the religion. The Hindu garden was informal and profuse and, as a concept, influenced the development of the Chinese prototype when Buddhism was introduced to China.

As one would expect, however, the Moghuls, who were avid garden makers, adopted the Persian garden as their model. In time, differences evolved out of the specific conditions of the region. For example, the narrow rills of water expanded into large expanses which helped to modify the heat. The ultimate expression of this was a pavilion set on an island in a broad lake. It has been suggested that the Moghul garden was a dwelling place in its own right, and was an enclosed, protected setting for life, in general, and pleasure, in particular. Horticulture was an obsession and the gardens were filled with all kinds of trees, especially fruit and flowering. Brimming raised channels ran through the gardens and provided the necessary water.

The gardens of Kashmir reflected the different geography in the plants that were grown and being typically linear on sloping sites with more water in the form of cascades and fountains.

Another variation on the Islamic garden theme in India was the tomb garden of the Moghuls. The worship of ancestors, adopted by the Moghuls, was a Mongol concept, not Persian. The tomb was built with a garden which was used for pleasure until the death of the individual. It was thus enjoyed by both the living and the dead (Fig. 2.13).

MEXICO AND CALIFORNIA

We have seen that the courtyard or patio closely linked to the living rooms and corridors of the house is the distinguishing characteristic of the Spanish garden. If we pursue this cultural tradition and climatic type, we find them not surprisingly in the Spanish Empire of the New World. From Mexico, the Spanish influence extended into what are now New Mexico and Texas leaving behind a substantial heritage. Expeditions explored Alta California in the late eighteenth century and the series of missions built by Junipero Serra and his monks between 1769 and 1821 incorporated courtyards with central fountain or well, diagonal paths, and plantings of imported fruit trees, herbs, and flowers, surrounded by arcades (Fig. 2.18). Domestic homesteads, too, adopted similar arrangements, well-suited to the California climate and style of life at that time and clearly derived from the Spanish pattern (Fig. 2.19). This phenomenon and its subsequent revival in the 1920s will be discussed later. But consider at the moment the compelling qualities of this garden concept which evolved from the experience and form of the Persian and early Middle Eastern cultures 5,000 years earlier and 10,000 miles away. In suitable climates, a house type with a private family patio and direct indoor/outdoor connections remains a valid form in the second half of the twentieth century regardless of all social and material advances.

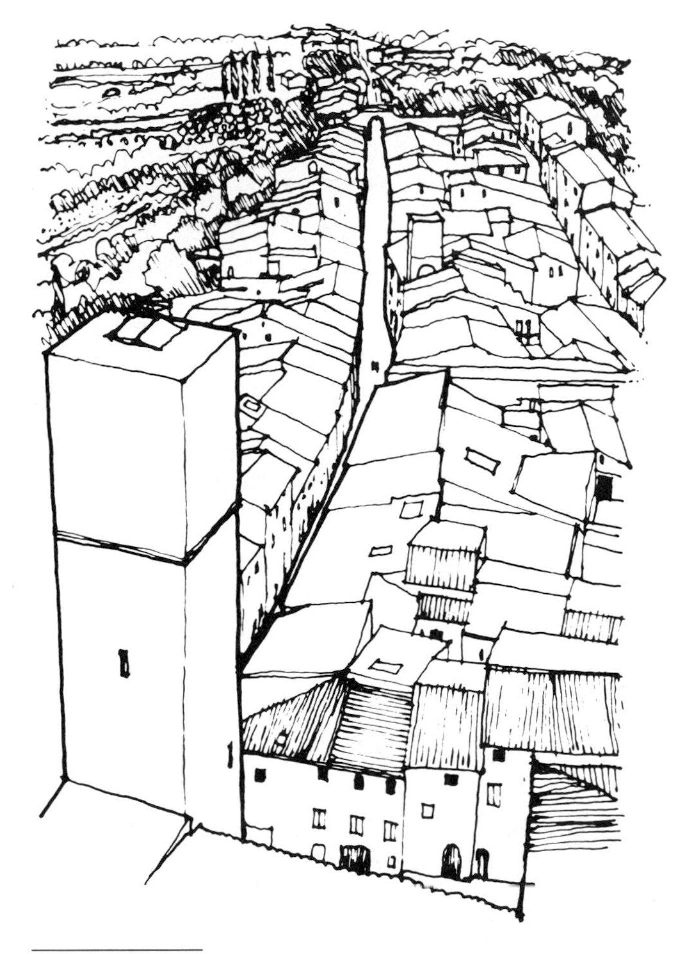

FIGURE 2.20
Italian hill town of the Middle Ages—little space or need for gardens and parks.

MEDIEVAL EUROPE

The Medieval period of European history occupied the time between the disintegration of the Roman Empire and the emergence of Modern Europe in the fifteenth century. The sense of community isolation within a hostile landscape is perfectly evoked in Hesse's novel *Narcissus and Goldmund*. The dark ages were characterized by war, turmoil, and plague. Pleasure gardens were unusual within the dense fortified cities and towns (Fig. 2.20). Space which was available was used functionally for growing food or medicinal herbs. Gardens also were devoted to this purpose within the walls of castles and baronial strongholds (Fig. 2.21). In the monasteries more extensive areas were planted with fruit trees, vines, vegetables, and altar flowers (Fig. 2.22), but the most important element was the physic garden planted with sixteen different herbs which were the basis of drugs and medical science (Fig. 2.23). These herbs were concocted into lotions and preparations to treat various illnesses. For example, lemon balm was used for dog and scorpion bites, chamomile for disease of the liver and also for migraine. Myrtle was recommended for many ailments including ulcers, spitting of blood, and fractured joints. Toward the end of the period, with the easing of political conflict, the development of trade and accumulation of wealth, Medieval gardens attached to castles and country houses became larger, more elaborate, and designed for pleasure as well as utility. Herb gardens and orchards were important basic elements of the walled gardens, which were embellished with grass-covered seats, fountains, flower beds, arbors, clipped shrubs, and fish ponds. Within the enclosure, pleasure pursuits took place; jesters entertained their lords and ladies who danced, ate meals, and made love in the gardens (Fig. 2.24).

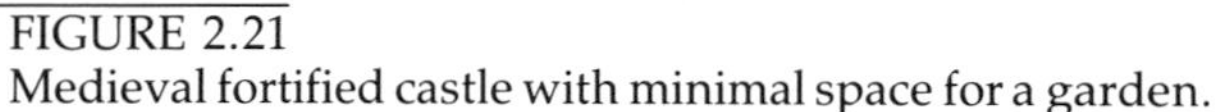

FIGURE 2.21
Medieval fortified castle with minimal space for a garden.

The ballads of troubadors and early manuscripts describe Medieval gardens in terms of an emerging idyllic image of nature. The grass is always intensely green, lawns always sprinkled with fresh wildflowers. The water emanating from fountains and wells is crystal clear. There is no pollution. The air is fresh, the sky is cloudless and bright blue. Trees are in blossom. Birds sing sweetly and mate happily. The time is always spring. The garden provided sensuous pleasures: the scent of flowers and blossom, the coolness of shade cast by the trees and arbors, rest and relaxation, and the acoustic delights of bird song and running water. This is the image of the Medieval garden and no doubt it matched the reality. Its intimacy, simplicity, beauty, and delight are appealing and appropriate to twentieth-century lifestyles.

Carl Theodore Sorensen, the Danish landscape historian, suggests that the great sense of craftsmanship associated with these gardens of the Middle Ages forms the basis for the gardener working as an artist in the subsequent history of garden design. Craftsmanship, an essential component of the Middle Ages, with

FIGURE 2.22
A Medieval monastery with a series of enclosed gardens for herbs, vines, and vegetables.

FIGURE 2.23
A monastery herb garden. Detail of a woodcut by an anonymous artist from Fior di Virtu Hystoriato, Florence, 1519. The Metropolitan Museum of Art, Harris Brisbane Dick Fund, 1925.

FIGURE 2.24
A Medieval garden. Woodcut from Crescentius' De Agricultura Vulgare, Venice, 1519. The Metropolitan Museum of Art, Harris Brisbane Dick Fund, 1934.

its craft guilds and an inventiveness capable of solving all kinds of practical problems, ultimately became associated with aesthetics or ornament. This combination raises life to a higher level or to what British art historian Kenneth Clark defines as civilization.

Thus in gardening the craft produced edges and divisions, plots, dimensions, and shapes suited to cultivation practice, irrigation, tilling, and gathering. But as the idea of an ornamental pleasure garden developed, so the edges and divisions of functional origin became less practical and became ends in themselves. Thus their arrangement became an art as well as a craft.

ITALY

As the Middle Ages progressed from barbarism into an ordered political system based on commerce, so the wealthy aristocracy which it supported turned their attention to refinement. Circumstances made this possible first in Italy in the fifteenth century. Kings, princes, and merchants of the Italian city-states looked back to the Roman Empire for inspiration and guidance. Thus the Renaissance was initiated. Music, art, literature, science, and architecture became major preoccupations of the new enlightened age. In garden design, which held an equal place with the other arts, the most important influence was the writing of Pliny on gardens, paraphrased by Alberti in the second half of the fifteenth century. The theory proposed that the garden be strongly linked to the house by loggias and other architectural extensions into the landscape. The villa should be located on a hillside. Terraces and stairways were recommended to overcome the difficulties of uneven terrain, and an avenue or axis should link up all elements and spaces of the plan.

The gardens of the early Renaissance were designed as intellectual retreats where scholars and artists could work and debate in the coolness of the countryside away from the heat and frustrations of the cities in summer. The Villa Medici, designed by Michelozzo for Cosimo de´ Medici around 1450, is an early expression of Alberti's principles (Fig. 2.25). The banker Medici selected the site on a hillside outside Florence overlooking the plain where it would catch the breeze. Thus it allowed the view which Alberti prescribed. Because of the hillside location, several terraces were required to fit the villa into the land. The entrance driveway followed the contours along the hillside arriving at the top terrace in front of the villa. The house was connected to the garden by a loggia or arcade. However, the relationship between the upper and lower terrace is indirect. The necessary connection was not celebrated with an elaborate staircase as it would have been in the sixteenth century. Behind the house and cut off from the rest of the garden is the giardino segreto, or secret garden. This was a place in which to be alone, secret, hidden and quiet, as opposed to the rest of the garden which would be more public, used by visitors and guests, and permeated with servants.

Bramante's plan for the Belvedere Garden of the Vatican (1503) introduced architectural steps as a major garden design feature to link terraces. The great hill-

FIGURE 2.25
The Villa Medici (1450).

side Italian gardens of subsequent dates developed this new element to its fullest potential. The use of water, which was readily available in the hills, favored for summer villas, was also exploited in elaborate gardens.

Perhaps the greatest example of expertise in stairways and waterworks is the Villa d'Este, designed by Pirro Ligorio in 1575 (Fig. 2.26). Here all the essential characteristics of the prototypical Italian garden are in evidence. Dense shade as a contrast to the bright Mediterranean sunlight was provided by the arrangement of avenues of tall cypress, pleached alleys, and arbors. Sculpture and architectural features were placed throughout the garden to enliven it by contrast with natural forms and textures and also to provide an architectural relationship with the house or villa. On the steep slopes, terraces and flat areas were carved out, supported by retaining walls, and connected with a variety of stairs, flights of steps, and ramps. Water, diverted from a river at a higher point, was directed through the gardens in the form of cascades, fountains, jets, and reflecting pools. These provided visual

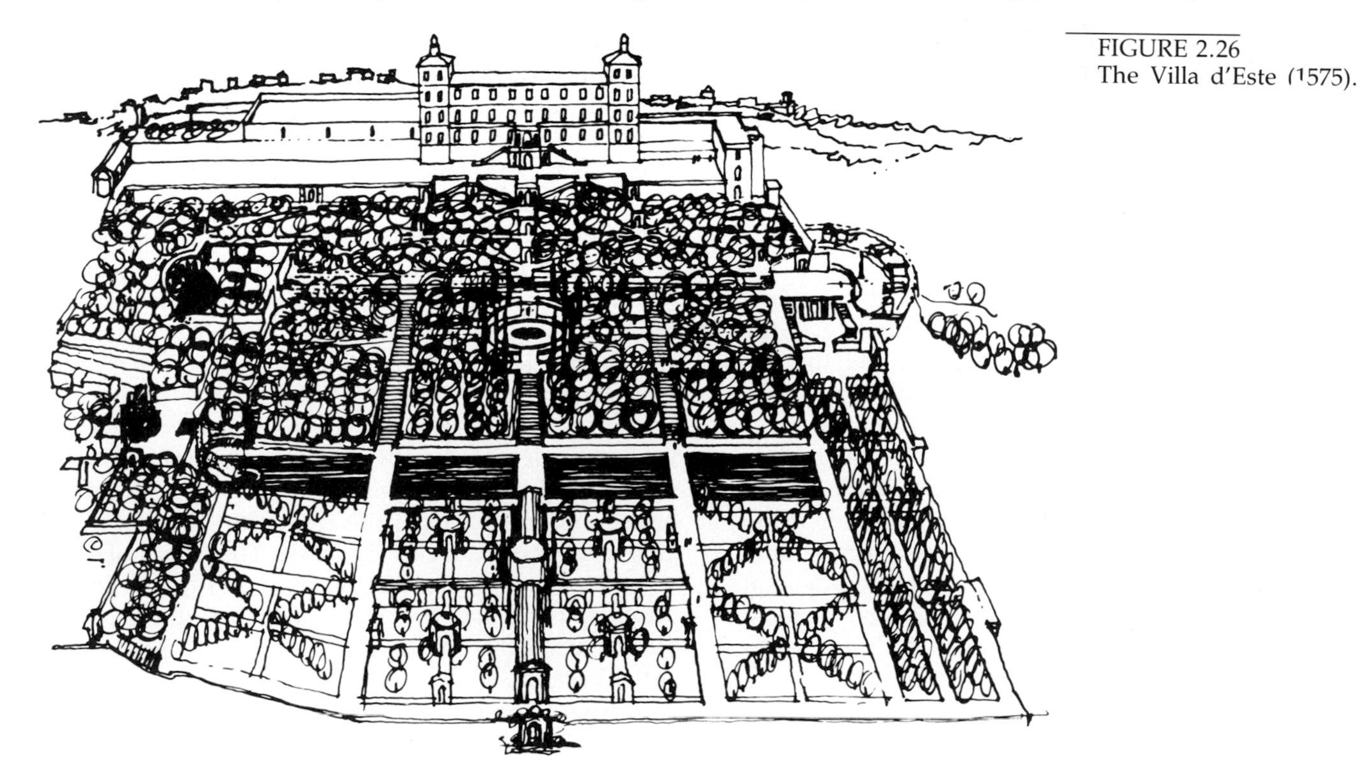

FIGURE 2.26
The Villa d'Este (1575).

FIGURE 2.27
The Villa Lante (1560).

and sensuous delight and also served as an irrigation system. The presence of water together with shade contributed to the much desired coolness which the garden was expected to provide. Boxwood and other shrubs were clipped and arranged in linear patterns to be seen from above, but the use of flowering plants was rare. The entire layout was organized axially. Avenues of trees were used to emphasize perspective and to frame views of the landscape beyond the garden. The house and garden were designed in one process, as a unity.

The entrance is at the lower level and the visitor progressed through the garden with its various sculpture and fountains and other features and points of interest to the palace above. this provided a kinetic and sensuous experience, an unfolding of events before entering the building. A spectacular composition, it was designed for effect and to impress those who visited it.

The Villa Lante, built earlier than d'Este, is less Baroque, on a smaller scale, and more intimate (Fig. 2.27). Its design was directly related to an existing village (Fig. 2.28). An avenue runs between its marketplace and the front gate. The villa itself is two houses, or one house split into two by the garden, whose axis divides it. In addition, since the garden runs from the front gate between the villas to the top of the hillside, there is a front garden and a back garden. These two facts make it an unusual and interesting design. Sylvia Crowe speaks of the progression of water from a rustic quality at the top, gradually increasing in sophistication as it is channelized and formed into jets and waterfalls until it reaches the bottom in an elaborate architectural water parterre.[3] On the other hand, since (as in the Villa d'Este) the garden is approached from

FIGURE 2.28
Plan of the Villa Lante, showing the relationship of the garden to the adjoining village. Note also the large enclosed informal woodland.

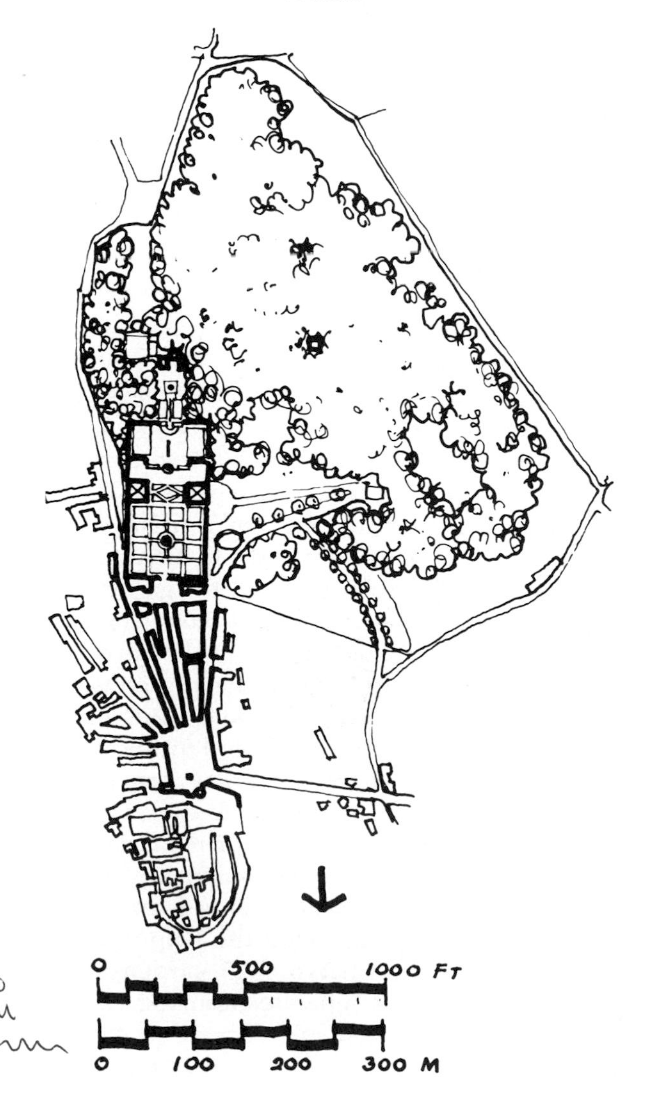

[3] Sylvia Crowe, *Garden Design* (London: Country Life, 1958).

the bottom, the actual experience sequence would in all probability be the reverse. The garden is a progression of events with changing views, symbolic meaning, and increasing enclosure. At certain points jets of water were designed to spray unsuspecting guests, and a stone dining table in the upper garden utilized the water in its center for cooling wine and floating dishes back and forth. As one rises up the hill, the parterre on the lower level is revealed and the surrounding town and landscape beyond the wall also become progressively more visible. The enclosed garden was an oasis or paradise in contrast to the misery and squalor in the adjacent village and surrounding agricultural landscape.

In both of these gardens there is an inspired combination of site and concept. The qualities of the site are respectfully molded into a strong architectural composition. This provides an intense contrast between natural and man-made forms, which is often the essence of visual satisfaction in landscape design. Moreover, the site is enriched with detail appropriate and related to the overall concept yet providing variety and surprise within an intelligible whole. This relationship between detail and site plan is handled in such a way that each would be incomplete without the other. These are enduring principles in design.

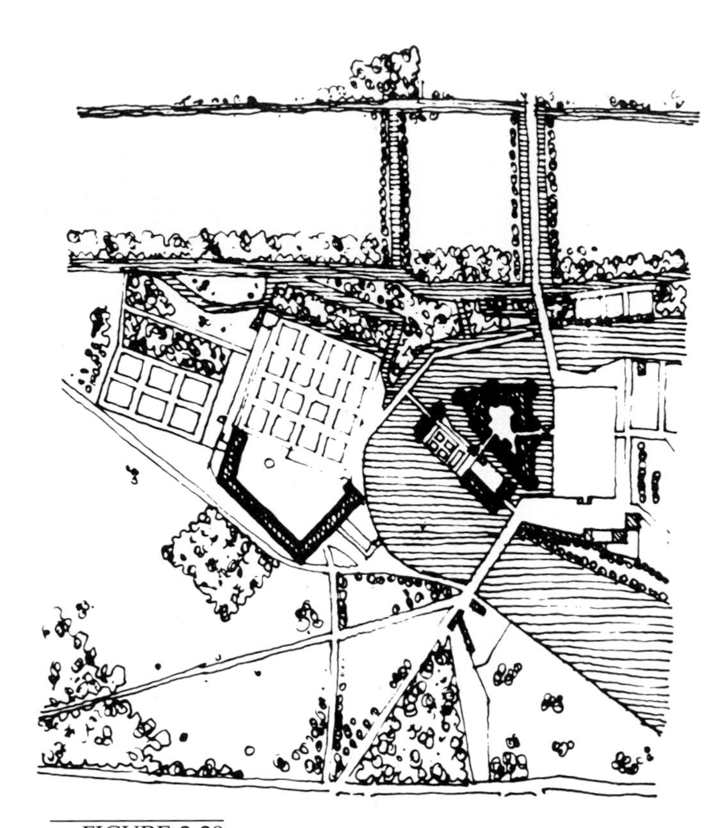

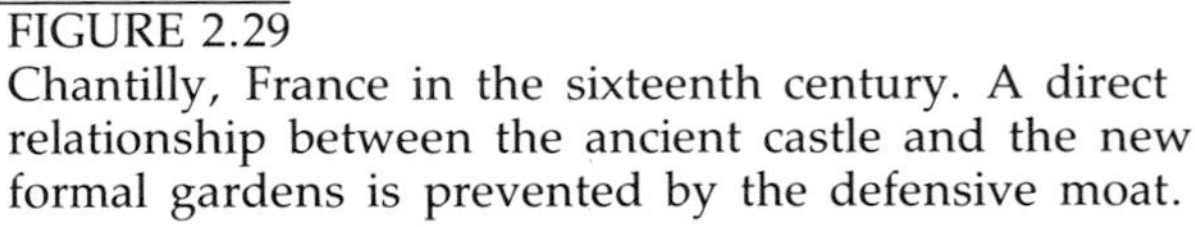

FIGURE 2.29
Chantilly, France in the sixteenth century. A direct relationship between the ancient castle and the new formal gardens is prevented by the defensive moat.

FRANCE

Conditions of peace and prosperity essential for a renaissance came to France later. The aristocracy's enthusiasm to assimilate the artistic developments of Italy was dampened by the Hundred Years' War with England until the end of the fifteenth century. In 1495 Charles VIII of France made an expedition to Naples and returned with twenty-one Italian artists, a considerably quantity of *objets d'art*, and ambitions to build in the Italian manner. Subsequently, the gardens of the ancient châteaux at Amboise and Blois were altered and additions were made to reflect the Italian aesthetic. But it was difficult to achieve the prescribed unity between the new gardens and the existing buildings surrounded by protective moats and fortifications. At Blois, due to the lay of the land, new formal gardens were laid out at an oblique angle to the châteaux. At Chantilly, the original castle occupied an island, making a direct house and garden relationship impossible (Fig. 2.29). At Fontainebleau, where Francis I rebuilt and decorated the palace with the help of a second importation of Italian artists in 1525, gardens were laid out beyond the moat separate from the châteaux.

It became obvious that only by building completely new châteaux and gardens at the same time could the proper effect be realized. This was done at Ancy-le-Franc (1546) and Château d' Anet (1548) and at numerous places thereafter. However, even though the protective moat served no defensive function after the invention of gunpowder, the French insisted on including a symbolic moat around many of the new châteaux.

In the seventeenth century France reached her greatest period of wealth and power and, in addition, became the major arbiter of taste throughout Europe. The French garden is particularly noted for its use of parterres. The origin of the parterre lay in the use of low hedges to separate one kind of herb from another in the Medieval physic garden. The functional divisions became ornamental in themselves and frequently there was nothing contained within them. Sometimes colored gravel or clay and sometimes flower and foliage plants were used. The optimum effect was seen from above. Jacques Boyceau developed the art of the parterre and a theory of garden design which prepared the ground for the celebrated work of André Le Nôtre in the mid-seventeenth century. Whereas the Italian gardens were typically designed by architects, in France they were designed by professional gardeners trained in design.

The climate and landscape of northern France played a role in determining the basic characteristics of the French garden and also accounted for some differences between the prototypical French and Italian gardens. Northern France is comparatively flat and wooded. The gardens thus tended to appear as clearings in a forest and the gentle topography had to be treated with subtlety to create distinct differentiation of levels or terraces from which to view the parterres. Views out were limited. Slowly moving rivers and low-lying marshland lent themselves to the development of canals, moats, and expanses of still water. The use of fountains and cascades is thus less typical in the French than in the Italian garden. The few fountains in northern France were achieved at great expense and with considerable ingenuity.

The strong axial layout, symmetry, mathematical proportions, and infinite perspective of the seventeenth-century French garden reflect the wealth and power and rigid social structure of France and the evolving concept of man's ascendancy over nature. Hunting practices in the forest land surrounding the gardens required the cutting of alleys radiating from a central point. These provided sight lines and facilitated maneuverability. This "star" pattern was incorporated in the design of the garden and also in urban form, as demonstrated in the radiating avenues of Versailles, Paris, and Washington, D. C.

Two masterpieces by André Le Nôtre, Vaux-le-Vicomte (1650-1661) (Figs. 2.30 and 2.31) and Versailles (1661) (Figs. 2.32 and 2.33), represent the ultimate expression of the concept of a geometrically ordered landscape. Vaux is a perfect example of house and garden unity. It was designed by a team consisting of André Le Nôtre, the gardener, and Le Brun and Le Vau, architects. The scale of the enterprise was, for those days, enormous. The project provided employment for hundreds of workers, some of whose families were displaced by the removal of three villages which lay in the way of the design. The area of the estate measured approximately ¾ mile by 1½ miles. However, the formal garden itself was a smaller area around the palace. The plan looks simple, rigid and symmetrical, but it is actually rich and varied on either side of the main axis with a number of surprises. The land was carefully shaped as it sloped away from the palace in such a way that the river, which was canalized, could not be seen until the last minute. In addition, from a particular position looking back along the axis, the entire facade of the palace is seen reflected in the square pond. The garden is a mathematical exercise with carefully worked out proportions and optical effects. The palace itself is surrounded by a moat, a symbolic feature carried over from earlier traditions.

The garden belonged to Fouquet, Finance Minister to Louis XIV, and was frequented by large crowds of courtiers and officials, nobles, and their servants. It was a stage set for display and ceremony where fêtes and concerts were held, boating took place on the river and hunting in the surrounding park, and the whole environment and social routine had all the qualities of an exclusive country club.

The King, jealous of Fouquet's social and artistic triumph, imprisoned him and took his design team to a small hunting lodge at Versailles. Within seven years, the original garden of 250 acres was enlarged to

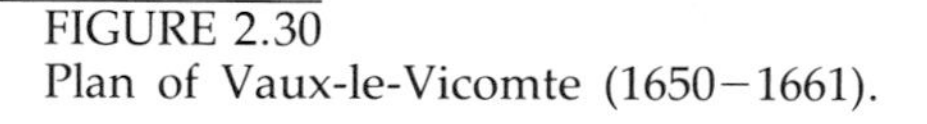

FIGURE 2.30
Plan of Vaux-le-Vicomte (1650–1661).

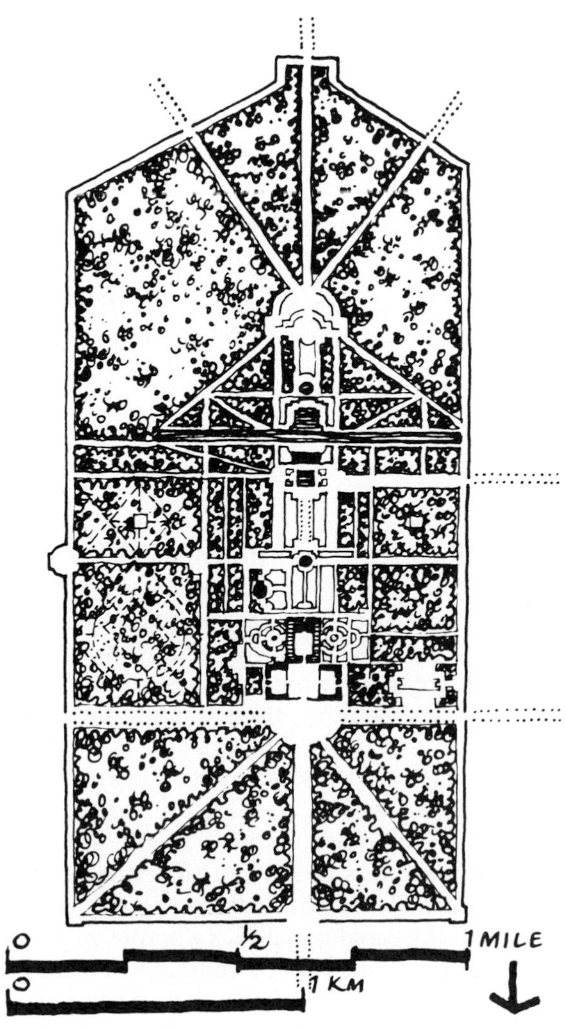

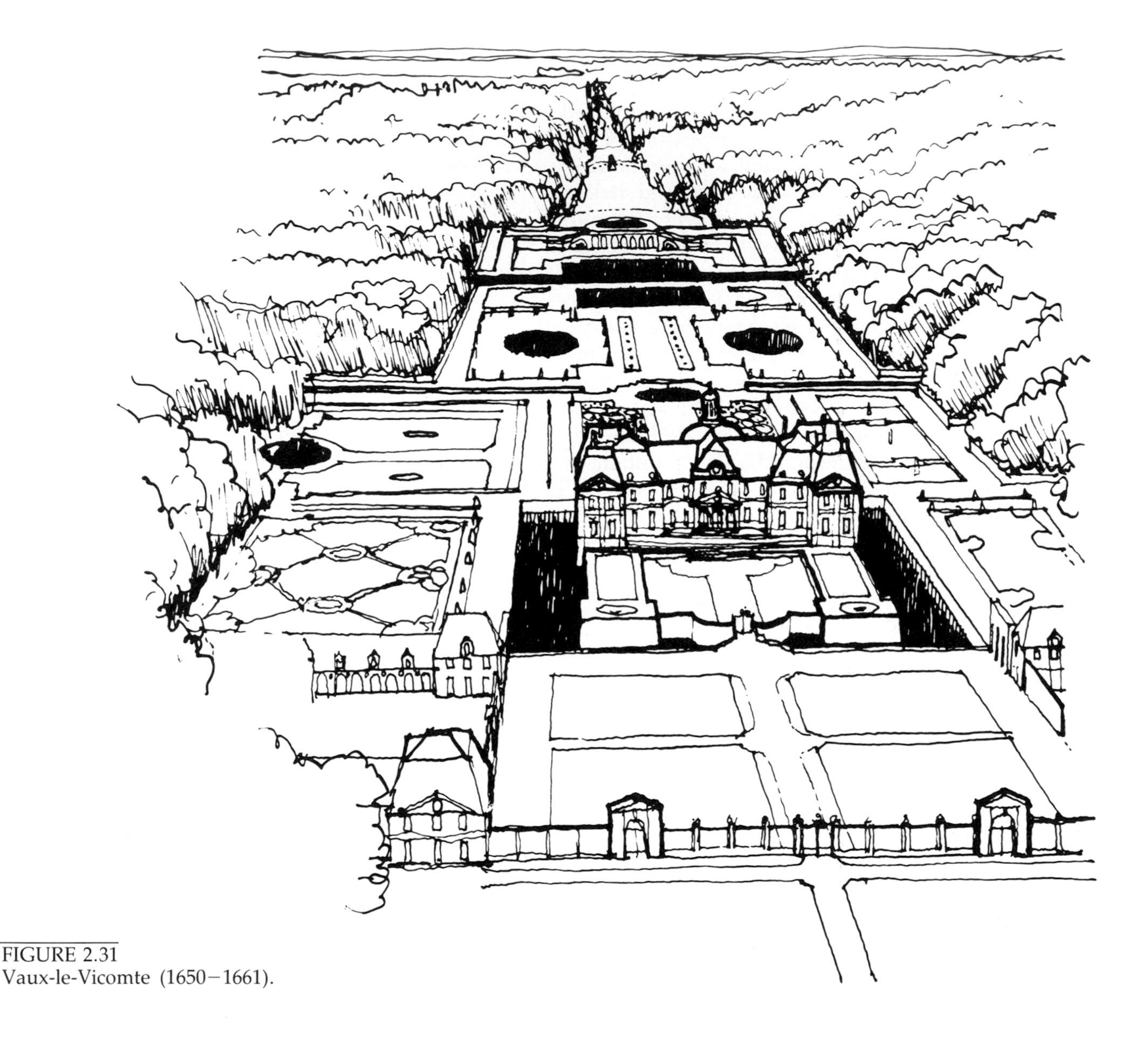

FIGURE 2.31
Vaux-le-Vicomte (1650–1661).

an estate of 15,000 acres, and the facade of the palace was extended to 1,325 feet in length. Although the garden itself may seem small in relation to the entire planned area, its axial lines are extended out into the landscape in the form of hunting rides forming star intersections where they meet and reradiate. It was an even greater undertaking than Vaux-le-Vicomte.

In spite of the technical difficulties, there were 14,000 fountains at Versailles. The palace was the focus of a new city of Versailles built to house the 20,000 people connected with the French Court. The palace itself accommodated 1,000 noblemen with their 4,000 servants. The distance from the palace to the beginning of the canal is ¾ mile (a gentle slope). The canal is 4,000 feet or almost 1 mile long beyond that and 300 feet wide. The principles of the French garden are clearly illustrated; the strong central axis leading to the horizon runs straight through the Sun King's bedchamber. It is a clear expression of the power of man over nature and, of course, of one man over other men, of divine right. The surrounding forest forms a strong enclosure to the garden. Views out are restricted to those provided by the alleys. The garden space is tightly closed around the main axis at the tapis vert. Within the forest to the left and right of the central open space are all kinds of gardens, waterworks, small theaters, and other contrived fantasies for the amusement of King and courtiers. As at Vaux-le-Vicomte, the gardens were designed for use by many people at one time. Versailles was the center of government with all the diplomatic, political, and entertainment functions that it implied. The gardens provided an outdoor setting in keeping with the grandeur of the palace.

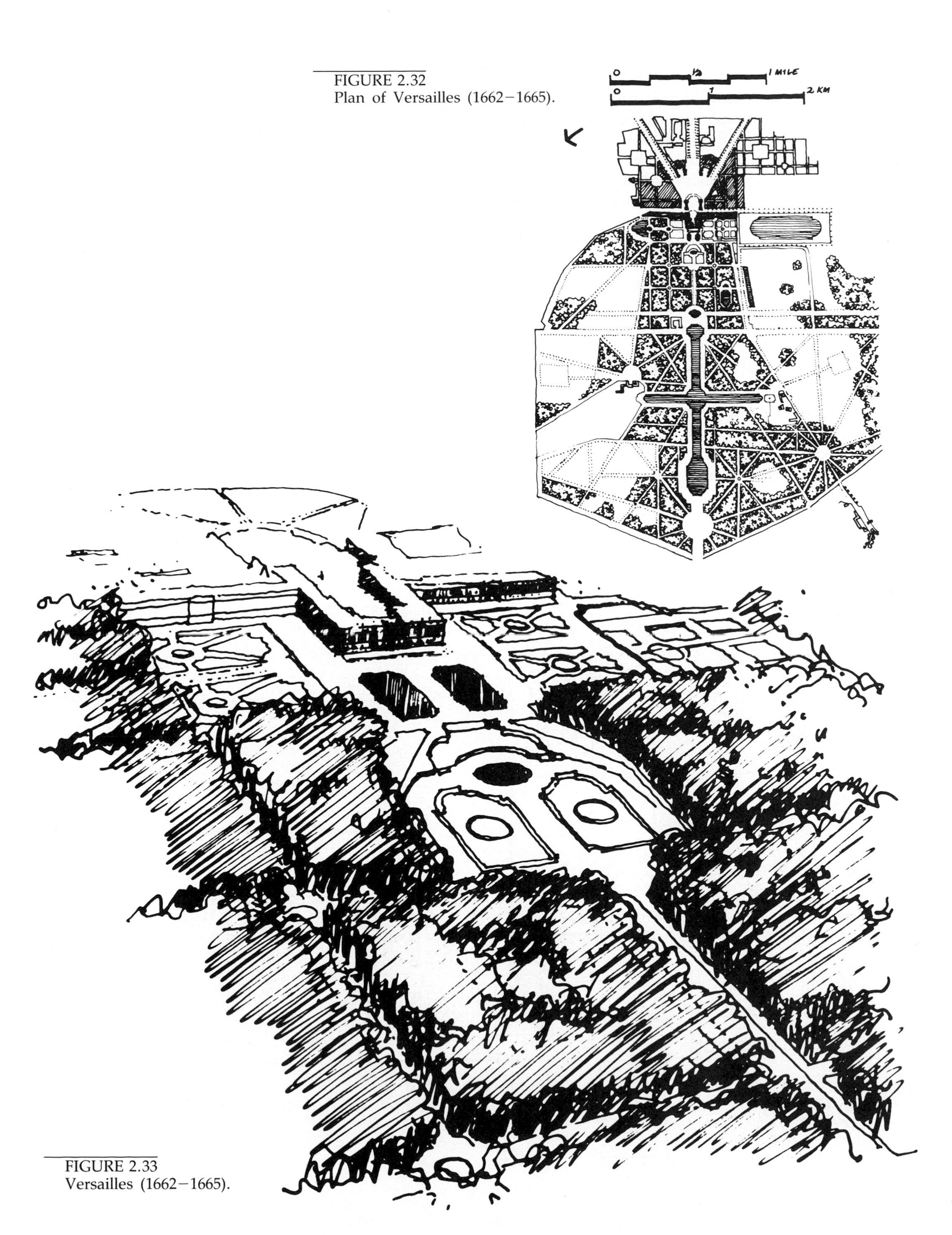

FIGURE 2.32
Plan of Versailles (1662–1665).

FIGURE 2.33
Versailles (1662–1665).

THE TUDOR GARDEN

In England in the sixteenth century, improved agriculture, trade, and global expansions brought prosperity. The upper class, with their newfound wealth and aspirations, expanded and altered their walled medieval gardens according to ideas imported from Italy via France and Holland. The gardens which resulted form a distinct prototype: a human scaled, architectural garden which made a logical and fitting extension of the manor house that it served (Fig. 2.34). The prototype is of interest because it served as the model for Colonial gardens in northern United States and also in the late nineteenth century served as the major example for those who argued in favor of the formal garden as an antidote to the Victorian landscape garden.

The brick manor house would be reached by a straight road terminating in a fore court with associated functional buildings, stables, storerooms, and servants' quarters. Orchard, kitchen garden, and pleasure or flower garden would be arranged to the sides and in front of the house to which they related geometrically. The house would be set up off the ground and have a terrace on the garden side. The pleasure garden, enclosed by high walls or yew hedges, would be divided into square or oblong plots by straight walks and narrower crosswalks at right angles. These would be either filled with flowers and protected by painted wooden fences or trellis or consist of knotted beds (complicated geometric patterns made out of low boxwood or thrift filled with flowering plants or colored gravel). Grass areas or bowling greens were also common and walks were shaded by regular plantings of trees. Summer houses or pavilions, connected to wide terraces built against the outer wall, provided pleasant places to sit with a view. And at ground level, openings in the wall in the form of gates or grills created a visual link with the landscape beyond. The clipping of plants into shapes, human and animal images, was also popular in the sixteenth century garden as it had been in the gardens of ancient Rome. Hedges of yew, box, privet, or thorn were used extensively to divide the garden into sections. Some-

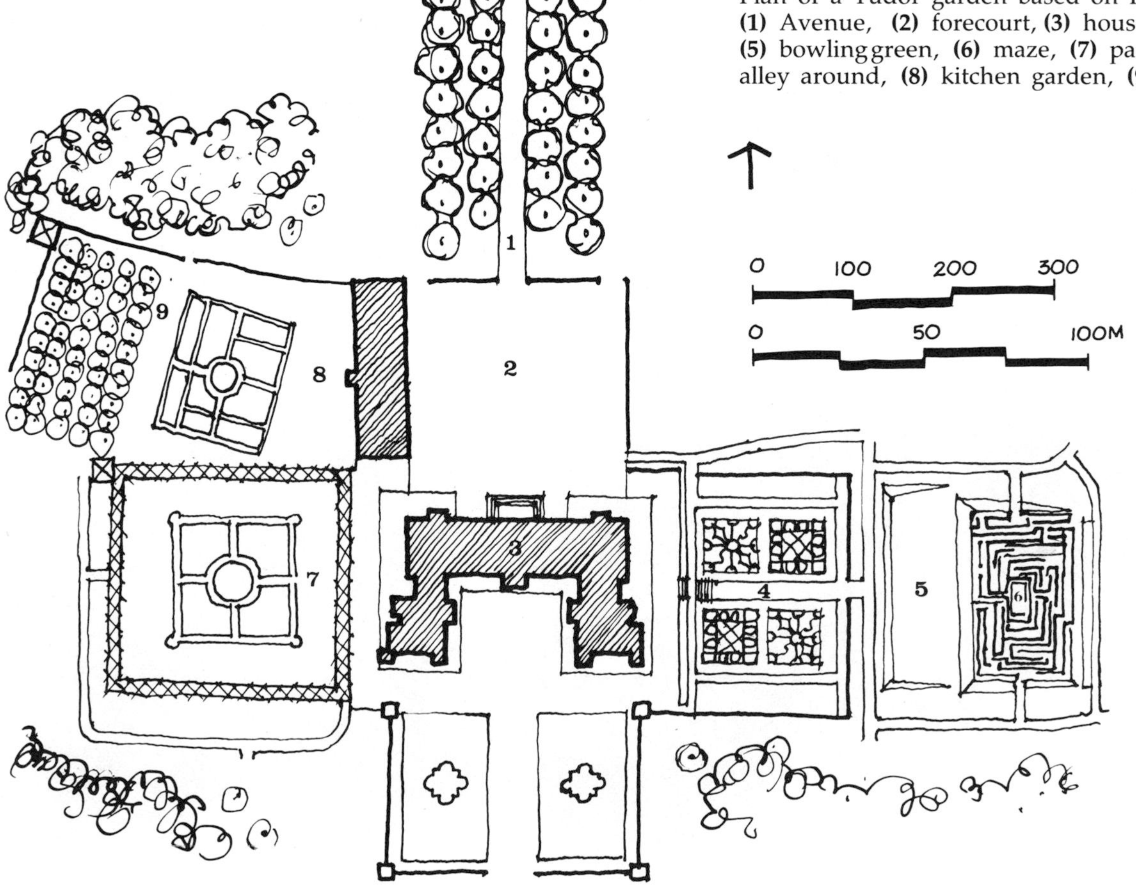

FIGURE 2.34
Plan of a Tudor garden based on Hatfield House. **(1)** Avenue, **(2)** forecourt, **(3)** house, **(4)** knot garden, **(5)** bowling green, **(6)** maze, **(7)** parterre with pleached alley around, **(8)** kitchen garden, **(9)** orchard.

times a maze was planted for entertainment. As time went on and the continental influence became more pervasive, statues and fountains were introduced. The fountains were used for watering the plants. Some spouted water in unexpected directions, drenching visitors, to the amusement of the owners. Flowers were planted profusely. The orchard, regarded as much as a source of pleasure, was located, if possible, to the windward of the vegetable, herb, and flower gardens, but not so as to cast shade on them. And likewise, tall forest trees such as oaks, ashes, and elms (the wilderness), sheltered the orchard.

THE FORMAL GARDEN IN ENGLAND

The influence of the French garden was enormous, especially in Holland and England. Their scale and rich design were impressive to all who saw them. The French tradition in England became preeminent after the restoration of the Stuart kings at the beginning of the seventeenth century. Contemporary views show the unsuitability of the rigid forms when superimposed on the undulating English agricultural landscapes. The intimate outdoor room quality of the Tudor garden was destroyed, simple parterres and knot gardens were replaced by more elaborate designs, wells and simple fountains were replaced with formal pools and elaborate waterworks. Le Nôtre is thought to have designed the gardens of Greenwich Palace for Charles II, but the professional gardeners London and Wise were the chief exponents of the French garden in England, and they completed work which attempted to recreate the essential symmetry and monumentality of the French style at Hampton Court (1699), Longleat (1685–1711) (Fig. 2.35) and Chatsworth (1680–1690).

At Longleat, the natural river was formed into square and rectangular basins and furnished with fountains. Parterres were laid out within an architectural framework, but the avenues of trees superimposed on an open, undulating agricultural landscape looked quite different from the hunting rides cut out of

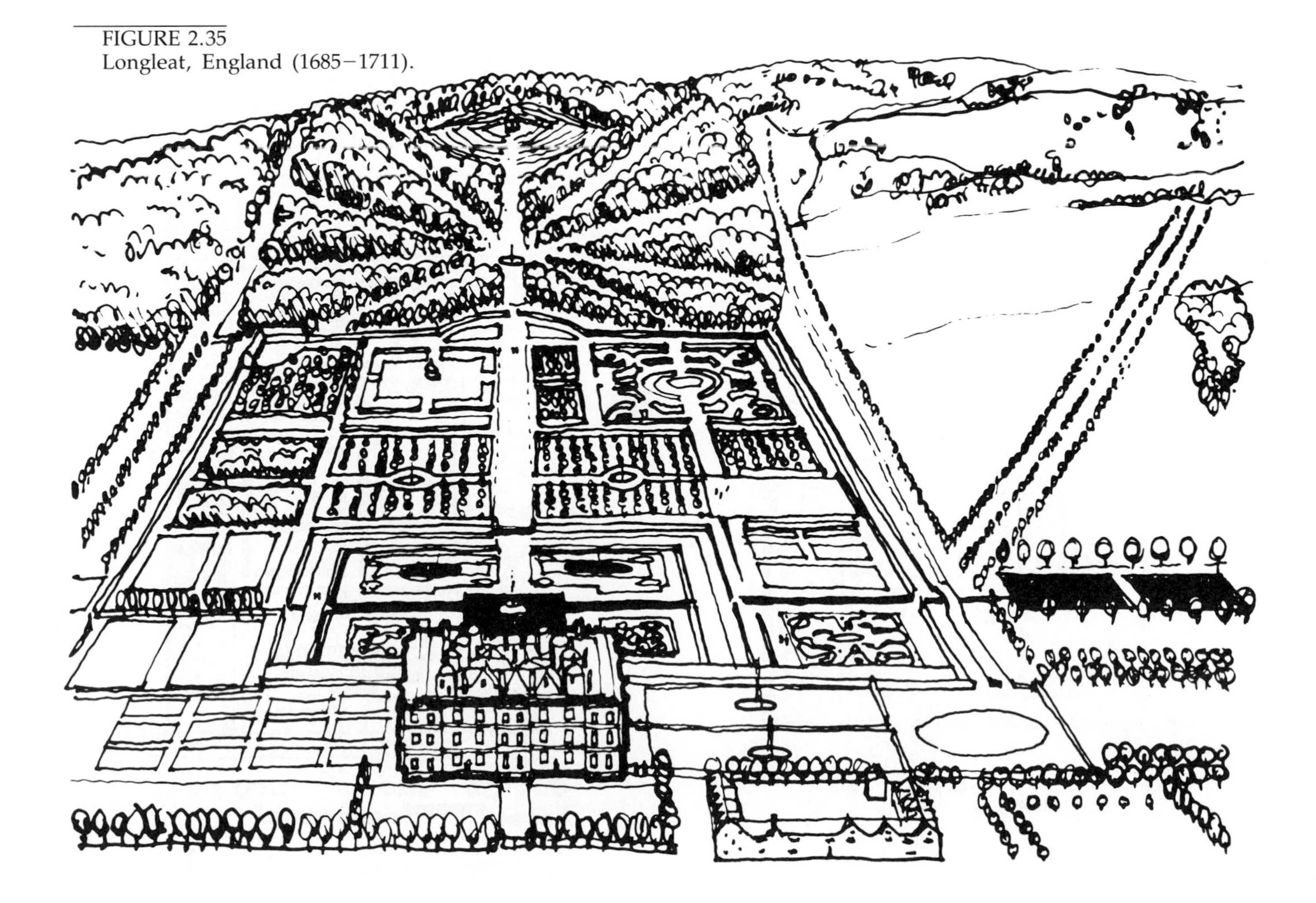

FIGURE 2.35
Longleat, England (1685–1711).

the forests of France. At Greenwich, the topography of the site did not match the formality of the plan, nor was anything done to make it do so. Even at Hampton Court, where the land was more level, the French garden style did not fit well on the open landscape. In other words, due perhaps to inept design and certainly to the different qualities of the English landscape, the French gardens in England were poor imitations of the great models on which they were based.

COLONIAL GARDENS

In was inevitable that both French and British settlers should bring to the American colonies the seventeenth-century garden forms from their homelands. In the north settlers of predominantly yeoman stock perpetuated the cottage gardens they had been accustomed to in England. This was essentially a utilitarian garden with little sense of aesthetics in its plan. In Massachusetts settlers from a higher economic background took the English manor house and garden as a prototype. Typically, these early American gardens were not large, were enclosed with fences or hedges, and had a central axis path leading through beds of flowers and vegetables, edged with clipped plants, to an arbor, summer house, or dovecote at the end (Fig. 2.36). The formal arrangements hinted at a desire to be stylish in the French manner but gardens

FIGURE 2.36
A town residence, Salem, Massachusetts (eighteenth century). **(1)** Stable, **(2)** tool yard, **(3)** arbor, **(4)** flower garden, **(5)** vegetables, **(6)** beehives.

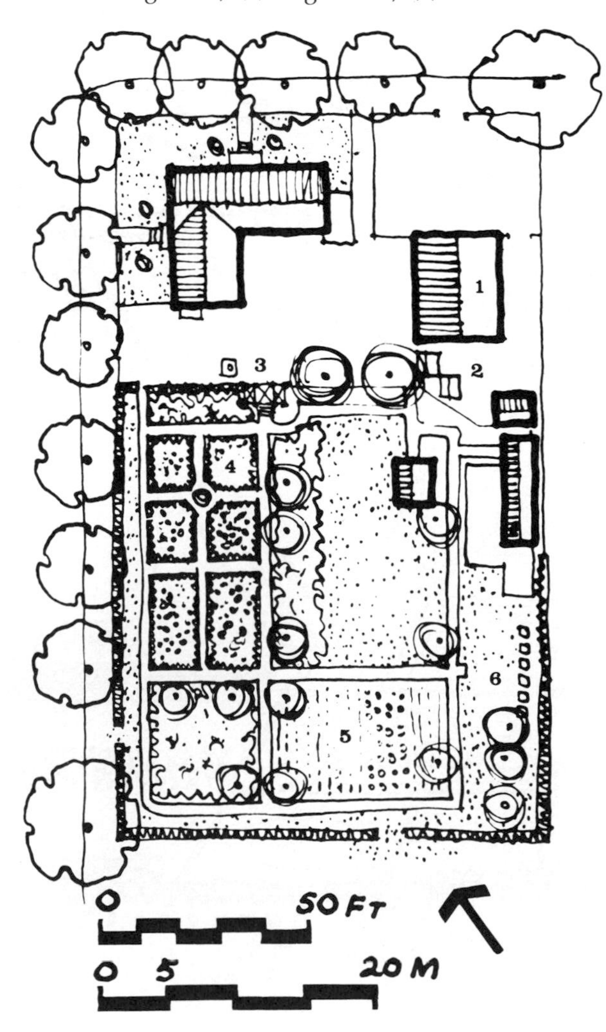

FIGURE 2.37
Typical town garden in Virginia (eighteenth century). **(1)** Kitchen, **(2)** dairy, **(3)** smoke house, **(4)** stables, **(5)** vegetables, **(6)** grapes.

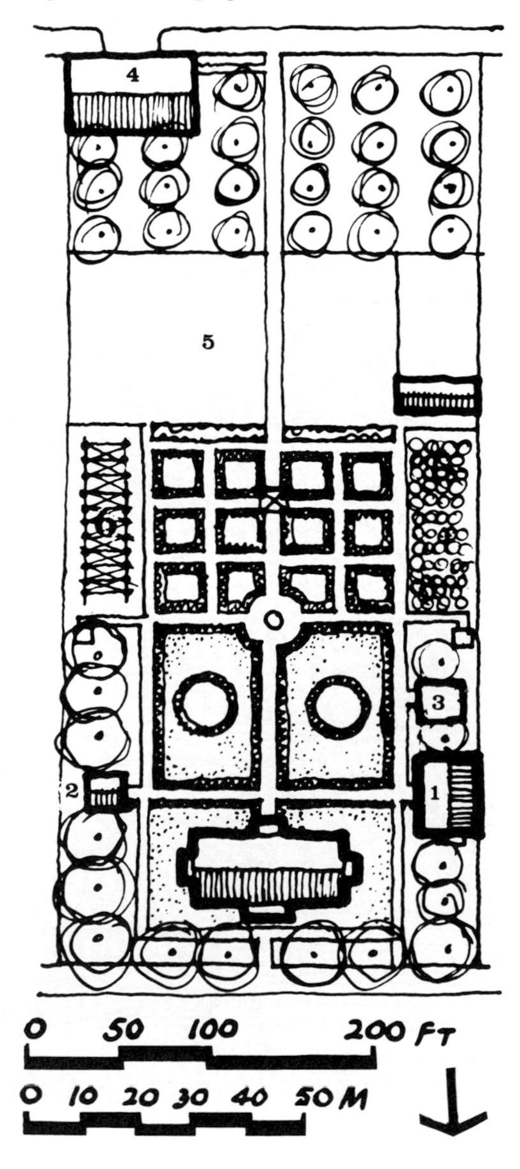

FIGURE 2.38
The garden of the Governor's Palace, Williamsburg, Virginia, 1699.

in the United States were created under very different social and economic conditions.

The south, with its tradition of landed gentry and a different type of society and government, was more conducive to the development of extensive gardens (Fig. 2.37). Their inspiration came from imported gardening literature and European travel. The fine palace gardens of Williamsburg (1699) show clearly the European formal garden influence (Fig. 2.38). This influence in America stretched well into the nineteenth century despite the evolution of the landscape garden in England in the early eighteenth century.

ENGLAND, THE LANDSCAPE GARDEN

The landscape garden was an entirely different concept and its origins were varied. The English countryside with large fields made possible by enclosure, rolling hills, winding streams, and scattered trees, inherently unsuited to the French garden, was an important element in English country life. The formal gardens of France were associated with despotic government distasteful to the democratic and rights-conscious Englishmen of the eighteenth century. An antithesis to the formal garden would thus be more acceptable. The emerging Romantic movement produced poetry and paintings which extolled the beauties of nature and landscape. The grand tour which all cultured Englishmen made through the Alps to Italy brought them in contact with rugged, picturesque scenery. Scenes such as they would see on the tour were represented on the canvases of Nicolas Poussin, Salvador Rosa, and Claude Lorrain (Fig. 2.39). The paintings were not actual views but compositions of typical elements selected and arranged for emphasis— craggy mountains, rivers, pastoral plains, ruined castles and monuments, lakes, and windblown trees. Many included classical temples and groups of allegorical figures. In addition to the landscape and its stylization in the paintings, the visitor to Italy saw the famous villas and their gardens in an appealing, romantic state of disrepair. The travelers began to see landscape through the eyes of the painter and consequently on their return to England found their stiff formal gardens uninteresting and unattractive. One other influence was the Orient, which was opened to trade in the seventeenth century. Scenes on imported porcelain and lacquer work depicted natural gardens, lakes, and waterfalls and the aesthetic and attitude which they represented were influential in the development of a new system of gardening in England (Figs. 2.3 to 2.8).

The landscape garden was a product of the Romantic movement. Its form was based on direct observation of nature and the principles of painting. Surprise,

FIGURE 2.39
"Hilly Countryside" 1640 by Claude Lorrain. Courtesy Norton Simon Art Foundation.

variety, concealment, and the development of idyllic prospects became the goals of the art of landscape. The manipulation of nature's undulating contours according to Hogarth's serpentine "line of beauty" and the articulation of light and shade much as a painter would do became the preoccupation of all men of taste and culture in eighteenth-century England and ultimately all over Europe and in America in the nineteenth century. Where they existed, the parterre and terrace of the formal garden were replaced with rolling grassland, clumps of trees, lakes, meandering rivers, and serpentine drives (Figs. 2.40 and 2.41). In the early

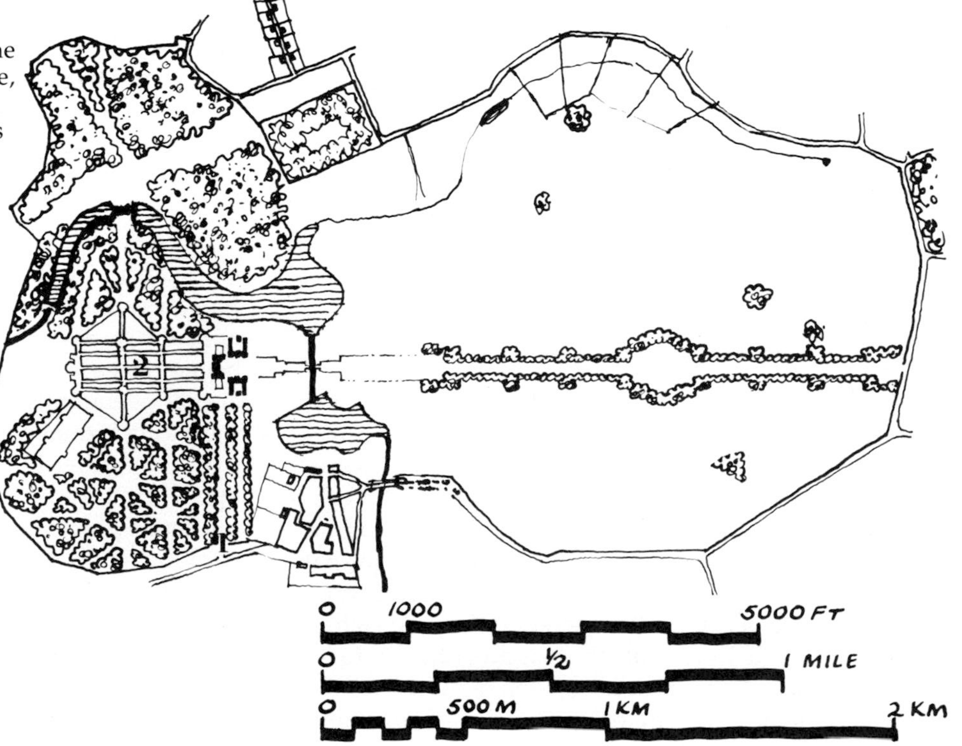

FIGURE 2.40
Blenheim Palace as laid out by Henry Wise in 1705. Note **(1)** the straight entrance from the village, **(2)** the parterre in front of the house and the radiating avenues in the woodland.

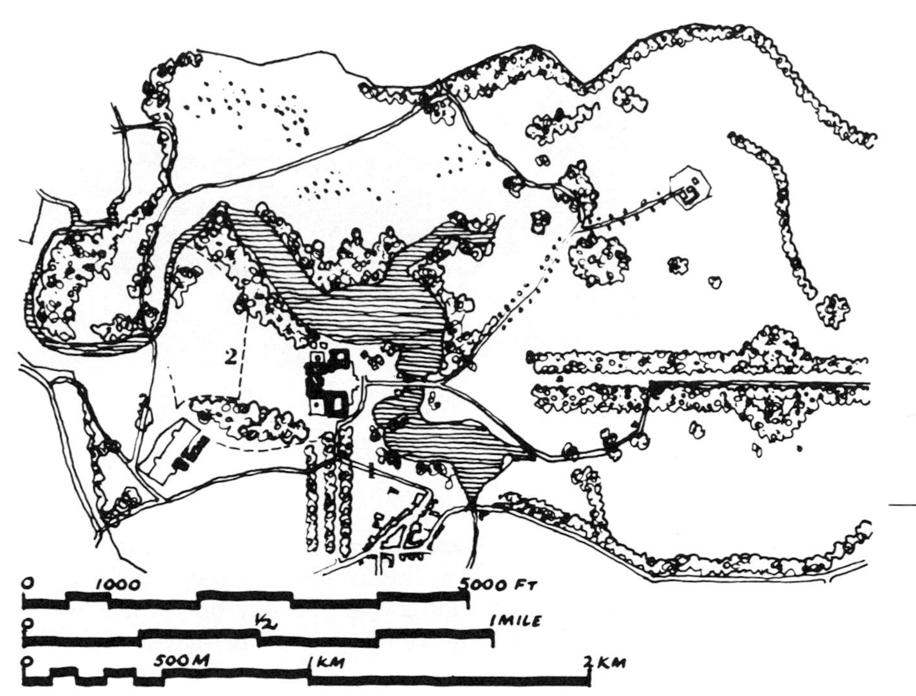

FIGURE 2.41
Blenheim Palace as altered by Lancelot Brown in 1758. Note **(1)** the new winding approach from the village, **(2)** the irregular plantings and the sunken fence in front of the house replacing the parterre.

examples the scene was embellished at suitable points with temples, bridges, and sculptures.

Of fundamental importance was the elimination of the visual break between garden and landscape. One of the techniques for eliminating this break was the sunken fence. This allowed the eye to see straight out to the countryside while at the same time keeping deer and stock out of the garden proper. It is a technique with potential for use today in contemporary landscape design (Fig. 2.42).

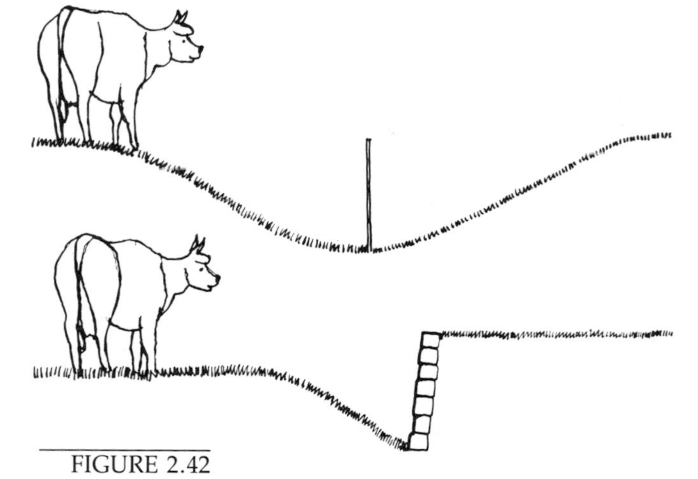

FIGURE 2.42
Two versions of the sunken fence—a technique of the eighteenth century landscape garden used to eliminate visual boundaries between garden and landscape.

William Kent argued that the validity of the system was due to two important factors: first its moral integrity and second its classical derivations. For example, he said that bronze fountains cast to look like trees, trees clipped to look like stone, and other such trappings found at Versailles were dishonest or at least foolish. A natural cascade or serpentine stream was purer in concept than a jet of muddy water drawn up at great expense from a marsh. The taste for the irregular and natural was thus considered highly moral. The classical origins of irregularity were more difficult to identify. However, it was found that classical authority practiced regularity in building and irregularity in gardens. The Valley of the Tempe at Hadrian's villa was evidence of this (Fig. 2.12). Thus, just as Palladian architecture was established as classically correct, so too was the irregular garden.

By the third decade of the century, the revolution in garden design was well under way. It was led at first by so-called amateurs such as Henry Hoare, who started work at Stourhead in 1743 (Figs. 2.43 and 2.44).

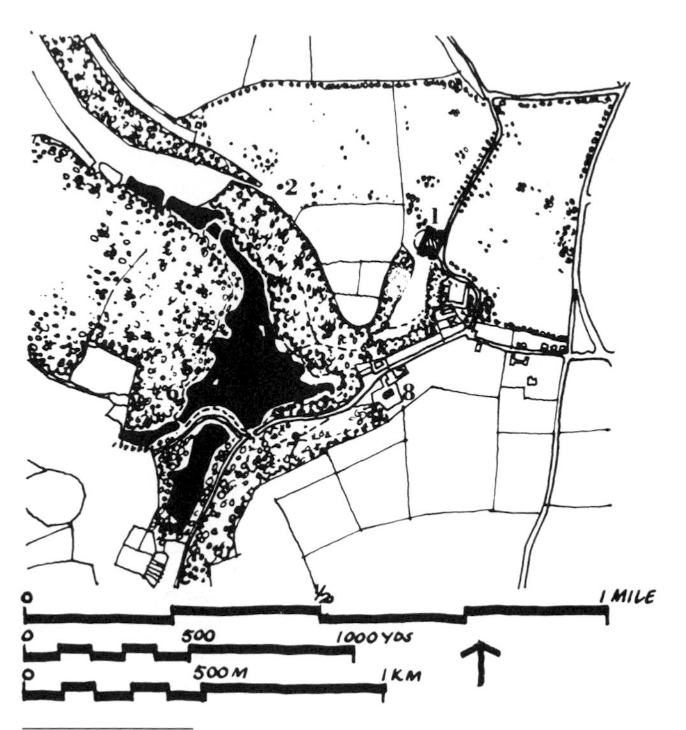

FIGURE 2.43
Stourhead, England (1744). Key to plan: **(1)** house, **(2)** obelisk, **(3)** Paradise Temple, **(4)** grotto, **(5)** watch cottage, **(6)** Pantheon Temple, **(7)** Sun Temple, **(8)** St. Peter's Church.

FIGURE 2.44
Stourhead, England (1744).

The garden was set in a valley in which a stream was dammed to create an irregular lake. This cannot be seen from the house above, a Palladian villa, and, conversely, the house is not seen from the garden. The only connection between the two is an obelisk, which can be seen both from the house and from a specific point in the garden. A path was laid out around the shore of the lake connecting a series of "events," and the garden was properly experienced by following the route in the prescribed direction. The tour might take a day even though the distance was not great. The garden was arranged according to the rules of landscape painting, and in fact in this particular case the garden was based on a painting by Claude Lorrain. The bridge at the starting point, the Temple of Flora, and the Pantheon set out in the garden are similar in form and disposition to those in the painting.

A further level of appreciation was the mythological or literary allusions associated with each feature. As one walked, new vistas and views were revealed and the visitor was brought obliquely to buildings and places seen earlier. At one point the path leads underground into a cool grotto with a moss-covered statue of Neptune, ferns, and the sound of running water. It is a conscious change in environment to evoke physiologically, as well as intellectually, images of a legendary underwater kingdom. A rocky opening at water level reveals the Temple of Flora across the lake already visited.

Stourhead is thus a sequence of experiences. Many have intellectual meaning and are conceived and appreciated on the basis of a knowledge of mythology and poetry. In addition, the environmental qualities of light, temperature, texture, and sound together with visual impressions add sensations which, combined with the first level of reaction, make a complete experience. A modern movie is perhaps the closest comparison in which an image, the meaning associated with it, and the response can be predetermined.

Bright flowering plants were not favored in the landscape garden. The rhododendrons that can be seen at Stourhead today were not part of the original planting. These were planted later and now stimulate a controversy between "purists" and the National Trust, who own and maintain the garden for the public. The National Trust say that the visiting public like azaleas. The purists would like the rhododendrons removed.

William Kent was the first professional to design gardens in the new manner. At Rousham, built between 1738 and 1740, Kent planned the entire view from the existing house and built a miller's cottage and a ruin on a distant hill to complete the romantic composition (Fig. 2.45). Thus the design consideration extended to the entire landscape visible from the house. The cumulative effect of this approach has resulted in the way the English landscape looks today. It has been designed and is a composite of views from many country houses. The garden at Rousham lies to one side of the house and includes a classical arcade, a serpentine rivulet, a grotto, cascades, and evocative

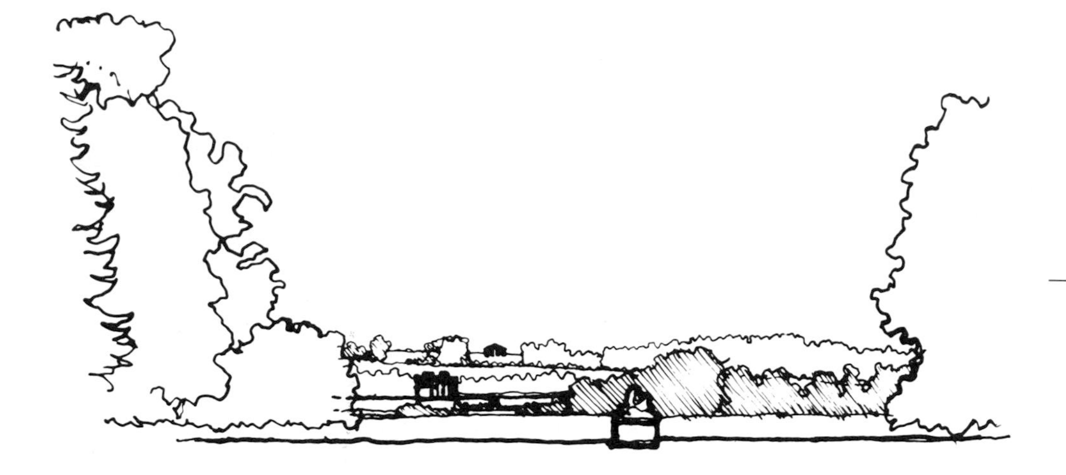

FIGURE 2.45
Rousham, England (1738–1740). View from the house into the landscape embellished with a mill and distant romantic ruin.

statues placed within clearings in a woodland and connected with vistas and walks (Fig. 2.46).

By the mid-eighteenth century, the new style in gardening was widely accepted. Lancelot Brown, called Capability Brown, became the leading exponent and was in great demand. Unlike Kent, he did not approve of architectural features in the garden. Terraces and parterres were to be cleared away from the base of the house until nothing was left except grass, which came right up to the foundations. A sunken fence would eliminate the visual boundary, and the seemingly contiguous landscape would be planted irregularly with trees in clumps or groups on undulating ground. If possible, a stream would be dammed to form a lake as at Blenheim, and made to fit naturally without awkwardness into the landscape (Figs. 2.41 and 2.47). The appearance of these landscapes depended on good estate management and productive agriculture, for they encompassed working farms and fields. In addition, the making of picturesque landscapes which would blend visually into the existing natural system depended on an understanding of ecological principles.

In the late eighteenth and early nineteenth century Humphry Repton published a theory of landscape gardening and became the leading exponent of the style.[4] Repton modified Brown's ruthless formula and favored the restoration of the terrace to connect the house to the garden. In a satirical essay Repton was referred to as Mr. Milestone because of a trick whereby the milestones set on the driveway leading to the house were set at less than a mile apart.[5] In this we see

[4] Humphry Repton, *Sketches and Hints on Landscape Gardening* (London: W. Bulmer, 1794).

[5] Peacock, Thomas Love, *Headlong Hall* (London: Pan Books, Ltd., 1967). (First published in 1816.)

FIGURE 2.46
Rousham, England (1738–1740). Plan shows the placing of elements in the landscape to improve the view. **(1)** mill and miller's house, **(2)** ruin, **(3)** house, **(4)** garden.

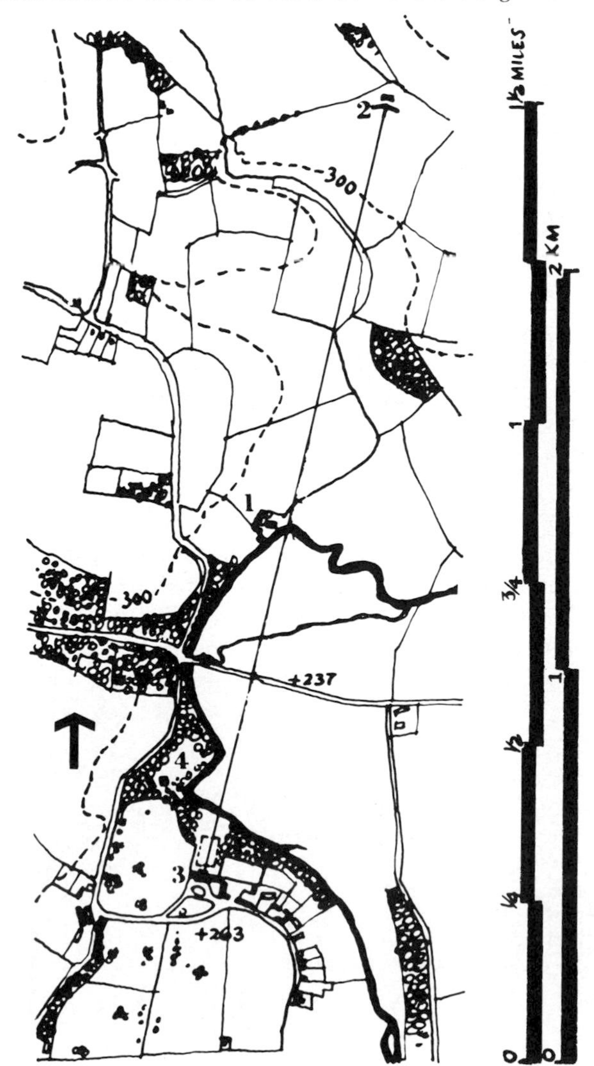

FIGURE 2.47
Blenheim, England (1758)

FIGURE 2.48
An impression of Redbook drawing by Repton showing a house in a bland landscape—a parody of Brown's formula (1803).

FIGURE 2.49
The "after" illustration by Repton showed the introduction of a terrace and outbuildings, a romantic lake and picturesque planting (1803).

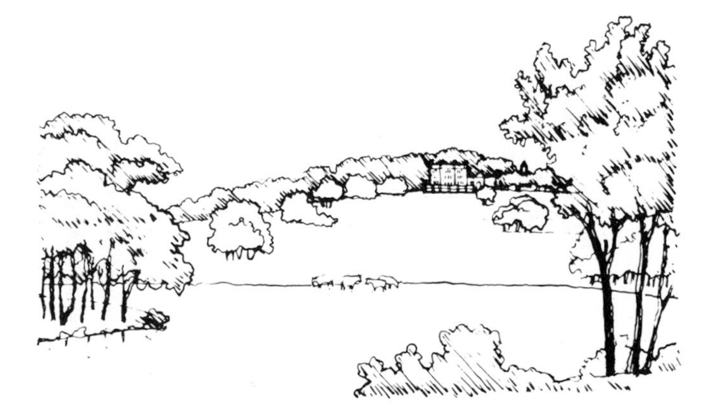

evidence of appreciation based on quantity and size reflecting on the prestige of the owners. A technique of more importance were his "redbooks," which illustrated his proposals with "before" and "after" drawings or watercolors (Figs. 2.48 and 2.49). Comparison of these showed how a quiet, uninteresting meadow and stream could be transformed into a beautiful landscape with serpentine lake and irregular plantations as an environment for a castlelike establishment set on a broad terrace (Fig. 2.50).

THE LANDSCAPE GARDEN IN THE UNITED STATES

In due course the romantic landscape garden was adopted in America. Thomas Jefferson's remodeling of the Monticello gardens (Fig. 2.51) and the simple lawn and plantations introduced at Mount Vernon in 1737 (Fig. 2.52) are early indications of a change in American taste. Some of the first completely new landscape gardens were designed by Andre Parmentier, a Belgian who established a nursery in Brooklyn in 1824. In 1828 he wrote an essay praising the picturesque style and opposing the formalism then prevalent in America. He subsequently laid out the grounds of several large estates along the Hudson River before his death in 1830.

Parmentier was succeeded by Andrew Jackson Downing as champion of the landscape garden. Downing's theory,[6] published in 1841, was based on the work of Repton and embodied the same theory

[6] Andrew Jackson Downing, *A Treatise on the Theory and Practice of Landscape Gardening: Adapted to North America* (Boston: C. C. Little and Co., 1841).

FIGURE 2.50
Proposal for a country house by Repton (nineteenth century).

of the picturesque. His arguments in favor of the beauties of natural landscape, woods, and plantations and the aesthetic and moral values to be obtained from them were so convincing that all new gardens in association with the increasing number of suburban villas were laid out in the Romantic idiom (Fig. 2.53). His book was moralistic in tone, stressing the refinement and sophistication needed to appreciate the subtleties of natural forms. By the middle of the nineteenth century Downing had established himself as a tastemaker in gardening matters on the East coast in America. He was adopted by the wealthy owners of estates on the Hudson River. Here he created very creditable landscapes in the English manner but with care to emphasize the particular qualities of each site. Illustrations in his book show prototypical villas for people of middle income (Figs. 2.54 and 2.55). Families

FIGURE 2.51
Monticello, Virginia (1796)

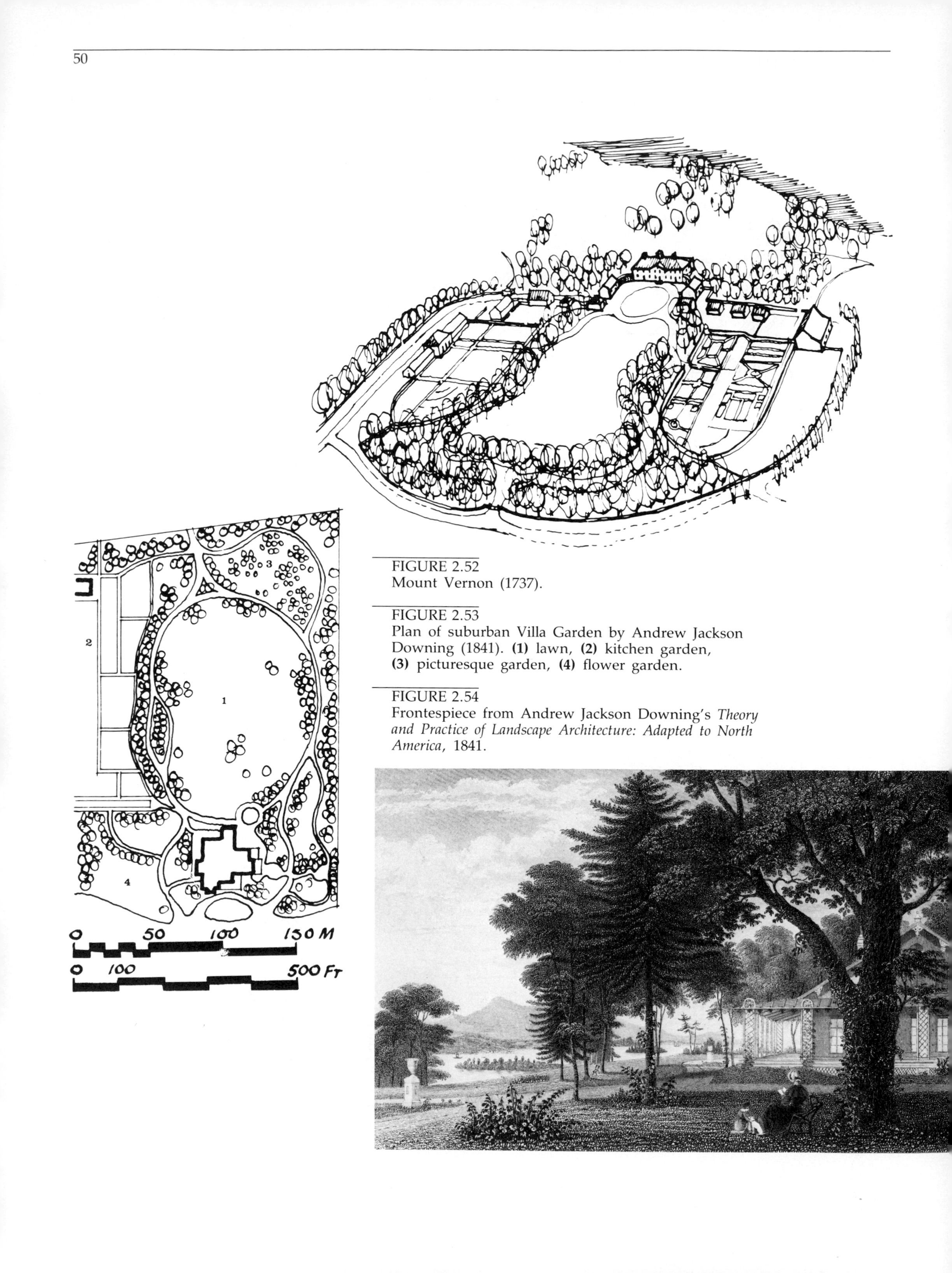

FIGURE 2.52
Mount Vernon (1737).

FIGURE 2.53
Plan of suburban Villa Garden by Andrew Jackson Downing (1841). **(1)** lawn, **(2)** kitchen garden, **(3)** picturesque garden, **(4)** flower garden.

FIGURE 2.54
Frontespiece from Andrew Jackson Downing's *Theory and Practice of Landscape Architecture: Adapted to North America*, 1841.

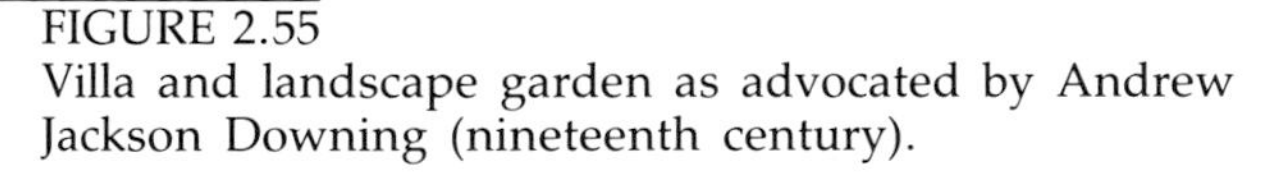

FIGURE 2.55
Villa and landscape garden as advocated by Andrew Jackson Downing (nineteenth century).

are seen posed somewhat awkwardly or having tea on a lawn enclosed with conifers and shrubberies or commanding a view of a distant mountain landscape.

Downing established and popularized the Romantic landscape garden as a tradition in America. It was part of a larger interest in nature and the American landscape, which will be discussed in Chapter 3. In the adoption of an informal and natural style of landscape design which recognized the constraints and potentials of each site we can detect the roots of a landscape philosophy held and advocated strongly by Frederick Law Olmsted as he entered practice in 1856. This East coast tradition, which emphasized nature and natural looks with soft edges and curving lines as a contrast to urbanism, persisted well into the twentieth century and remains popular today in contrast to the modern garden.

THE LANDSCAPE AND FLOWER GARDEN AND THE ECLECTIC REVIVAL GARDEN

By the end of the nineteenth century gardens and gardening in Britain and the United States became heavily influenced by a fascination with plants on the one hand and architectural eclecticism on the other. This influenced gardens wherever western ideas were adopted. The result was often a fusion of the two but each represented different attitudes and concepts which we can relate to two premodern prototypes; the landscape or flower garden and the architectural garden, both achieving definition in the period between 1880 and 1930.

The combined result of villa gardens, which were too small to achieve the landscape effect advocated by Repton and Downing, and an increased availability of plants from around the world led to the disintegration of the landscape garden into a hodgepodge of flower beds, shrubberies, and specimen trees planted singly in lawns. The prototype is difficult to define because it was largely formless. The essential characteristic was a collection of plants, the more unusual the better, some of which required the climatic protection of a greenhouse or conservatory attached to the house. Such gardens and their villas were situated along tree shaded streets on the edge of expanding industrial cities or were located in the country, being adaptations of earlier landscape gardens (Fig. 2.56).

In an effort to restore order to the nineteenth century garden, designers turned to earlier traditions, notably those of the Tudor and Italian gardens. The Italian style practiced by Barry and Nesfield in England in the 1830s was characterized, as at Shrubland, by stone terraces, flights of steps, balustrades, fountains, and classical sculptures. Geometric flower beds and parterres were planted with half hardy annuals and clipped dwarf conifers were distributed in symmetrical patterns related to house and terrace. The end result was an expanded architectural garden around

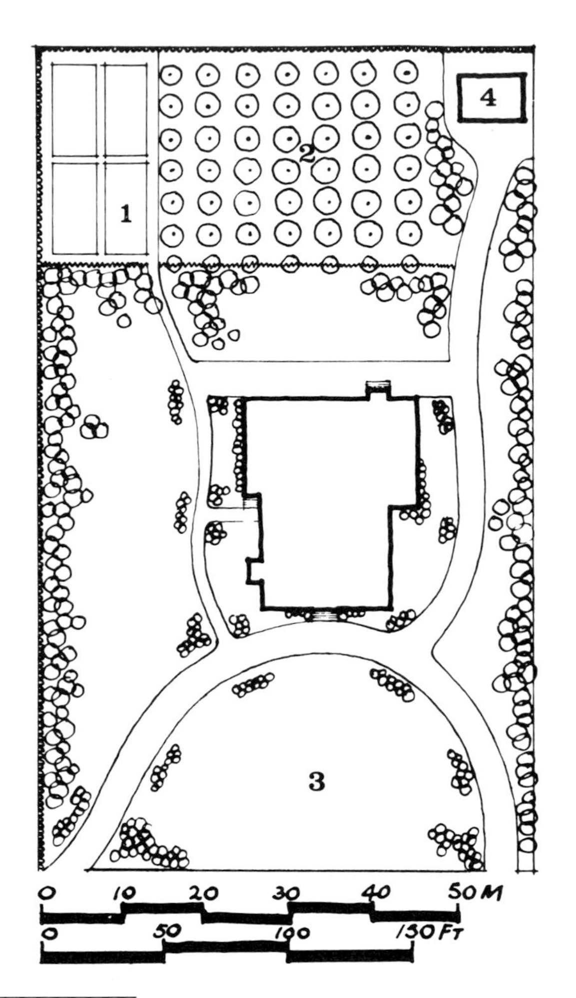

FIGURE 2.56
Plan for a villa garden (1900) by John McLaren superintendant of Golden Gate Park. Note the similarities with A. J. Downing's plan (Fig. 2.53). **(1)** Vegetable garden, **(2)** orchard, **(3)** front lawn, **(4)** garage.

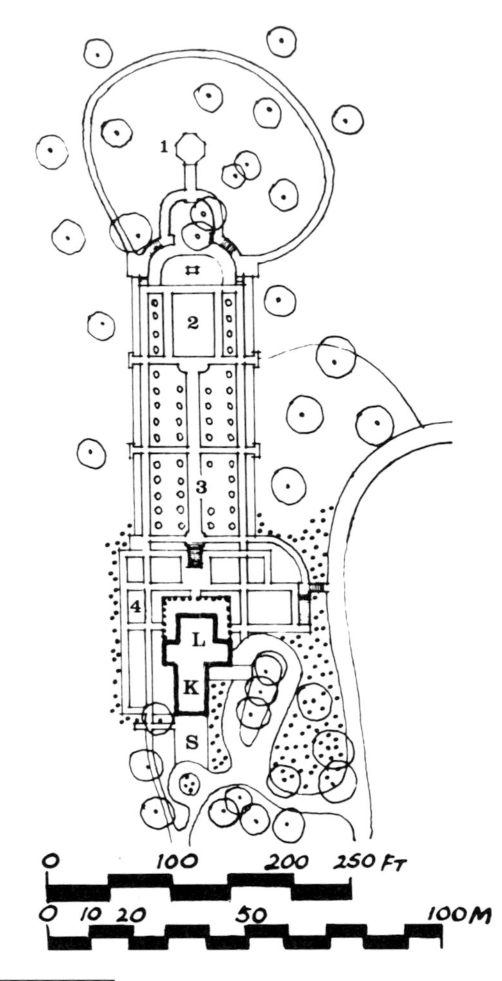

FIGURE 2.57
The eclectic revival in California and elsewhere produced formal gardens and houses with more intimate connections between indoors and out. Key: **(L)** living room, **(K)** kitchen, **(S)** service yard, **(1)** gazebo, **(2)** fountain pool, **(3)** parterre, **(4)** terrace.

the house. Later, historical authenticity provided the theoretical basis for the new formal garden of modest but imposing proportions (Figs. 2.57 and 2.58).

In the United States, one of the first gardens in the new architectural style was Biltmore, the Vanderbilt estate in North Carolina (started in 1888). A French chateau, designed by Richard Hunt, it included a formal garden designed by none other than Frederick Law Olmsted. This was toward the end of Olmsted's career and his participation in the Chicago exhibition.

The two garden types could not have been more different and lead to sharp controversy (and in England a bitter debate between Robinson and Blomfield). Architectural gardens, which became associated with carpet bedding, were criticized by those who wanted to combine horticultural variety with a natural effect. Alternatively the natural garden was criticized by advocates of the architectural garden for whom it had no form and lacked the necessary setting for the house.

Yet each in its own way had merit. The natural garden provided a laboratory for the plant enthusiast who arranged plants ecologically, according to the best growing conditions. It was an experimental environment in which the owner participated enthusiastically, exchanging notes with others, constantly making changes and additions. The architectural garden, on the other hand, while often simply a show of wealth and a longing for a visible sign of class and style, did strengthen the house and garden relationship compared with the landscape garden in which the villa sat on high foundations surrounded with

FIGURE 2.58
An eclectic house and garden in California, 1920. Notice the similarity in form and situation with the Villa Medici (Fig. 2.25).

shrubbery and flower beds. It was the English gardener, Gertrude Jekyll, who brought sense and resolution to the debate. A keen horticulturist with an interest in painting, she brought to her work and writing a certain rationale that had widespread significance in Europe and the United States and presaged the modern garden. She held no blind prejudice against the architectural garden as was evident by her lifelong association with Edwin Lutyens, an English architect who designed many formal gardens which Miss Jekyll planted. She approved of formal garden design near the house, but she was also interested in the wild garden and planted small woodlands with trees and shrubs selected because of their ecological compatibility growing in rough grass planted with bulbs. Transversed with mown glades, these gardens were largely self-sustaining.

For the flower garden, she invented the herbaceous border, a collection of hardy perennial flowering plants which provided a succession of flowers throughout spring, summer, and fall (see page 210). Flower and foliage color were combined as an impressionist painter would do, the borders were framed and the plants set off against a solid background of hedge, brick, or stone walls. Her practice and writing during the late 1800s and the first 30 years of the twentieth century were extremely influential in opening up the question of what a garden should be.

Her philosophy seemed to be that the garden design should respond to the use and characteristics of the site and also the interests and desires of the owners. The only requirement was that it should be appropriate and perfectly carried out.

The eclecticism which this point of view favored involved careful studies of sixteenth- and seventeenth-century Italian, French, and English architecture and gardens. Reginald Blomfield's *The Formal Garden in England* (1892) and Charles Platt's *Italian Gardens* (1894) published in America were two influential books which advocated garden design based on recreating the best of the past and spawned a spate of similar volumes. Italian villas, French châteaux, and English manor houses provided inspiration for the designers and satisfied the fantasies of the clients. In general, they were not imitations but rather interpretations, and many were successful and remain to this day as examples of good proportion and spatial organization. The products of Lutyens and Mawson in England, Platt, Farrand and Lockwood de Forest in the United States, Forestier in France, (to name only a few of the prominent practitioners of the period) were imbued with formality and order and typically featured an integration of house and garden (Platt and Lutyens, e.g., designing both) as frequently found in the originals. On a small scale, this type of design was most suitable. On a large scale, in the country, a progressive transition from architectural order to the natural setting was achieved and considered a desirable relationship (Jekyll).

THE MODERN GARDEN

In 1917, Hubbard and Kimball, the American educators and authors of *An Introduction to the Study of Landscape Design* (1917), agreed that there were two current styles of garden design: the Classic and the Romantic. The Classic was formal, implying restraint and stability. The Romantic was informal, its attraction lying in variety, contrast, and an emotional appeal (not to mention the horticultural interest). In spite of their attempt at objectivity, the text suggests that Hubbard and Kimball favored the classical as illustrated in the revival of the Tudor Garden in England (Blomfield) and as practiced by Charles Platt and others in America. However, the ideal situation would be to combine both, to have formality in the garden close to the house (fore court and terrace) which together would form a unit set in a larger estate. The natural features of this would be emphasized and the landscape planted with native species. Even in smaller gardens (½ acre or so), it might be possible to achieve such a combination but the informal portion could only be a representation of nature: an open irregular lawn, with two or three freestanding trees and shrub plantings.

Hubbard and Kimball's discussion of the garden as an enclosed, protected unit within an estate or simply of small suburban gardens as adjuncts to a house, suggests a change in the way people thought of a garden, its form and use at the turn of the century. Although the authors are critical of the excessive rationality of German garden design of the period, they were clearly impressed with the concept (generated by the Darmstadt School of Design, forerunner of the Bauhaus) that the house and its surroundings were all part of one architectural scheme. This, together with a propensity for sitting, eating, and drinking outdoors, led to the idea that the ground surrounding a house should become a series of outdoor rooms. Such was the typical modern German garden. It incorporated rectangular shapes that were more convenient as outdoor rooms, easier to maintain, and fitted most economically into rectangular lots.

In California, in the early 1900s, with its increasing population of families of modest income, a new house type became popular. Typically consisting of six to nine rooms, these single-story houses with many windows, ample porches, and wide eaves were built on small lots in a variety of architectural styles (Fig.

FIGURE 2.59
California bungalow.

2.59). The Gamble house by the Green Brothers in Pasadena, although not a bungalow, initiated the concept. It has many porches related to the rooms of the house, permitting outdoor living. The bungalow became a prevalent house type and did recognize, as Olmsted put it, the advantages of health and comfort which could be provided by a direct relationship with the outdoors. The back porch was an important element. Overlooking a small garden, its use included the serving of meals and family activity somewhat similar to the Spanish-Mexican courtyard (Fig. 2.60). The quality of life afforded by the California bungalow was described by C. F. Saunders as "informal but not necessarily bohemian" and "simple without being sloppy."[7]

FIGURE 2.60
Plan of a California bungalow and garden. **(1)** Porch, **(2)** veranda, **(3)** vegetables, **(4)** lawn, **(5)** summer house, **(6)** garage.

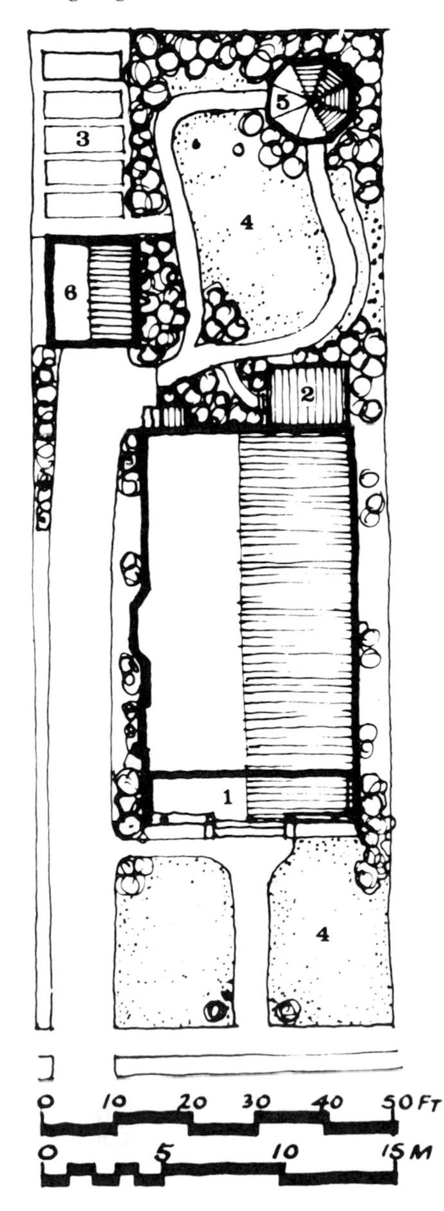

In the 1930s, after the Depression, the urban areas of California continued to expand. Smaller building lots and the presence of the ubiquitous automobile resulted in the reduction of usable garden space for the average homeowner. There was a shortage of gardeners and a lack of time and enthusiasm for gardening. At the same time there was an increasing change in attitude toward gardens and a realization of their potential for providing additional living space in a mild and agreeable climate. *Sunset Magazine* encouraged the development of a life-style in which the garden and all its components—terrace, barbecue, and swimming pool—combined into a home environment with the ambiance of a resort.

In 1938, Tunnard, an English landscape architect, proposed three interrelated approaches to landscape design: the functional, the emphatic, and the artistic.[8] The functional approach decreed that the garden must be pleasant to live in as well as to look at. It must provide for social necessities, rest, recreation, and aesthetic pleasure. It must also be economical and rational. The emphatic approach was based in the aesthetic principles of the Japanese garden, especially asymmetry (likely to result from the functional approach above), the deep appreciation of form and texture, and the goal of unity between architecture and landscape. The artistic approach assumed, first, that garden design was an art (not simply a craft), and second, that its practice was akin to modern sculpture in which form and quality were derived from the materials being used.

Developments in art and architecture in Europe, cubism and abstract expressionism, functional architecture, and the modern movement, had their impact first on the East coast but also in California. Modern architecture needed modern landscape architecture. Thomas Church and later Garrett Eckbo on the West coast, James Rose on the East, Christopher Tunnard and others in England became the avant-garde of modern landscape architecture in the late 1930s. The landscape garden and the eclectic neoclassical garden were rejected.

[7] Charles Francis Saunders, *Under the Sky in California* (New York: McBride, Nast, 1913).

[8] Tunnard Christopher, *Gardens in the Modern Landscape* (London: The Architectural Press, 1939).

The career of Thomas Church is considered here in detail for several reasons. First, he was an innovator like the other great designers in history whose works have already been discussed. Second, he evolved an approach to design suited to the environment and social context in which he practiced. Third, his practice was almost exclusively in private gardens, which is the subject of this chapter.

Church adopted a theory which followed that of the new architecture. This recognized three sources of form. The first consisted of human needs and the specific personal requirements and characteristics of the client. The second comprised the technology of materials, construction, and plants, including maintenance and a whole range of form determinants derived from the site conditions and quality. The third was a concern for the spatial expression, which would go beyond the mere satisfaction of requirements and into the realms of fine art.

At first the garden forms he used were traditional with clipped hedges and eclectic motifs. He designed small town gardens and wrote about the challenge they presented. He said that the small garden could not be "natural" if it was to serve as an extension to the house. Their scale and use called for hard surfaces, screens to separate areas, and design forms that would increase their apparent size (Fig. 2.61). Church recognized that many people had small gardens, especially in urban settings, where the garden could serve a vital

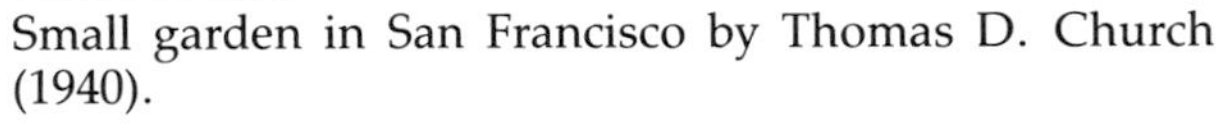

FIGURE 2.61
Small garden in San Francisco by Thomas D. Church (1940).

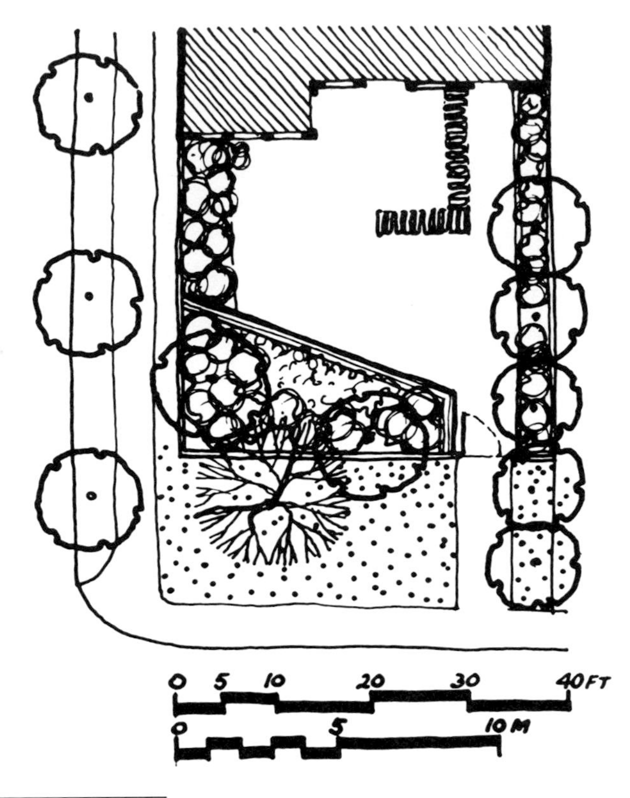

FIGURE 2.62
Treatment of front garden by Thomas D. Church.

function as an outdoor room or as a giardino segretto such as his own small garden behind a wall in San Francisco. Like it or not, he said, the function of the house had spilled out into the garden and must be provided for. The landscape architect no longer had a choice between the functional and the aesthetic approaches.

The increasing use of garden space was encouraged by modern architecture which provided direct access between house and garden (Fig. 2.62). The use of the garden for outdoor entertaining, games, and children's play combined with the need to reduce maintenance resulted in the widespread introduction of paving materials and ground cover plants designed as simple shapes. Church recommended that the spatially wasteful front lawn should be dispensed with and showed the advantages of this in several examples in which the street was screened off by walls or fences, providing usable private space (Fig. 2.63).

Church developed an aesthetic theory based on cubism. A garden should have no beginning and no end and it should be pleasing when seen from any angle, not only from the house. Asymmetrical lines were used to create greater apparent dimensions.

FIGURE 2.63
Exhibition garden by Thomas D. Church (1940).

Simplicity of form, line, and shape were regarded as more restful to look at and easier to maintain. Form, shape, and pattern in the gardens were provided by pavings, walls, and espaliered or trained plants.

Two small gardens designed for the 1940 Golden Gate Exposition marked the beginning of this new phase (Fig. 2.64). They demonstrated the possibilities for the evolution of new visual forms in the garden while satisfying all practical criteria. The central axis was abandoned in favor of multiplicity of viewpoints, simple planes, and flowing lines. Texture and color, space and form were manipulated in a manner reminiscent of the cubist painters. A variety of curvilinear shapes, textured surfaces, and walls were combined with a sure sense of proportion and the gardens incorporated some new materials such as corrugated asbestos and wooden paving blocks. Stylistically they were a very dramatic advance on all previous garden designs.

The genius of the California garden thus lies in the combination of numerous concepts and traditions which preceded it and are based on the people, climate, and landscape of the region. Landscape architects in Britain, Scandinavia, Germany, and Switzerland produced a European synthesis with equally distinctive results. The East coast struggled with its obsession with the landscape tradition and Burle Marx in Brazil developed an approach to design that is based on modern painting and botany. Louis Barragan developed an equally vivid but different vocabulary of form in Mexico.

The modern garden prototype emerged out of a changed conception of what a garden should be. Again, because of its basic design philosophy and because of its international appeal, there is no absolute specificity to the prototype. It is typically small and enclosed by fences or walls, frequently confined to the back of the lot, the front being occupied with garage, guest parking and entry. The entire garden space is

FIGURE 2.64
Modern garden design by Garrett Eckbo (1945) shows uses allocated for all parts of a small lot and sculptural structuring of space. Key: **(1)** play area, **(2)** childrens' yard, **(3)** flower area, **(4)** grass, **(5)** decomposed granite, **(6)** service yard, **(7)** fruit trees, **(8)** shrub hedges, **(B)** bedroom, **(L)** living room, **(K)** kitchen, **(G)** garage.

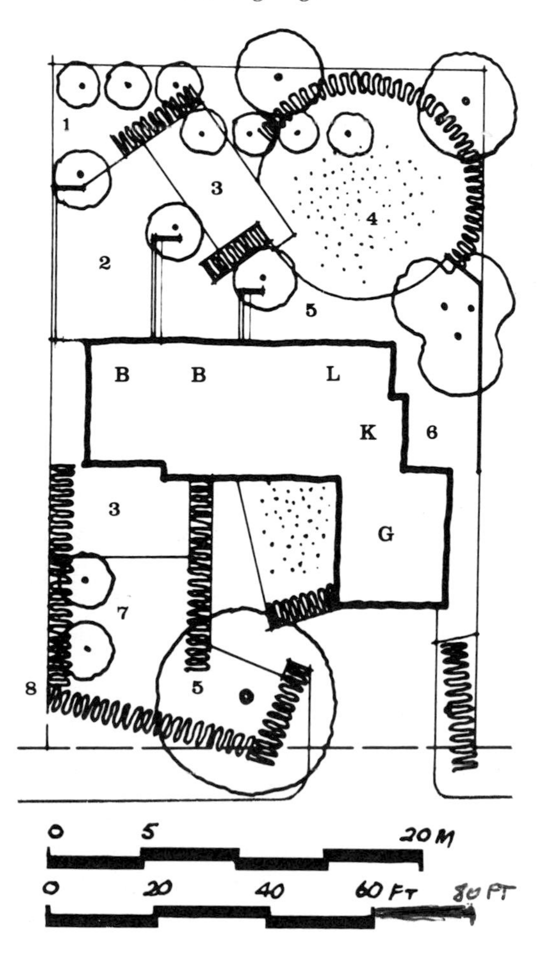

FIGURE 2.65
A garden by Thomas Church in California in 1948 showing the interrelationship of indoors and out, characteristic of the modern garden.

divided according to uses and the outdoor areas are connected by doors to the rooms of the house, e.g., kitchen to herbs, vegetables, garbage, and storage, living room to terrace and barbecue (Fig. 2.65). It is used intensively for outdoor recreation, games, sunbathing, swimming, eating, and drinking. Privacy is desirable. This garden type seems to represent the ideal for people of all income groups in many parts of the world today.

FUTURE OF THE GARDEN

It is difficult to say what future there is for the private garden. There seems to be a revival of interest in gardening and in organic vegetables but in some areas the cost of a single family house is becoming prohibitive. In most California gardens irrigation is required for lawns and because many "exotic" plants are favored over the native or drought-tolerant species. In any place where water is not plentiful, this is wasteful. So the future of the garden in California at least must take account of this environmental factor. But the survival of private gardens as a concept is a separate issue. The increasing popularity of condominiums and cluster developments (Fig. 5.15) is fostering, or may be the result of, a change in attitude. It seems that many people do not want to have anything to do with gardens and gardening. They would like to look at grass, trees, and flowers but prefer maintenance crews to take care of it. This may be more a reflection of real estate economics than popular preference. For most people the garden or a symbol of it which they nourish themselves seems to be an important part of life.

Most contemporary landscape architects, with a few notable exceptions, have given up designing private gardens. Perhaps this is appropriate. There is certainly a case to be made for more participation in the design process by clients. However, professional technology is definitely required, especially in fragile environments where the impact of inept construction could be devastating and widespread. Also, the imagination and conceptual thinking of a designer is still a valid input in a process whose purpose is to reveal possibilities and develop unthought of solutions suited to the specific setting.

THE GARDEN IN FILM, MUSIC, AND LITERATURE

Films, music, and novels describing or produced in particular periods of history contribute to an understanding of the social and environmental context of the gardens. For example, the opera *Aida* (Verdi) gives us a flavor of ancient Egypt as does the film *Cleopatra* (1963) which, like Julius Caesar (1950), portrays ancient Rome. The Middle Ages is evoked by the religious and secular music of Dunstable, Binchois, and

Dufay, the novel, *Narcissus and Goldmund* by Herman Hesse and the films *The Seventh Seal* (1956) (Bergman), *The Lion in Winter* (1968) and *Becket* (1964).

The film *El Cid* (1961), *Alhambra* by Washington Irving (1829), and thirteenth century troubador and trouvere music and de Fallas *Nights in the Gardens of Spain* evoke a Spanish ambience. For Italy, we may turn to the masses and madrigals by Monteverdi, Palestrina, and Gabrielli and two Zefferelli films, *Romeo and Juliet* and *Taming of the Shrew* (with Taylor and Burton). Seventeenth century France may be represented by operatic, religious, dance and ballet music composed by Charpentier, de Lalande, and Lully (court musicians to Louis XIV), *The Three Musketeers* by Dumas, *Sun King* by Nancy Mitford and the films, *The Rise of Louis XIV* (1965) and *Last Year at Marienbad* (1961). The stage, religious, string and keyboard music, madrigals, masses and lute songs by Tallis (for Henry VIII at Hampton Court), Morley, Byrd, Purcell, Boyce complement the Tudor era in England while the compositions of Hayden and Handel (Royal Firework music written for an open air concert in 1749) evoke the eighteenth century. Films such as *Tom Jones* (1963), Oliver Goldsmith's restoration comedy, *She Stoops to Conquer* and Jane Austen's *Pride and Prejudice* (1813) contribute to our understanding of England in the eighteenth century. Many films about Japan such as *Chusingura* and the novel *Shogun* provide an excellent sense of historical Japan. For more modern times, Sinclair Lewis's novels, *Babbit* and *Main Street*, and F. Scott Fitzgerald's *The Great Gatsby* deal with American society in the first half of the twentieth century, and the film, *Mon Oncle* (Jacques Tati) pokes fun at the modern garden.

This is a personal, rather than a definitive list. Gardens described in this chapter did not and do not exist in a vacuum, but rather in a context of the other arts and within the framework of society. The more these connections can be made the better will be our understanding of the garden in history and the better our ability in design for today.

SUGGESTED READINGS

General Histories of Landscape Architecture and Garden Design

Berral, Julia S., *The Garden: An Illustrated History.*
Clifford, Derek, *A History of Garden Design.*
Crowe, Sylvia, *Garden Design*, pp. 17–77.
Fairbrother, Nan, *Men and Gardens.*
Gotheim, M. Louise, *The History of Garden Art.*
Hadfield, Miles, *Gardens.*
Hyams, Edward, *A History of Gardens and Gardening.*
Jellicoe, Geoffrey and Susan Jellicoe, *The Landscape of Man.*
Newton, Norman T., *Design on the Land.*
Sorensen, Carl Theodore, *The Origin of Garden Art.*
Thacker, Christopher, *The History of Gardens.*
Tobey, George, *A History of Landscape Architecture.*
Wright, Richardson Little, *The Story of Gardening.*

China

Graham, Dorothy, *Chinese Gardens.*
Keswick, Maggie, *The Chinese Garden.*
Siren, Oswald, *Gardens of China.*

Japan

Bring, Mitchell, *Japanese Gardens.*
Holborn, Mark, *The Ocean in the Sand.*
Horiguchi, Sutami, *Tradition of Japanese Gardens.*
International Federation of Landscape Architects, *Landscape Architecture in Japan*, 9th Congress, 1964.
Morse, Edward S., *Japanese Homes and Their Surroundings.*
Newsom, S., *A Thousand Years of Japanese Gardens.*
Siren, Oswald, *Gardens of China.*
Tamura, Tsuyoshi, *Art of Landscape Gardens in Japan.*
Treib, Marc and Ron Herman, *A Guide to the Gardens of Kyoto.*

Ancient Mediterranean

Clifford, Derek, *A History of Garden Design*, Ch. 1, "Pliny and the Renaissance Garden."
Tobey, George, *A History of Landscape Architecture*, Chs. 1–9.
Wright, Richardson Little, *The Story of Gardening*, Ch. 2, "How Gardening Began."

Islam

Persia:
Lehram, Jonas, *Earthly Paradise—Garden and Courtyard in Islam.*
Moynihan, Elizabeth, *Paradise as a Garden.*
Spain:
Crowe, Sylvia, *Garden Design*, Ch. 3.
Villiers-Stuart, Constance M., *Spanish Gardens.*
India:
Crowe, Sylvia, et al., *The Gardens of Moghul India.*
Villier-Stuart, Constance M., *Gardens of the Great Moghuls.*

The Medieval Garden

Crisp, Frank, *Medieval Gardens.*
Harvey, John, *Medieval Gardens.*
McLean, Teresa, *Medieval English Gardens.*

Italy

Crowe, Sylvia, *Garden Design*, Ch. 4, "The Italian Garden."
Coffin, David, *The Italian Garden in First Colloquium on the History of Landscape Architecture*, Dunbarton Oaks.
Jellicoe, Geoffrey A., *Studies in Landscape Design*, Ch. 1, pp. 1–15, "The Italian Garden of the Renaissance."
Masson, Georgina, *Italian Gardens*, pp. 142–144, "Villa Lante," pp. 136–139, "Villa D'Este."
Shepherd, John C., and Geoffrey A. Jellicoe, *Italian Gardens of the Renaissance*, pp. 1–24.

France

Adams, William H., *The French Garden, 1500–1800.*

Clifford, Derek, *A History of Garden Design*, Ch. 3., "France."

Crowe, Sylvia, *Garden Design*, Ch. 5, "The French Tradition."

Fox, Helen, *André le Nôtre.*

Giedion, Sigfried, *Space, Time and Architecture*, pp. 133–160, "Organization of Outer Space."

Hazlehurst, Franklin H., *Jacques Boyceau and the French Formal Garden.*

Hazlehurst, F. H., *Gardens of Illusion, the Genius of André Le Notre.*

England

Chadwick, George F., *The Works of Sir Joseph Paxton*, pp. 19–43.

Clark, H. F., *The English Landscape Garden*, pp. 1–35, 37–38, Chiswick.

Crowe, Sylvia, *Garden Design*, Ch. 6, "The English Landscape Garden."

Dutton, Ralph, *The English Garden.*

Green, David, *Gardener to Queen Anne*, "Henry Wise and the Formal Garden."

Hunt, John Dixon and Peter Willis, *The Genius of the Place.*

Hussey, Christopher, *The Picturesque.*

Hyams, Edward S., *The English Garden.*

Jourdain, Margaret, *The Work of William Kent*, pp. 15–26, Introduction by Christopher Hussey.

Massingham, Betty, *Miss Jekyll.*

Pevsner, Nikolaas, "The Genesis of the Picturesque," *Architectural Review*, Vol. 96, November 1944, pp. 139–166.

Strong, Roy, *The Renaissance Garden in England.*

Stroud, Dorothy, *Capability Brown*, pp. 13–20, Introduction by Christopher Hussey.

Stroud, Dorothy, *Humphry Repton.*

American Colonial Garden

American Society of Landscape Architects, *Colonial Gardens.*

Favretti, Rudy J. and J. P. Favretti, *Landscapes and Gardens for Historic Buildings*, pp. 11–26.

Leighton, Anne, *Early American Gardens.*

Lockwood, Alice, G. B. for Garden Club of America, *Gardens of Colony and State.*

Tobey, George, *A History of Landscape Architecture*, Ch. 15., "Conquerors of Wilderness."

Landscape Garden in America

Cleveland, Horace W. S., *Landscape Architecture* (1873), Ch. 2, pp. 6–9.

Downing, Andrew Jackson, *Landscape Gardening: Adapted to North America.*

Eaton, Leonard K., *Landscape Artist in America: The Life and Work of Jens Jensen*, pp. 81–211, "The Private Work."

Newton, Norman T., *Design on the Land*, Ch. XVIII, "Early American Backgrounds."

Tobey, George, *A History of Landscape Architecture*, Ch. 16, "United States 1800–1850."

Flower Gardens and the Eclectic Revival

Blomfield, Reginald, *The Formal Garden in England.*

Brown, Jane, et al., *Frederick Law Olmsted*, pp. 86–89.

Massingham, Betty, *Miss Jekyll.*

Newton, Norman T., *Design on the Land*, Ch. XXIII., "Eclecticism," Ch. XXX., "The Country Place Era."

Platt, Charles, *Italian Gardens.*

Taylor, Geoffrey, *The Victorian Flower Garden.*

Robinson, William, *The English Flower Garden.*

Tobey, George, *A History of Landscape Architecture*, Ch. 18., "The Arcadian Myth."

The Modern Garden

Brookes, John, *Room Outside.*

Church, Thomas, *Gardens are For People.*

Eckbo, Garrett, *Home Landscapes.*

Laurie, Michael, "The California Garden," *Landscape Architecture*, October 1965, pp. 23–27.

Tunnard, Christopher, *Gardens in the Modern Landscape.*

Tobey, George, *A History of Landscape Architecture*, Ch. 21., "Form Follows Function."

LANDSCAPE AND NATURAL RESOURCES

3

Two themes from the historical review of landscape and resources are important in the study of landscape architecture. The first comprises the events or movements that led up to government action or intervention in the conservation of resources such as forests, wildlife, soil, and water, and the establishment of such agencies as the U.S. Forest Service, the Geological Survey, Soil Conservation, and the Bureau of Land Management at the federal level, and Departments of Fisheries and Wildlife at the state level. The second theme involves the events that led up to governmental support for the conservation of natural scenic landscape for public use and enjoyment resulting in the U.S. National Parks Service and the state parks movement. These themes are intertwined yet separate. They deal with the attitudes of people and changes in those attitudes toward landscape and resources in the nineteenth century. It is important to understand the background of these agencies and the reasons for their

FIGURE 3.1
Section lines of the land survey (1878) are one mile apart. The American Midwest. Photograph by William A. Garnett.

establishment. Many employ landscape architects. Others provide information useful in land use planning and design. The work of some is changing in response to concepts of multiple use and the increasing demand for recreation.

SETTLEMENT OF THE AMERICAN LANDSCAPE

In 1620 when the Mayflower landed on the East coast of America, the Indians who populated the land had been present on the continent for countless generations. The Indians held beliefs about landscape different from those of the West Europeans. The land ethic of the American Indian was an I-thou ethic (as defined by Gutkind), involving a reverence for the life-sustaining landscape, its plants and animals. The Indians related to a particular landscape region by ties of kinship and nature rather than by an understanding of property ownership. There was a close relationship between settlement and resources; the amount of food available determined the population and its distribution.

By contrast, the European settler thought in terms of estates and land parcels he could own, cultivate, and use as he wished. His concept of land ownership involving exclusive possession of land was supported by legal documents and deeds. The landscape was thus divided into rectangles. William Penn's plan for Philadelphia (1683) and the land survey of 1878, which sectioned the entire American landscape west of the Appalachians, are clear expressions of that attitude (Fig. 3.1).

The first task of forest-bound colonists was to develop woodsmanship; homes and stockades had to be built, land cleared, and firewood cut. Clearings for agriculture could be carved out of the forest only by great effort or the deliberate use of fire. Tree cutting preceded the establishment of agriculture and the worst forest destruction was justified with this reasoning. Either the original vegetation was replaced with a crop which was harvested, or else the land was used for cattle and sheep grazing. The shock was often too great. The crude techniques of lumbering employed in early Colonial times resulted in soil erosion. Cropping without replenishing the soil with nutrients reduced its fertility. Overgrazing resulted in thin grass cover, resulting in poor yield and soil erosion.

Late eighteenth-century illustrations show primitive clearing of fields and space for farmhouse and buildings surrounded or enclosed by the native forest. When the land was exhausted, the farmer would move on to a new site.

Some who unwittingly destroyed land were simply poor farmers ignorant of the processes of nature and techniques of sound agriculture. The homesteaders in the plains states created the dust bowl by not understanding the laws of drought and the importance of grass in an arid land.

The virgin forests of North America were some of the finest in the world. East of the Great Plains every acre was originally covered by trees and to the west coniferous forests flourished in the Rocky Mountains and along the Pacific Coast. A growing nation needed wood for housing, shipbuilding, and fuel, and by the 1800s cities began to need lumber in very large quantities. Machines, circular saws, and steam mills were organized to provide it. The invention of the wood pulp process for paper manufacture also led to an increased demand for timber. Thus, in addition to the farmers' desire for cleared land, there were great incentives to cut timber for economic return. Lumbering quickly became America's largest industry. Although there was a great quantity of forest, the wasteful techniques of cutting and the fires that were a side effect resulted in rapid depletion of the resource and by 1900 the myth of superabundance had been revealed as a fallacy (Fig. 3.2).

FIGURE 3.2
Wasteful clear cutting practices. Photograph by U.S. Forest Service.

FIGURE 3.3
"A lively scene on an American prairie—a buffalo hunt by steam." From Frank Leslie's illustrated newspaper, 28 November 1868.

FIGURE 3.4
Hydraulic mining in California. See also Fig. 1.7. Courtesy of the Bancroft Library, University of California, Berkeley.

The wildlife of the country was equally plentiful and varied and was equally plundered. The fashionable beaver hat resulted in the depletion of that species. Hunters shot buffalo from railroad cars (Fig. 3.3). Seals and other animals and birds, including the American eagle, symbol of the nation, were practically eliminated. The passenger pigeon was extinguished completely.

Resources such as oil, coal, and mineral ores were mined as easily as possible and then, as soon as it became difficult or uneconomical, the process stopped, leaving half-finished workings, dereliction of landscape, and heaps of overburden. This strip and run process was not only wasteful of the sought after resource but also resulted in severe soil erosion and destruction of the natural system. For example, hydraulic mining in California removed soil and overburden covering gold deposits by a jet of water (Fig. 3.4). The soil was thus washed into rivers, which carried the silt to lower levels where a raising of the river beds caused flooding on farmlands. There was therefore a conflict between agriculture interests and mining. Ultimately hydraulic mining was made illegal by the state legislature. Excessive erosion was also caused by cattle overgrazing and the growing of annual crops in grassland country. Overfarming and overgrazing were as disastrous in terms of soil loss as were overlogging and mining (Fig. 3.5).

FIGURE 3.5
Denudation gullies, Kennett, California, 1934. Photography by U. S. Forest Service.

CONSERVATION OF RESOURCES

In 1864 George Perkins Marsh inquired into the balance of nature and the interrelationship of plant and animal communities and concluded that "The ravages committed by man subvert the relations and destroy the balance which nature has established." He was convinced that the balance could be restored only if man used wisdom in managing resources.[1]

Marsh had considerable influence in the legislature and his efforts and writings contributed to the passing of the Public Lands Bill of 1891, which empowered the President to set aside forest lands as public reservations. The Forest Reserve Act was passed in 1891. Millions of acres of forest were thus made public reservations by succeeding presidents and Congress. This conserved the country's future lumber supply and also saved scenic lands from being divided haphazardly into homesteads. However, the Forest Management Act of 1897 advocated multiple use and required that in addition to providing a continuous supply of timber, the forest should be open to mining and grazing. The U. S. Forest Service was established in 1905 within the Department of Agriculture to manage these lands. The Forest Service leases timber rights to commercial operators and is thereby a self-supporting government agency. Part of the revenue is directed to the needs of local communities and to provision of recreation facilities for the public.

At the same time, soil and moisture conservation became the concern of government. It was estimated that the annual cost of erosion in terms of production was $400 million. In 1935 the Soil Conservation Service was established in the Department of Agriculture. Today the Soil Conservation Service devotes much of its efforts to mapping soils in terms of their quality and best use. These data can now be used in assessing the agricultural capability, susceptibility to erosion, and foundation suitability of soils.

It was the economic depression of the 1930s which precipitated much government action in connection

[1] George Perkins Marsh, *Man and Nature* (New York: Scribner, 1864).

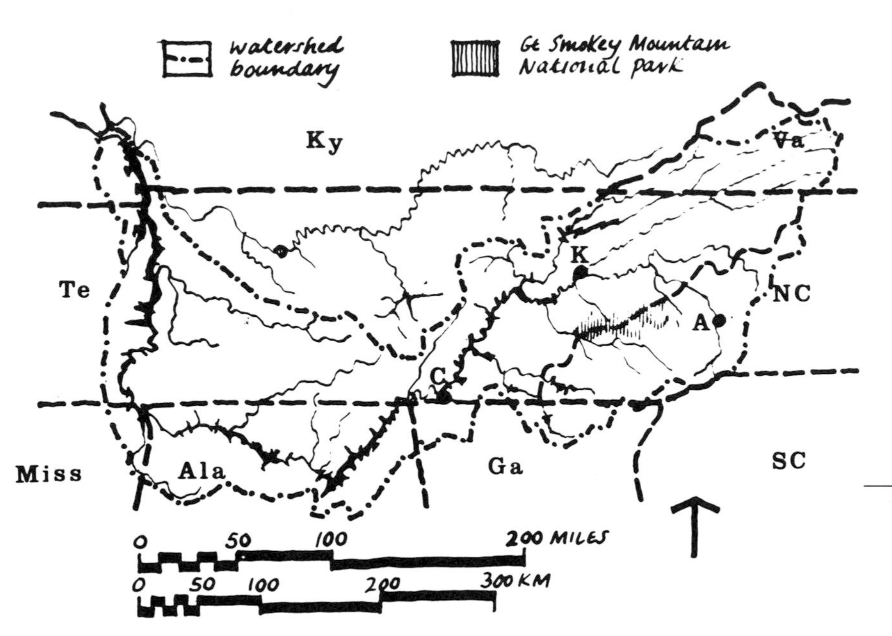

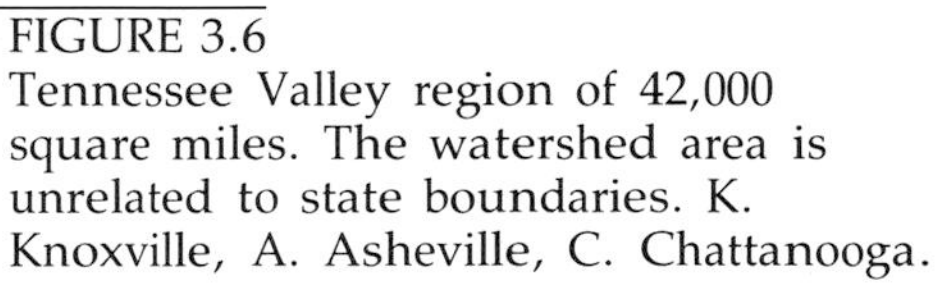
FIGURE 3.6
Tennessee Valley region of 42,000 square miles. The watershed area is unrelated to state boundaries. K. Knoxville, A. Asheville, C. Chattanooga.

with conservation. The New Deal introduced conservation as an integral part in the war against economic depression. After his election in 1932 President Franklin Roosevelt sponsored conservation of forests, soil, and water and initiated the Civilian Conservation Corps to achieve it. Many of the features—buildings, outlooks, trails, roads, and camps—to be found in the state and national parks today resulted from these efforts.

One bill of the New Deal established the Tennessee Valley Authority. Under this legislation, a broad plan was proposed for a physiographic region which included parts of seven states (Fig. 3.6). A semiindependent regional authority was created and given wide powers to promote the economic and social well-being of the people of the entire valley. The Tennessee Valley had been rich in timber and petroleum resources, but its ruthless exploitation resulted in a

FIGURE 3.7
The T.V.A., Tims Ford Reservoir. Photograph courtesy of Tennessee Valley Authority.

derelict landscape and a depressed population. In 1933 no region of the United States had lower incomes or more families on relief. The Tennessee River had superior hydraulic power sites, yet it flowed unchecked through counties and states where few farmers had electricity. In addition to the T. V. A. dam building program, the plan included navigation, reforestation, soil conservation, outdoor recreation, the retirement of marginal farmland, and the manufacture of fertilizer. In ten years the river was harnessed, over 700 miles were made navigable, and the dams provided low-cost power and flood controls. Scientific agriculture and contour plowing were introduced. Reforestation added to the revitalized landscape, and attractive scenery was created in which lakes provided opportunities for water-oriented recreation (Fig. 3.7).

LANDSCAPE QUALITY

The conservation of scenic landscape for public use and enjoyment has a different source from the movement that led to the conservation of forests, soil, and land as a governmental policy. To understand the background it is necessary to return to eighteenth-century England and to the Romantic movement, source of the landscape garden and new forms in literature and the arts. This coincided with or inspired a changed attitude toward wilderness and large scale scenery which, up until the end of the seventeenth century, had been considered hostile and uninteresting.

Published accounts of tours through England, Scotland, and Wales by William Gilpin led to the development of tourism in the countryside (Fig. 3.8).[2] The concept that the landscape itself was worthy of attention was advanced in essays such as Gilpin's "Picturesque Beauty"[3] and Price's "The Picturesque as Compared with the Sublime and the Beautiful".[4] William Wordsworth, writing of the year 1750 in his *Guide Through the Lakes*, noted: "Travellers, instead of confining their observations to towns, manufacturies [sic] or mines, began to wander over the island in search of sequestered spots, distinguished, as they might accidentally have learned, for the sublimity of the forms of nature there to be seen." William Gilpin described the objective of picturesque travel as "Beauty of every kind. . . . This great object(ive)," he wrote, "we pursue through the scenery of nature, and examine it by the rules of painting, we seek it among

FIGURE 3.8
Sketch in the style of William Gilpin which contributed to the popularity of romantic landscape in England in the eighteenth century.

all the ingredients of landscape—trees, rocks, broken grounds, woods, rivers and lakes, plains, valleys, mountains and distances. These objects themselves produce infinite variety—no two rocks or trees are the same. They are varied, a second time by combination, and almost as much a third time, by different lights and shades and other aerial effects." Thus the landscape was described as though it were a painting. It is also a description of all the qualities which we enjoy in landscape today, particularly diversity and contrast.

English painters of the nineteenth century also stimulated the new generation of native tourists who were eager to see the scenes they depicted on canvas. The best known of these were Turner and Constable. Their work was central to the Romantic movement. The Industrial Revolution also fostered interest in the beauty of natural landscape as a contrast to urban ugliness. The concept of ideal landscape as depicted earlier by Claude Lorrain and Poussin in the eighteenth century and on which the landscape garden was based became less credible under the impact of the economist Malthus (who argued that there were limits to the population the world could support) and Darwin, whose theory of evolution helped to dispel the notion that some god had given perfection to nature in a moment of original creativity. In the course of the nineteenth century, paintings which were close imitations of nature (not idealized landscapes) became the most popular form of art. Some paintings depicted rocks almost as though the painting were a scientific study, accurate and geologically correct. A peaceful scene with water in the foreground reflecting a luminous sky and set off by dark trees was something which everyone agreed was beautiful, as in previous ages they had agreed about a naked athlete, a madonna and child, or an idealized Classical landscape by Poussin or Claude Lorrain (Fig. 2.39).

But in spite of Darwin there was still a moralistic

[2] William Gilpin, *Mountains and Lakes of Cumberland and Westmoreland* (London: R. Blamire, 1772).
[3] William Gilpin, *Three Essays: On Picturesque Beauty; On Picturesque Travel; and On Sketching Landscape* (London: R. Blamire, 1792).
[4] Uvedale Price, *An Essay on the Picturesque as Compared with the Sublime and the Beautiful* (London: J. Robson, 1794).

overtone to this interest in natural landscape. Constable believed, for example, that nature was the clearest revelation of God's will and thus landscapes painted in the spirit of humble truth could be a means of conveying moral ideas. Both Wordsworth and Constable believed that there was something in trees, flowers, meadows, and mountains that was imbued with divinity and so it was felt that if nature was contemplated with sufficient devotion it would reveal a moral and spiritual quality of its own. In this argument, the landscape was regarded as a symbol of the self and as a symbol of God, rather than as evidence of the divinity.

The publication of picture books and the development of the railroads in England gave impetus to and made possible tourism on a popular scale. In 1841 Thomas Cook started his business of arranging tours for working people from the cities to the coast or the mountains.

Interest in nature and the out-of-doors was further stimulated by the growth of the natural sciences in the nineteenth century. Botany, biology, and geology all involved field trips into natural areas. Geologists who went to the Alps to study the rocks were overwhelmed by the beauty of the landscape and incidentally developed mountaineering as a pastime.

But even in these early days the possibility of destroying the beauty of natural landscape was evident. In his *Guide through the Lakes in the North of England*, written in 1810, William Wordsworth warned about the despoliation of the landscape and the disfigurement of the lakes by new settlers and their houses. "The author has been induced to speak thus at length by a wish to preserve the native beauty of this delightful district." Then, anticipating a solution and the concept of national parks Wordsworth wrote: "The author will be joined by persons of pure taste through-

FIGURE 3.9
Spring Mountain on the Hudson River, painted by Thomas Cole about 1827. Courtesy Museum of Fine Arts, Boston.

out the whole island who by their visits (often repeated) to the lakes (in the North of England) testify that they deem the district a sort of national property in which every man has a right and interest."[5]

The United States had its own set of influential poets, painters, naturalists, and philosophers, who persuaded the American public of the inspirational qualities of natural landscape. In an essay on American scenery written in 1836, Thomas Cole, founder of the Hudson River school of painting, listed the components of scenery as, "mountains, lakes, waterfalls, forests, the sky and its associations" (Fig. 3.9). Emerson, in his essay "Nature" written in the same year, emphasized the beneficial effects that contemplation of nature had on both body and soul. Goodness and natural beauty were inseparable. Beyond that he proclaimed, a little snobbishly that " . . . love of (natural) beauty is Taste." In addition, Emerson felt strongly that the individual should enjoy an original relation to the universe as opposed to (reading) books and second-hand experience (about nature).[6] Thoreau believed that the order of the week as set out in the Bible should be reversed. The seventh day should be a day of work and sweat and toil; in the remaining six days man should be free to feed his soul with sublime revelations of nature. He was one of the nation's first preservationists, believing that some landscapes should be left unspoiled and that animals should have inviolate places of refuge.[7] In 1858 he made a plea for "National Preserves," in which wild animals would be protected not for sport but for "inspiration and our own true recreation."

By the 1840s in the United States, the Romantic movement and a tourist industry to go with it was centered on the Hudson River, the Adirondacks, and the White Mountains of New Hampshire.

CONSERVATION OF SCENERY

Frederick Law Olmsted, son of a New England middle-class merchant, farmer, traveler, author (and as already mentioned, inventor of the title "landscape architecture"), came to California in 1863 as a land manager for the Fremont lands in the foothills of the Sierra Nevada.

Like the poet Wordsworth and the painter Constable in England, and like Emerson and Thoreau in the United States, Olmsted felt the strong moral appeal in natural landscape beauty and studied the potential of the landscape for the advancement of human morality and happiness. He was also a keen student of the books of William Gilpin. He was a serious and energetic man who, in the course of his own work, became familiar with the natural qualities of Yosemite Valley and also with the threats to its natural beauty and ecological stability, due to sheep farming, tree cutting, and mining (Fig. 3.10).

The valley, discovered in 1851, had already attracted attention for the drama of its physical features. Photographs from as early as 1829 illustrated the awesome statistics, a valley 2,300 feet deep and the Yo-hamite Falls, 1,300 feet high (Figs. 3.11 and 3.12). Lithographers and artists also reproduced the scene and in 1868 Bierstadt painted his famous view of the valley. In the short time that he was in California, Olmsted worked for its preservation under the guiding principle that enjoyment of scenery of this kind could have a profound influence on mankind and it should therefore be conserved and made accessible to the public. In 1864 he was appointed one of several commissioners of Yosemite Valley, which by act of the Federal Government was granted to the State of California "for public use, resort and recreation." This act provided through government action the first scenic area for public enjoyment in the United States and, indeed, the world. Olmsted prepared a report and plan of action. It recognized the essential principles of land management in terms of preservation of natural scenery and public access. The philosophy and principles in the report were to become central in the work of the National Parks Service, founded subsequently in 1916.

A few years later, in 1870, members of an expedition exploring the Yellowstone Region of Wyoming were impressed by the natural beauty they saw there: canyons, hot springs, waterfalls, lakes, and forests. And though they could legally have filed homesteads or mining claims, they decided that the area should be a permanent public preserve and such action was subsequently taken by the government in 1872 when it was designated as the first national park.

The battle lines were drawn in the conflict of interest between the exploiters of resources, the lumbermen, miners, hunters, on the one hand, and, on the other, such figures as naturalist John Muir. Muir and the Sierra Club gathered national support for the preservation of the entire Yosemite region surrounding the relatively small state-managed valley. Muir worked and wrote passionately against the destruction of watersheds, scenic landscape, and forests through overgrazing and exploitative lumbering. In 1890 the government created a forest reservation (including the valley) of more than 1 million acres.

---

[5] William Wordsworth, *A Guide Through the District of the Lakes in the North of England* (London: R. Hart-Davis, 1951). (First issued anonymously in 1810.)

[6] Ralph Waldo Emerson, *Nature* (New York: Scholars Facsimiles and Reprints, 1940). (First published in 1836.)

[7] Henry David Thoreau, *Walden* (Boston: Ticknor and Fields, 1856).

FIGURE 3.10
Yosemite Valley (see also Figs. 9.18 and 9.19). Photograph by Wilford Hoover.

FIGURE 3.11
Travellers arriving in Yosemite Valley (late nineteenth century). Courtesy of the Bancroft Library, University of California, Berkeley.

FIGURE 3.12
Tourists in Yosemite (late nineteenth century). Courtesy of the Bancroft Library, University of California, Berkeley.

FIGURE 3.13
Niagara Falls. A scenic wonder that became popular in the nineteenth century.

John Muir continued his campaign and was a major force behind the 1916 bill establishing the National Parks Service, which has now developed into a large scale manager of land, interpreter of landscape and natural history, and provider of recreational facilities.

Thus John Muir combined his emotional love of wilderness and natural landscape with the scientific teachings of George Perkins Marsh to achieve in stark political reality that which Emerson and others had only dreamed of.

As interest grew in the outdoors, it was recognized that a system of state parks was necessary to accommodate the increasing demand for recreation in the countryside made possible by the automobile. The State Parks movement was initiated in 1921. New York and California began the development of extensive systems in the late 1920s. In 1928, New York State with a population of 12,580,000 had 56 units ranging in size from the near wilderness Adirondack preserve to the Niagara Falls (designated in 1885) (Fig. 3.13), and the intensively used Jones Beach. The California State Park system, with its nucleus of redwood groves, was established in 1927. The report by Frederick Law Olmsted, Jr. is considered an important and prophetic document. It particularly noted the role of the automobile in recreation and the special importance of the limited coastline resource.

The system now includes more than 725,000 acres in parks, beaches, and recreation and historic areas. Similar park systems were developed in most states, with much progress being made in the 1930s.

A role for the landscape architect became defined as bringing people in contact with landscape in such a way that scenic qualities were maintained at the same time that convenience and services were provided. Up to World War II, when the numbers of visitors were relatively small, this could be done with little conflict. However, in recent years the increase in numbers and the satisfaction of their demand for lodging, campgrounds, road access, and so forth, by a parks service eager to please, has finally been found to lead to conditions at odds with the original intent. Yosemite National Park has in excess of 2 million visitors annually. There is overuse and overcrowding in virtually all national and state parks (Figs. 3.14 and 3.15). Reservation of campsites is necessary in many, and various strategies are being devised to maintain the experience of nature.

FIGURE 3.14
Yosemite campground (1933).Photograph courtesy National Park Service, Yosemite.

FIGURE 3.15
Yosemite campground (1959). Photograph courtesy National Park Service, Yosemite.

Some reappraisal of recreation needs as they relate to the setting is necessary. Less spectacular scenery than that found in the national parks may be acceptable for the social kind of vacation that many seek at Yosemite and elsewhere (Fig. 3.16). In Britain the country park concept has been developed to meet this need. These parks are situated closer to urban centers than most national parks or wild areas of landscape, and they are designed for intensive use. They either relate to existing amenities and features or depend on the creation of entirely new recreation environments out of derelict land (Fig. 3.17).

The record of mismanagement and exploitation of land and landscape outlined here is not unique to the United States. It seems to have been the pattern for all Western cultures and industrialized nations. In all cases, government has responded sooner or later with conservation measures of one sort or another.

But the conservation struggle continues. Conflicts occur between the economic interests of corporations

FIGURE 3.16
Camping in Yosemite. Photograph by Bruce Davidson.

FIGURE 3.17
Motorcycle riding, one of many new sports in need of suitable terrain in the hinterland of urban communities. Photograph by Cynthia Anderson.

and individuals and the long-term values of conservation for present and future generations. Conservation organizations lock horns with corporations and sometimes government agencies in protest over pollution, destruction of natural resources and scenery, and so on. Government often finds itself in the middle. The goals of the environmentalist sometimes seem at odds with those of the working man—ecology versus jobs. But these are simply short-term problems that must be seen in broader perspective. Enlightened government must protect resources and environmental quality as part of a viable economic program.

It does seem important, however, that the professionals should be more involved in initiating projects and proposals than they appear to have been. As the supply of natural landscapes in need of protection dries up and even before then, there will be a need to improve and create areas of natural landscape where presently there is dereliction and ugliness.

SUGGESTED READINGS

Coyle, Davis C., *Conservation, An American Story of Conflict and Accomplishment.*

Huth, Hans, *Nature and the American.*

Jones, H., *John Muir and the Sierra Club.*

Laurie, Michael, *A History of Aesthetic Conservation in California.*

Leopold, Aldo, *A Sand County Almanac.*

Nash, Roderick, *Wilderness and the American Mind.*

Marsh, George Perkins, *Man and Nature* (1864).

Muir, John, *Yosemite,* Doubleday Anchor Book.

Mumford, Lewis, *The Brown Decades,* pp. 59-80.

Newton, Norman, *Design on the Land,* Ch. XXXV and XXXVI, "The National Park System," Ch. XXXVII, "The State Park Movement."

Udall, Stewart, *The Quiet Crisis,* Ch. XX, pp. 109–125, "Wild and Park Lands," Ch. XIII, "Conservation and the Future."

Music

Grand Canyon Suite (1931), Ferde Grofé.

Appalachian Spring (1945), Aaron Copland.

Amid Nature, op. 91, Antonin Dvorák.

URBAN PARKS AND RECREATION

ORIGINS

In the ancient civilizations of Greece and Rome a number of urban open spaces were traditional: the marketplace (the agora in Greece, the forum in Rome); gymnasia for athletes; and sacred burial groves. Each of these was designed or set aside for a specific purpose. On special occasions when a private estate was opened to the public, people had an opportunity to enjoy planted gardens.

By 300 AD, thirty such gardens are said to have been open to the public in Rome. In addition, according to Mumford, there were at least eight campi: grass covered commons used for informal games. There is also evidence of public gardens in ancient China.

The Medieval towns of Europe were densely populated but the small scale of the cities meant that the countryside and fresh air were readily available and accessible (Fig. 2.20). There was little room and no particular need for land set aside within the city for recreation. The urban marketplace and the church steps and square were the major open spaces in which the public could gather in crowds. The church plaza was used for the performance of symbolic or mystic plays and the marketplace was, of course, used for the exchange and sale of goods and fresh produce brought in from the surrounding countryside. Those open spaces that did exist in the Medieval town were largely set aside for uses other than recreation, although they were in fact used in a variety of unplanned and recreational ways. For example, areas near churchyards and odd spaces beyond city walls were typically used by youth for sports and games.

In Renaissance Europe we see the periodic opening of private grounds or palace gardens to the public. In London the large Royal Parks, property of the Crown, were in time completely given over to public use. The same applied in other royal capitals. These cities richly endowed with parks were uniquely favored and were exceptional in the early nineteenth century in having a considerable amount of public park land, albeit unplanned and accidentally placed in relation to the population. In London a ready-made park system was provided by the opening to the public of St. James, Hyde, and Green parks and, later, Regents Park. Some of the older parks went through transformations related to changes in taste. In the seventeenth century, St. James Park was laid out with a straight-edged canal and parallel avenues of trees. In the eighteenth century the layout was converted into the romantic landscape setting that exists today (Fig. 4.1). In Paris there was a pattern of royal open space similar to that of London. The Champs Elysées, Tulleries, the Royal botanic garden and parc Monceau were all open for public use by the early 1800s.

In 1810 Regents Park, property of the Crown, was planned by John Nash partly as a public park and partly as a real estate venture (Fig. 4.2). The terraces and crescents that surrounded the park were conceived and built at the same time as the central core, which was a landscape park open to the public. This landscape also served to increase the desirability and value of the property. The park was laid out in the landscape style with meandering lakes and plantations and was like a country gentleman's estate and at the same scale. Each leaseholder of a terrace house and each individual roaming through the landscape could imagine that it was his own. Thus in the heart of the city the feeling and appearance of a large landscape garden were achieved for many people at a fraction of the cost to each.

However, the expanding industrial cities had very little provision for parks; moreover, parks were randomly distributed as a result of individual philanthropy. Frequently there were no parks at all. The expanding urban populations were housed in minimum housing built back to back with virtually no yards and only narrow access alleys between rows (Fig. 4.3). Because of these conditions, the poor were unhealthy and their performance at work was low. This fact became a major concern for industrialists and

FIGURE 4.1
St. James Park, London.

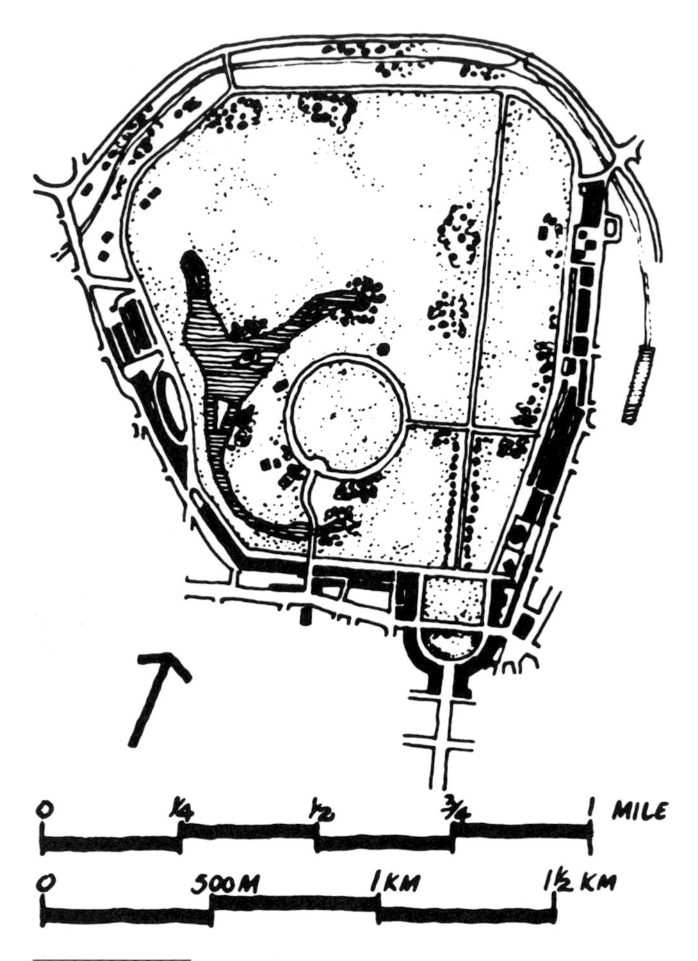

FIGURE 4.2
Regents Park, London (1810).

manufacturers who relied on the work capability of the people for their profits. Dickens' *Oliver Twist* provides a vivid description of these times and conditions. Many died at an early age due to ill health, attributed to crowding, poor buildings and services, polluted air, bad working conditions, and long working hours for men, women, and children. As a result of concern for the health of the workers, various acts of Parliament were passed in England between 1833 and 1843. These allowed for the use of public monies or taxes to provide improvements, sewers, and sanitation systems and to provide public parks.

Birkinhead Park

The city of Birkinhead near Liverpool was the first municipality to use these powers. Joseph Paxton was asked in 1843 to prepare plans for a park and also a real estate venture conceived by the park commissioners.

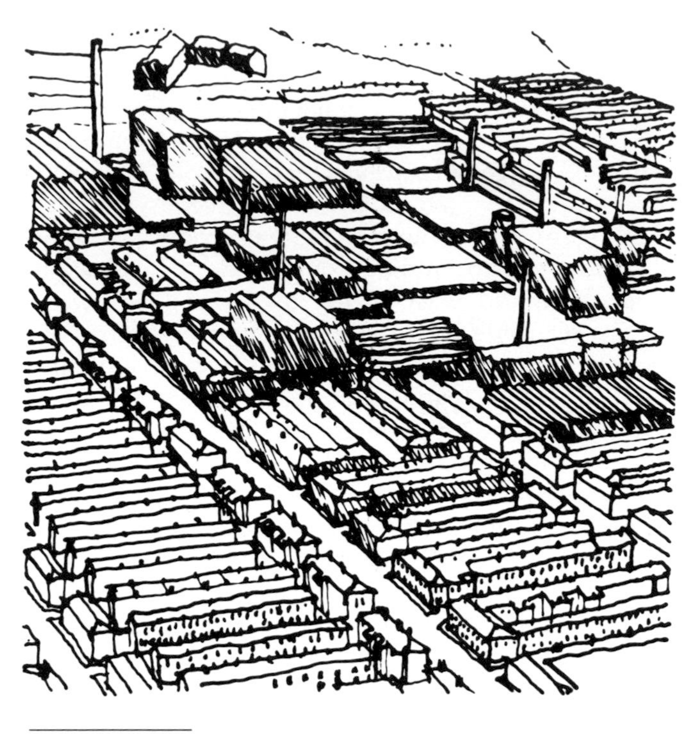

FIGURE 4.3
Typical nineteenth century English industrial town with back-to-back housing in close proximity to factories.

The act permitting the use of taxes stipulated that 70 acres were to be set aside for the free recreation of the inhabitants. In fact, 226 acres of sterile clay land, unsuitable for agriculture, were purchased. Of these, 125 were appropriated for public use and the remainder was set aside and sold for building sites. The two functions, private housing and public recreation, were planned together as Nash had done earlier at Regents Park. A special attraction of this combination was its financial success. The sale of the surrounding building land at enhanced values due to its situation covered the cost of the park itself. The plan (Fig. 4.4) included meadows for sports such as cricket and archery. There were winding carriage drives and separate pathways meandering through trees and around the edge of irregular lakes or fish ponds. Undulating topography was created with the excavated material from the lakes. Running from one side to the other is a wide road to permit business traffic to cross the park, which otherwise broke the extended grid of the street pattern. Although the house sites were adjacent to and overlooked the park, vehicular access to them was provided by roads outside the park. In 1852 Frederick Law Olmsted, who visited Birkinhead,wrote in his book *Walks and Talks of An American Farmer in England*

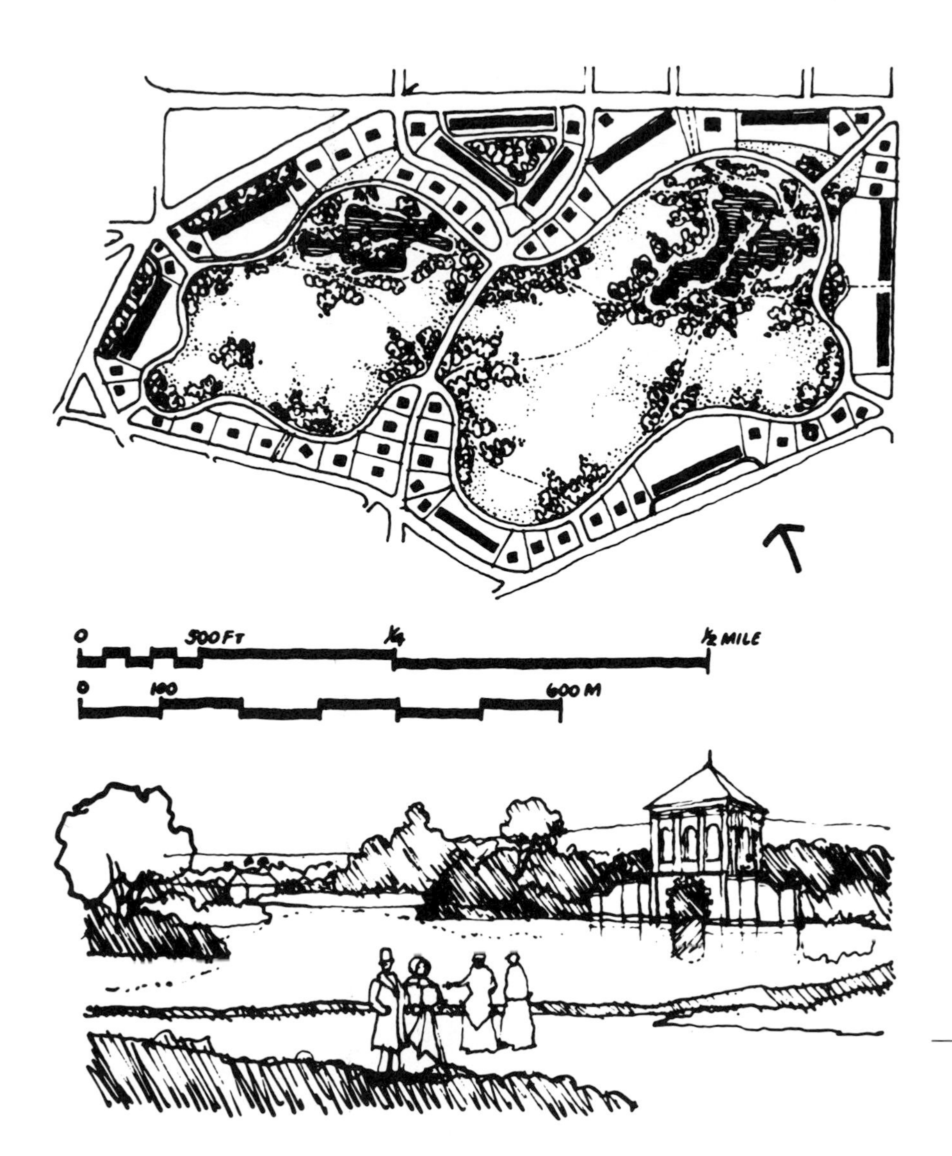

FIGURE 4.4
Birkinhead Park, England (1843).
(a) Plan, **(b)** view.

that he was "Amazed at the manner in which art had been employed to obtain from nature so much beauty."[1] Birkinhead Park was a success and stimulated a period of park building in Britain. Many of the new parks were designed by Paxton.

UNITED STATES

In the United States there was, of course, no tradition of royal parks. Open space specifically set aside for recreation was rarely embodied in urban developments of the eighteenth century, nor was it needed. However, such functional areas as the New England common, originally for the grazing of stock or for military parades, began to assume the role of public parks in the early nineteenth century.

Some planned cities such as Philadelphia and Savannah included residential squares planted with trees in the manner of Georgian London. These squares were not public parks but usually were reserved for use by residents of the surrounding houses. However, they do represent acceptance of the concept of bringing green areas into the city.

In 1848 Andrew Jackson Downing expressed concern over the lack of public parks in the United States. Despite the earlier traditions of the New England commons, the courthouse square in the south, and the planned towns of the eighteenth century, public parks were essentially unknown in America.

[1] Frederick Law Olmsted, *Walks and Talks of An American Farmer in England* (New York: Putnam, 1852).

Rural Cemeteries

Grotesque though it may seem, the closest approximation to a public park was the embellished rural cemetery. Many of these were laid out adjacent to the large cities in the nineteenth century: Laurel Hill (1836) in Philadelphia, Mount Auburn (1831) in Boston, and Greenwood (1852) in New York (Fig. 4.5). A description of Mount Auburn in 1831 tells that "The avenues are winding in their course and exceedingly beautiful in their gentle circuits adapted picturesquely to the inequalities of the surface of the ground and producing charming landscape effects from this natural arrangement." These areas of naturalistic landscape included monuments and tombstones, buildings and planting, and they were extremely popular with the inhabitants of the large cities. Guidebooks were prepared for visitors, suggesting routes through the grounds which would take in the most impressive monuments and viewpoints. On fine days hundreds of visitors, mostly on pleasure outings and picnics, would visit the cemeteries. It is said that 30,000 people visited Laurel Hill in Philadelphia between April and December of 1848 and almost twice that number visited Greenwood, New York. Downing argued that the general interest shown in the cemeteries proved that public gardens "established in a liberal and suitable manner near our cities would be successful."

Park Values

The case for public parks in the nineteenth century was built largely on the same concerns as that for improved housing. There seem to be five basic arguments: the first is concerned with public health, the second with morality, the third is related to the development of the Romantic movement, the fourth is concerned with economics, and the fifth with education.

A concern for public health led to reform in housing and improved sanitary sewers and drains. Included in the concept of better health was the availability of

FIGURE 4.5
Greenwood Cemetery, New York, 1852. Reproduced from the collections of the Library of Congress.

parks allowing the circulation of fresh air and providing space for exercise, rest, and refreshment in a sunny landscape setting. The concern for public health also resulted in the building of rural suburbs for the rich, who wished to get as far away from the urban conditions as possible. Thus began the exodus from the city based on the opinion that cities were ugly, unhealthy, and dangerous, a viewpoint which has grown in popularity and resulted in the critical disintegration of contemporary American cities. Now more people live in the suburbs than in the cities, with those in the cities mostly minorities.

Second, the concern for morality is associated with the idea that nature itself is a source of moral inspiration. The advocates of this concept felt that if the workers had an opportunity to study and contemplate nature, this would improve their mental stability and provide them with beliefs that would transcend day to day drudgery and substitute for the oblivion which the "gin palaces" provided. Parks were thus associated with this concept of morality in nature inasmuch as they would provide landscape for contemplation. Later, sports facilities and allotments in which vegetables could be cultivated were also considered to serve this moral purpose.

The aesthetic argument was that the visual qualities of the expanding industrial cities were generally considered ugly (although there were some artists who found beauty in blast furnaces and other industrial installations). Essentially, the city was equated with ugliness and public parks as large landscapes inserted into this ugliness would thus serve as an antidote.

The economic argument derives from the first three arguments. These propositions are the basis for a money-making system whereby public parks provide qualities of health, morality, and beauty to the workers, whose productivity is thus improved. At the same time, real estate values are increased by proximity to the romantic landscape in an otherwise drab environment. This in turn produces revenue for the city through higher taxes. Finally, the park was seen as a place of instruction in natural science through arboreta and zoos.

Although the landscape style of gardening was not specifically a response to the depraved urban conditions, it might well have been. The eighteenth-century theories of landscape design based on informality, naturalism, Romanticism, and the picturesque became the logical antithesis to urban conditions of the nineteenth century. Park designs included all of the elements one would expect: curvilinear drives and paths, rustic gates, Gothic architecture, irregular lakes, and informal landscape planting. In fact, the public park was to become the only place of sufficient size where the landscape garden style could be carried out successfully and parks were thus laid out as though they were large private estates with accommodations made for the greater number of people.

Andrew Jackson Downing became a strong advocate of public parks for America in the manner of Birkinhead. He advanced the revolutionary idea that, as in England, parks should be maintained at the expense of the taxpayer. He also recognized the real estate, money-making possibilities for land adjacent to public parks. In addition, he argued the moral case that "such park projects would civilize and refine the national character, foster the love of rural beauty and increase the knowledge of and taste for rare and beautiful trees and plants." He saw the park as a piece of rural scenery in which people could walk, ride, or drive in carriages. It would be a relief from the city streets: "Pedestrians would find quiet and secluded walks when they wished to be solitary and broad alleys filled with happy faces when they would be gay." Downing died in 1852, but his advocacy persuaded the city of New York that it should plan a major public park.

Central Park, New York City

As early as 1785, New Yorkers had seen the need for "a proper spot where the city's numerous inhabitants can enjoy, with convenience, the exercise that is necessary for health and amusement." Political difficulties and arguments preceded the selection and purchase of land in the center of Manhattan island. Eventually a board of commissioners advertised for designs of the layout and offered prizes for the four best plans submitted.

The competition was won in 1858 by Frederick Law Olmsted and his partner, Calvert Vaux (Fig. 4.6). The statement with the plan justified the largeness of the area (843 acres) with the assumption that the city would some day be built up on all sides and that this park would be, to a large extent, the only chance the inhabitants would have of seeing such a landscape. Olmsted intended that the park be the precise center of the population of a city of 2 million, an estimate which was farsighted at the time. (However, by the time of his death in 1903, the population had already reached 4 million.) He predicted the day when the park would be surrounded by an artificial wall twice as high as the great wall of China, composed of urban buildings. The workers who could not spend holidays

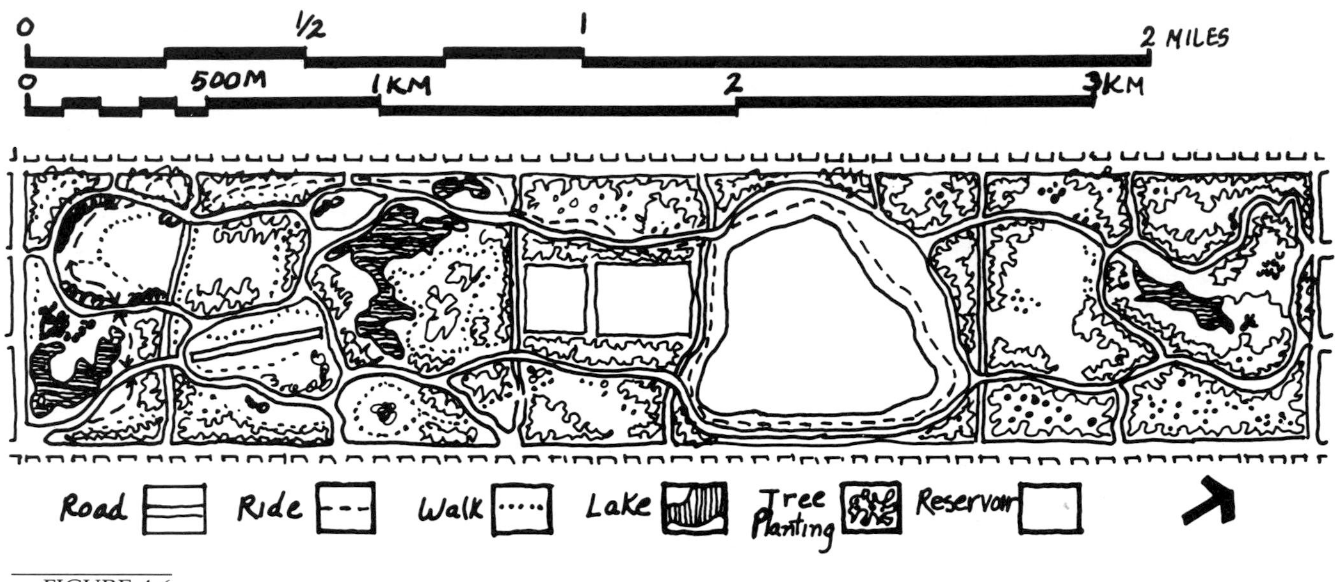

FIGURE 4.6
Central Park, New York, 1858.

in the country, he argued, should be supplied with some semblance of it within the park. It was laid out as a piece of rural scenery and a deliberate attempt was made to screen out the anticipated buildings beyond the park boundaries (Fig. 4.7). One formal element was included in the plan, the central mall: "An essential feature of a metropolitan park—level, spacious and thoroughly shaded." This provided for a very human need: a stage for parading and also a place in which to sit and watch other people, which was what Downing had in mind when he talked of broad alleys filled with happy faces.

The circulation system in which traffic types were separated was particularly innovative. Four roads for crosstown traffic connecting the east and west sides of the park were arranged with underpasses, which would avoid any conflict with park uses and remain unseen below grade. People in the park, walking, riding, or driving in carriages, were thus separated from and unaware of the ordinary city traffic. Carriage

FIGURE 4.7
Central Park, New York.

drives, riding trails, and footpaths were also separated within the park itself.

In the early days the park was too far away from the center to be visited by the majority of New Yorkers except on special occasions, holidays, Saturday afternoons, and Sundays. Nonetheless, in 1871 the number of visitors was estimated at 10 million, or 30,000 average per day (at a time when the city had less than 1 million inhabitants). On days that were not holidays the average was 23,000, of which about 9,000 came on foot and 14,000 in carriages or on horseback. Attendance was greatest on Sundays and band concert days. The number of pedestrians would be as many as 50,000 on the finest days of the season. Use of the park was stimulated by the facilities. Riding and driving in carriages were provided for by winding roads and bridle paths and as the park came into greater use, new habits and customs developed. Skating was one activity that grew amazingly in popularity.

In addition to these benefits to the people, Central Park was also considered a financial success. In 1872 it was estimated that the annual increase in taxes directly related to the development of the park exceeded the annual interest on the cost of the park lands and improvements by over 4 million dollars.

But careful control was necessary to prevent the park turning into a repository for features that would negate its original intent. In 1863 Olmsted catalogued the "encroachments" that had been proposed for Central Park which had been "warded off" in the previous five years. These included "Towers, houses, telescopes, mineral water fountains, cottages, Aeolian harps, gymnasiums, observations and weighing scales, steam engines, snow shows and ice boats, and the use of the ice for fancy dress carnivals, the sale of vegetables, velocipedes, perambulators, Indian work, tobacco, and cigars." His journal records without alarm, however, the introduction of seven pairs of English sparrows.

PARKS MOVEMENT

This first major park in the United States, and the public's approval of it, gave momentum to an urban parks movement. Olmsted became the major practitioner and designed parks for Boston, Brooklyn, Buffalo, Detroit, and many other major cities. Other landscape architects including Horace Cleveland, George Kessler, and Jens Jensen made important contributions in Minneapolis, Chicago, and Kansas City. In Boston Charles Eliot worked with Olmsted to combine an engineering solution to flooding and sanitation problems with a greatly needed open space system.

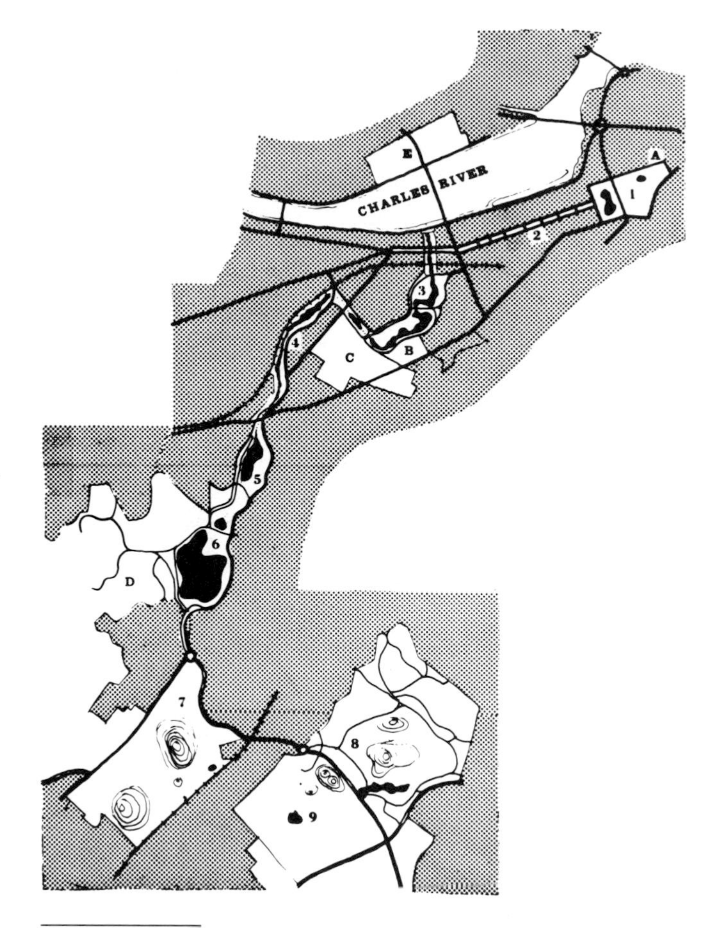

FIGURE 4.8
Boston Park system. Key: **(1)** Boston Common, **(2)** Commonwealth Avenue, **(3)** Back Bay Fens, **(4)** Muddy River, **(5)** Olmsted Park, **(6)** Forest Hills Cemetery, **(A)** State House, **(B)** Fine Arts Museum, **(C)** Colleges, **(D)** Brookline, **(E)** M.I.T.

The Boston parks system connects the Common to Franklin Park through driveways planted with trees, running in a continuous landscape expanding to 1,500 feet in places and contracting to as little as 200 feet in others (Fig. 4.8). The idea of a system of parks linked with parkways was a unique American concept later associated in planning with the automobile.

It is interesting to note that land which was considered useful for more economic purposes was rarely selected for a park. At Birkinhead the land was heavy clay. Central Park included the unbuildable granite ridge of Manhattan Island. The Boston parks system was created out of marshes. And in San Francisco, which was not to be left out in the fashion of building large city parks, the land which was purchased in 1870 consisted of 1,000 acres of wind-swept sterile sand dunes well outside the built-up area (Figure 4.9).

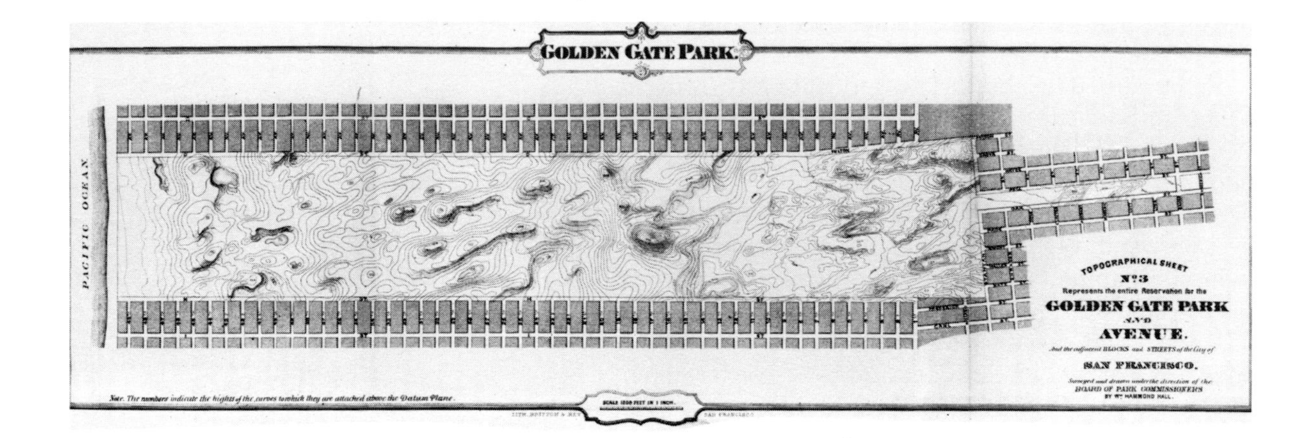

FIGURE 4.9
Golden Gate Park (1872). Original state of site. Courtesy of the Bancroft Library, University of California, Berkeley.

FIGURE 4.10
Golden Gate Park. Plan for eastern portion of the park, published in 1872. Key: **(A)** dressed ground or lawn, **(B)** flower garden, **(C)** conservatory, **(D)** the Manor House, **(E)** croquet or children's playground, **(F)** plateau—carriage concourse, **(G)** botanical garden, **(L)** lakes, **(M)** meadow, **(P)** parade, cricket or baseball ground, **(S)** Strawberry Hill, **(H)** space for large pavilion, **(a)** small observatory, **(b)** bridges, **(f)** fountains, **(k)** rustic pavilion, **(p)** the lodge, **(r)** traffic road.

William Hammond Hall was appointed Park Engineer for Golden Gate Park. He started by preparing a plan for the quarter nearest the city, and while this was being constructed a program of planting was begun on the remaining land in a successful attempt to stabilize the shifting sands. Hall corresponded with Olmsted, whose influence was no doubt responsible for some of the park's features, especially the circulation system separating wheeled traffic from pedestrians with bridges at critical intersections (Fig. 4.10). In 1887 John McLaren became superintendent of the park and through his horticultural expertise brought the park to maturity and completed the transformation of barren sand dunes into today's Golden Gate Park: 1,000 acres of well-watered forests, glades, and lakes connected with drives, paths, and riding trails (Fig. 4.11).

Although there is no consistent pattern, it seems that derelict land or land in some other way unattractive or unsuitable for other uses will always be the land most likely to be available for parks and recreation.

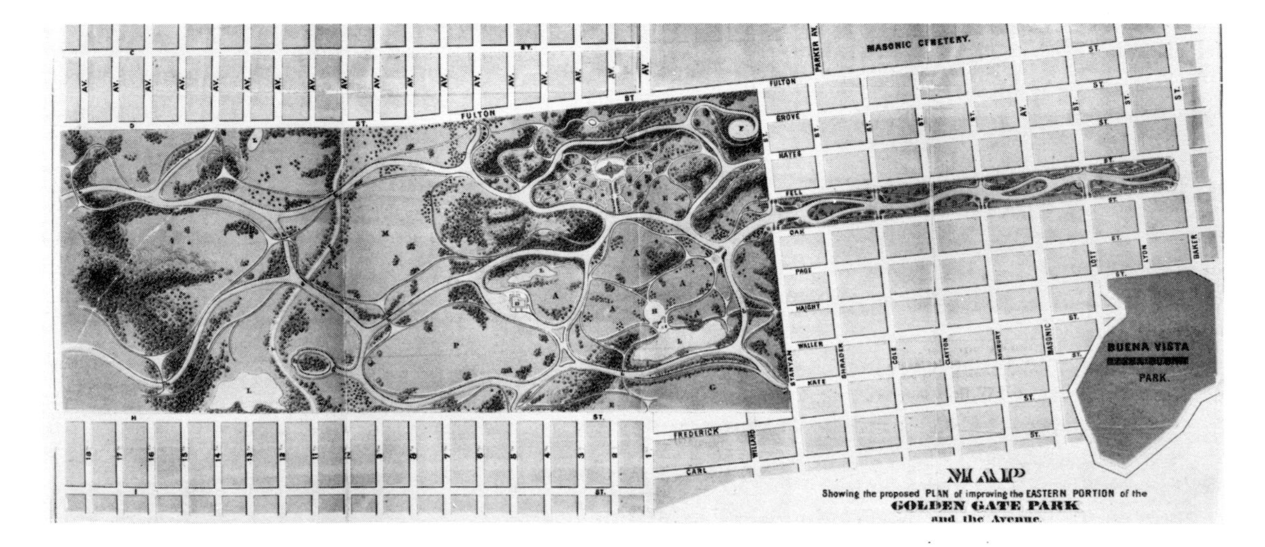

The disused canals and railroad tracks of England have in some cases been cleaned up and turned into public amenities. Worked-out coal mines, waste disposal areas, and old gravel pits have also found new use as recreational areas. This pattern in history suggests other possibilities for today. Power line rights of way (Fig. 4.12), river flood plains, and other land unsuited for anything else may be linked up in open space systems.

It is another fact of changing times that the real estate benefits of location next to a public park do not necessarily apply in all cases. It may still be true of Central Park and Regents Park, but there are other instances in which the once expensive housing situated near a park is now a slum and the park is relatively unused. The building of new parks, which in the eyes of local residents might attract illicit behavior, is sometimes seen as a threat, especially where nearby homes already have private gardens. The frequently discussed lack of safety by day as well as by night in the larger city parks, although not always supported by statistics, is also a new social factor to be contended with.

FIGURE 4.11
Golden Gate Park.

FIGURE 4.12
Park on a power line right of way. Oakland, California (1969).

PARKS AND RECREATION AREAS

Since the nineteenth century "parks and recreation" have become a major industry with a large civil service in cities, counties, states, and regional districts. Smaller neighborhood parks and playgrounds were introduced at the end of the nineteenth century as centers of sport and physical fitness and other social programs. In an attempt to measure the effectiveness of a city's provision of parks, organizations such as the National Recreation Association formulated standards in terms of acres per unit of population. By these standards there was never enough. Although they are generalities, which must be weighed with the variables of the specific place, it is still true that cities and other agencies tend to think of recreation facilities in terms of such standards.

The standards and acreages cited below are based on a combination of several sources. It should be noted, however, that the recommendations in the California guide for recreation and parks vary according to the climatic zones of the state. Thus larger acreages are recommended in the warmer zones to permit more extensive tree planting.[2]

In the conventional system, recreation units are classified in terms of their scale and distribution. The play lot, or block playground for use by preschool-age children, is the smallest unit and should, according to the standards, be within walking distance of a majority of homes, located perhaps in the interior of a city block. They should be between ⅛ and ¼ acre in size and are especially important where the density is high. The recent "mini-park" building program in run-down sections of cities indicates the value of play lots in such areas; low-density suburban housing may have less need.

The next category is at the neighborhood level: the neighborhood park, playground, or recreation center, or a combination of all three. In this case the neighborhood is usually described as the area served by an elementary school. (Busing of children between neighborhoods to achieve racial balance in the schools may conflict with this concept.) The facility should provide indoor and outdoor recreation for children between 5 and 14 years of age. Pre-school children and family groups should also be provided for and a landscape area of at least 2 acres is desirable. Ideally the neighborhood playground would be situated within ½ mile of each home. Recent standards argue that it is logical to combine the park with the elementary school and its yard. The standards suggest that if the school is 10 acres, then the related park should be 6 acres. If separate, 16 acres would be needed. Another standard suggests that there should be 1 acre of neighborhood park for every 800 of population. But the facilities and parks should reflect the population. Old people who do not drive may have realistic needs for open space equivalent to the tot lot close to home.

The standards also call for community recreation areas, or playfields. A community is defined as a number of neighborhoods, or a section or district of a city. It is suggested that these facilities should provide a wider range of recreation possibilities than those at the neighborhood level, including fields, courts, and swimming pool, and a center in which arts and crafts, clubs, and social activities may take place. The recommended size is 32 acres or 20 acres if connected to a school, and they should be located between ½ and 1 mile of every home. Another measure is that 1 acre of community park should be provided for every 800 population.

Finally, city-wide recreation areas are described as large parks providing the city dweller a chance to get away from the noise of the city, its dirt and traffic (Fig. 4.13). If the automobile was permanently prohibited from the large nineteenth-century parks this would be possible. They should provide the variety of activities and possibilities to be found in Central Park and Golden Gate Park. The desired effect can hardly be provided in less than 100 acres. There should be sports centers and facilities for golf, boating, and so on. The 1956 standards for California suggest that a city of 100,000 should have 883 acres of city park, of which 21 would be needed for parking. Beyond these park standards lie special items. Every city should have golf courses, outdoor theater, zoos, botanic gardens, or similar facilities.

These standards are, of course, abstractions, created by the parks and recreation industry. They may not take into account the extent to which recreation patterns have changed in recent years, but in general they make sense.

To what extent have recreation patterns changed since the nineteenth century? Shorter working hours and automation tend to result in boredom rather than exhaustion for the blue-collar worker. At the adult level, Wayne Williams has observed that the traditional leisure triangle has been reversed.[3] Those with the most leisure time today tend to be the unskilled, the semiskilled, and the skilled, in that order. Thus it is perhaps obvious that the need is for diversion rather than for recuperation and that the majority of people need and will seek challenging and active recreation

[2] *Guide for Planning Recreation Parks in California* (Sacramento: State Printing Office, 1956).

[3] Wayne R. Williams, *Recreation Places* (New York: Reinhold, 1958).

FIGURE 4.13
Hyde Park, London. A city wide recreation area within the city but large enough to be isolated from it.

and meaningful involvement. For children, Williams believes that the whole city should be considered a playground, a park, and a classroom and that ways should be found to incorporate the public and especially children into the various workshops of the city—bakeries, auto repair shops, and so on. In this concept, recreation is regarded as an integral part of living, as it should be, rather than as something to be enjoyed in a playground.

New concepts of recreation, changes in population, and patterns of work and leisure come at a time when many of the parks designed over a hundred years ago have reached maturity and are in need of renewal. Major opportunities exist, therefore, for the landscape profession in collaboration with parks and recreation departments and commissions and with community participation, to reevaluate their role in society, leading toward the development of new forms rather than historical restoration.

SUGGESTED READINGS

Butler, George D., *Introduction to Community Recreation*, Ch. 5, "History of Municipal Recreation in the United States," Ch. 11, "City Planning for Recreation."

Chadwick, George F., *The Park and the Town*, Ch. 1, pp. 19–36, "The English Landscape Movement and the Public Park," Ch.4, pp. 66–93, "Sir Joseph Paxton," Ch.9, pp. 163–220, "The American Park Movement."

Chadwick, George, *The Works of Sir Joseph Paxton*, Ch. 3, pp. 44–71, "Paxton and the Wider Landscape."

Cleveland, Horace W. S., *Landscape Architecture* (1872).

Cranz, Galen, *The Politics of Park Design*.

Creese, Walter, *The Search for Environment: The Garden City Before and After*.

Fabos, Julius, et al., *Frederick Law Olmsted*.

Fein, Albert, *Landscape into Cityscape*.

Fein, Albert, *Frederick Law Olmsted and the American Environmental Tradition*.

Giedeon, Sigfried, *Space, Time and Architecture*, pp. 618–626, "The Dominance of Greenery in London Squares," pp. 641–666, "The Transformation of Paris, 1853–68."

Heckscher, August, *Open Spaces*.

Jackson, J. B., *American Space*, pp. 211–219, "Central Park."

Kelley, Bruce, et al., *The Art of the Olmsted Landscape*.

Laurie, Michael, *Nature and City Planning in the 19th Century*, Laurie, Ian, (ed), "Nature in the Cities."

Meyerson, Martin, *Face of the Metropolis*, pp. 11–37, "The Changing Cityscale."

Mumford, Lewis, *The Brown Decades*, pp. 80–96.

Scott, Mel, *American City Planning*, Ch. 1., "The Spirit of Reform."

Reps, John W., *The Making of Urban America*, Ch. 12, "Cemeteries, Parks and Suburbs."

Tunnard, Christopher, *American Skyline*.

Udall, Stewart, *The Quiet Crisis*, pp. 159–172, "Cities in Trouble."

Zaitzevsky, Cynthia, *F. L. Olmsted and the Boston Park System*.

HOUSING

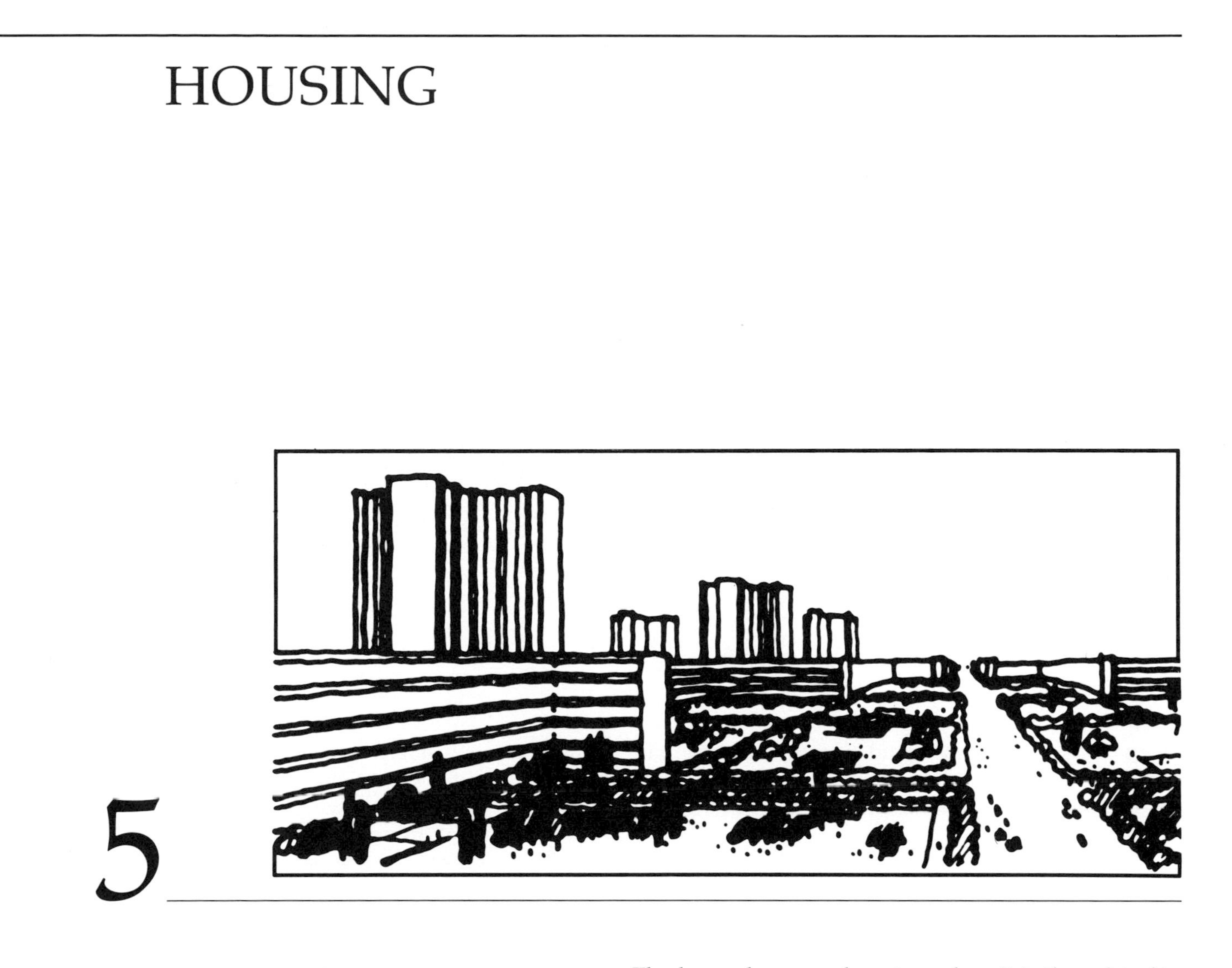

5

The house becomes housing when it is thought of in multiples either as a set of separate entities on individual plots of land or as row housing, condominiums, or apartment complexes. This chapter deals with the relationship of open space for public or private use to the individual domestic unit in a variety of housing systems. We will see the historical transformation from layouts in which the garden is held within the form of the house itself, as at Pompeii (Fig. 2.10), to others in which the dwellings are set in a larger landscape, as in cluster developments of new towns and planned unit developments (Fig. 5.1). We must ask ourselves the meaning of this reversal in concept and the implications in social and ecological terms.

The Medieval city may be thought of as large multiple dwellings somewhat similar to Soleri's Arcologies.[1] They were built piecemeal and slowly.

---

[1] Paolo Soleri, *Arcology: The City in the Image of Man* (Cambridge, MIT Press, 1969).

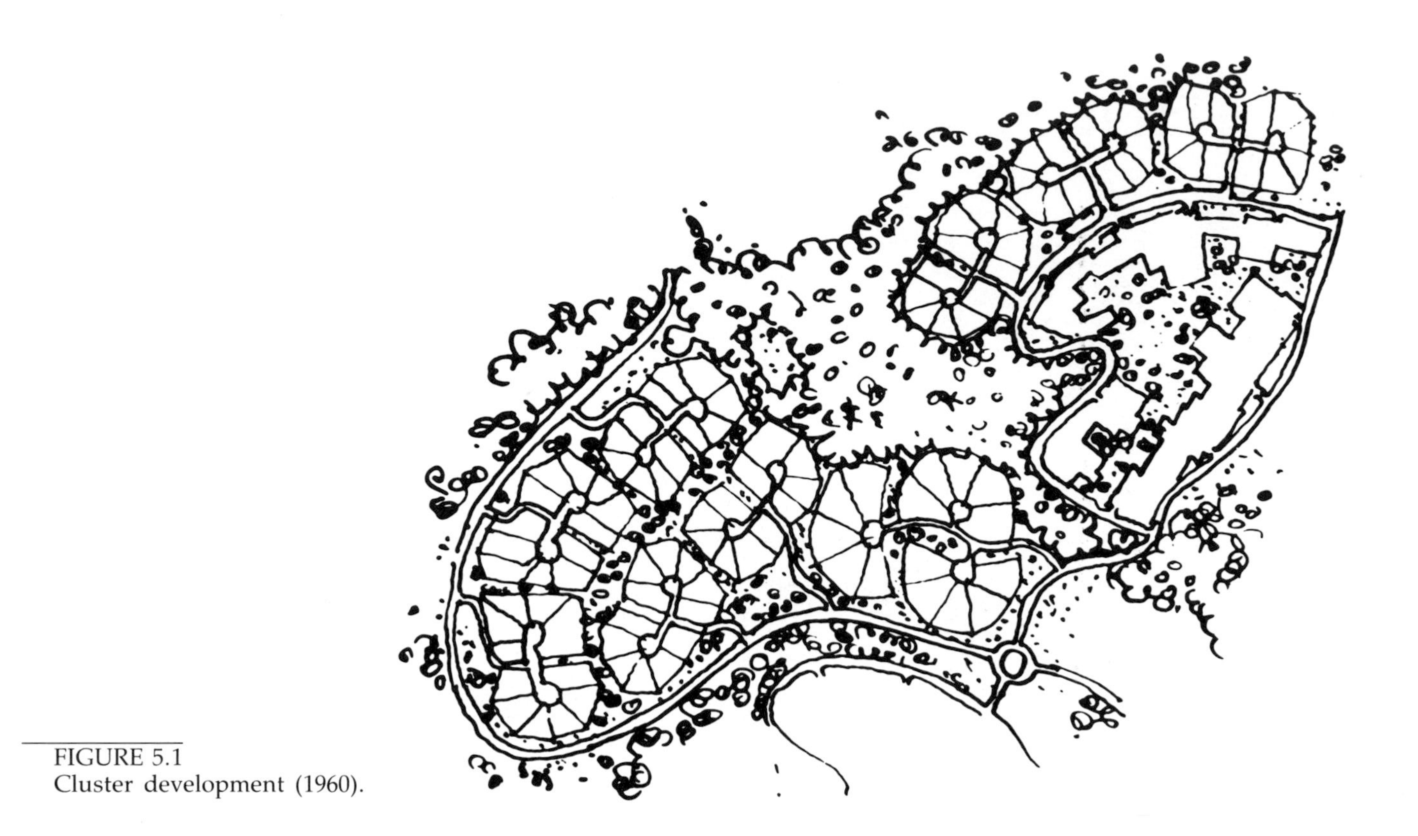

FIGURE 5.1
Cluster development (1960).

Open landscape and farmland surrounded the urban organism, whose texture included small courtyards, public streets, and squares intimately related to the dwelling units (Fig. 2.20).

It is not until the seventeenth century in France that we find the conscious planning and design of multiple housing on a large scale influencing the form of the city. In Paris residential squares were favored by a rising middle class who had aspirations they could not afford. The aspiration in seventeenth-century France was to live in a palace like Versailles (Figs. 2.32 and 2.33). This being impossible, housing was built around urban squares in which the sides of the squares were designed to look like modest-sized palaces. In fact, each side contained six or eight individual row houses of four or five stories.

THE LONDON SQUARE

This concept was developed especially well in England in the eighteenth and nineteenth centuries. In London, squares were built in which the sides were designed as one architectural facade (Fig. 5.2). At the back of each row house was a private garden at the bottom of which were stables with access from a mews, or alley. Formal access to the houses was from the roadway surrounding the square. In the middle of this was a fenced garden enclosure for the exclusive use of the residents whose houses faced it; each resident had a key to the gates. In the seventeenth century these gardens were quite urban, paved, and with a formal arrangement of trees.

The gardens in the squares of the eighteenth century were laid out in the newly fashionable landscape style providing a refreshing view from the windows of the houses. The square itself was usually designed with shrubbery, large trees, and ground shaping in an attempt to screen out the urban surroundings. This paradise was separated by a fence from physical intrusions by the masses, and it was an arrangement of privilege. It was a symbol of the countryside carefully framed, representing a cautious acceptance of nature in the city. The urban form that was developed at Bloomsbury in London included several degrees of privacy, from the total privacy of the house, to the open but private back garden, to the public street, and then to the semiprivacy of the central garden in which other residents but not the general public would be encountered. Variations included one in which the central area of a city block was developed as a garden for the residents of surrounding terraces, who reached it through a very small private garden at the back of the house, the other side of which faced onto the street. Such systems of housing achieved quite high density since the units were often only about 20 feet wide. At

FIGURE 5.2
A London square (eighteenth century).

the same time private gardens were provided for each house and community gardens for the entire block.

The extension of the idea that such pieces of nature were desirable elements of city life can be seen in the development of crescents or terraces of houses which looked onto larger or more extensive landscapes than the small square could provide. The crescents of Regents Park (Fig. 4.2) and Bath confront nature in much the same way as Versailles did. Nature is accepted. There is no longer fear or apprehension associated with the natural world and the city is no longer confined by walls and a limited concept of urbanism. The Royal Crescent at Bath built in 1767 was a product of the eighteenth-century landscape movement (Fig. 5.3). Landsdowne crescent with its undulating naturalistic form is even more responsive to the

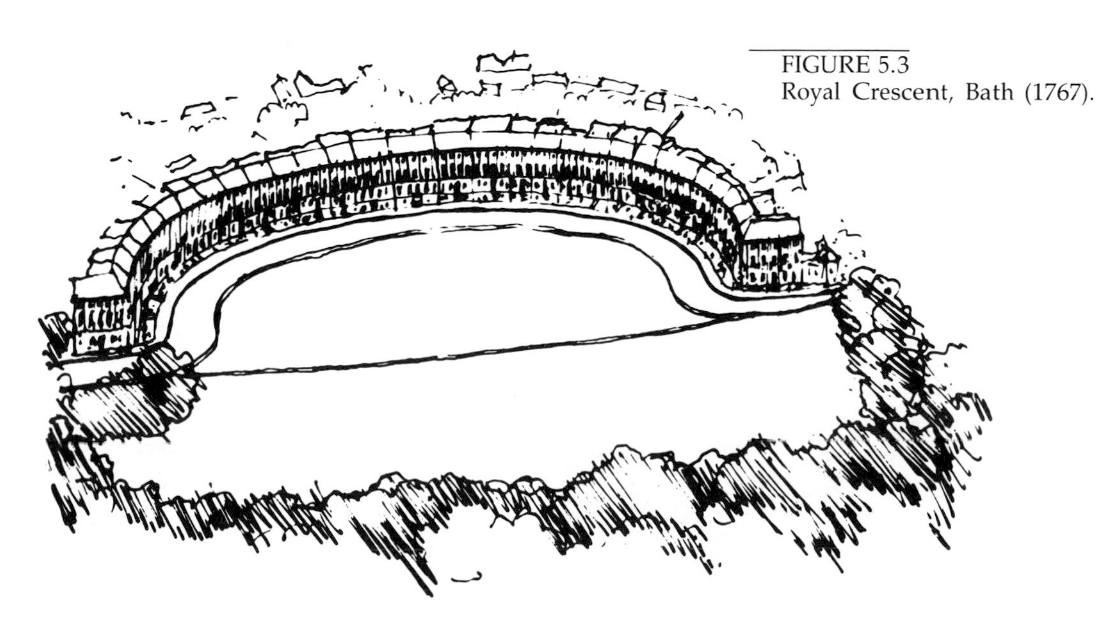

FIGURE 5.3
Royal Crescent, Bath (1767).

new spirit or attitude. Both reflect the increasing enjoyment of natural landscape and command views of parkland and the countryside beyond. The terraces surrounding Regents Park were considered sophisticated because of their landscape outlook and consequently commanded higher values. The residential square had burst its bounds and grown into a public park.

In the United States the concept of the London square was incorporated to some extent into the urban developments on the East Coast. Penn's plan for Philadelphia incorporated five squares, four of them for the exclusive use of the residents around them. The plan of Savannah was also based on the residential square. In Baltimore, New York, and Boston there were squares and terraces, but in general the "London" square does not appear to be a typical element in American cities of the nineteenth century. This may be due to the pervading Jeffersonian ideal that country life was preferable to that of the city.

THE ROMANTIC SUBURB

The major American contribution to urban form was the romantic suburb in the nineteenth century. This served as an escape from the conditions of the industrial cities and was conceived visually and aesthetically as a contrast to the typical grid pattern of streets in expanding urban areas. In the second half of the nineteenth century landscape architects and others became critical of this grid pattern, which was described as tedious and monotonous on flat land and hideous when set on undulating ground. It was said that natural beauty was thus sacrificed for speculative convenience. Olmsted, Downing, and others developed a new concept of residential site planning which became known as the romantic suburb. In 1852 Alexander Davis laid out a suburb at Llewellyn Park, New Jersey. Its entrance gate was Gothic, the roads were winding, and the sites for housing were set in a framework of trees and shrubs. In addition there was a central landscape park.

Another example is Riverside in Chicago, laid out by Frederick Law Olmsted in 1869 (Figs. 5.4 and 5.5). Curvilinear roads and irregular-shaped parcels of land were held together by a linear park which followed a river. This was the social meeting place for the community. There were no continuous rows of buildings forming architectural units as in the London squares and in Regents Park. There was very little architectural definition. The buildings or villas were separated from a close association with the street and were embosomed

FIGURE 5.4
Plan of Riverside, Chicago, Illinois as proposed by Olmsted and Vaux (1869).

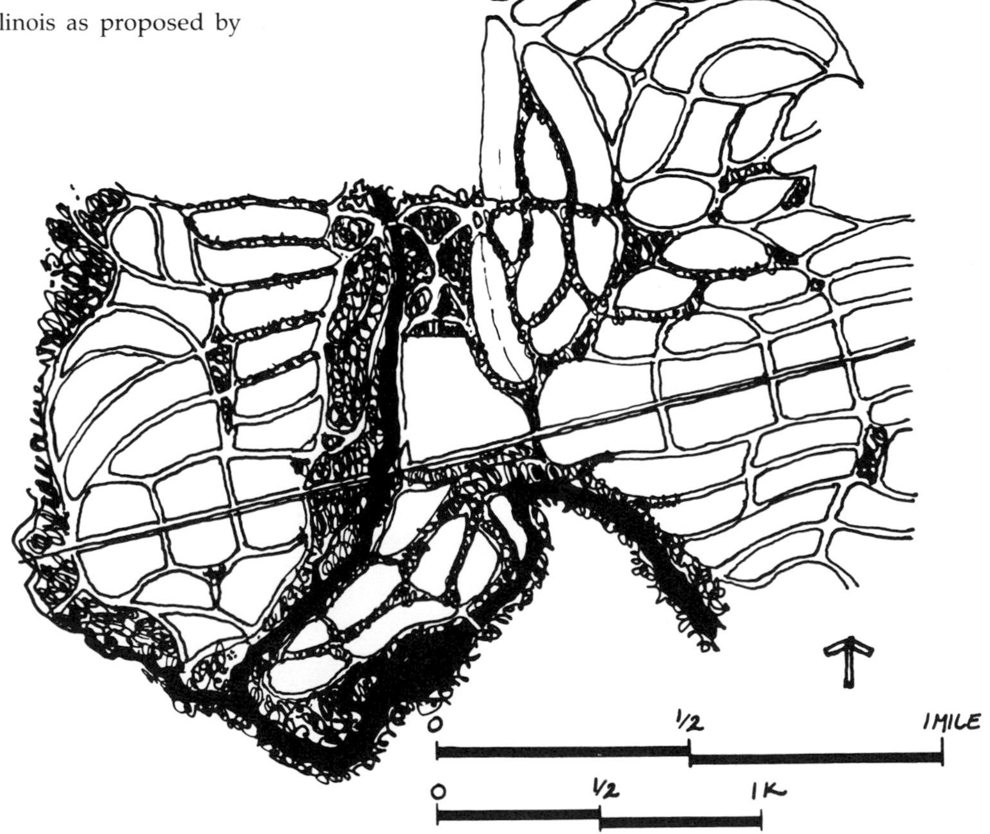

FIGURE 5.5
Riverside, Chicago, Illinois (1869).

within a green landscape and deliberately absorbed by it. Once the planting reached maturity the houses would be secondary in the view from the streets.

This kind of planning called for variations in the size and shape of the traditional residential block. It represents a new concept of a continuous city/park/garden resulting in what Chadwick calls the urban–rural continuum.[2] Infrared aerial photography reveals the extent and degree to which a green matrix does exist in the current suburban and also central city environments. If the romantic suburb represented the best kind of residential setting in 1852, there seems to have been very little change between then and now. The highest priced residential areas in the United States, with the exception of a few stylish downtown sectors, seem to have a similar appearance with perhaps the addition of a high security fence. Although these suburbs were intended for wealthy merchants, the ideas of the romantic suburb could be, and later were, easily applied to garden cities, industrial communities, and new towns.

THE COMPANY TOWN

The concept of company towns in which housing was built by industrialists next to their factories was developed in Europe and in New England in the nineteenth century. Originally the arrangement was one of convenience, with most of the advantages on the side of the capitalist, but in time productivity was seen to be related to the health and welfare of the workers. Thus toward the end of the century industrial communities responded to this point of view. It was believed that the effects of mass production procedures on the workers could be counteracted with attractive homes and gardens and community facilities and open space. The earliest significant examples were built in England.

At Port Sunlight, Lever built a town to house the workers for his soap factory. The location he chose had all the attributes of a good industrial site: cheap land, water frontage, transportation, and an available labor supply. Of the 52 acres Lever acquired, the factory occupied 24 and the remainder was devoted to the model village. It was Lever's dream that the workers would no longer have to walk out to the country to experience the beautiful world but that natural beauty would constantly surround them. Port Sunlight near Birkinhead was a vivid contrast to the back-to-back slum housing in Liverpool. It incorporated the concept of the romantic suburb with curvilinear roads, private gardens, public parks, recreation areas, and community facilities. The houses were attached and designed by notable architects as clusters of ten or more units to look like large manor houses. The visual quality appears as a collection of mansions set in a park instead

[2] George F. Chadwick, *The Park and the Town* (London: Architectural Press, 1966).

FIGURE 5.6
A row of workers' houses, Port Sunlight (1887).

of the collection of modest workers' dwellings which it actually was (Fig. 5.6). The factory was present in the background and easily reached on foot.

In 1879 the Cadbury brothers moved their chocolate factory from Birmingham to open fields four miles away and established a garden village at Bourneville (Fig. 5.7). The goal was to prevent speculative building as well as to provide housing for key workers. Bourneville is thus unlike Port Sunlight, not strictly a company town. The most influential concept at Bourneville was the Cadburys' belief that the workers would benefit physically and psychologically from the most

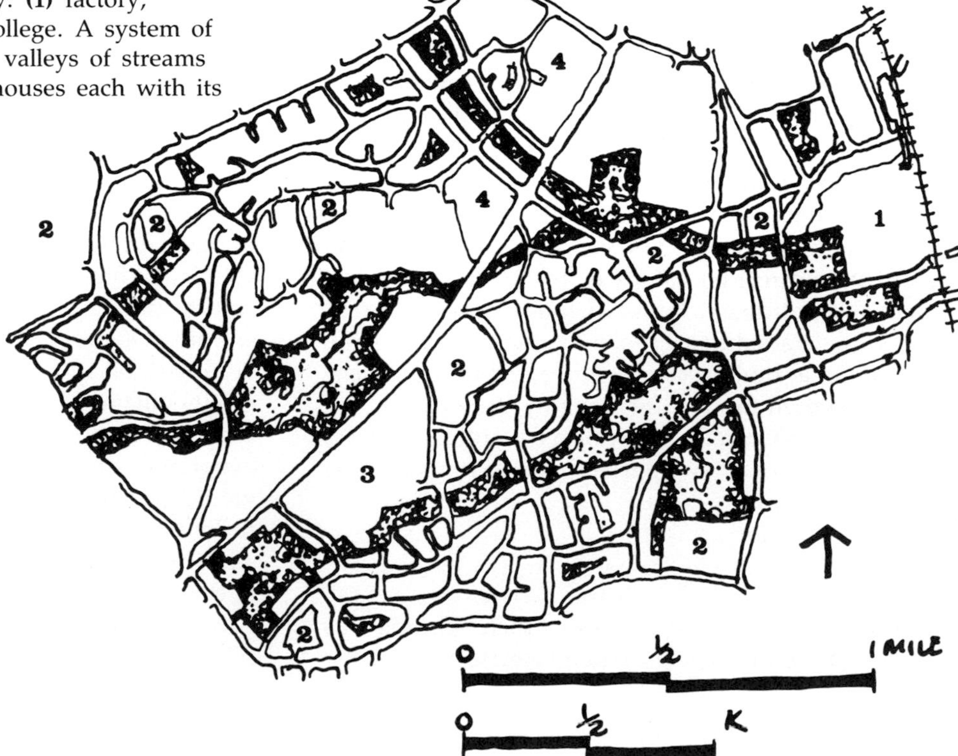

FIGURE 5.7
Plan of Bourneville (1879). Key: **(1)** factory, **(2)** school, **(3)** hospital, **(4)** college. A system of public open space follows the valleys of streams and runs between groups of houses each with its own garden.

natural and healthful of all recreations, gardening. Gardens would also help to lower the density, which in itself would be an improvement on the industrial city. One hundred and twenty acres of land around the factory were developed. Sixteen acres were set aside for public open spaces, which included a village green, two parks, and two playgrounds, one of which provided supervision and care for children under 12. Streets were laid out and planted with trees. The houses built in groups were architecturally attractive and provided with ¼-acre gardens at the back. These were laid out, dug, and planted for the tenant in advance. Planted in each garden were eight fruit trees (pears, apples, and one plum) and twelve gooseberry bushes. Significant quantities of food were grown. Once the town was established, figures indicate that the death rate in Bourneville was half that of the rest of the country, and that the stature of the children was greater on average than that of Birmingham children.

The industrial or company towns built in America after these experiments reflected some of the new ideas but were, with a few exceptions, less philanthropic and usually laid out with the economic grid pattern of streets. Pullman, Illinois (1885), was one such planned community in which housing was built in groups and public buildings, schools, and a park with a lake were provided. Gary, Indiana (1907), a steel town, depended on private initiative for infilling the grid layout of streets within which land for two public parks and various public buildings was set aside by the company.

THE GARDEN CITY

There is a direct line from these towns planned by philanthropic industrialists to improve living conditions for their own workers to the garden city movement. This was a very influential concept in the early twentieth century. Its origins also lie in the romantic suburb. The garden city idea was formulated by a law court clerk named Ebenezer Howard in 1898.[3] The economic essence of the theory was that the community should own the land, but this was not necessarily what happened in practice. Howard sought the abolition of the evils of the industrial revolution. Like Lever and the Cadburys, he was a reformer and wished to see the elimination of slums, overcrowding, and urban squalor. He conceived the city as a series of concentric circles, the inner core of which would be a civic center in a common or park. The outermost ring would be set aside as a green belt for agriculture and institutional use. Between these would be housing and a section for industry. The diagram was an abstraction to be applied according to the specific conditions of topography and transportation of the selected site.

This concept was attempted twice in England, at Letchworth (1908) and Wellwyn Garden City (1924) (Fig. 5.8). Letchworth was supposed to have a population of 30,000 but failed to attract it after 25 years. It was not an economic success. Wellwyn was more successful because by 1924 the garden city idea had parliamentary approval as a method of improving urban housing, and in 1921 legislation was passed enabling the government to give financial assistance for the building of the new city. As a result of the failure of Letchworth, changes were made. The com-

FIGURE 5.8
Wellwyn Garden City (1924).

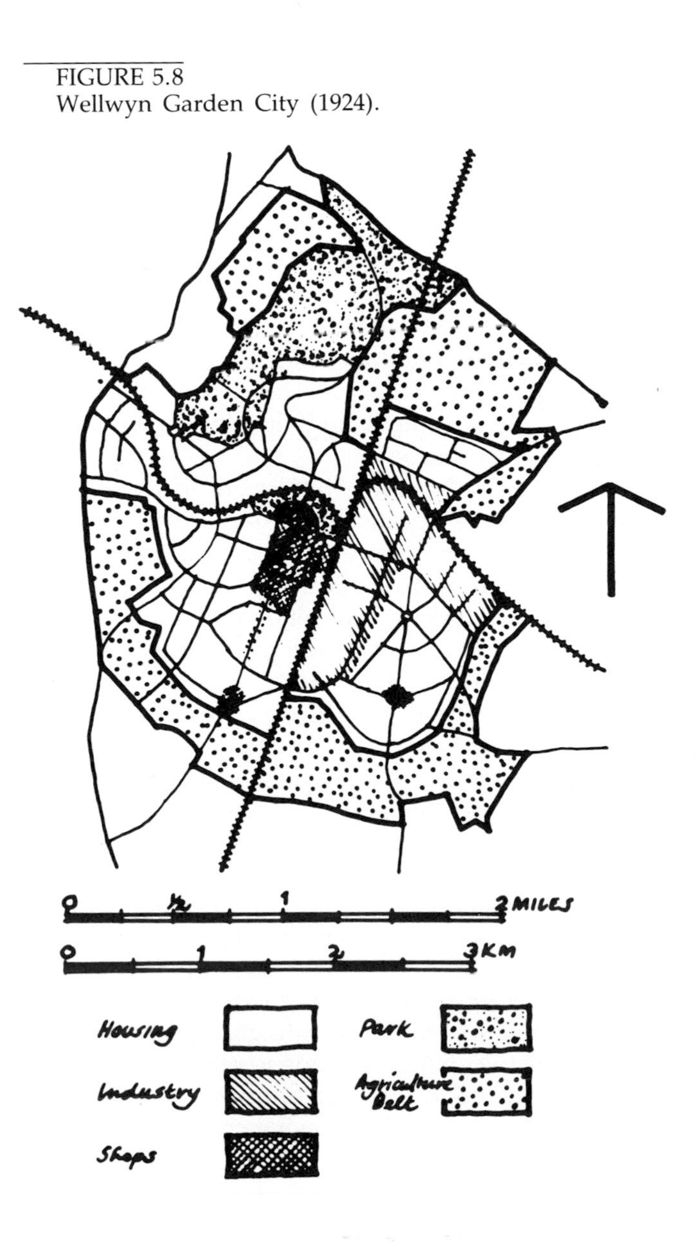

[3] Ebenezer Howard, *Garden Cities of Tomorrow* (London: S. Sonnenschein, 1902). (First published as *Tomorrow; A Peaceful Path to Real Reform*, 1898.)

pany set out to design a town of definite size to accommodate between 40,000 and 50,000 inhabitants on 24,000 acres. The location was chosen 20 miles from London so it was near but definitely separate from the big city. After 12 years there were 9,000 inhabitants, 2,500 houses, and 40 industries, and Wellwyn was well on its way to fulfillment. The romantic suburb concept transformed to a popular scale in the industrial villages or company towns was now expanded into full-scale garden cities. Landscape and greenery as a background for life became the popular taste, available to a broader segment of society than before. Improvements in transportation, rail, streetcars, and automobiles, contributed significantly to its success.

In the 1920s the garden city concept was seen as a possible solution to better housing in the United States. The architects Clarence Stein and Henry Wright were two of its champions. Under their guidance the City Housing Corporation of New York built some tentative new forms in 1924. Common green spaces were provided in the interiors of otherwise fairly conventional blocks. More radical innovations came at Radburn, New Jersey (Figs. 5.9 and 5.10). The community was planned in 1929 but unfortunately coincided with the economic depression and was never fully completed. Radburn, as built, was not a garden city by definition, although Stein and Wright did believe strongly in Howard's ideals of green belts and towns of limited size planned for work as well as living. At Radburn they recognized the limitations of the conventional block system and developed what they called the superblock.

In spite of only partial fulfillment of the original plan, Radburn is significant for demonstrating some new forms for community development suited to the early twentieth-century life-style. The houses were designed for middle-income white-collar families. The floor plan reversed the usual relationship of living rooms to the street, new kinds of circulation were provided, and safety for children was given special importance. The typical superblock was about 40 acres. The hierarchy of roads begins with the expressway linking the town to the outside world. Main through roads connect the neighborhoods to each other and to the expressway and then secondary connector roads encircle the superblocks. Finally, culs-de-sac serve as access roads to clusters of twelve to fifteen houses (some semidetached). The average density is four families per gross acre. Pedestrian circulation connects the private gardens at the back and runs between them leading to a central park area. Paths lead through this area and underpass the secondary connector roads, allowing children traffic-free routes to other superblocks and to an elementary school which serves several blocks lying within a half-mile radius which comprises a neighborhood.

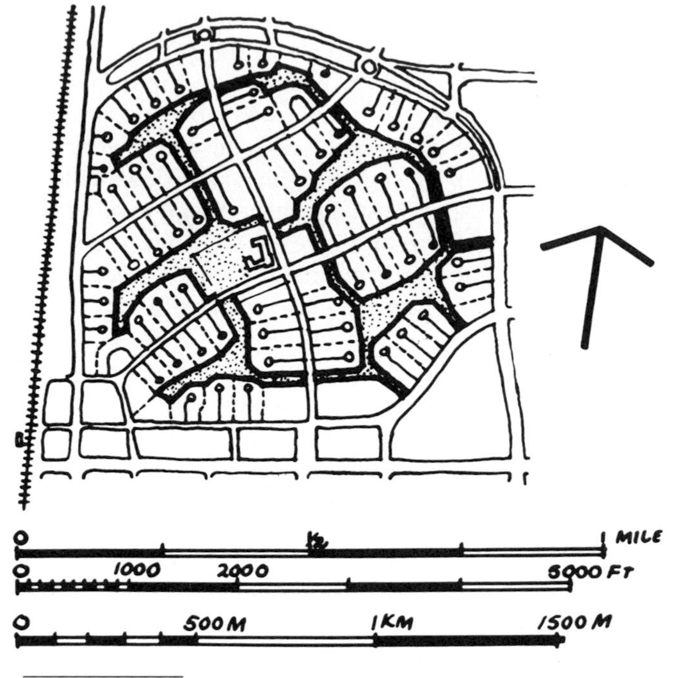

FIGURE 5.9
Radburn, New Jersey (1929). A neighborhood of six superblocks.

The plan reflects the preoccupation with the automobile both from the point of view of circulation and ease of driving access, but it also recognizes that the automobile has its place and that it is desirable to be free of it. The street or cul-de-sac is considered a service function and the living rooms face onto the garden at the other side. There has always been a tendency for children to find the service side more interesting (auto repairs, hard surface for cycles, and so on), but at least the cul-de-sac is not filled with fast-moving traffic. The park contains community facilities, swimming pool, and play areas. The form of housing was found to be satisfactory. A housing association to which all homeowners belonged and contributed took care of maintenance in the park and provision and running of the recreation facilities.

Other communities were built on similar patterns at Pittsburgh (Chatham Village), Greenbelt, Maryland, and elsewhere, often in wartime housing and government projects. But in spite of the apparent advantages and environmental quality the system provided for people, the layout was not widely adopted. Real estate developers preferred the single family conventional

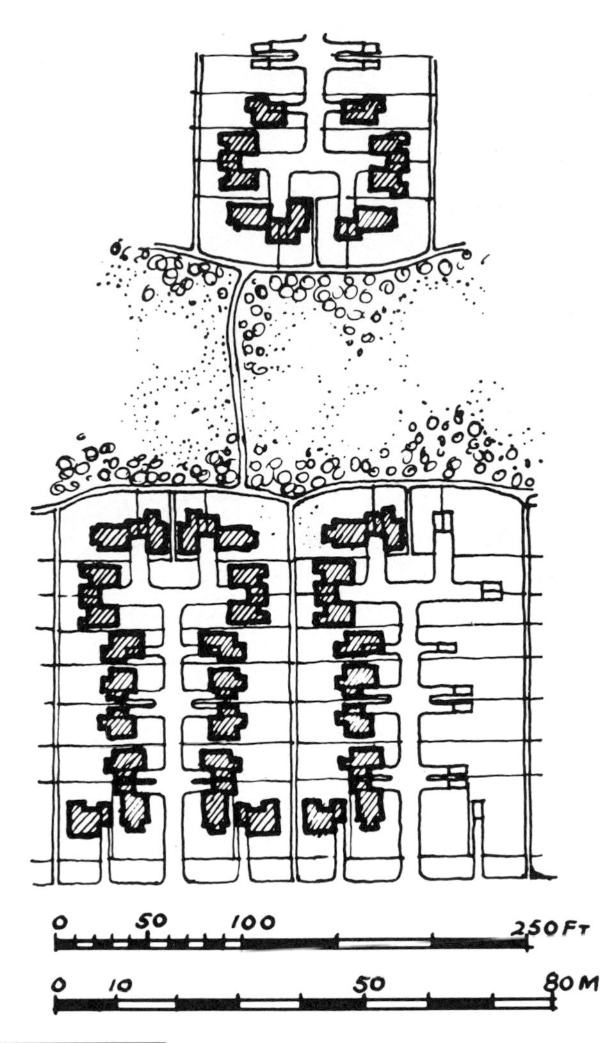

FIGURE 5.10
Radburn, New Jersey (1929). Relationship of culs-de-sac to central green.

subdivision, which was easier to handle, and the public had little choice in the matter.

The Radburn idea was adapted to a rental apartment development at Baldwin Hills in Los Angeles in 1941. One large superblock of 80 acres includes 627 dwelling units. The density is thus 7.8 families per gross acre. The automobiles are restricted to garage courts separated from the buildings and connected to them by walkways. The parking ratio is three spaces per house, much higher than at Radburn. The units have small patios with access to a central "village green," ½ mile long and varying between 50 and 250 feet wide. In this way, many people are brought together with amenities at fairly high density. It is an ideal plan for children but also well suited for older or retired people who want seclusion and quiet.

NEW TOWNS

In Europe after the war there was an urgent need for new housing and reconstruction. In Britain, the government supported an extensive public housing program through which, as in the rest of Europe, the current thinking in housing was expressed in physical form and in large quantities. There were two basic sources of inspiration: the *Ville Radieuse concept* of Le Corbusier,[4] in which high-rise buildings stood in a landscape park (Fig. 5.11), and the Radburn plan, in which compact planning allowed the provision of public open space within the framework of the housing. One way or another, the new towns had a great deal of open space. By comparison with the urban areas from which the people came, the density, at ten families per gross acre, was low. "Prairie planning," as it was called by cynics, meant long distances to walk to schools and shops. The environments were alien to people who had grown up in the warm closeness of the East End of London, and thus to some extent the physical form of the new towns destroyed or prevented social interaction of the type they had been accustomed to.

A second group of new towns built in the 1950s tried to adjust to some of the criticisms. At Cumbernauld, for example, a more dense town was planned, with average densities twice that of the earlier attempts (Fig. 5.12). Even at the higher densities, however, considerable open space was included, but it was distributed differently. The larger areas, sports fields and parks, were situated around the built-up area, not within it as at Stevenage. Cumbernauld closely fits Howard's conceptual plan for a garden city. In the middle is the town center, within ten minutes' walk of the farthest house (theoretically, and weather permitting). The circulation system, derived from the Radburn superblock principle, is arranged so that no traffic lights or traffic policemen are needed. Pedestrians are separated from automobiles, which are frequently stored in auto courts, as at Baldwin Hills. Even though the density is high, the housing areas are predominantly low rise and have private gardens or accessible small scale open space within the layouts and connected to the green belt. Although the new towns in Britain consisted of low-rent public housing so that the houses are relatively small for economic reasons, the layouts are innovative and have application in other circumstances.

New town building in America has been carried out

[4] Charles Edouard Jeanneret-Gris, *The Radiant City* (New York: Orion Press, 1967). (First published in 1933 as *La Ville Radieuse*.)

FIGURE 5.11
High-rise concept. La Ville Radieuse (1933).

only on a limited scale and on a privately financed basis. Reston, West Virginia, Columbia, Maryland, and Irvine in Southern California are three examples. These private enterprise towns are planned as garden cities with housing, industry, and green belts.

Reston was planned for 75,000 people with a variety of housing types at various densities, oriented toward village centers. In addition, the town seemed to be planned around sporting interests. Riding, water sports, swimming, fishing, canoeing, and golf are available. An advertising brochure states that "In all cases the resident of Reston can locate for leisure with his favorite recreation activities waiting for him just beyond his doorstep." Thus in this case open space in housing takes on specific recreational uses as well as providing aesthetic beauty. This justifies the incorporation of so much landscape in the plan. Walking and cycling paths, separated from the roads, run through the open spaces and connect the schools and village centers.

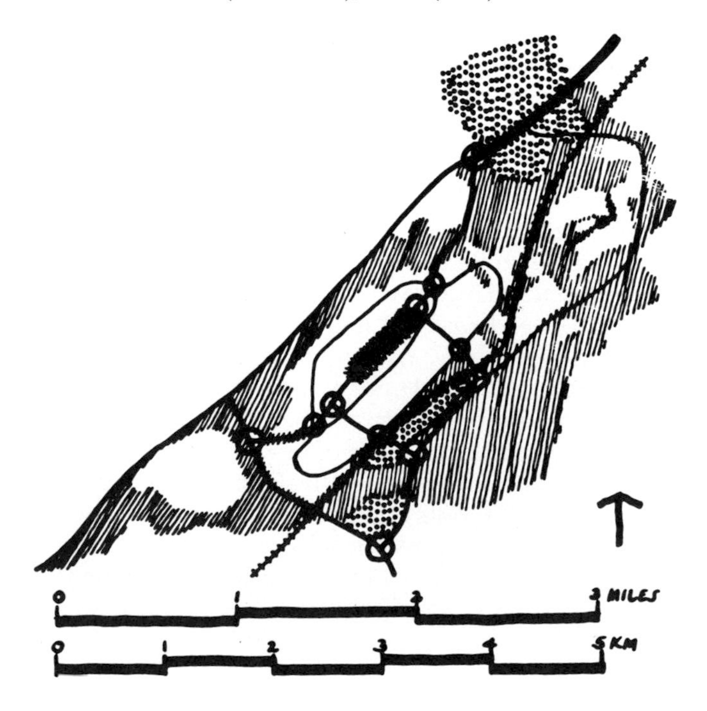

FIGURE 5.12
Cumbernauld (new town), U.K. (1958).

Although all this open landscape may sound like an ideal environment in which to raise a family, social life at Reston still depends on at least two cars in the garage. Another problem is illustrated by the disruption caused in the community when a child was drowned in the lake. The amenities were then seen to some to represent social problems and physical hazards to health and safety.

Columbia, near Washington, D. C., is a similar kind of new town planned for 105,000 people by 1980 (Fig. 5.13). Much of it is already built on an area 5 by 9 miles. It has a hierarchy of neighborhoods, villages, and a town center:

> As we drive through, some other qualities start to come into focus, striking qualities, new ones. The first sensation comes abruptly. There is no urban geometry here, no precise roadway grid, no ninety degree intersection every 400 feet. The streets are all curved

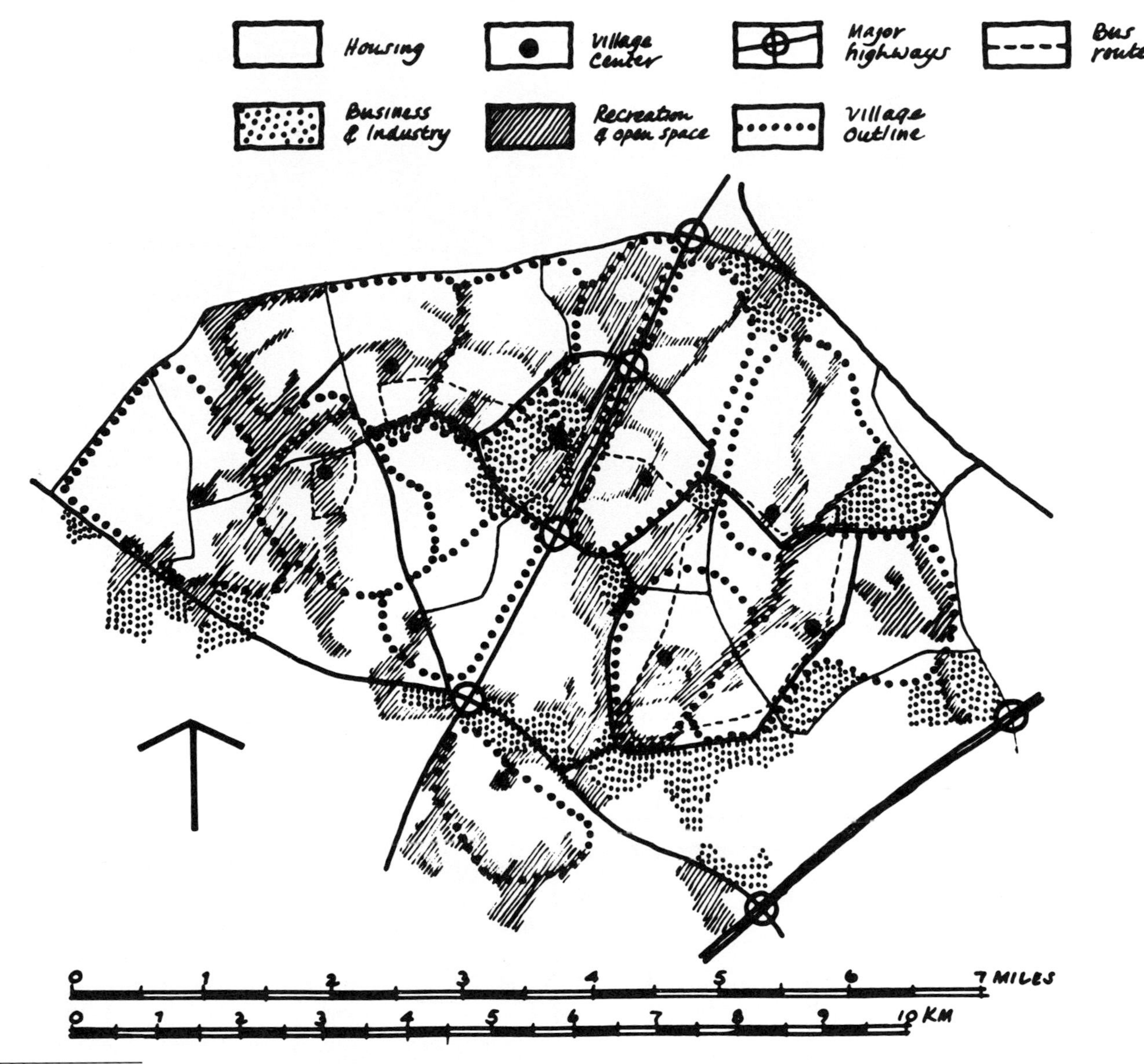

FIGURE 5.13
Columbia (new town), Maryland (1964).

> gently. Most of the houses are built on oval culs-de-sac. There is no overhead lattice of utility lines and poles. All that is underground. There is no tin forest of T.V. aerials. Gone, in short, are the straight lines, the hard edges that rigidify and segment the typical residential neighborhood. And that absence leaves, in the scene of swaying willows, old oaks and spreading greensward, a softness, an openess, a newness. (Fig. 5.14.)

This description in *The New York Times* recalls the quality of the romantic suburb of the 1850s. And although it seems that most people who live there consider it the "American dream," there are unexpected social problems. For example, such open-plan communities with lakes, restaurants, and facilities present ambiguities about who may use what and how.

In condominium developments the surrounding landscape and facilities are usually provided and taken care of by a homeowners' association (Fig. 5.15). Even the houses are maintained this way. Although some similarity may exist between their plan forms and the Radburn superblock, there is often very little similarity in life-styles. In Radburn the inhabitants wanted to lead conventional family lives with a community of

FIGURE 5.14
View, typical of both Reston and Columbia new towns.

FIGURE 5.15
Woodlake, California. An apartment complex with a large central park and recreational facility. Wurster, Bernardi and Emmons, architects. Lawrence Halprin, landscape architect.

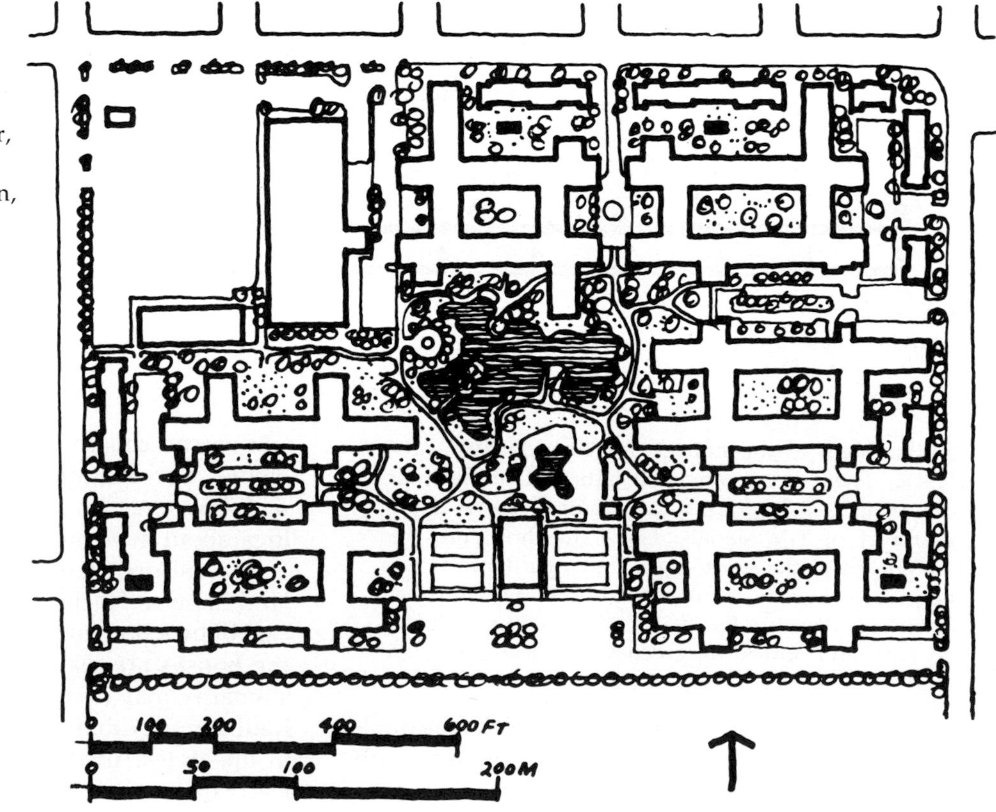

FIGURE 5.16
Radburn-type housing layout in Denmark provides privacy as well as common open space at densities similar to or less than conventional subdivision.

like-minded people. In condominiums, children often are not allowed. People frequently leave at weekends and there is very little sense of community. Such homes often are thought of as investments.

This review has shown a complete change in concept from the Roman house, tightly enclosing its symbols of nature, through the intermediate stages of the urban square and romantic suburbs, to the new towns and cluster developments in which landscape surrounds and permeates the dwellings.

Two techniques in housing have been used to provide substantial areas of open space in close proximity to the dwellings. One is the high-rise apartment block which frees the land that would otherwise have been covered by conventional houses and gardens. This leads to a degree of isolation from neighbors and disconnection from the ground in some societies and situations. It is successful in some ways, in others it is not and high-rise public housing has come to be associated with social problems (Fig. 5.11).

Another technique is the cluster concept, which concentrates building in high-density groups allowing views out into a landscape that would otherwise be subdivided if the same number of houses were spread out at an overall low density (Fig. 5.1). This system provides attractive views and open space which may be used for community facilities as in a condominium, or for pedestrian cycle and riding trails as in a new town, or for unstructured children's play. Whichever way, the land has to be maintained and managed at someone's expense. Both schemes may be wasteful of land. Neither seems to understand the different kinds of open space that are needed or the real values to be gained by more compact planning, which should be part of a larger urban policy in which conservation zones for water catchment and flood control are assembled as a system related to and incorporating the open space component of residential areas.

In Scandinavia, where land is perhaps more highly valued, one finds numerous examples of housing with private gardens and common greens (Fig. 5.16). They are essentially Radburn-type layouts. The minimum garden opens onto a public lawn. Privacy is provided with hedges and fences and there is a free flow between public and private areas, the family and the community. Planning is compact and densities are high.

Continuing down in scale, the patio house enclosing its garden and providing extreme privacy in the Roman manner is in fact an economic and socially appropriate solution where land is scarce and society is complex—and where is it not? A private terrace or

FIGURE 5.17
Minimum garden: balcony and window boxes.

balcony sheltered from wind is the minimum outdoor unit where plants can be grown in pots and window boxes, and where one can relax in the sun (Fig. 5.17). All dwellings should have at least this possibility.

The typical subdivision which has not been discussed in this chapter may soon become subject to adaptation and be influenced by some of the concepts of group housing reviewed here. Concern for improved social cohesion, affordable housing, distance to work, efficient land use, and conservation of agricultural land may lead to infill housing in low density suburbs and the inclusion of shops, offices, apartments, and parks.

SUGGESTED READINGS

Chermayeff, Serge and Christopher Alexander, *Community and Privacy*.

Breckenfeld, Gurney, *Columbia and the New Cities*.

Creese, Walter L., *The Search for Environment: The Garden City Before and After*, pp. 108–143, "Neat and Clean at Port Sunlight and Bourneville," pp. 203–218, "The First Garden City of Letchworth," pp. 315–344, "The New Towns."

Howard, Ebenezer, *Garden Cities of Tomorrow*.

Reps, John W., *The Making of Urban America*, Ch. 15, "The Towns the Companies Built."

Stein, Clarence, *Towards New Towns for America*, pp. 37–74, Radburn.

LANDSCAPE PLANNING

6

ENVIRONMENTAL CRISIS

In recent years there has been a marked change in public sensitivity and interest in the environment. Ecology and planning have become household words. Air and water pollution, agricultural land, nuclear power plants, toxic wastes, highways, and billboards are a few of the issues. Literature on the subject has come forth steadily, and public figures, elected and hereditary, have given their prestigious support to the cause. Commissions, agencies, and programs have been established with varying powers to regulate, control, and beautify the environment. The extent to which it has become a public concern may be measured to some degree by increased television coverage and the use of conservation and ecological terminology in the advertising industry. This broad interest in the environment is, of course, not enough. Experts who believe in the future of mankind, do so only with severe provisos. For example, we should realize that the problems of the environment, pollution, and waste of resources are the result of the stated goals currently given primacy in our society: to produce for profit and to utilize one's land in any reasonable way one wishes. The geographer Philip Wagner states the problem: "Until we are willing to pay for aesthetic and ecological improvement, until we are willing to sacrifice some degree of economic benefits, our environmental problems are going to persist and get worse."[1]

In spite of the fact that we all inhabit the same earth, each society naturally tries to solve its own problems within its own socioeconomic framework and with the resources available to it. This is a practical but short-term view. Although it is easy to accept the trends of society and, as they arise, to deal with environmental problems such as water and air pollution, depletion of agricultural soil, energy shortages, and higher food prices, we might also begin to think in terms of dealing with the trends before they are generated. If a widespread understanding of the ecological facts of life together with a concern for the common good and the long-term survival of mankind were to permeate the lawmakers' chambers, the advertising agencies, and the industrialists' design studios, many potential problems might never arise. Planning under these circumstances would be a positive rather than a negative procedure. Having said this, we now turn to some specific conflicts.

POPULATION AND RESOURCES

The environmental context in which we are operating today in the United States and in the world is one in which we are faced with the impact of an immense increase in population associated in some places with rising standards of living. We can expect the 3 to 6 billion people in the world today to almost double in the next 30 years. Some authorities estimate that the earth's population could eventually level off at 15 billion and that these people could be supported by the earth's resources provided we go about it in the right way. The problem facing mankind in the immediate future is how to house and feed these people.

The implications of these population projections tend to vary, depending on one's viewpoint and geographical location. In the United States, with vast resources and a relatively slow population increase compared with the Asian countries, the American consumes 130 times more than the average Indian. In a world view this represents a peculiar imbalance. Locally, however, the environmental problems of the advanced technological societies have their own degree of importance when seen out of global context.

The effect of expanded populations can be expressed and made comprehensible in a variety of ways. For example, it is predicted that by 1990 more than half the population of the world will be living in cities of 100,000 or more. In 1967, Herman Kahn suggested that perhaps 80 to 90 percent of the developed world will be urbanized by the end of the century and cities of the less developed nations will double their population every 15 years.[2]

Kahn predicts the evolution of a "San–San Pacific Megalopolis," a continuous urban area centered around Los Angeles stretching from San Diego to Santa Barbara and ultimately to San Francisco. The same is expected on the East coast between Boston and Washington. Reston and Columbia are manifestations of this infilling process. In Europe the concentration of population centered in the southeast of England around London is seen as developing into a conurbation stretching from Manchester to Milan. However, because of the implied concentration, the projected population of the United States in the year 2000 will occupy only 2 percent of the land and the population of England and Wales will take up only 16 percent. Currently half the population of the United States lives within 50 miles or one hour's drive of the oceans, the Gulf of Mexico, or the Great Lakes. The fact quite simply is that certain areas of countries and regions throughout the world are more attractive for settlement than others for a variety of reasons—economic, political, geographical, and so on—and these locations, already urbanized, are likely to continue to attract the major portion of population increase, even if its rate of growth is reduced. New York, Los Angeles, San Francisco, London, Tokyo, and Paris will continue to be attractors. The water's edge is particularly attractive.

Increasing urbanization, together with ultimate limitations on convenient territorial expansion of cities, poses the question of population densities. Currently there is a wide range. For example, the greater Los Angeles area, comprising some 4,000 square miles, is at present occupied by 9 million people, at an overall average density of 2,250 per square mile. By contrast, the 7 million people in Calcutta occupy 400 square miles at an average density of 50,000 per square mile. Manhattan is even higher with 68,000, and between the extremes there is every conceivable rate. There is no conclusive evidence that the higher densities are bad and the lower are better. Density cannot be equated with quality of environment without further

[1] Philip L. Wagner, *Constraints Necessary to Achieve the Quality of Life: The Geographer's Viewpoint*. Man and His Total Environment (Los Angeles: University of California Water Resources Center, 1967).

[2] Herman Kahn, *The Year 2000* (New York: Macmillan, 1967).

qualification in terms of dwelling type, accessibility, and distribution of open space. Evidence suggests, however, that certain ill-defined aspects of the urban environment do lead to a high incidence of neuroses and social pathologies such as delinquency and mental and physical ill health.

The consequences of urban expansion are enormous in terms of additional housing, schools, recreation facilities, industry, retail centers, and transportation systems. The problems of water supply and sewage and waste disposal are also critical and these involve the relationship of the expanding metropolis to the hinterland. In addition, it is no accident that the highest concentration of population tends to coincide with or adjoin the areas of the most productive soils in the world (Figs. 6.1 to 6.3). The loss of such land due to urbanization is of major concern and its impact must be evaluated in the larger terms of world food production, supply, and consumption. The statistics can be expressed in a variety of dramatic ways. For example, it is estimated that the United States has lost as much as 1 million acres of its best farmland in a year. Britain has been losing it at the rate of 10 acres a day.

FIGURE 6.1
Competing uses, housing and agriculture, on the richest agricultural soil in the world. Davis, California.

FIGURE 6.2
Arlington, Virginia, suburb of Washington, D.C., consumes woodland landscape (1957). Photograph by William A. Garnett.

FIGURE 6.3
West Covina, Southern California. Orange groves being replaced with subdivisions (1952). Photograph by William A. Garnett.

PLANNING AND POLITICS

Whatever planning concepts are employed in the accommodation and distribution of increased population, there seem to be two major implications. First, land not hitherto urbanized will be required for new development. Second, the interaction between expanded urban populations and the surrounding hinterland will be greatly increased and intensified in terms of recreation and the supply of resources. Also implied is the redevelopment and environmental improvement of existing urban centers and a questioning of the widely held belief that high-density living is undesirable.

The crisislike proportions of the population and resources problem, which can now be clearly seen, and a worldwide historical record of squandered resources and environmental chaos, make a comprehensive approach to planning the environment imperative for survival if for no other reason.

Some problems are, of course, much larger than a matter of physical planning and design. Clearly designers cannot themselves create the social and economic stability necessary for a healthy and great society. Yet it is the planner's and designer's role to create the environment of society, and in doing this he must be aware of the possibilities inherent in the arrangement of the environment for the encouragement, permission, or frustration of human aspirations and human needs, for social and cultural interaction and fulfillment, and for economic stability, efficiency, health, comfort, and human happiness. The environment and its design and planning cannot be separated from these fundamental social factors.

In *The Home of Man*, Barbara Ward places the future of the world squarely in the realms of economics and politics.[3] The issues are described in three contexts: (1) population, which will increase, (2) justice, which is a democratic ideal, and (3) resources, which are diminishing. She believes (1) that the population increase should and can be accommodated by intention and design, (2) that housing for the poor, with basic minimum standards, should form a major goal for societies dedicated to ending human deprivation, and (3) that the constraints posed by limited resources challenge us to design sustainable environments.

For her, then, these are goals that can be achieved by political decisions which include an appropriate distribution of funds (taxes) and human resources to procure (for example) conditions for population stability, conservation of energy resources, and a massive reduction in defense spending (which she claims reached a global 250 thousand million dollars in 1976). She advocates a planned economy, control of land prices to remove speculation, and the separation of development from property rights. In another sphere she advocates national inventories of farm land, soil, and water resources, recreation areas and areas of ecological and aesthetic sensitivity and, in short, a national plan for land use, shelter, utilities, traffic, work, recreation, convenience, and beauty. Within this, the individual will be comfortably housed in mixed, lively urban communities created by modification of the existing urban framework, provided continuity with the past rather than by total clearance schemes. Degraded land will be restored, neglected areas will be turned into playing fields and adventure playgrounds. Recreation areas will be created on the fringe of cities and there will be a closer relationship of food growing areas to the market. That all of this is possible is demonstrated by examples from various countries. Her point is simply that a concerted policy, and therefore one with broad equitable impact, depends on and requires national commitment rather than ad hoc local enterprise.

URBANIZATION AND THE LANDSCAPE

Regardless of whether socioeconomic and political considerations suggest the establishment of new towns, the continued physical expansion of existing cities to accommodate population increase, or some other solution, the selection of land suitable for urbanization should depend on an assessment of its fragility and its value for other uses. The fragility of a landscape is a function of geology, soil, slope, climate, vegetation, wildlife, and scenic quality, and the extent to which landscape degradation would result from its disturbance and change in use. Symptoms of landscape degradation are excessive soil erosion, silting of streams, landslides, flooding, and loss of wildlife (Figs. 6.4 to 6.6). Moreover, assessment of alternative uses or higher values depends on a concept in which landscape and its social content are regarded as a resource. Thus clean rivers and aquifers, rare vegetation and wildlife, high-quality agricultural soil, and areas of historic interest and scenic quality would be considered for conservation on the basis of their uniqueness, scarcity, or irreplaceability and therefore their value to society (Fig. 6.7).

Clearly the ability to make decisions based on these criteria of fragility and value depends on an understanding of the evolution of the landscape, the essential elements of environment, and the basic natural

[3] Barbara Ward, *The Home of Man*, 1976.

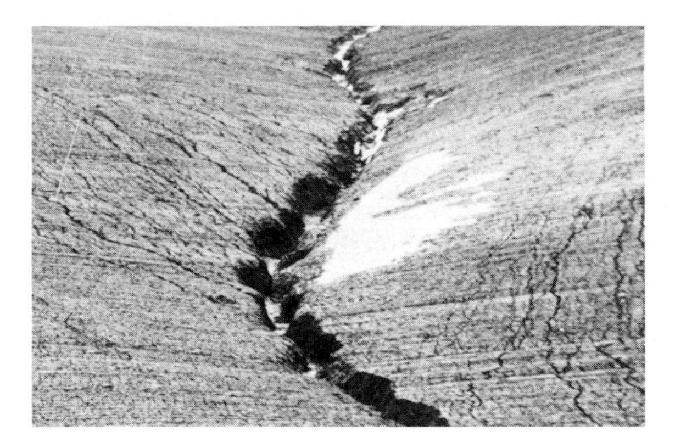

FIGURE 6.4
Soil erosion.

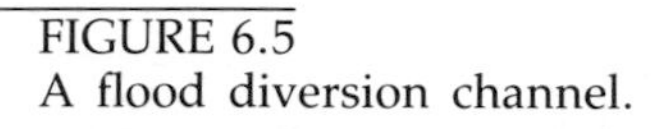

FIGURE 6.5
A flood diversion channel.

FIGURE 6.6
The same channel about a year later silted up as a result of erosion caused by subdivision development.

FIGURE 6.7
Productive agricultural soil, a scarce resource of value to society.

processes and ecological interrelationships within which we operate. It is then necessary to find a way to evaluate the variables of the natural system so that they can become powerful and manageable determinants of land use policy and of form in project planning and design.

LANDSCAPE PLANNING

What is meant by the term landscape planning and how does it differ from social and economic planning? Hackett sees the role of the landscape planner as the locating and welding of various land uses in a process based on a technical knowledge of the physiology of landscape and an aesthetic understanding of its appearance. The result would be another stage in the evolution of the landscape.[4] Crowe suggests that landscape planning is a wider concept than land use planning, because it includes appearance as well as use, pleasure as well as fertility. She sees the function of landscape planning as guiding the intricate intermeshing of functions and habitats, as separating the incompatible, reconciling diverse uses, and relating each specialized use to the overall landscape seen as setting for life.[5] McHarg asks that we view man-made changes to the landscape in terms of creativity. He argues that man as part of nature is required to be creative in the evolutionary process and that changes should be judged in terms of the laws of nature and evolution. His system of landscape planning is based on the proposition that nature is process and value exhibiting both opportunities and constraints for human use.[6]

Landscape planning consists of a scientific aspect concerned with research and a shaping aspect based on the research; the two parts result in the production of a policy statement. The landscape plan sets out the

[4] Brian Hackett, *Landscape Planning* (Newcastle: Oriel Press, 1971).

[5] Sylvia Crowe, The Need for Landscape Planning, in *Towards a New Relationship of Man and Nature in Temperate Lands* (Morges: IUCN, 1967).

[6] Ian McHarg, *Design with Nature* (New York: Natural History Press, 1969).

FIGURE 6.8
Landscape type: mountains versus wilderness. Absaroka Range, Wyoming. Shoshone National Forest. Photograph by R. Burton Litton, Jr.

framework and lines of action by which the landscape is to be adjusted in accordance with ecological principles to meet the needs of changed circumstances.

These views describe the intentions of landscape planning. Its process can be divided into four stages: (1) survey and analysis; (2) evaluation; (3) policy or design solution; and (4) implementation.

The Landscape Survey

The landscape survey is an assessment of the facts and forces that have formed the landscape. Three classes of information comprise the survey: the landscape—ecological factors; the human, socioeconomic, and cultural factors; and the visual appearance representing the interaction of these two.

Natural Factors. The survey is concerned first with the identification of landscape types. These can be defined on the basis of ecology and visual quality. Land in whatever state of cultivation or wilderness is clearly not a uniform commodity. Every landscape is unique as a result of the variables involved in its formation and its basic structure and geographical location. Each landscape type or ecosystem is thus a dynamic reflection of the facts and forces of its evolu-

FIGURE 6.9
Landscape type: Coastline. Tomales Bay, California. North and leeward exposure supporting live oak and California Bay. Photography by R. Burton Litton, Jr.

FIGURE 6.10
Landscape type: Riparian meadow. Taylor Creek, Eldorado National Forest, Lake Tahoe. Photograph by R. Burton Litton, Jr.

tion. Thus deserts are different from coastal strands, mountains are different from marshlands, and so on (Figs. 6.8 to 6.10, and 11.7). Within each basic type lie microenvironments related to differences in geology, soil, exposure, slope vegetation, and use by man (Fig. 6.11).

The level of detail required in the analysis depends on its purpose. Where the study is of a broad nature dealing with intrinsic suitabilities of land for some use, then a comprehensive evaluation of all natural factors is essential.

The landscape–ecological factors survey must include a description of the historical–geological processes responsible for the basic form of the landscape and the distribution and outcropping of various geological formations. These strata must be located and described in terms of permeability and water-holding capacity, stability, and other variables (Fig. 6.12). Fault lines, landslides, river cutting, and other dynamic aspects must also be recorded and mapped. The soil is an extension of geology, although not always located where it was formed. The composition of the soil varies according to its geological parentage and its

FIGURE 6.11
Landscape types and values mapped for Nantucket Island (Zube, 1966).

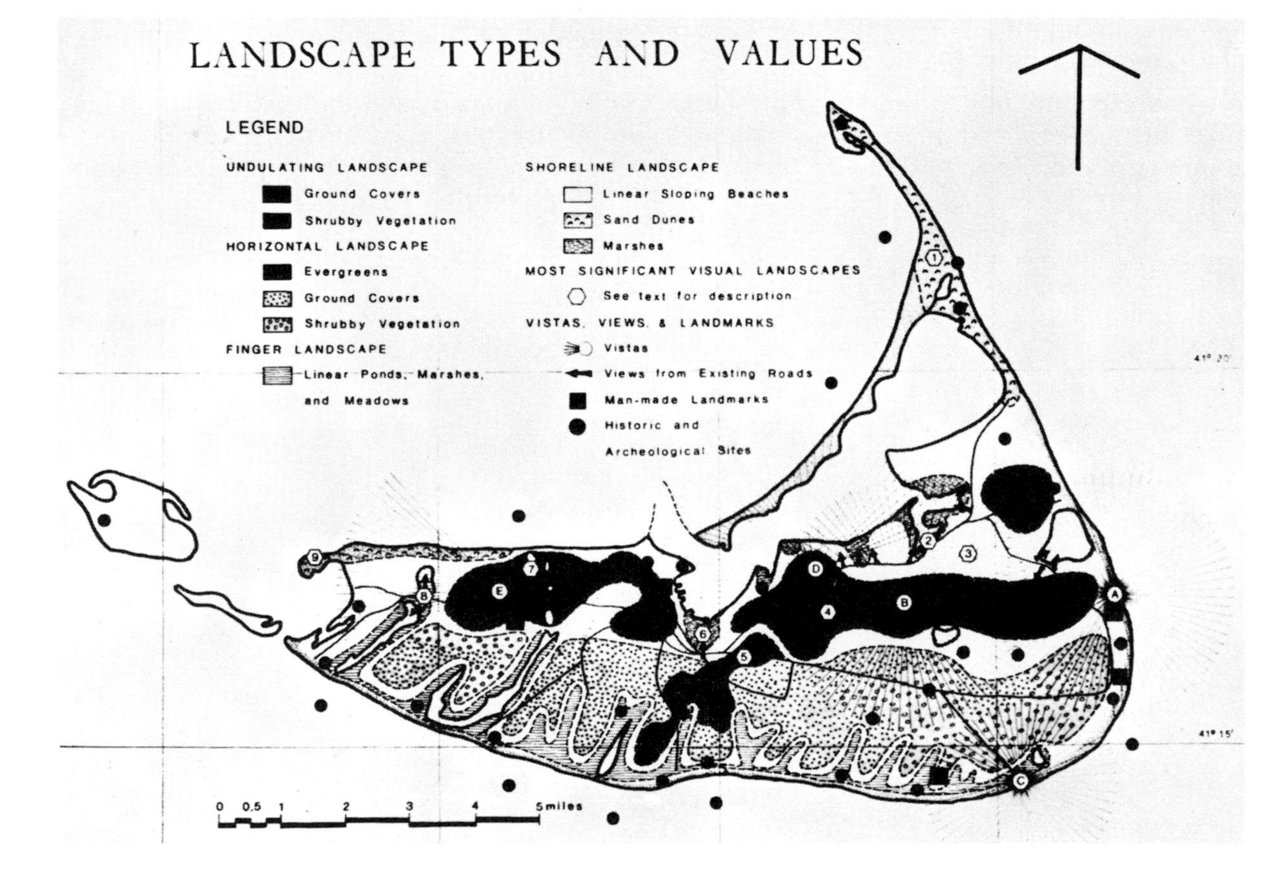

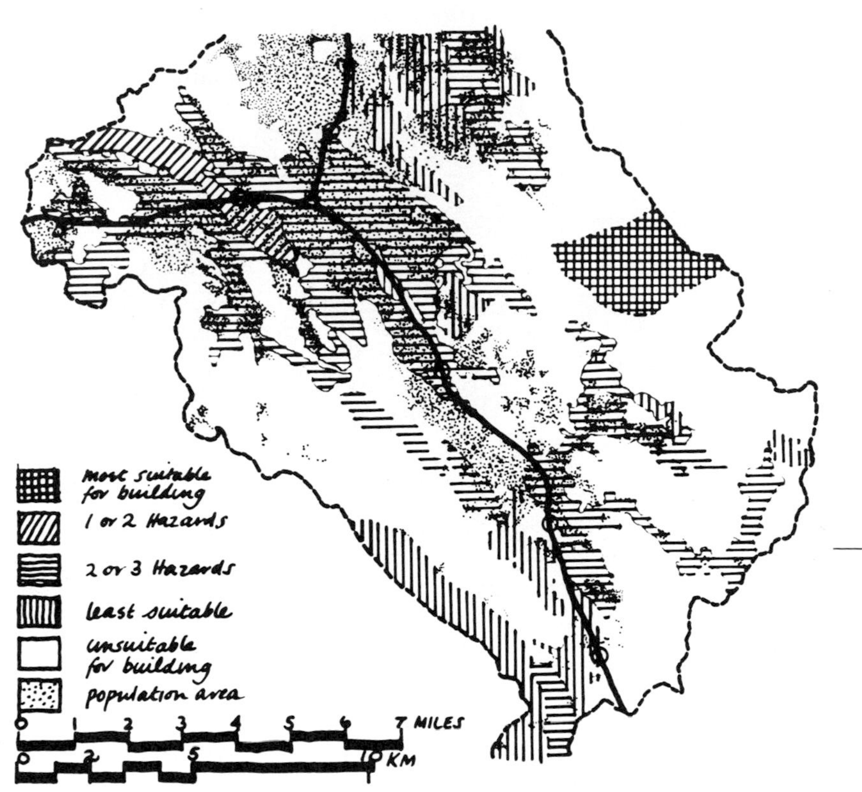

FIGURE 6.12
Building suitability map based on a combination of geological factors. It will be noted that the distribution of population does not correspond to the areas of least hazard. Study by students of Landscape Architecture, University of California, Berkeley (1972). (Robin Chiang and Robin Nelson.)

method of formation and the subsequent weathering process and use by man. Soils are classified and named on the basis of these and other variables and are described in terms of stability, erodability, shrink–swell factor, fertility, and so on.

Water is not only an important factor in giving form to the landscape, but all life depends on it. Its presence is a major ecological determinant. In addition, water is the link between all dynamic aspects of the environment. Our analyses must therefore show where it comes from, where it runs to, and where it is stored above and below ground. The climate is responsible for the amount of water that is precipitated on land. Temperature and winds, together with water, make up the components of erosion which have shaped the landscape over millions of years. The variables—temperature, water, soil—determine the distribution of vegetation. The variety of vegetation and its location in a natural landscape is an indicator of these variables. The topography of the landscape represents other determinants in the distribution of vegetation (elevation and slope orientation) and the stability of geological formations and soils (steepness of slope). Wildlife is dependent on the quantity and distribution of the vegetation. All these data must be assembled and mapped in such a way that the variables can be related to each other and to the purpose of the study. Computerization of data and the capacity to produce maps based on several factors facilitate the evaluation phase.

Social Factors. The human, socioeconomic, and cultural factors included in the survey will vary depending on the particular situation. The cultural marks of man resulting from habitation and land use may cover considerable periods of time before the survey. Thus historical associations, events, and landmarks should be recorded as well as the present disposition of land and population, settlement, and industry. Land ownership and political jurisdictions may also prove useful information in the evaluation stage. This section also includes information reflecting pressures for change or conservation, land values and sales, and activity of environmental groups.

Visual Quality. Visual analysis is included in this list of basic data on the assumption that dramatic scenic landscape or the picturesque combination of settlement and physiography are themselves potential resources that may be evaluated according to their uniqueness and the principles of the artist.

As we have seen in Chapter 3, since the mid-nineteenth century, landscapes of outstanding visual quality such as Yosemite and Yellowstone in the

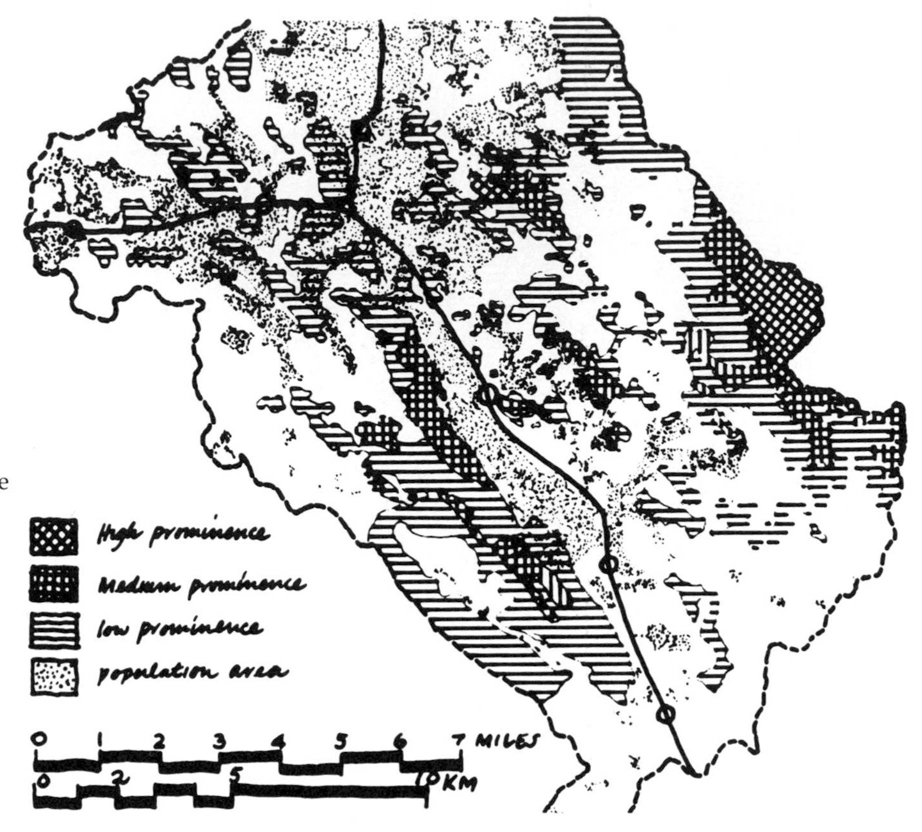

FIGURE 6.13
A visual analysis that maps the most dominant features in a watershed. The assessment is made by observations taken at ten accessible places within the region. Areas of high prominence can be seen from seven or eight positions. Areas of medium prominence from three or four and those of low prominence from only one or two positions. Study by students of Landscape Architecture, University of California, Berkeley (1972). (Brian Lynch and George Lefler.)

United States or the Lake District in England have been considered worthy of protection for aesthetic enjoyment. In more recent years, concern for visual quality has spread to the more ordinary environment. The Natural Beauty Conference and the Highway Beautification Act of 1965 were products of this concern and preceded more comprehensive legislation in the form of the National Environmental Policy Act (1969) and similar state legislations in California, Vermont, and Maine (all 1970). In addition to the protection of resources and control of adverse impacts, such as soil erosion, deforestation, flooding, removal of wildlife habitat, air and water pollution, and unfavorable social and economic changes, the various acts included visual quality as a factor of the environment to be considered in the impact assessment process (discussed on page 128).

The National Environmental Policy Act and the California Environmental Quality Act require an evaluation of unquantifiable environmental amenities and protection of aesthetic, natural, and historical environmental qualities. This requirement has led to the development of methodical systems of landscape assessment by which landscape can be described and evaluated for planning and conservation purposes and as input to Environmental Impact Statements (EIS) and Reports (EIR). Research has followed two main directions. One involves perception and preference studies by which landscape quality is judged by aggregating human responses to landscape images and types. The results have shown a basic preference for naturalness, and complexity, uniqueness, and the presence of water (Vohl).[7]

A second direction involves descriptive inventories as a means of representing the landscape which is then evaluated according to a set of aesthetic criteria and professional judgment. Landscape inventories describe the landscape in terms of land form, water, vegetation, land use, and settlement patterns. Inventories are either related to a specific set of viewpoints, for example along a road, trail, or stream, or they are regional and comprehensive, concerned more with conservation of scenic landscapes as a whole than simply the view from the road. Both are important and in both, the inventory determines the landscape type as previously discussed (page 107). The visual attributes take precedence over the ecological, although they are interdependent.

[7] R. Viohl, Jr. *Landscape Evaluation* (Albany, N.Y.: New York State Sea Grant Institute, 1975).

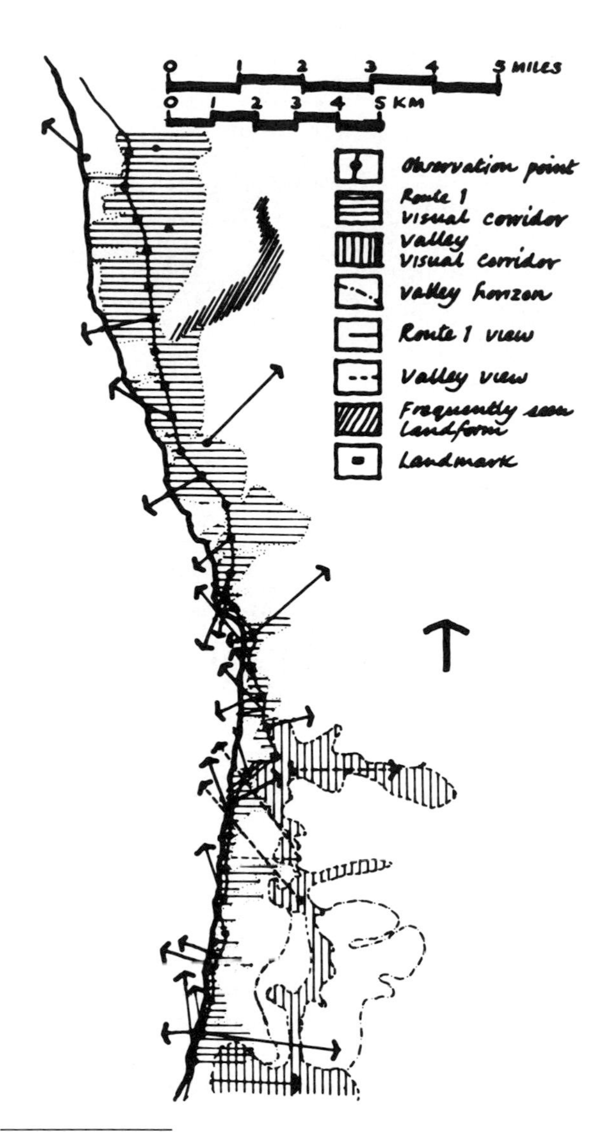

FIGURE 6.14
Observations taken at regular intervals along a road results in the definition of a visual corridor and provides a notation of vistas and changing scenic quality. Study by students of Landscape Architecture, University of California, Berkeley (1973). (Michael Knox, Steve Lang, Brendan Doyle.)

The description of the landscape (inventory) is objective and includes typical features as well as unique ones. The landscape is represented by photographs, drawings, and maps. Whether the inventory is routed or regional, it leads to the definition of basic landscape units defined by land form and vegetation. These units may be large (characterized by repetition of land, e.g., foothill region) and small (characterized by topographic enclosures, e.g., valley). Terms such as feature landscape, focal landscape, panoramic landscape are applied (Litton).[8] The regional landscape unit is not necessarily visible from any one point, since its definition is not based on visibility. It comprises an area spatially defined in which a similar landscape quality is encountered. A routed visual unit, on the other hand, consists of land or lands that are visible from specific observer location and may include noncontiguous areas beyond the immediate foreground (Figs. 6.13 to 6.16).

The U.S. Forest Service's Visual Management System (1974),[9] although related to its particular objectives of maintaining a productive landscape that is also a scenic and recreational resource, employs two measures for landscape quality. These are "variety class," and "sensitivity level." The variety class calls for the division of the landscape into three types: distinctive, common, and minimal. These terms are a function of uniqueness in the composition of landscape features such as land form, water, vegetation, and so on. The zones are identified and mapped using aerial photos and field observation. The second measure, "sensitivity level" is related to people's concern for scenic quality. Landscape visibility from places of high use such as primary scenic roads, major campgrounds and lakes provide the basic data. Again, there are three levels of importance determined by the number of people likely to see the landscape. The zones can also be mapped and combined with the "variety class" map. In this way landscape areas of greatest visual importance are identified. It is a rough but clear system and employs the traditional aesthetic criteria of line, form, texture, and color. It is not without its critics, however, and other measures of landscape quality such as vividness (memorability), unity and variety, multiple visibility, complexity, and diversity have been used and different systems of evaluation developed in this complex field.

In another method, visual units are ranked in terms of twenty scenic factors (e.g., vegetation, slope) as a function of four levels of vividness or distinctiveness applied to five characteristics of the landscape based on its geomorphology: (1) skyline, (2) profile, (3) floor and water forms, (4) lakes, (5) rivers and streams.[10]

In addition to natural scenery, the visual quality of towns and villages, agricultural and heritage landscape are becoming more important and in need of evaluation as society seeks to preserve aspects of the past against the onslaught of commercial develop-

[8] R. B. Litton, *Forest Landscape Description and Inventories*, 1968.

[9] U.S. Forest Service, *The Visual Management System*, 1974.

[10] R. J. Tetlow and S. Sheppard, *Visual Resources of the NorthEast Coal Study Area*, 1976.

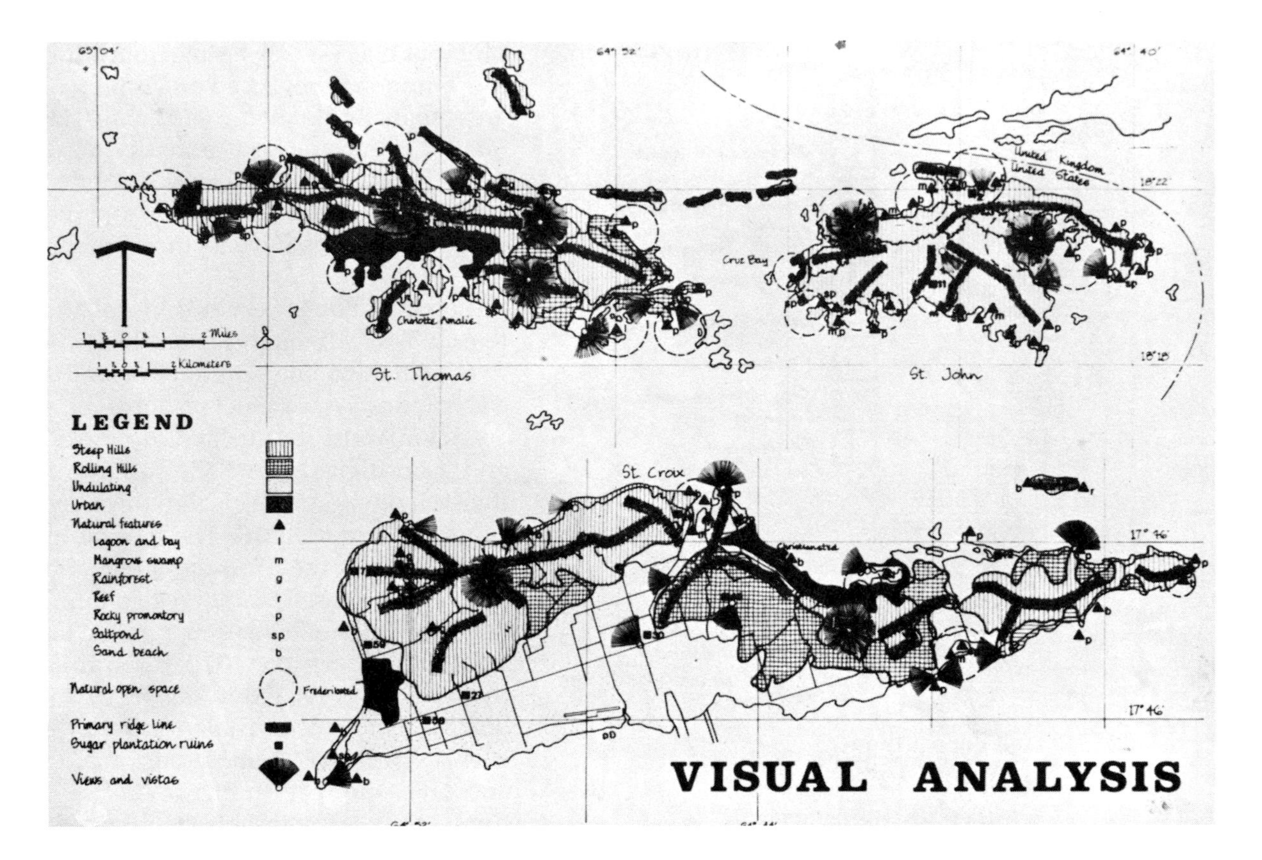

FIGURE 6.15
Visual analysis. The Virgin Islands (Zube, 1968).

FIGURE 6.16
Method of calculating landscape visibility from specific points using contour maps and section lines. A computer program is also available to do this.

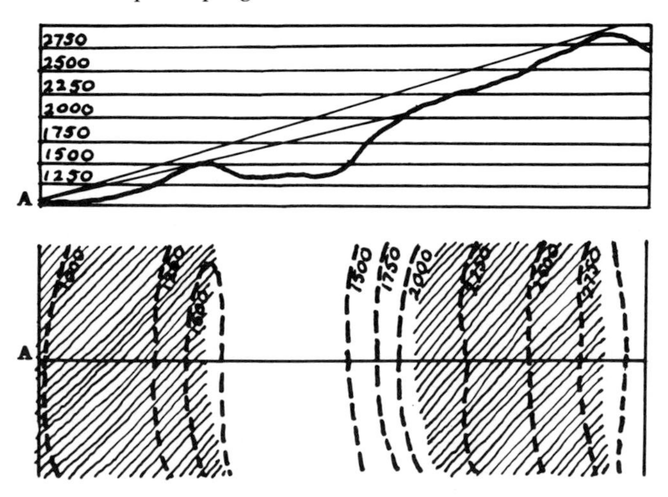

ment. In these the element of time, vegetation management, and authenticity complicate the process and objectives.

An essential goal of all methods of landscape evaluation is to determine the qualities and features that give it identity. Thus, the impact of change and development can be assessed and constraints, mitigation, or conservation measures prescribed accordingly. Measures of vulnerability to change or the ability of a landscape to absorb development with minimal effect are often necessary as a component of landscape evaluation when there is choice about where change may occur such as in road alignment and ski slopes. These are usually based on steepness of slope, vegetation pattern, complexity of land form, and so forth. As the methods of evaluation become more objective, visual quality as a factor in landscape planning is likely to carry more weight in the process.

Photographs and sketches taken from likely viewpoints and zones of landscape, which are part of important views, constitute the raw data. Prominent landmarks and all elements fundamental to visual quality can be mapped in the same way as the other survey information (Figs. 6.13 to 6.16).

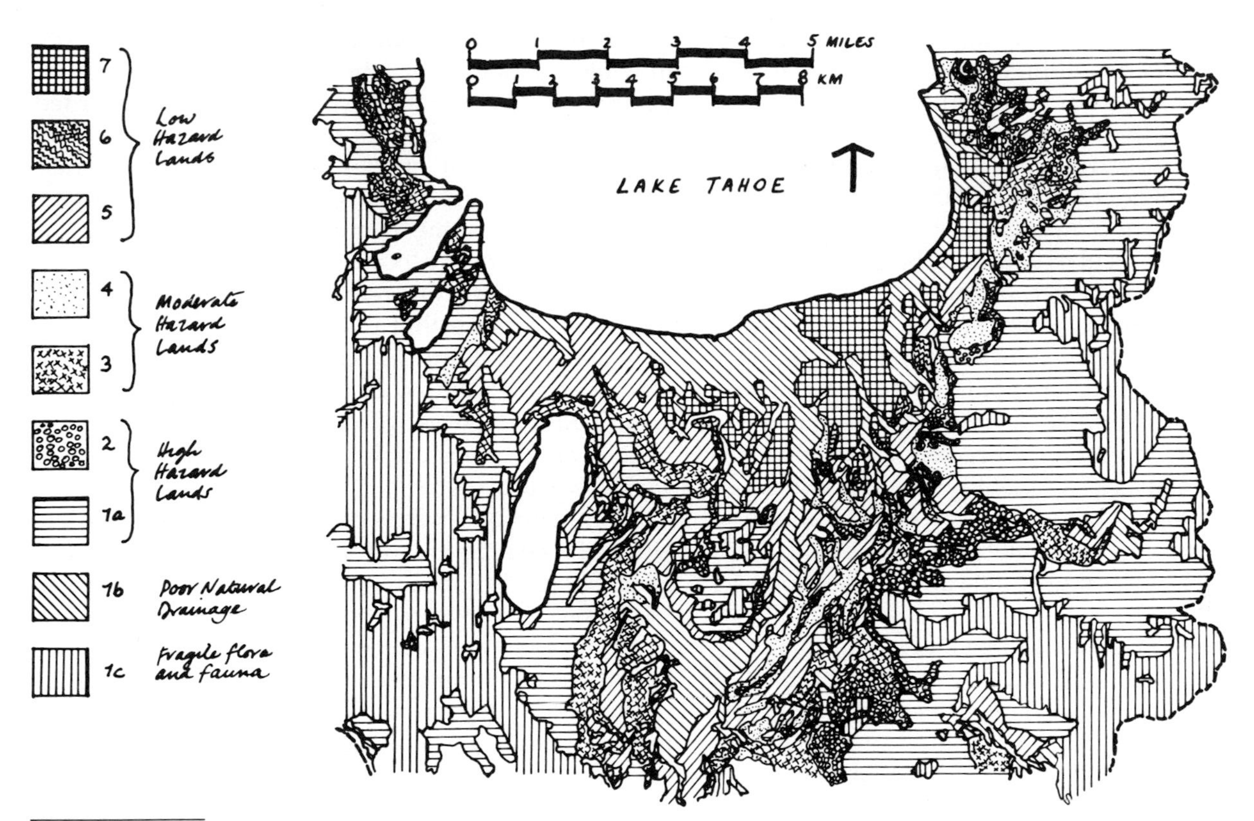

FIGURE 6.17
Lake Tahoe Basin, Land Capabilities. A portion of the map prepared by the U.S. Forest Service in cooperation with the Tahoe Regional Planning Agency (1971). The map shows seven land capability classes designated by number in order of increasing tolerance for use without sustaining permanent damage. Land capability involves consideration of (1) risks of land damage from erosion and other causes and (2) the subsequent impact of such damage on vegetation, sedimentation, flooding, wildlife, and water quality.

The land capabilities are determined according to the frequency and magnitude of the hazards encountered: floods, landslides, high water tables, poorly drained soils, fragile flora and fauna, and easily erodible soils. Class 1 represents areas that exhibit the greatest frequency or highest magnitude of hazardous conditions, or both. Class 7 represents areas where hazardous conditions are negligible.

The map can be used to judge the risk of land damage and to assign use activities and intensities within hydrologic and topographic limitations. The study does not suggest that development should occur on the locations shown.

The land rated lowest has the least tolerance for use, the steepest slopes (over 30 percent), the greatest potential for erosion and the highest runoff potential, or the poorest drainage and flora and fauna.

Evaluation

Wagner suggests in a general way that we should assess the landscape in terms of economic, aesthetic, and ecological values.[11] Our management of the land should aim toward the optimization of ecological fitness and health, visual beauty, and employment. Put another way, the evaluation stage should be concerned with a balance between the natural potential and the economic and technical requirements of the human society. The survey information collected thus must be interpreted and evaluated in terms of the existing natural processes, intrinsic suitability of the land, and pressures for change to that land. Features must be evaluated in terms of their scarcity value, their limitations for development, and their opportunities for various land uses, in terms of their impact or lack of impact on the natural system.

The evaluation is made in terms of potential land uses and the degree to which the natural system can sustain disturbance. We can therefore look at the landscape in terms of potential uses and the optimum

[11] Wagner, *op. cit.*

criteria of those uses and thus find areas where they can best be fulfilled within the allowable level of disturbance. We are concerned with two basic questions: first finding the optimum landscape criteria for those uses that are adequately defined, and second determining the impact of various land uses on different types of landscape. We can arrive at degrees of suitability for a particular land use based on these factors. The point at which a degree of suitability becomes unacceptable is a function of the values of society and the role of mitigation measures in reducing adverse impact. The reliability of the data is of course critical, and the development of new technology might render some criteria obsolete or reduce the estimated environmental damage. "Capability" usually refers to a scientific evaluation of land in terms of its capacity for change, whereas "suitability" is related to the criteria for specific uses and social values in relation to capability (Fig. 6.17).

The issues of criteria and impact are clearly interrelated, but for the moment let us look at them separately. The criteria for land uses vary to some extent depending on the geographical and cultural context. The specification for each is written from two points of view, that of the operator or user and that of the public. The criteria fall into three categories: (1) economics, (2) health and safety, and (3) ecological and visual relationships. Thus optimum agricultural use will have criteria for soil, slope, drainage, aspect, and access. High-speed highways will have criteria for curves and gradients. Housing will have criteria for geological stability, sewage disposal, and microclimate. Flood plains and land subject to subsidence or slippage are obviously unsuitable for housing or schools. In addition, earthquake fault zones and filled land in earthquake-prone areas should be regarded as unsuitable. Even though residents of such areas frequently are unconcerned or fatalistic about the danger, there can be great cost to society (Fig. 6.18). When disaster strikes, it is usually the public that pays for repair of roads and services and special loans to the victims. In other words, there is a loss to society. Nuclear power plants are a special case where stability of foundations is of widespread concern.

Choosing the location of a house should be done in terms of achieving the best microclimate for people. The warming effect of lakes in winter, the cooling effect of winds, and the presence of vegetation can be taken advantage of to achieve the best outdoor living conditions and the least cost of heating and cooling. Conversely, zones of land in temperate climates which by virtue of their slope or orientation receive little direct sunlight throughout the year, and particularly in winter, should, from the points of view of health, heating costs, and energy conservation, be regarded as relatively unsuitable for human occupation. From an economic point of view land that will increase building costs is unlikely to be attractive to developers unless there is some compensating factor, such as location or view. The location of housing in relation to areas of visual quality requires some special criteria which will ensure that quality.

Suitability is simply indicated by the concurrence of a number or a majority of positive factors in any one area. Multiple use is, of course, possible and compatible; alternatives are likely to occur as part of the evaluation process.

The impact question is concerned with the possible effect of a change in land use on the environment in general and also on nonrenewable resources such as fertile soil, pure water, economic minerals, and outstanding landscape beauty, however difficult that may be to define. The impact may simply be the loss of such resources. In addition, this definition of resources that may be damaged should include habitats: the soil and vegetation supporting the food chains of ecological communities whose presence is often associated with the control of insects which cause damage to agricultural crops. Thus, as Fraser Darling points out, chunks of underdeveloped landscape and woods are in themselves, without any other use at all, extremely important and productive elements of the environment not to be given up lightly.[12] Some elements of the landscape which do not appear to have any use actually do, if an overall view is taken of the environment and its processes. It is generally true that when man alters natural ecosystems by design or ignorance, they are usually simplified (as in agriculture) or made less complete, and they lose something of their holistic quality of resistance to invasion by foreign species. There is a potential conflict between economic food production and the natural ecology of the area, especially if fields are large and of one main crop. Complexity and richness are essential attributes of an ecologically sound landscape.

Soil erosion is one of the major likely impacts of housing construction, highway construction, and forestry. Steep slope, lack of vegetative cover, and highly erodable soil types are the causal variables. Construction techniques and machinery are the socioeconomic variables. Excessive erosion caused by the interaction of these factors results in the loss of soil and

[12] Fraser Darling, *New Scientist*, April 16, 1970.

FIGURE 6.18
(a) and **(b)** The San Andreas fault runs through the lake at the top right hand corner and out to the Pacific Ocean in the foreground. Evidence of land failure can be seen and the highway has been closed indefinitely. Oblivious to the dangers, subdivisions, schools and other construction has taken place within the fault zone with effects such as that shown even without a significant earthquake. Photograph 18 (a) by William A. Garnett (1958). Photograph 18 (b) by Jean Stein (1973).

vegetation and causes flooding at lower levels by silted up streams.

The disposal of sewage by septic tanks can cause pollution of rivers and groundwater. Water quality is thus related to sewage disposal systems whose capacities and service areas may limit the growth of communities.

Extensive paving and roofing covering the natural surface of the land increases the rate of runoff and may result in flooding if the storm sewer system is inadequate or nonexistent. Or if rainwater is removed in storm sewers or otherwise prevented from seeping into the soil, the water table may be lowered with resulting impact on trees and vegetative cover, some of which may die as the availability of water decreases. The excessive removal of water by wells from aquifers may also have a similar effect and may cause subsidence. The microclimate can be altered by the filling or creation of lakes and by new topography giving rise to variations in temperature and wind. For example, if San Francisco Bay were filled to the extent that was, until recently legal, the temperatures in San Jose would have increased significantly that buildings would need air conditioners as an essential rather than as a luxury. This may in itself sound as though only money would be involved, but the additional power needed would lead to an increase in the chain of events involved in the production of that power. Many links of this chain have their own detrimental ecological repercussions on resources and environment elsewhere in the region.

There is always an impact. Its extent or degree of destructiveness varies according to the closeness of the fit between the use and the suitability of the land for that use in ecological and social terms. The evaluation phase of landscape planning is involved, then, with matching the uses to the landscape so that the criteria for the uses are fulfilled with the least possible impact.

Policy and Implementation

The results of the evaluation may then become the basis for regional policy or determinants in design and planning at a smaller scale. Implementation of policy requires legal measures democratically approved and enforced in such forms as zoning, performance standards, building codes and ordinances, and means of compensation for reduction of potential for development in the common interest. Although not dealt with in detail here, this phase is of course critical, for without it all the ecological concern, analysis, and evaluation would be to no avail. Increasingly and appropriately, professionals are becoming more involved at this level in an attempt to reach an accord between conflicting and sometimes unnecessarily conflicting positions.

The example that follows is a gross oversimplification of the landscape planning process, which is, in reality, highly complex. The East Lothian Study is a theoretical caricature of the method just outlined. The value judgments and the criteria by which decisions were made were not those approved by any legislative body, although they may someday be. They are assumed to be reasonable for the benefit of present and future populations within the context of environmental quality and conservation of resources.

CASE STUDY 1. EAST LOTHIAN

East Lothian is a county of Scotland comprising about 416 square miles. The area lies to the east of the city of Edinburgh with ½ million inhabitants. This may sound small if you live in New York or Los Angeles, but Edinburgh, in the overall scale of the country, represents a considerable center of population and is associated with an industrial belt stretching west to Glasgow. The study area was based on the watershed of the Tyne River running from the highlands in the south to the North Sea. The boundary of the watershed does not quite coincide with the county boundaries. Thus the planning unit includes a portion of an adjacent county and not all of East Lothian. In addition, the coastal area, which did not lie within the watershed, was included because of its obvious geographical relationship and its popularity for seaside recreation. All of these conditions are prototypical and occur with local variations anywhere in the world.

In addition to evaluating the land in terms of its suitability for a variety of probable uses, one chief objective of the study was specifically to locate areas that could be designated as country parks for recreation. These were to provide places where people from Edinburgh and as far away as Glasgow could go for active recreation and social vacations. The country park concept was conceived as having an attractive landscape setting with buildings for group facilities and provision for sports, sailing, and even auto repair work; some place close to but away from the everyday environment, that is, within the hinterland of population centers.

The uses considered likely, in addition to recreation, were housing of three different types (densities); industry (since there was a source of labor as agricultural employment declined); forestry (in relation to a national policy to increase the production of home-grown timber); motorway or freeway route alignment (in relation to the major transportation connection to the south, which, by virtue of the topography, had to pass through the region); and agriculture (which was traditionally a major use of the land due to the excellent soil and a climate suited to the growing of wheat and potatoes). Six possible land uses were thus selected: agriculture, housing, industry, forestry, motorway, and recreation.

The study did not result in a plan for the future of the county or watershed. The objective was rather to examine all the alternative uses, to look at the landscape types in the area, and to recommend the best possible use for that land. This provides quantities of land suited for one use or another if a demand for it should arise. The recommendations are based on a desire to optimize the potential.

Note on Figs. 6.19 to 6.34:
The East Lothian Study was done by graduate students in Landscape Architecture at the University of Edinburgh in 1969–70. They were Messrs. Bauld, Filor, Hasting, Desau, Rice, Shihabi, and Smith, and Miss James.

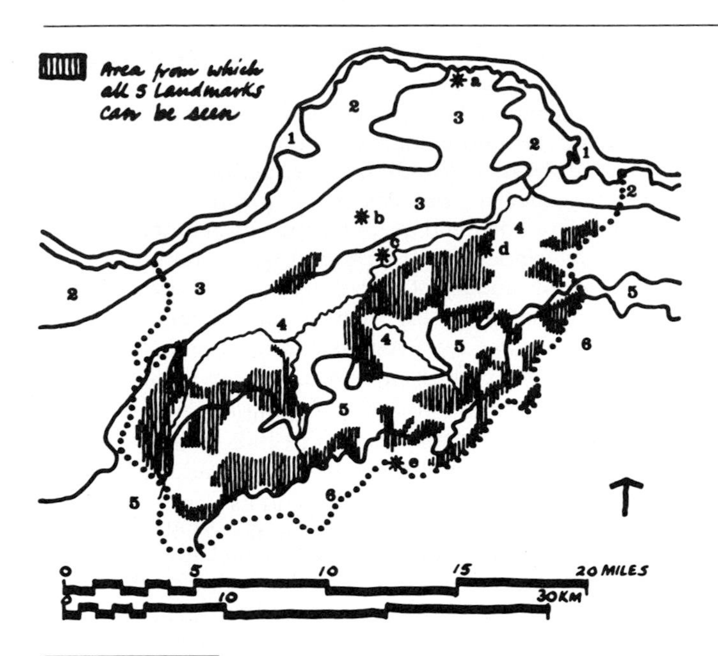

FIGURE 6.19
East Lothian Study: Visual analysis. **(1)** Coastal zone **(2)** Coastal plain **(3)** Tranent ridge **(4)** Tyne valley **(5)** Foothills **(6)** Moorland **(a)** Berwick Law (volcanic plug), **(b)** Hopeton monument, **(c)** Church tower, **(d)** Traprain Law (volcanic plug), **(e)** Lammer Law.

Thus if at some stage a policy for promoting more industry is established, then the land most suited for this according to optimum criteria is already pinpointed and can be examined in detail for its availability, dimensions, and so forth, related to the specifics of the case. The demand for any land use can be evaluated in terms of an assessment of the land's capability and suitability as already described. Alternative futures can thus be presented to legislators and the public. Decisions can then be made openly in the knowledge of what will be lost if land most suited for one use is used for another.

The survey and analysis began with visual impressions. The area was divided into six basic landscape units on the basis of their variations in topography, land use, and vegetation patterns and because of their separateness or unique identity: (1) the coastal zone; (2) the coastal plain; (3) a ridge area separating the former from (4) the valley itself; (5) the rolling foothill country; and (6) high moorland landscape (Fig. 6.19). The coastal zone, attractive and popular for recreation, was itself varied according to its edge: beach, rocks, marshes, and so on (Fig. 6.20). The coastal plain was flat and extensive, with rich soil; because of its flatness it was suitable for arable farming and also suitable, topographically at least, for building and trailer parks (caravans) (Fig. 6.21). The ridge area was wooded, providing views to the coast and to the moors (Fig. 6.22). The valley included several historical monuments, battlefields, and country houses, all valuable recreation resources (Fig. 6.23). The foothills, rather more rolling, commanding fine views to the north, were predominantly used for sheep farming (Fig. 6.24). The moorland was bleak and cold, almost at the timberline, and generally without major tree cover (Fig. 6.25).

Within this framework several conspicuous landmarks were identified: volcanic plugs, distinctive land forms which can be seen for miles around; a monument on a hill; a church spire in the county town (Fig. 6.26). These were selected for their prominence and a map was prepared which showed the visibility of the landmarks. Zones from which all of the landmarks could be seen at once were plotted (Fig. 6.19). Clearly the views from such areas would be panoramic and this information was considered useful in the selection of scenic routes and the location of country parks and picnic areas.

The visual analysis indicated that the quality of the landscape was to a large extent the product of numerous skylines. Skyline zones were thus plotted as areas that should be protected from land uses, which would se-

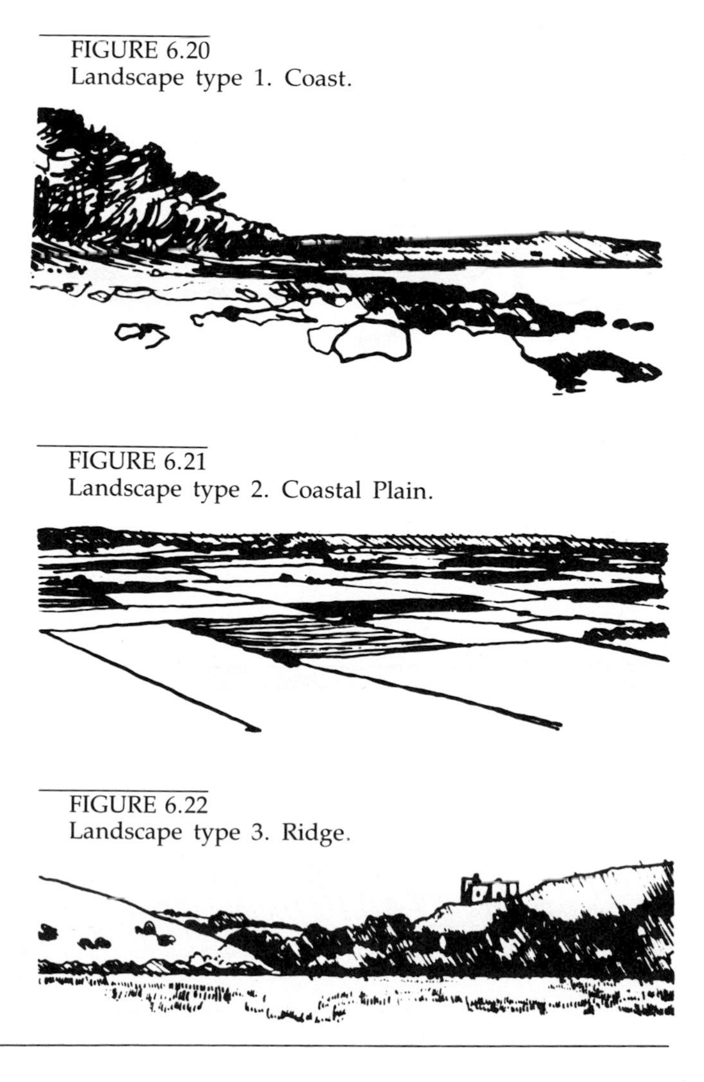

FIGURE 6.20
Landscape type 1. Coast.

FIGURE 6.21
Landscape type 2. Coastal Plain.

FIGURE 6.22
Landscape type 3. Ridge.

verely alter their character and where special requirements may be imposed to maintain it (Fig. 6.27).

The sociocultural factors were easily obtainable from maps. Land use information was supplemented with a record made by schoolchildren of the specific use of each field in a particular year. An overall picture was compiled showing woodland, pasture, and wheat and potato farming. A comparison of historical maps showed the changes in the amount of woodland that had occurred, much being added in the eighteenth and nineteenth centuries and some removed later in the trend toward larger fields. The existing landscape includes windbreak plantings, hedgerows, and plantations associated with country estates. The diversity and quantity of these was considered an ecological asset as well as an important component of the visual quality.

The landscape is intensively used for various forms of agriculture with associated small market towns and villages. In addition, there is a considerable quantity of historic and archeological sites scattered throughout the area, representing hundreds of years of settlement and use and a considerable potential for recreation. It is a humanized landscape, attractive in its contrasts and combinations of town and countryside. It is not untypical of well-used landscapes anywhere in the world. People from the cities like to visit the villages, fish in the rivers, have picnics at the seaside, and hike in the hills. Meanwhile, the landscape is a working concern, growing food and fiber. The coexistence of these two perceptions of the landscape is vital to both town and country.

The natural factors analysis began with an examination of the geology. The faults associated with the basic divisions of the landscape were no longer active. Minerals of economic value in the area were unimportant. Coal mining which had taken place in one district was no longer operational but left zones of land liable to subsidence for a period of years. A large limestone deposit located adjacent to the study area was being actively extracted and was supposed to satisfy all the predicted future needs of the cement industry. This indicated that the limestone deposits lying within the area need not be considered as potentially valuable. Road stone might be

FIGURE 6.23
Landscape type 4. Valley.

FIGURE 6.24
Landscape type 5. Foothills.

FIGURE 6.25
Landscape type 6. Moorlands.

FIGURE 6.26
East Lothian Study. Overview of landscape types from foothills to coast and showing one of the prominent topographic landmarks.

the only material to be extracted from the area and in fact its quarrying was slowly destroying one of the volcanic plugs. The geological analysis in this case was not a significant determinant of land use and the formations were all considered relatively stable.

A study of slopes, however, proved more significant (Fig. 6.28). Slopes over 25 percent were considered too steep for any building use. Mapping of slopes was carried out in relation to criteria for housing and building in general. These involved building costs and the likelihood of excessive erosion caused by construction. Thus by our selected standards, high-density housing and industry should be located on the flattest land under 2.5 percent. Medium-density housing could occur on land up to 10 percent. Single houses at low density could occur on land up to 25 percent. Mapping of these slope categories showed considerable constraints on the location of high- and medium-density housing and industry.

Climatic studies showed the amount of rainfall and the variation in its distribution within the region. As the land increased in height so did the rainfall (to 40 inches). At the coast, the rainfall was considerably less (25 inches) and the number of hours of sunshine in the year was one of the highest in the country. Cold easterly winds and sea fog also contributed to the pattern of climate. The rainfall information with other data became particularly important in the assessment of different areas of land for various forestry species.

The soil study rated the soils according to their capability for agriculture. This involves not only the soil type but other related values including the slope of the land, exposure, wind, and rainfall. Agricultural value then was rated from class 1 (best) to 7 (urbanization). The position was adopted that since good agricultural land was an invaluable resource, as much as possible should be reserved for that purpose. The Ministry of Agriculture usually was prepared to fight court battles to preserve classes 1 and 2, and on the basis of this all class 1 and 2 land was allocated for agriculture as a primary value to which all else would take second place. In this way the agriculture suitability map was derived (Fig. 6.29).

The suitability of land for economic forestry depends on the slope of the land (to facilitate operations), rainfall (different species have different optimums), soil (different species thrive best on different soil types), and elevation (colder temperatures affect the growth of certain species). All the data maps showing slope, elevation, rainfall, and soil were thus used in the production of suitability maps for several forest species considered economic in the area: beech, larch, Scots pine, and Norway spruce (Fig. 6.30).

Criteria for the motorway alignment were established. From an economic standpoint, the motorway should not interact with slopes over 2.5 percent. It should also avoid streams and flood plains. From a conservation viewpoint

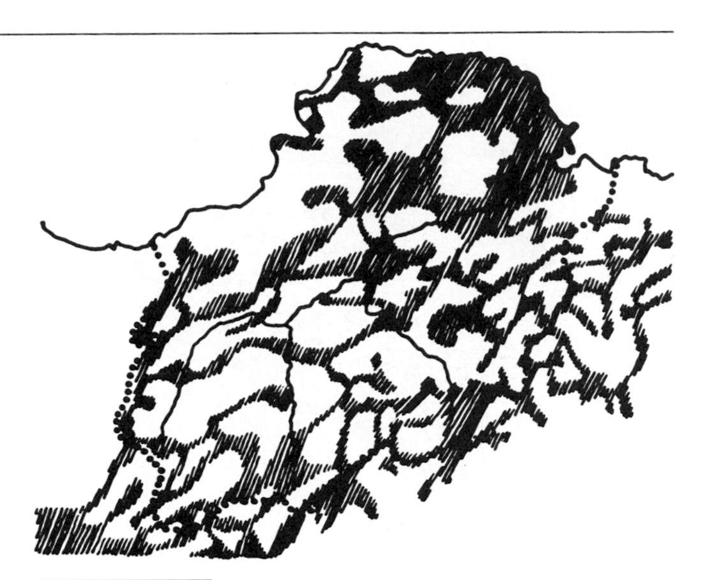

FIGURE 6.27
East Lothian Study: Skyline zones.

FIGURE 6.28
East Lothian Study: Slope analysis.

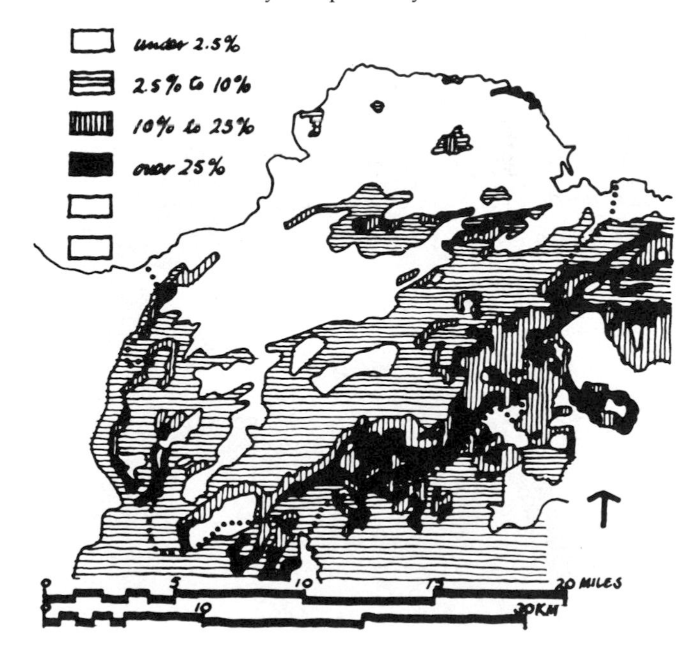

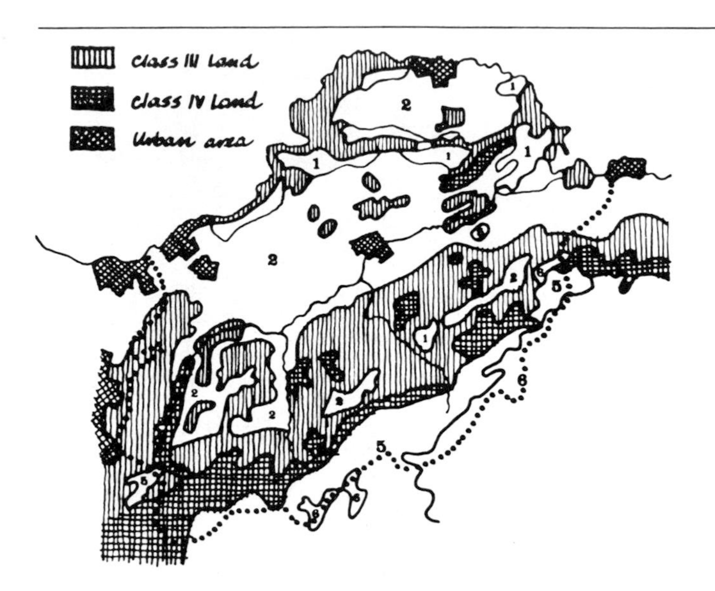

FIGURE 6.29
East Lothian Study: Agricultural suitability. **(1)** class I land, **(2)** class II land, **(5)** class V land, **(6)** class VI land.

FIGURE 6.30
East Lothian Study: Forestry suitability.

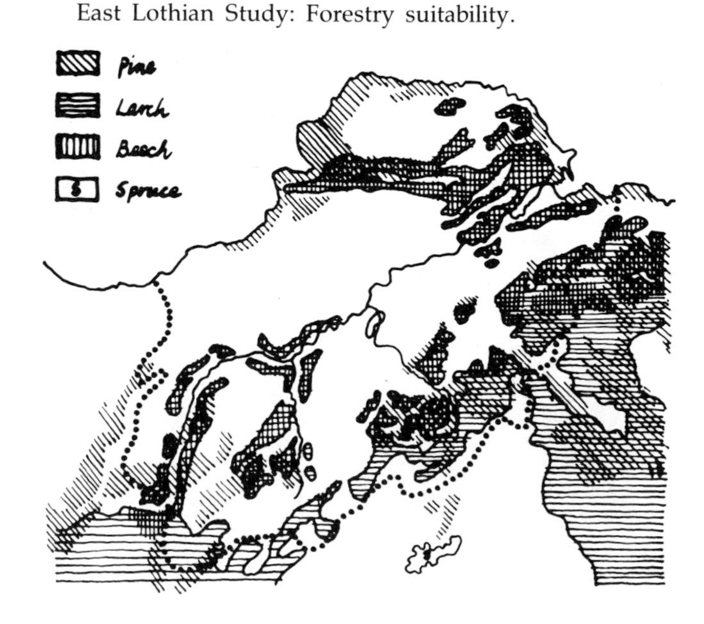

the motorway should not cross A1 or A2 agricultural land. It should not go through existing settlements and should avoid scenic areas and historic monuments. Many of the criteria applied were based on reducing the cost of construction. In selecting the route, short areas of higher value had to be sacrificed for the sake of distance. The system of overlaying constraints indicates that the route should follow the line of least resistance (Fig. 6.31). We find, however, that if the constraints are valued equally, this may mean the loss of high-quality agricultural land and disruption of farms. When this is the only constraint, longer or more costly alternatives may be proposed on the grounds that the loss of nonrenewable resources may be of longer term importance than short-term cost in cash.

A hydrology map indicated the watershed areas, water catchment and reservoirs, and flood plains of streams and rivers. Degrees of pollution were also noted. These data were useful in the recreation suitability study and also in the motorway alignment. The natural habitats were identified. The vegetation and habitat changed according to the land use and the differentiation in topography and natural environment. The various plants and animals to be found in the area were related to these habitats: marshland, sea coast, estuarine, riverine, fields, grassland, uplands, moorland, and others. This variety in habitat contributed to a richness in vegetation and wildlife.

All land with the exception of A1 and A2 agricultural land and skyline zones was considered in the housing and industry suitability studies (Fig. 6.32). The higher density, equivalent to town expansion and public housing (twenty units per acre), was permitted on remaining land with a slope of less than 2.5 percent but not where woodland occurred. The same land areas were also considered suitable for industry but with the added condition of proximity to major road and rail transportation routes. Areas with a slope of less than 10 percent, not on good agricultural land, woodland, or skylines, was considered suitable for medium-density housing (four to six units per acre). Low-density housing suitability covers virtually all the land except the skylines. A1 and A2 land was included to permit the building of farmhouses or farm workers' dwellings. The housing could go anywhere except on the skylines and slopes over 25 percent. In many cases the housing would be best situated within woodland and "absorbed" by it. Although it may appear possible from the map that the countryside could be covered with low-density housing, building would be permitted only in relation to farms or on large acreages.

A composite map for housing and industry showed the areas most suited for each use within the criteria established, and it showed areas where there were competing or alternative uses for the same land. From a visual standpoint, one area rated suitable for industry was tested to see how visible it would be from the surrounding landscape, and it was found to be relatively unseen (Fig. 6.32).

The landscape was rated in terms of recreation suitability by giving a value to squares in a kilometer grid according to the number of recreation components they contained (Fig. 6.33). These were identified as woodlands, water, architectural or historical features, and existing recreation facilities; in addition, the lower agriculture values were considered an added positive value in the rating. The squares with the most components were considered at least worthy of consideration for recreation. A further refinement of the system weighted the factors in relation to the amount of each component in the square. This produced a more sensitive and positive map with clearer definition of areas endowed with good recreational opportunities.

A composite of all the suitabilities was prepared by overlapping all the suitability maps. There were some areas where uses competed, providing alternatives, for example, recreation and mixed farming; low-density housing, recreation and mixed farming; low-density housing, recreation, and forestry. However, the criteria selected and the values decided upon actually resulted in very little conflict. Changes in criteria and values would, of course, produce different maps and possibly more conflict. The composite map is in itself not important. It should be understood that this kind of study is not a plan for the future. It is an assessment of the land and gives some potential uses of that land to be used as a basis for planning. It exposes some values that are not always understood and makes available to planners and the public a picture of what is to be lost or gained when any particular planning decision is made. The criteria adopted for any land use may vary. Interpretation of the natural factors data may also vary, but the system shows what could happen if criteria and interpretations were applied consistently and how the public sector might benefit from this procedure.

The recreation study was geared toward the selection of areas suitable for country parks. A map delineated recreation nodes. These occurred within the areas from which views of the landmarks could be obtained and coincided with the coming together of features such as rivers, footpaths, and historic sites. The location of country parks was recommended within the multiple view areas, within the low-density housing suitability areas (to permit structures), and in relation to the highest scoring recreation squares (Fig. 6.34). This is a generalized system of focusing quickly on the most likely areas. The decision to designate one or more sites for country parks depends on the demand, the policy of the county, and the availability of funds for the purpose. These areas or nodes must, of course, be analyzed in detail for final site selection, but the search need not go outside the areas of

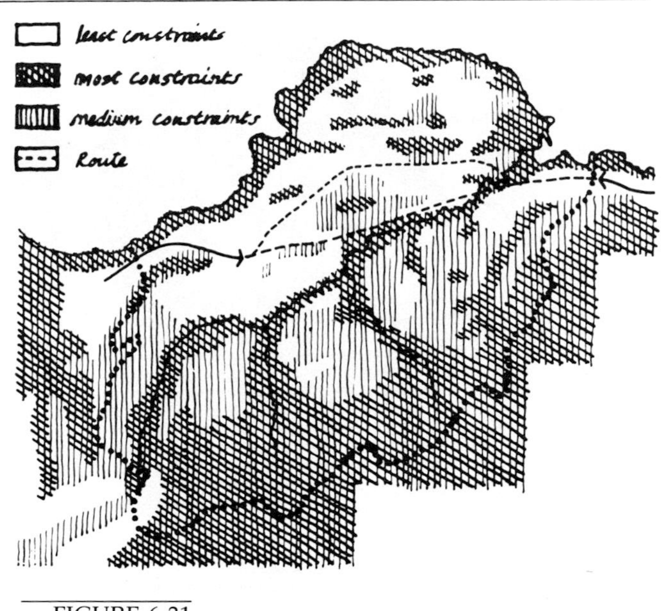

FIGURE 6.31
East Lothian Study: Motorway alignment.

FIGURE 6.32
East Lothian Study: Housing and industry suitability.

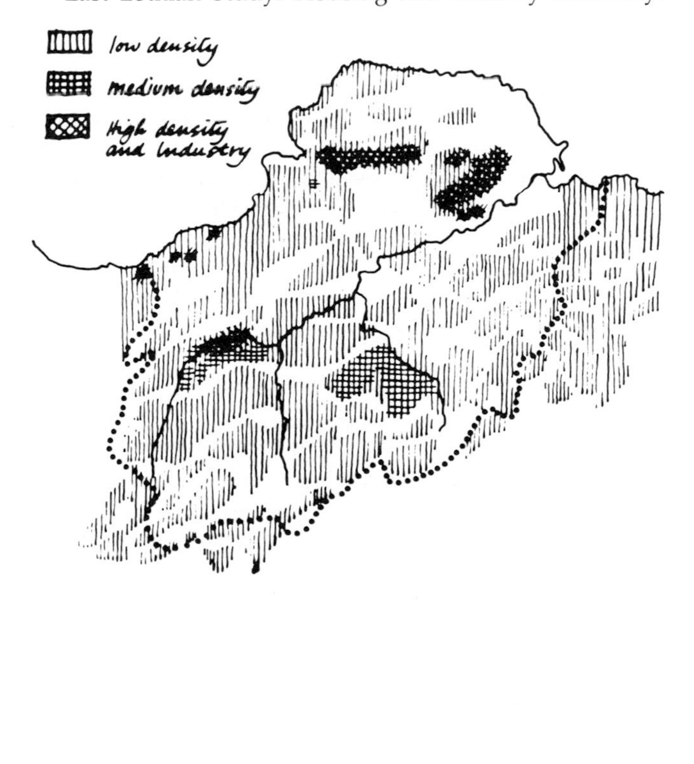

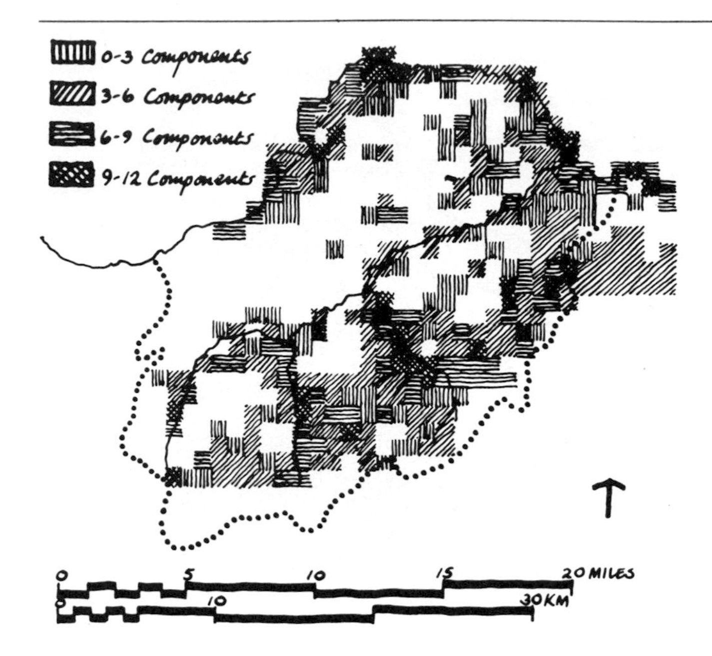

FIGURE 6.33
East Lothian Study: Recreation suitability.

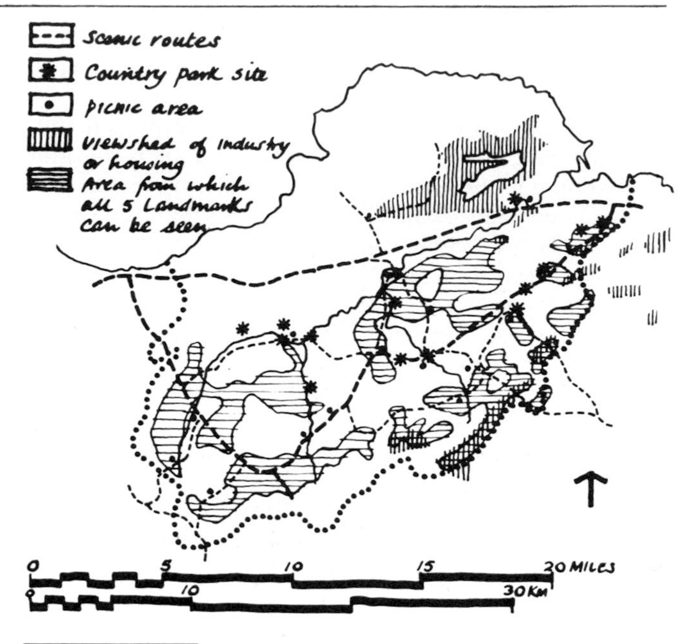

FIGURE 6.34
East Lothian Study: Map of recreation possibilities including country parks, scenic routes, and picnic areas.

highest potential. In other cases, derelict or reclaimed land might be selected on the assumption that landscape quality would be created by design and planting.

Selection of scenic routes was suggested by bringing together the existing road map, areas of good views, and the location of historic monuments. "Conservation corridors" were also proposed. These consisted of woodlands, hedgerows, and rivers connected as reserves for wildlife whose seasonal migration and food gathering involves movement within the countryside pattern.

A discussion of planning large regions of landscape in private ownership may seem idealistic. The political process involved is far from established. The process whereby land owners are persuaded that their land should be used in a certain way for the common good and the long term advantage of society, and then are compensated at public expense for any loss incurred is, as yet, not well worked out or popular. The planning laws of Great Britain and other European countries are perhaps more suited for this strategy than are those of the United States, but the costs are high and the definition of public good often is hazy at best.

LANDSCAPE PLANNING IN THE UNITED STATES

In the United States many plans and planning studies have attempted to relate the principles of landscape planning to the realities of land speculation and ad hoc development practices. Some are concerned with the future expansion of cities (Minneapolis,[13–15] Baltimore,[9] Santa Cruz Mountains[10]), others with the control of housing and recreation development in resort areas of scenic value (Lake Tahoe[16]), others with islands (Hawaii,[17] the Virgins,[18] Nantucket[19]), and others with the conservation of recreation sources (Wisconsin[20]). The principles are essentially the same in all cases: resources and landscape types are surveyed and evaluated in terms of uniqueness and

[13] Wallace, McHarg, Roberts, and Todd, *An Ecological Study for the Twin Cities Metropolitan Area* (Metropolitan Council of the Twin Cities, 1969).

[14] Wallace McHarg Associates, *Plan for the Valleys* (Philadelphia, 1963).

[15] Tito Patri, David Streatfield, and Tom Ingmire, *Early Warning System* (Berkeley: University of California, Department of Landscape Architecture, 1970).

[16] U.S. Forest Service (in cooperation with the Tahoe Regional Planning Agency), *Land Capabilities and Land Use Plan* (U.S. Department of Agriculture, 1970).

[17] Eckbo, Dean, Austin, and Williams, and Muroda, Tanaka and Itagaki, Inc., *A General Plan for the Island Kauai* (Honolulu: State of Hawaii, 1970).

[18] Ervin H. Zube, *The Islands* (Amherst: University of Massachusetts, Department of Landscape Architecture, 1968).

[19] Ervin H. Zube, *An Inventory and Interpretation of Selected Resources of the Island of Nantucket* (Cambridge: University of Massachusetts, 1966).

[20] Philip H. Lewis, *The Outdoor Recreation Plan* (Wisconsin Department of Resource Development).

impact. Some stop short at capabilities whereas others combine capabilities with socioeconomic pressures and propose optimum form for counties and urban expansion.

There are two difficulties in implementing these plans. The first is to match the administrative unit with the natural regional planning unit. The second is the question of imminent domain, always an unpopular concept, and compensation for landowners whose aspirations are in conflict with the long-term common good. Such a system in which potential land users are guided as to where they should or should not develop in terms of the larger overview of the common good appears to require sociopolitical changes and enlightenment. More difficult to accept, yet desirable even now, is the idea that in certain cases the removal of development along coasts and lakes would be in the public interest and worth the cost.

CASE STUDY 2. SEA RANCH

Sea Ranch is on the north coast of California within 3½ driving hours from San Francisco, lying in its recreation hinterland. In 1965 a developer proposed a second-home community along 16 miles of the coast and associated coast range. The building program called for an economic density to satisfy the existing demand for vacation houses. At the same time, the landscape had to be maintained visually and ecologically. Lawrence Halprin and Associates made planning recommendations for the use of the land and suitable building forms on the basis of an ecological study. It was felt that these recommendations would enhance rather than destroy the landscape, which would inevitably have been destroyed if uncontrolled growth had been permitted as seen elsewhere on the coast.

A survey and an analysis were completed. An understanding of what would be changed with the imposition of new uses plus an understanding of the nature of a second home and especially in this case an understanding of the climate led to criteria for density, location of buildings, and principles of land use and conservation.

The landscape consisted of three zones: the beach and rocky shoreline or cliffs, the ocean terrace or raised beach, and the forested hillside behind (Fig. 6.35). Windbreaks of Monterey cypress existed on the terrace, having been planted fifty years earlier for agricultural purposes. Grazing practices had kept the terraces in grassland but in places overgrazing had taken place. The hillsides were covered in mixed coniferous forests (primarily Bishop pine) within which a thick underbrush had grown as a result of strict fire control over the previous fifty years, thus increasing the fire hazard.

The soil and geology study was not particularly relevant in this case, since foundations for large structures were not considered. A few minor restrictions were revealed. There were some areas of soil erosion and some marshy places which were considered unsuitable for building.

The climatic studies had a major impact on the form and distribution of the development. On the Northern California coast, one intuitively expects fog in the summer and persistent strong winds, a certain unreliability about the weather, and considerable rainfall in winter. The study set out to determine how bad the climate really was. Would it deter people from buying land there? And if the climate was a liability, could it be ameliorated or compensated for by design and planning? Analysis revealed that this part of the coast did not in fact have as much fog as elsewhere. Aerial surveillance over a year showed the overall fog pattern tended to reach Sea Ranch last as it moved in from the ocean. This was at least a favorable finding.

The temperatures were influenced by the combined effect of sun, fog, and wind. A radiation chart expressed the heat that was available throughout the year. In spring and fall there was found to be high solar radiation. Even in the summer temperatures were relatively high. Architecturally, the designers interpreted this fact as suggesting the need for skylights and large windows which would capture as much heat as possible. This would save heating costs and ensure warmth in the house, even though it would be used only on weekends.

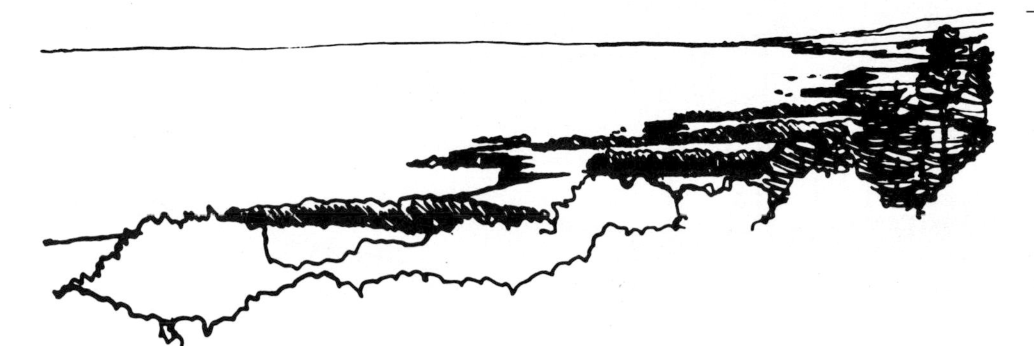

FIGURE 6.35
Sea Ranch: View showing the basic components of the landscape beach, ocean terrace, and wooded slopes.

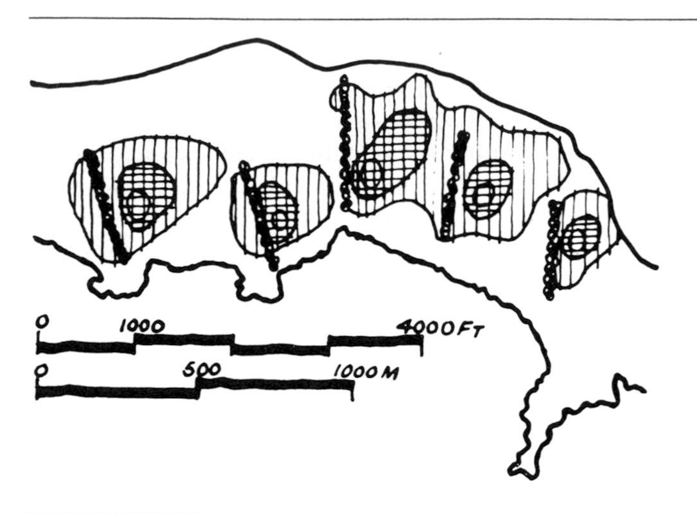

FIGURE 6.36
Sea Ranch: Diagram of shelter provided by wind breaks on ocean terrace. (See also Fig. 10.10.)

The existing shelter belts provided areas of shelter. On the lee side, zones of land were found to have wind speed reductions of up to 50 percent (Fig. 6.36). Study of the direction of the winds, their force and the possibility of providing shelter indicated that for 60 percent of the year the winds came from the northwest and were in excess of 12 miles per hour, a speed in which walking was difficult. Shelter was considered essential for any dwelling on the ocean terrace area. It was proposed that houses be oriented toward the south, with outdoor areas and parking spaces situated on the leeward side of the building. The wind-clipped cypress trees provided inspiration for the form of the demonstration houses by Esherick. Monopitched roofs, which would deflect the wind, and fences with air foils were recommended to provide sheltered open spaces and gardens (Fig. 6.37).

Olgay's Bioclimatic Chart was used to produce a table of bioclimate needs.[21] The prevailing temperature, humidity, and sun hours at Sea Ranch were compared with the ideal climate of Olgay's chart; temperatures in the 50 to 80 degree Fahrenheit range and humidity in the 40 to 70 percent range. The differences at any time of day or year were translated into the amount of cooling or heating that would be required to maintain such ideal conditions for human comfort. Additional heating to maintain comfort (warmth) was further described in terms of clothing for better understanding of the climate and what it would be like sitting out in it. The range runs from shirtsleeves and shorts to overcoats in relation to the months of the year and the times of the day. It is a vivid way to describe the climate. The conclusion was that the climate was reasonable (although not excessively warm) and would permit outdoor activity and passivity with reasonable comfort, plenty of fresh air, and absolutely no smog—an ideal climate for a vacation home. Wind and solar radiation were the two aspects of the climate of greatest importance; protection from the one and capture of the other were indicated.

The plan was prepared in 1965 (Figs. 6.38 and 6.39). The goals were to achieve a relatively high population density consistent with a habitable environment and a vacation type of life-style. The program included sites for condominiums: groups of units joined together into a larger structure, covering less land than separate homes. This allowed large expanses of open space consistent with an economic number of dwellings. This was one technique used to maintain the landscape. The program also called for single-family house lots because this was the major demand. Included were a restaurant, village center and hotel, recreation center, golf course, and air strip. It was designed as a village or community and more than just a subdivision of the land. Having regard for the requirement of conserving the quality of the landscape and coping with the natural elements, the plan proposed limited housing situated along existing hedgerows so

[21] Victor Olgay, *Design with Climate* (Princeton, N.J.: Princeton University Press, 1963).

FIGURE 6.37
Sea Ranch: Demonstration houses by Joseph Esherick.

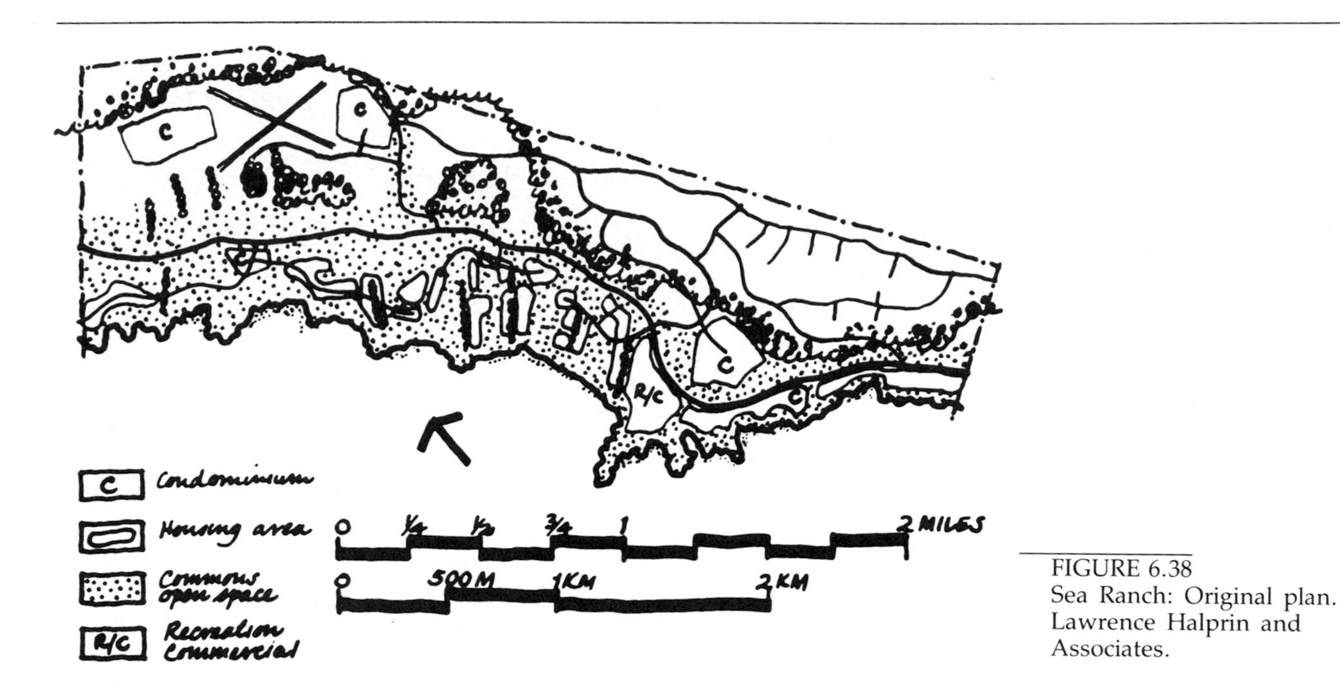

FIGURE 6.38
Sea Ranch: Original plan. Lawrence Halprin and Associates.

that dwellings would be sheltered and also relatively inconspicuous. But the meadows between these strips were designated as open space. New planting was included to create other zones of shelter. Most of the housing was proposed within the coniferous forest (with brush cleared). Views from the hillside were spectacular and the density and building codes were such that the forest cover would essentially remain intact.

The demonstration houses by Esherick and the condominium by Moore/Turnbull demonstrated the kind of architecture that was considered appropriate for the landscape and the weather. The recreation center was also designed to counteract the ill effects of the wind. Berms of earth were created and the pool and tennis courts were sunk into the ground to protect them from the wind (Fig. 6.40). The beach was reached by stairs from the upper terrace.

Sea Ranch is an example of an ecological study undertaken for a large area of land in single ownership. The results were influential architecturally and the respect for the landscape determined the distribution of building sites. The specifically ecological implications are not certain.

There are different levels of ownership. First there is total ownership (private property)—home and land within a fence. A second level is private restricted land which is owned by the individual outside house and fenced garden, but its use is restricted to natural vegetation. Third, there is common land which is owned by all the property owners in the development and is managed at their expense. Architectural quality is controlled by a design review committee.

FIGURE 6.39
Sea Ranch: Detail of development showing meadows and access to the beach.

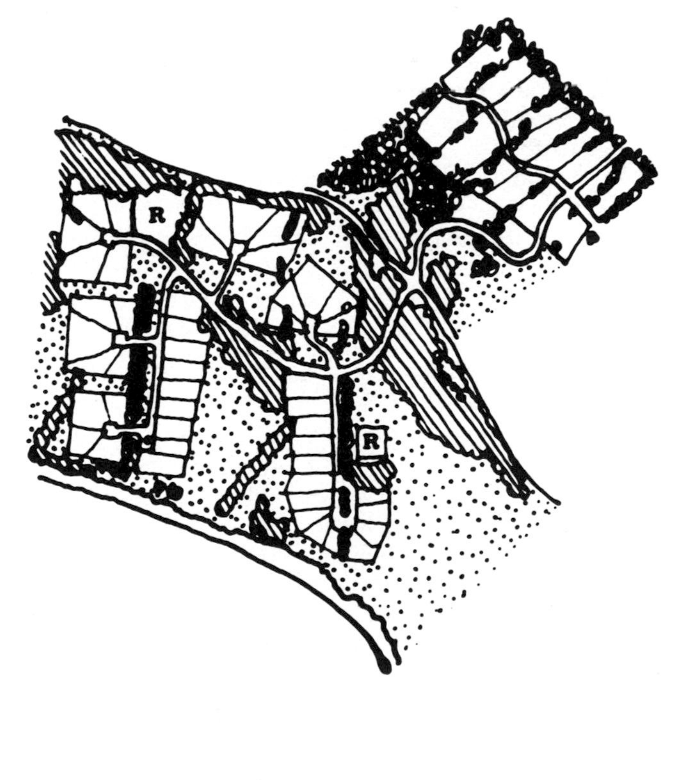

FIGURE 6.40
Sea Ranch: Recreation complex incorporating protective land form. Moore, Lyndon, Turnbull and Whitacker.

Whether or not the intent of any plan is fulfilled depends on its administration. The interpretation of the plan and policy may change as personnel changes. This occurrence is characteristic of landscape architecture in general. Landscape plans are always plans for the future by definition, and as such require a certain continuity of administration and management if the objectives are to be achieved. Like others, the Sea Ranch plan has been modified.

At another level of planning, the Sea Ranch project is controversial.

Before the project was begun, debate over whether this coast land should be in private or public ownership might have been valuable. At a time when only 300 miles of California's 1,300 miles of coastline were open to the public, a strong case could have been made for public acquisition. It is probable that if an overall study of the coast had existed in 1965, as it now does under the Coast Planning Act of 1972, these lands might have been considered a scenic and ecological resource to be managed for public use and enjoyment, recreation, conservation, or scenic easement. As it is, all building was halted while the Commission completed its plan and there has been considerable litigation as a result of it, notably concerning public access to the beach and view corridors from the public road. Be that as it may, this project is interesting because of the way in which the planning and design decisions were made in relation to the natural processes and especially the climate.

CASE STUDY 3. THE VALLEYS

A planning proposal for the Valleys, an area consisting of 60 square miles of Baltimore county lying in the development-prone hinterland of the expanding city, is described in *Design with Nature*.[22] A group of landowners who had a long-standing attachment to the landscape decided that they should attempt to control growth and change so that the inevitable demand for housing could be satisfied without the destruction of a beautiful landscape heritage. The study area was politically defined and included two streams and their valleys and a high plateau area between them.

Ian McHarg and David Wallace, who made the study, sensed the beauty of the landscape and pictured the changes that would occur under the normal subdivision procedures. It was accepted that housing should and could be situated in the landscape as part of the regional goals of the county, but it was agreed that development should be controlled to avoid loss of amenity. It was believed that guidance from the principles of soil and water conservation would indicate the most suitable way to develop the land and ensure a measure of natural beauty. It was also argued that planned growth would be as profitable as uncontrolled growth. The realization of the plan was seen as a joint venture between the public and private sectors. That is, the good will of the landowner would need to be backed up with legal county ordinance and zoning regulations.

Much of the study involves measures of change, housing costs, and the appropriate population target for the area. The proposition that observation of conserva-

[22] McHarg, *op. cit.*

tion principles can avert destruction to the landscape and ensure enhancement is perhaps the most important from the landscape planning technique point of view.

The geology and the physiographic features—slopes, vegetation, flood plains, rivers and streams, soil types, and topography—were studied. The highest values were given to two resources, water quality and soil, and their conservation. Wherever development and construction on the land would adversely affect these resources either through pollution or excessive erosion, these areas were eliminated from consideration for housing. An extensive groundwater resource (or aquifer) was found to be associated with a permeable limestone geological formation underlying the valleys. This meant that the streams and their flood plains were intimately connected with this underground resource, which provided drinking water from wells and which was also related to the river system that fed reservoirs outside of the study area. Because of the potential pollution of this water from septic tanks, and even sewers which leak to some extent, the flood plains and valley bottoms and strips of land 200 feet wide on each side of the streams running into them were considered unsuitable for any housing development. Thus the groundwater recharge area was eliminated in order to maintain water quality.

The higher plateau land between the two valleys was of less permeable geological nature and was therefore suitable for development from this and other points of view. The slopes between the valleys and plateaus presented a variety of conditions with implications for soil erosion. The slopes or valley sides tended to be largely covered with forest or deciduous woodland. The slopes varied in steepness, the steepest tending to face north. Slopes greater than 25 percent with or without forest cover were considered vulnerable to soil erosion and were eliminated from use altogether (on the recommendation of the Soil Conservation Service). The forest cover is important in conserving soil by preventing the full erosional impact of rainfall and by holding the land together with root systems. Therefore it was decided that slopes of less than 25 percent with forest cover could have a housing density limit of one house per 3 acres. This would ensure that the construction of houses and access roads would have a limited impact on the forest and thus on erosion. Slopes under 25 percent without forest vegetation would be prohibited for development, at least until such areas were planted with forest and the trees reached a degree of maturity. Portions of the plateau were forested. In these areas the density was limited to one house per acre. This ensured the maintenance of a thinned forest. Elsewhere on the plateau land, any density would be permitted provided it was marketable; even high-rise apartment towers with low groundcover were situated at several strategic sites.

A density or residential zoning plan was developed from the application of these principles and criteria of

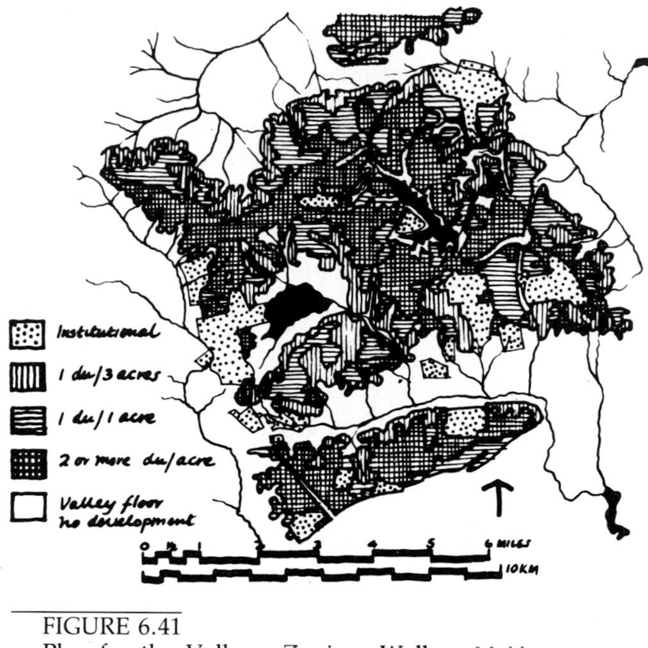

FIGURE 6.41
Plan for the Valleys: Zoning. Wallace McHarg Associates (1963).

FIGURE 6.42
Plan for the Valleys. Application of zoning principle at the scale of a project. Based on a study by Lindsay Robertson and Narendra Juneja.

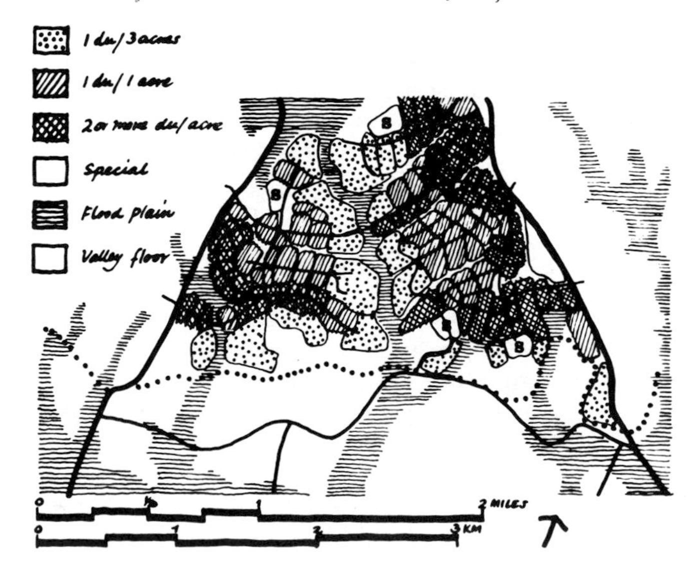

water quality and soil conservation (Fig. 6.41). From this a development plan was made with shopping and cultural nodes at hamlets, villages, and a town center. Two lakes were recommended as part of a water and soil conservation program. The valleys were essentially left alone for agricultural, recreational, and institutional use. It can be seen that the important visual features which gave the area its unique and attractive quality were in the process more or less conserved. The housing program was accommodated using 4,500 fewer acres of land than would be needed under the conventional land subdivision standards and techniques. At the same time, the essential landscape character was maintained. It was projected that by the year 2000, 27,000 new houses would be accommodated (according to the plan) on 17,000 acres. Cluster housing was recommended. The densities of the upper land would range from one house per acre to an average of four houses per acre. This is perhaps twice the density expected in the uncontrolled growth pattern. Variations in housing types and densities were recommended not only as a means to accommodate the program but also as a desirable mixture permitting a heterogeneous community.

A nonprofit corporation was recommended to control the development and to distribute the cash return from the land so that those whose land was limited in use would not lose. Some new zoning was needed at a county level: for example, 3-acre zoning for the wooded slopes, 25-acre zoning for the valleys, and natural resource zoning (providing for 200 feet on each side of every stream to be free of construction). These large scale zoning implications also had direct input to the operations of a developer of property. The physiographic features and the criteria for housing density associated with them could provide a zoning plan at any scale. Analysis of the landscape or site would reveal the optimum building program and identify areas to be reserved for conservation (Fig. 6.42).

This plan represents a long-term approach to economic development and planning. A number of landowners are involved but they are mostly owners of large holdings who have a common goal: to try to maintain the natural beauty of the area. They probably intend to stay on during and after development. It is thus a unique situation. But it is a case study which reveals very clearly the form that results from planning based on an understanding of the natural processes and an interest in conservation.

LANDSCAPE PLANNING AND ENVIRONMENTAL IMPACT

Landscape planning can be seen as a positive process to fit certain land uses to the most suitable land for the purpose and as a negative process designed to prevent ecological loss or waste of natural resources such as good agricultural soil or clean water. Its implementation would appear to be best suited at government levels (local, county, and state) in the development of a land use policy supported by local powers and by the resources for compensation where necessary (Fig. 6.43).

Whether or not there is an operational system of planning which guides development and land use, it is always important that the specific impact of any project be assessed in terms of its site and detailed ecological relationships. Such project impact assessment is conducted by means of a finer grain of data than those by which land use policy is set. It is possible therefore that even within areas designated as appropriate, a project may result in unforeseen and unacceptable side effects. These may require special design or technical solutions or, if the impact is deemed unacceptable, the project may have to be abandoned or placed elsewhere. This process of assessment is an essential component of good site planning, which may also be required by law.

The National Environmental Policy Act (1969) requires all federal agencies and certain industries which are licensed by the federal government to submit a detailed statement on the environmental impact of each new project or recommendation. The act directs these agencies to "utilize a systematic interdisciplinary approach which will ensure the integrated use of the natural and social sciences and the environmental design arts in planning and decision making which may have an impact on man's environment." They are also enjoined to develop methods whereby the currently unquantifiable environmental amenities and values may be included with technical considerations in the assessment of impact.

In addition to addressing itself to the general question of environmental impact, each report is required to specify any adverse environmental effects that are unavoidable should the proposal be implemented. It must also explore alternatives to the proposed action, including the alternative of "no project." It must show the extent to which resources will be lost, and is required to show the relationship between local short-term uses of the environment and the maintenance and enhancement of long-term productivity.

The State of California extended the purpose and intent of the national legislation to the state level with the California Environmental Quality Act (1970). This required all state agencies to prepare environmental

FIGURE 6.43
An oil tank farm, a steel plant, subdivision and shopping center in ill-planned juxtaposition with each other and with the natural resources of the shoreline and saltwater marsh. The tree-covered peninsula was scheduled to be transformed into harbor facilities for the steel works. Only a change in world markets saved it from this fate and a conservationists' struggle saved it from some equally unsuitable commercial venture. It is now part of a regional park system. The objective of landscape planning is to take the chance out of land use decisions and to match uses with the land most suitable for that use without loss of unique and valuable amenities and resources. Photograph by William A. Garnett (1966).

impact statements and, most significantly, as a result of a California Supreme Court ruling in the Friends of Mammoth case, required private developers of projects with significant effect to do the same. These were included, it was argued, because by virtue of local building permits they were, in fact, authorized by the government.

The purpose and requirements of the two acts are essentially the same. However, the California act includes an additional requirement to assess the extent to which the project will induce population growth.

A major difficulty lies in the methods by which the impact is assessed. Guidelines have been prepared in the form of a matrix which includes a list of environmental activities that might occur as part of or as the result of the proposed project and a list of existing environmental factors and conditions that might be affected by the activities.

The activities list is lengthy, including activities involved in construction as well as the end product. Ten categories enumerate every possible form of impact: those resulting from waste disposal, chemical treatment, accidents, transportation systems, resource renewal, processing industries, resource extraction, land alteration, construction, and modifications to the existing ecosystem.

The existing factors inventory is divided into three sectors: natural qualities, cultural qualities, and ecological relationships. The first is concerned with a listing of all earth, water, atmospheric, and biological resources and the natural processes of landscape evolution; the second with land use, ownership, and taxation, population distribution, and agricultural productivity. Transportation, pressures for change, and social factors such as life-style, comfort, enjoyment, and privacy are also included. Finally, the ecological relationships are concerned with food chains, plant succession, eutrophication, and wildlife habitats.

The matrix relates the two sets of information. The environmental activities involved in the project are checked and the existing factors on which the activities will have an impact are cross-checked. The third stage is the assessment of the magnitude of the impact. This is to be described as low, moderate, or significant.

Once the impact statement is completed, it accompanies the project through the usual agency review procedures. In the case of a private development, it would be reviewed by the appropriate planning commission. In addition, there is provision for public hearings on the report before the final decisions are made.

In principle, the concept of environmental impact statements is excellent. Questions of content and the organization of the content remain to be clarified. So, too, the question of who prepares the reports requires examination. The agency making the proposal is required to prepare the report or cause it to be prepared. Finally, the individual project impact statement procedure can in no way preempt long-term planning in which the cumulative effect of a series of projects is seen in a regional context. The two are complementary and are both essential in fulfilling the goals of the National Environmental Policy Act: "To create and maintain conditions under which man and nature can exist in harmony and fulfill the social, economic and other requirements of present and future generations of Americans."

SUGGESTED READINGS

Anderson, Paul F., *Regional Landscape Analysis.*

Bates, Marston, *The Forest and the Sea,* esp. pp. 246–262, "Man's Place in Nature."

Bates, Marston, *Man in Nature,* esp. pp. 94–104, "Ecology and Economics."

Belknap, Raymond, and John Furtado, *Three Approaches to Environmental Resource Analysis.*

Canter, Larry, *Environmental Impact Assessment.*

Colvin, Brenda, *Land and Landscape,* Ch. 17, pp. 254–258, "The Living Landscape."

Crowe, Sylvia, *Landscape of Power.*

Crowe, Sylvia, *Landscape of Roads.*

Crowe, Sylvia, *Tomorrow's Landscape.*

Darling, F. Fraser, *Wilderness and Plenty.*

Darling, F. Fraser and John P. Milton, eds., *Future Environments for North America.*

Dasmann, Raymond, *Environmental Conservation.*

Dickert, Thomas, ed., *Environmental Impact Assessment.*

Elsner, Gary, and Richard Smardon, eds., *Our National Landscape, A Conference on Applied Techniques for Analysis and Management of the Visual Resource.* 1979. U.S.D.A. Forest Service. Pacific Southwest Forest Range Station, Berkeley, California.

Fabos, Julius, et al., *Model for Landscape Resource Assessment.*

Fairbrother, Nan, *New Lives, New Landscapes.*

Forest Service, U.S. Department of Agriculture, *National Forest Landscape Management,* Vol. 2, Ch. 1, "The Visual Management System." Agriculture Handbook Number 462, 1974.

Hackett, Brian. *Landscape Planning.*

International Union for Conservation of Nature and Natural Resources, *Towards a New Relationship Between Man and Nature in Temperate Lands,* 1967.

Lassey, William, *Planning in Rural Environments.*

Lewis, Philip H., *Regional Design for Human Impact.*

Litton, R. Burton, "Aesthetic Dimensions in the Landscape," in *Natural Environments,* by John Krutilla, Johns Hopkins University Press, Baltimore, 1972.

Litton, R. Burton, *Forest Landscape Description and Inventories—A Basis for Land Planning and Design.* Pacific Southwest Forest and Range Experiment Station, Berkeley, California, 1968.

Litton, R. Burton, "Landscape and Aesthetic Quality."

Lovejoy, Derek, ed., *Land Use and Landscape Planning,* 2nd edition.

Marsh, William, *Environmental Analysis for Land Use and Site Planning.*

McHarg, Ian, *Design with Nature,* pp. 7–17, "Sea and Survival," pp. 79–93, "A Response to Values," pp. 127–151, "The River Basin."

McHarg, Ian, "Ecological Determinism," in *Future Environments for North America,* Frank Darling, ed., 1966.

Odum, Eugene P., *Fundamentals of Ecology,* pp. 419–447, "Applied Ecology."

Ortolano, Leonard, *Environmental Planning and Decision Making.*

Patri, Tito, David C. Streatfield and Thomas J. Ingmire, *Early Warning System.*

Progressive Architecture, May 1966, "Sea Ranch."

Rau, John, *Environmental Impact Analysis Handbook.*

Sears, Paul B., *Life and Environment.*

Sears, Paul B., *Where There is Life,* esp. pp. 214–216, "Reading the Landscape."

Simonds, John O., *Earthscape—A Manual of Environmental Planning.*

Tetlow, R. J., and S. Sheppard, *Visual Resources of the Northeast Coal Study Area,* 1977.

Thomas, William L., ed., *Man's Role in Changing the Face of the Earth,* pp. 453–469, "Environmental Changes through Forces Independent of Man," by Richard J. Russell; pp. 471–481, "The Process of Environmental Change by Man," by Paul B. Sears.

Twiss, Robert, David Streatfield, and Marin County Planning Department, *Nicassio: Hidden Valley in Transition.* San Rafael, California, 1969.

Way, Douglas S., *Terrain Analysis.*

Whyte, William H., *The Last Landscape.*

Zube, Ervin H., ed., *An Inventory and Interpretation of Selected Resources of the Island of Nantucket.*

Zube, Ervin H., ed., *The Islands: Selected Resources of the United States Virgin Islands,* 1968.

Zube, Ervin H., et al., *Landscape Assessment.* Dowden, Hutchinson and Ross, Stroudsburg, Pennsylvania, 1975.

SITE PLANNING

7

An understanding of landscape at the regional scale is an essential prerequisite to smaller scale site planning and detailed landscape design. Chapter 6 considered the relationship between the site and the larger ecosystem and the importance of evaluating the environmental impact which a development will bring to it. Conversely, many of the criteria for land use in regional land use planning should be based on an understanding of construction and grading techniques used in site planning and the optimum criteria for site planning and community form.

SITE ANALYSIS AND INTERPRETATION

To the real estate operator, a site is a parcel of land, a building lot with legal dimensions and boundaries, slopes, and sometimes very obvious distinctive features. Yet, although parcels of land may look similar on a map or subdivision plot plan, each has in fact differences (Fig. 7.1). Such differences in location, topography, and shape, and amenities are recognized and make land more or less valuable as a result. Buildable land closely associated to major transportation routes and sources of labor is clearly suited for industrial development. An island in a river commanding riverscape vistas and having access to water and water sports differs considerably from a lot in the urban flatlands of an average city and will be priced accordingly. Subdivisions and communities are named for amenities—Thousand Oaks, Lone Pine, Redwood Shores, and so on—and the sensitive developer is careful not to destroy the amenity, which is reflected in the cost of the houses and lots.

The matching of a given program for a project (school, subdivision, college campus, and so on) with a suitable site is a function of site analysis. Site selection may be determined by a comparative analysis of several available sites for the same predetermined program. Factors of importance include the location of the site within the region, its accessibility, its relationship to shops, industry, transportation, and so on, depending on the proposed use. Others will be concerned with the ability of the land to accommodate the proposed program. Which site can best satisfy the requirements?

Occasionally site analysis is carried out to determine what a parcel of land is best suited for. In this case the program is a direct reflection of the site's amenities and potential within its regional, social, and ecological context.

Whichever way the site and its programs are brought together, further analysis precedes planning and design. The level of detail depends on the nature of the program (simple or complex) and the type of site (urban or rural). An inventory and interpretation of the site's characteristics and its relationship with adjoining land will provide determinants of form, constraints, and opportunities for the location of buildings and the conservation of amenities.

In site analysis there are two important sets of factors: those established through reference to regional characteristics and those that are unique to the specific site. Regional factors include climate, vegetation zone, social organization and tradition, local government regulations, historical background, neighborhood provision of parks and playgrounds, and availability of sewage, water, and other services. All of these have an influence on a site and what can or should be done with it.

In the site analysis of a specific site there are two phases. A research phase, in which all relevant site data, maps, and other information are assembled and drawn to the same scale. Second is a site assessment phase in which visual values and relationships, feelings, and moods are recorded. With the establishment of a detailed program indicating building sites required and the dimension and requirements of other land uses to be included, the site planning process can begin. Most of the considerations in site planning have economic significance. In terms of development costs, the site plan should be efficient without sacrificing unique features of the landscape. The analysis and evaluation is directed to these considerations.

The categories of data in site analysis are similar to those for a landscape survey. The information is

FIGURE 7.1
A site has distinctive characteristics and relationships.

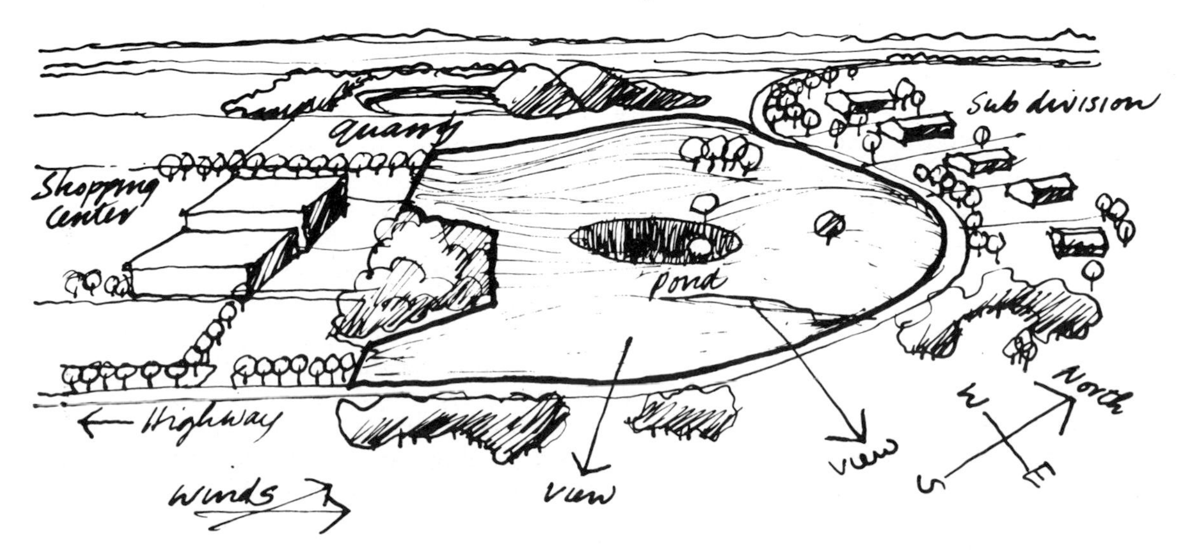

more specific, however, and its interpretation is related to the proposed project. Geology and soil, topography and slopes, drainage, vegetation, wildlife, microclimate, man-made features and existing use, visual qualities and relationships, legal regulations, and historical associations are typical headings for data collection.

Geology

Subsurface geological formations are responsible for the visible land form, the topography. In terms of building foundations, the bearing strength of near-surface geology can vary considerably over the area of a site and between sites. Hard sound rock may have a maximum bearing strength of 60 tons per square foot, whereas that of loose saturated sand–clay soil will have a capacity of 1 ton per square foot. Thus the location and depth of the various geological and soil conditions occurring on a site need to be known before large buildings are arranged and sited.

The ease with which subsurface material can be excavated is related to development costs and may be influential in plan arrangement. Surface drainage is also connected with the underground geology. The presence of aquifers will restrict the use of septic tanks and require the prevention of surface water pollution from other sources. The stability of the geological formation is also important. Geological description is important in assessing the stability of land. The dip slope and type of rock, the topographic slope, and its relationship to other strata may render an area subject to slides or slumping. Such areas are unsuited to construction.

Soil

The soil map is a mosaic of different soils, each with properties of importance in site planning. Soil is an extension of the geological formations. A soil is frequently, but not always, a direct product of the underlying rocks. Soil is an important factor in site planning in relation to stability of the land, foundation suitability, excavation, erosion hazard, drainage, and plant growth.

The stability of sloping land is a factor of soil type and its relation to geological strata. The bearing capacity of soil depends on its type and is a factor in the location of light buildings. The shrink-swell factor of certain clay soils in specific climates is another consideration of importance to the foundations of buildings and their siting.

Another economic factor may be the workability of the soil and the ease with which it can be graded. Sandy soil is heavier and less easy to work than loam. Some soils are more prone to erosion than others. This factor is determined by the texture of the soil and the slope of the land and the vegetative cover. Knowledge of the erodability of soils will determine whether or not the stable surfaces should be disturbed and if they are, what measures or controls will be needed to prevent excessive erosion. Soils vary in yet another way. The variables of texture and structure make some soils better drained than others. In a rainstorm, sandy soil will have sharp drainage whereas clay soils will quickly become waterlogged so that the rain will tend to run off the land instead of being absorbed. Thus runoff than can be expected from the surface of land will vary according to the soil. Drainage provision is therefore related to soil type.

Finally, the soil type will determine the plants that will be able to grow well and those that will not. Willows and poplars will thrive on wet clay soils, ericaceous plants on acid, and so on. The topsoil is the most important from the point of view of plant growth. It contains organic material and will have a more open structure conducive to root development, water and mineral uptake, and respiration. It has probably taken thousands of years to reach this condition of texture and fertility. Good soil is a resource that can be very easily and quickly destroyed.

The water table is the level below which the soil is saturated. It comes nearest to the surface in low-lying lands. It fluctuates seasonally and if the water table is high, basements will require special waterproofing and construction. A high water table that is connected to the sea and is saline is especially critical in the effect it will have on the growth of plants. Most plant roots will not grow in saltwater (except salt marsh types). Filled land developments at the coast or in saltwater estuaries and bays frequently encounter this problem. In this situation trees may be planted only in raised planters or watertight containers.

Topography

On the surface of the site, the topography is perhaps the most important factor to be assessed. We have already seen that the underlying geology and the slow processes of natural erosion are responsible for the form of the land and its slopes, valleys, ridges, and knolls. These topographic features may be quite influential in determining the organization of the site plan if we are to be in any way sensitive to the existing landscape characteristics. Visually, the topography and land form are important in the quality of the landscape. Site plans that intend to emphasize this quality must obviously understand the land's structure and pattern so that whatever changes are made can be done in the spirit of the original. In addition, the topographic survey will reveal badly drained areas and natural drainage channels. It will also show places that have good views and parts of the site which are visible or hidden from any selected point within or outside its boundaries.

The way in which different parts of the land can be used is a function of the land's slope and/or the ease with which it can be altered. The economic arrangement and location of buildings will also be influenced by slope. In general, building costs increase as the slopes become steeper. The existing slopes will indicate the minimum gradients of roads and paths that would be possible without grading. A map of the site with the land categorized according to its slope is a quick way in which the consideration of slope alone will be seen to organize the site plan. The categories of slope used in such a slope map will depend on the land uses being considered and the maximum permissible slopes selected for each use. Slopes under 4 percent appear quite flat but have positive drainage and are suitable for a variety of uses: building and sports fields, for example. Slopes between 4 and 10 percent can accommodate roads and pathways with little modification. For economic reasons, 6 percent might be selected as the maximum slope for housing at high densities. Slopes greater than 10 percent are considered steep, unfavorable for roads and paths without grading, and suited best for free play area and planting. A slope of 15 percent is considered a maximum for vehicular routes, and 25 percent is considered a maximum for lawn areas to be cut by machinery. For erosion control reasons, 25 percent might be the steepest land that could be altered. Topography also determines natural drainage patterns of the site. These should be kept operational if possible and buildings and structures should avoid natural swales unless the whole site is to be restructured.

Vegetation

The next aspect of site analysis is the vegetation. It is essential to record the plants that exist on the land and their maturity and health, important factors in determining whether to save particular trees and shrubs. Existing vegetation may provide protection from adjacent land uses and its conservation may therefore be important in maintaining a buffer from noise, airborne pollutants, or unpleasant views. The fire hazard nature of vegetation is also an important factor where new construction is planned. The erosion control capability of existing vegetation is vital in maintaining the stability of the land's surface. The type of existing vegetation together with the topography may be very important in the definition of the site quality and spatial relationships. Vegetation also gives a clue to the nature of the soil and the microclimate of the site. On large sites, variations in vegetation may exist between slopes with different orientation; this may be a reflection of available moisture, temperature, solar radiation, wind, and so forth. Those plants that are clearly growing well on the site provide an indication for the selection of new planting in site planning and design.

Wildlife

In association with vegetation, there is a wildlife population. The position of the site and its vegetation within the larger context of the world of insects, birds, and mammals should be carefully considered, especially in rural situations, before existing vegetation is removed or changed.

Climate

Each site has a general climate it shares with the region. These climatic factors have a general influence on architecture, site planning, and design. For example, excessive rainfall or long periods of high temperatures and sunshine suggest the need for covered walkways and shading. Frost and snow conditions indicate that the gradients on streets and sidewalks should be minimal.

The microclimate which is specific to the site is composed of variations to the general climate. It is created by topography, plants and vegetative cover, exposure to winds, elevation above sea level, and the relationship of the site to large water bodies and tall buildings. Microclimate information is not always available. Accurate measurements need to be taken at least over one year. If less time is available, some microclimate effects can be deduced from observation. Plants that show evidence of windshear indicate the direction of prevailing winds and differences in its effect within the site. The exposure and orientation of slopes can be used to infer probable conditions of warmth and sunlight, and the natural distribution of

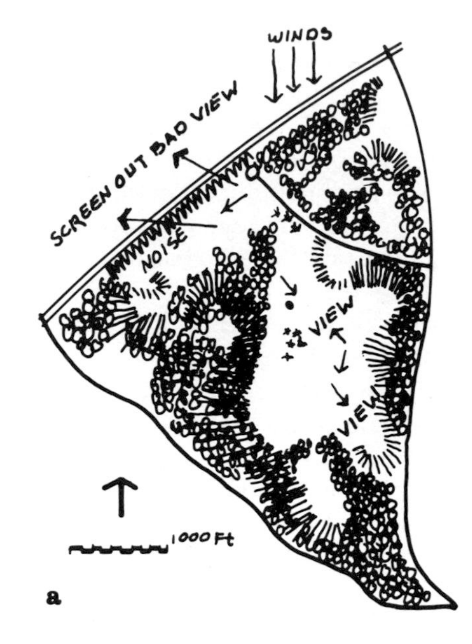

FIGURE 7.2
The site planning process is one in which a program for development is fitted onto an area of land of adequate size in such a way that it works efficiently and the characteristics of the site are expressed. These diagrams expressing four stages in the process are based on schematic drawings for a university campus for 5,000 students provided by David Gates. **(a)** The site—conditions, features, and relationship. **(b)** Evaluation of the site in terms of developable land. **(c)** Program requirements placed on the site with provision for expansion. **(1)** first phase, **(2)** second phase, **(P)** parking, **(S)** service. **(d)** The site plan.

vegetation may substantiate this. Sources of industrial pollution, dust, and sound can be specifically identified.

In addition, shade patterns caused by buildings and trees create microclimatic variations in temperature. Exposure and shelter are conditions of the site that also can be recorded. These factors are important in design, for they may be used to advantage or steps may be required to ameliorate their effects. The microclimate is an important factor in the way and extent to which the outdoor areas can be used. The selection of plant materials and their use to create more favorable microclimates in a generally unfavorable climate is a design response within the realms of site planning. Chapter 10 deals in more detail with the implications of climate in site planning and environmental design.

Existing Features

Frequently sites have existing features or buildings or are already in use. Buildings, roads, sewage systems, underground pipes and cables, the access to the site from public roads, and all other inanimate givens of the site which reflect its past and present use and which may form part of the plan for its future constitute essential data.

Social Factors

Related to this set of details are factors that affect the site but are invisible on it. These include, for example, building codes and development regulations which may vary from city to city or county to county. There may be other legal aspects such as rights of way and easements. To these should be added any historical associations or traditions that might legitimately influence the choice of materials or the design of the land. The site itself may have regional significance.

In addition, the concerns and life-style of the people affected by a site planning proposal require attention. There may be an existing population or a new one generated by the project. In either case, the goals of the program, developed by an economist, may be at odds with the needs and the aspirations of ordinary people. The program itself, then, may need analysis and discussion. The most responsible landscape architect will accept this challenge.

Visual Quality

Finally, there should be a visual analysis to record views and vistas that are attractive and adjacent areas that should be screened out. The color of the soil and the existing vegetation, the typical pattern of light and shade, the sky and clouds, the intensity of the sunshine, and the spatial characteristics of the landscape are factors worthy of note. The most successful design will be the one that is sensitive to these qualities. The intention is twofold: first, to develop the program with visually pleasing relationships within the site itself and, second, to fit the project harmoniously into the surrounding environment.

All these site dimensions and characteristics—the rocks and soil, the topography formed by them, the vegetative cover and associated wildlife, the climate

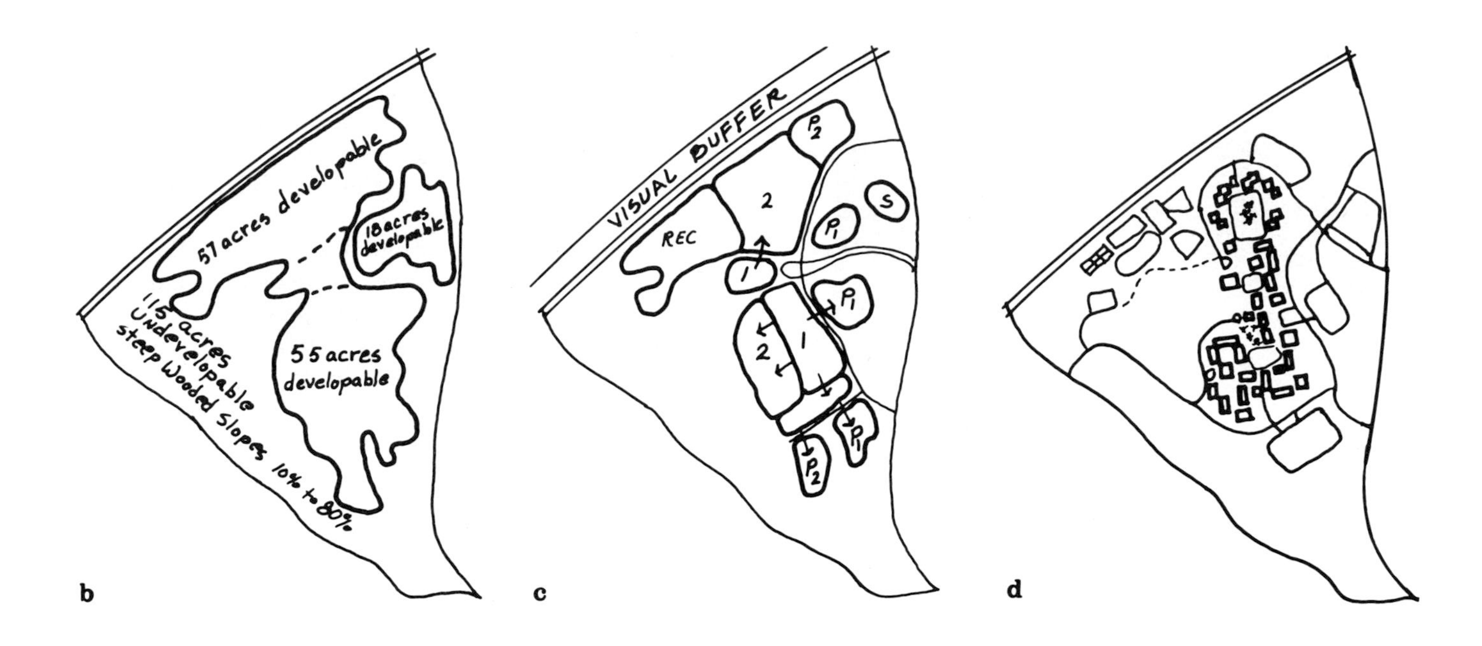

and microclimate, the man-made features, the legal regulations, the visual quality, and the historical association—constitute the site analysis. It is a complex set of information, tangible and intangible, objective and subjective varying in type and emphasis depending on the site's context: urban, suburban, or rural. At the same time, we may have a complex program for the development of the site. It is the bringing together of these two and the resolution of conflicts between them which is the process known as site planning (Fig. 7.2).

SITE PLANNING

Site planning may be thought of as a compromise between the adaptation of the site to fit the program and the adaptation of the program on account of the site. In joint ventures with architects and planners, it is important that the landscape architect be involved from the start of the project. The program and the site may be thought of as two sets of forces: one the site, which strives to express itself, its uniqueness; the other the uses in the program, which also have a generic form-giving process of their own.

Site planning is the process whereby the requirements of the program are provided, located, and connected to each other and to the outside world with minimum destruction of the site (if it has physical attributes), with imagination, and with sensitivity to the implications of the site analysis. The result must be, not only workable, but also easily maintained and serviced and (not the least) attractive to look at and be in. The extent to which the program and its physical manifestation eliminate the natural conditions of the site depends largely on whether the site has these conditions in the first place and second, on whether the program is too ambitious for the land available. Third may be a philosophical question: should the designer choose to remodel the site completely by giving total emphasis to the generation of form from the program (Fig. 7.3)? On the other hand, should the designer maintain an almost religious attitude to the land, basing the form and layout entirely on the utmost conservation of the original site features (Fig. 7.4)? A middle ground attitude is the most usual and

FIGURE 7.3
Air Force Academy, Colorado, in which the program was the prime generator of form.

FIGURE 7.4
House designed by Frank Lloyd Wright, Jr. built around and incorporating an existing tree.

appropriate. The site and the program should be combined and manipulated to produce qualities that neither alone would present. The interaction of the program with the site will result in a land use plan. This will show that the program can be physically accommodated on the site, that there is a system of circulation connecting the use areas and buildings, and how the project is physically related to the surrounding environment.

Each item in the program will have a set of criteria. Playing fields and courts are the most specific. The required area, surface, orientation, and microclimate are objective. The criteria for other outdoor uses such as picnic areas, flower gardens, and public plazas are more flexible. But optimum sizes, configurations, and climates can be stated and then provided. Where these and other features of the program are located is a function of the site characteristics that fulfill the criteria and the relationships that may be called for in the program for efficiency and servicing. As well as connecting elements of the plan, it is also appropriate to think in terms of separating uses that are incompatible. Circulation may be of several types, for example, auto, bicycle, and pedestrian. The directness of such circulation is a matter of function and economics.

In site planning we are involved then with the diagrammatic connections between buildings and outdoor space and with the arrangement of elements and allocation of areas for a variety of space needs and functions, all within the limits of a single comprehensive site and its program for development or change. The basis of this process is the resolution of conflicts. A conflict occurs when two functions, or needs, or uses, or systems are in opposition. Conflicts may already exist in the environment or may result from the imposition of one system on another. It may therefore be said that a design problem exists only when there is a conflict. Interrelationships between specific problems or conflicts occur when the solution of one affects the solution of another.

Problems or conflicts in site planning originate from two main areas of inquiry and the web of interactions which result. First we have the proposed or actual functions of buildings or uses of land. These may be called human factors. The scale may be that of a family of four or five and their dwelling and garden space, or that of a junior college campus or large comprehensive school with thousands of students and a variety of buildings and space needs. The second area of inquiry is the specific site or landscape, its relationships with adjacent land use, and its unique qualities of slope, soil, vegetation, microclimate, and so forth. These may be called the land factors and they vary from those found in a piece of wild coastline to those characteristic of a few blocks of a particular city.

Conflicts may exist entirely within the area of human factors. For example, where both groups are to be accommodated, a desire by older people for quiet and repose in outdoor space is likely to conflict with teenagers' preference for active sports, loud music, crowds, and spontaneity. Or conflicts may occur between human factors and land factors. For example, the exposure of a site to strong prevailing summer winds could conflict with a level of human comfort associated with outdoor relaxation. Further, conflicts may exist or be initiated entirely within the area of land factors. For example, we may regard excessive soil erosion or landslides as a conflict resulting from the interaction of a series of natural variables: slope, vegetable cover, and rainfall.

FIGURE 7.5
Glass windscreen providing shelter but still maintaining the view.

Another simple example may indicate the possible interrelationship of problems. The solution to the wind exposure difficulty can be solved to some extent by locating a shelter planting or fence in the appropriate place. But if a superb view also happens to lie in the direction of the prevailing winds, as at Sea Ranch (see page 123), we will have succeeded in negating an important quality in the enjoyment of the place. By grouping this requirement or problem statement with the first, we could arrive at a solution incorporating glass screens to break the wind, maintaining the view at the same time, although this might not be the only possibility (Fig. 7.5). This is simply a method of organizing the design process in such a way that all aspects will be taken into account in the production of form, which can thereby be emancipated from preconceived and arbitrary notions.

At this stage, site planning and detailed design begin to interact and merge. The site plan, once formulated, must eventually be implemented and it can be seen that the possibility of resolving conflicts at the detailed level affects the form of the site plan. This is the subject of Chapter 8.

The following examples will show how the site and the program are manipulated in the site planning process and the way in which overall concepts for a project are integrated with the process.

CASE STUDY 1. FOOTHILL COLLEGE

Foothill Junior College is a two-year community college for 3,500 students and also serves as a center for civic and cultural activities. Foothill College was designed in 1959 by the architects Kump Marsten and Hurd working with Sasaki, Walker, Landscape Architects. The designers were confronted with 122 acres situated in the east-facing foothills of the coastal range in Los Altos, California. Topographically, the site included two small hills separated by a ravine. The surrounding landscape consisted of a bowl-shaped form that was then in transition from orchard and agricultural use to suburban residential development (Fig. 7.6).

In addition to the building program which specified requirements for classrooms, laboratories, library, theater, gymnasium, sports field, student union, and administration building, the Board of Trustees stated general conceptual design criteria: (1) the scheme should be a solution related to the background and tradition of the area and (2) the scheme should avoid rigid formality or obvious geometric discipline yet produce an air of quiet dignity and sophistication appropriate to a college.

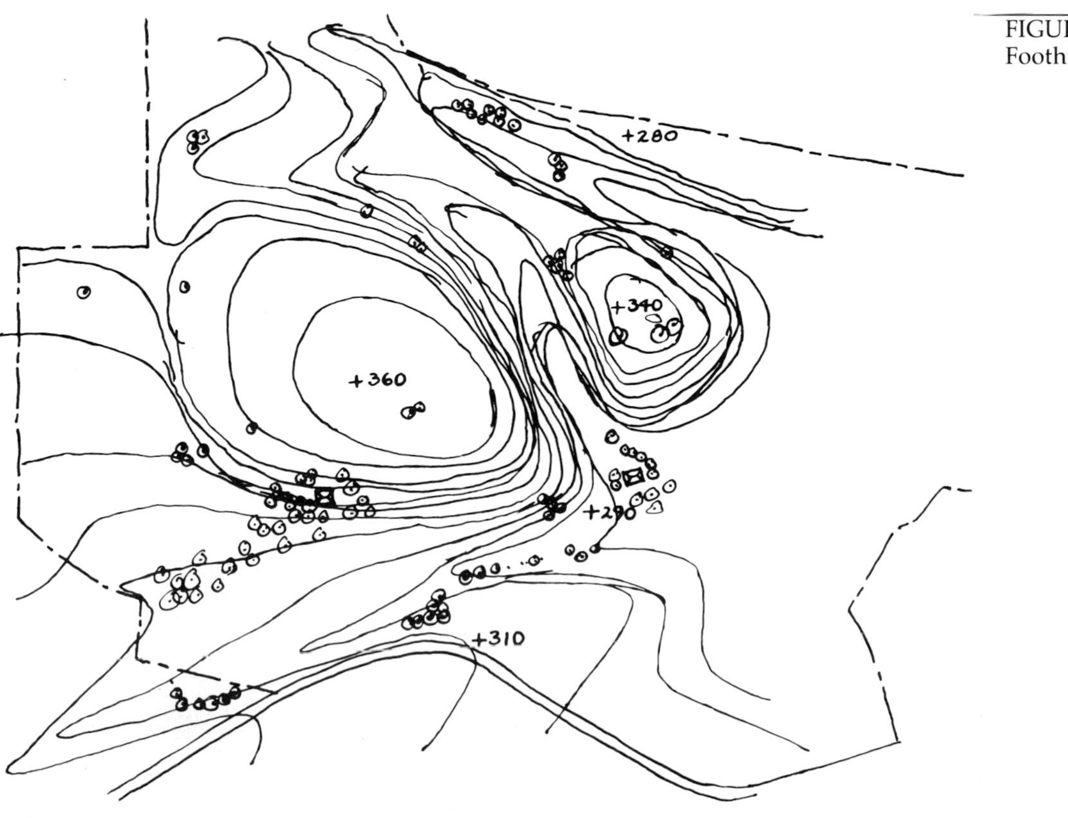

FIGURE 7.6
Foothill College: Original site.

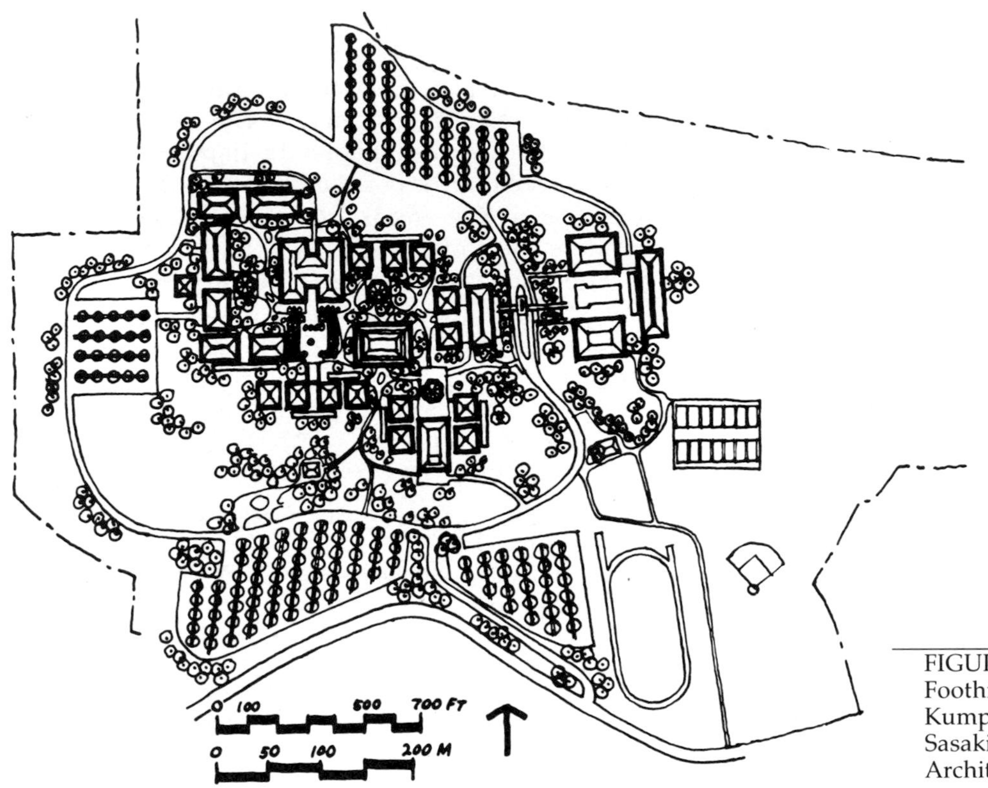

FIGURE 7.7
Foothill College (1959). Designed by Kump, Marsten and Hurd, Architects. Sasaki, Walker Associates, Landscape Architects.

Within the constraints of site and program a number of basic alternative solutions were possible. The topography could be flattened, the ravine filled, so that the college and its considerable parking facilities could be situated on flat land. On the other hand, parking lots could be situated on the high area in the center with the buildings below and around them, or the reverse. The latter arrangement was chosen. It was described as an "acropolis" scheme. The larger of the two hills was used for the academic and other buildings. The gymnasium was placed on the smaller knoll (Fig. 7.7).

The plan is simple: an entrance loop circulation road connects the four parking lots and a visitor arrival point. Pedestrian access from the parking lots is provided by footpaths up the side of the hill penetrating the outer wall at several points connecting to the internal path system leading to each building or destination. The distances between parking lots and buildings are about equal and not excessive. Minor roads lead to the edge of the "acropolis" for service purposes. The site plan type, with buildings in the center and circulation on the outside, suited the site conditions best. One major conflict between automobile and pedestrian traffic was resolved with a bridge connecting the academic area to the gymnasium. Others could have been avoided by placing the loop road on the outer edge of the parking lots.

Since the hills were too small to accommodate the diagrammatic arrangement of the buildings, 300,000 cubic yards of earth were moved in a restructuring operation which provided a more or less flat area of about 30 acres for the structures and the desired open space between them. So successful was the regrading that reviewers of the project remarked on the restraint with which the original land had been treated. One-story buildings to accommodate the academic functions were grouped around a central common or green. Special buildings, such as the library and theater, were larger but similar in design. The one-story buildings related in scale with the residential quality of the surrounding neighborhood. The teaching units were arranged around the small courtyards according to the academic disciplines: science, humanities, the arts, and so on. The student union was located near the visitor entrance at the end of the bridge leading to the gymnasium.

The architecture was wood framed. The roofs were clad with redwood shakes, which, with the outline of the roofs, contributed to the distinctive form and strong identity of the college. The roofs were extended in very wide eaves providing protection from sun and rain to the walkways surrounding all the buildings (Fig. 7.8). The walkways consisted of removable concrete slabs covering service ducts. Long, low brick buildings for faculty offices were located behind the classroom buildings forming the outside wall of the "acropolis."

The location of the buildings was determined not only by functional considerations and factors of convenience

FIGURE 7.8
(a) Foothill College, Zone 4. Photograph by David Arbegast (1966). **(b)** Foothill College, Zone 4. Photograph by Peter Kostrikin (1973).

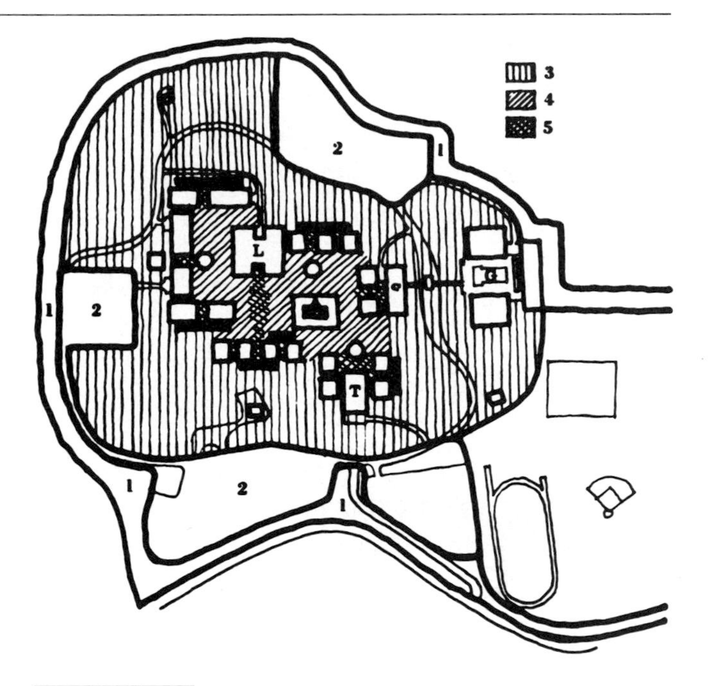

FIGURE 7.9
Foothill College: Conceptual diagram. Zone 1: edge Zone 2: parking areas, Zone 3: natural hillside, Zone 4: central open space, Zone 5: courtyards.

but also from the point of view of an aesthetic concept. The architect described the complex as having variety within unity, the unity being in the form of the buildings and the variety being in their informal arrangement.

There was also a landscape concept (Fig. 7.9). This recognized and emphasized five zones. The first was the edge, the boundary area connected with the adjacent land and its uses. Here, in whatever space was available (sometimes not much), planting was proposed to correspond with that which existed: eucalyptus or live oaks or orchard varieties. The second zone associated with the first included the parking areas and loop road. Here orchard-scale planting was proposed to serve as a foil to the large automobile parking capacity a commuter college requires. It was intended that these small-scale trees would help break the view of automobiles from the campus and help blend the development with its surroundings. Unfortunately, budget cuts and maintenance problems resulted in omission of this important element. The third zone, which is considered pedestrian, comprised the natural grass hillsides inside the loop road and up to the outside edge of the "acropolis." Here it was proposed to maintain the natural quality of the grassland and live oaks of the original site. There would be no irrigation and it was thought that this proposal, too, would relate sympathetically to the larger landscape context of summer brown foothills and sparse vegetation (Fig. 7.10).

The fourth zone was the major open space within the enclosure of the grouped buildings (Figs. 7.8 and 7.11).

FIGURE 7.10
Foothill College, Zone 3. The outer edge blends into the surrounding landscape. Photograph by Peter Kostrikin.

FIGURE 7.11
(a) Foothill College, Zone 4. Photograph by David Arbegast (1966). **(b)** Foothill College, Zone 4. Photograph by Peter Kostrikin (1973).

This to a large extent is separated visually from the immediate surroundings but commands distant views of the coast range to the west. Here the concept called for a rich and green landscape essentially enclosed and unseen from outside and representative of the foothill landscape in a more symbolic way than the other three zones. Incorporated in this zone were other program requirements: a circulation system and open space for informal use by students. By contrast to the arid third zone, this central area with undulating topography and planted shade trees is green and rich in quality as an oasis, and has come to be the most memorable landscape aspect of the college. The last zone consisted of the intimate courtyards situated between and within the buildings. They were to be refined in detail and quality using special pavings and ornamental plants to give each an individual identity (Fig. 7.12).

Foothill College is a classic example of site planning. There was a detailed and fixed program of requirements: the numbers of students and classrooms, facilities, and parking places were fixed. The site was selected as suitable in size and location. The community around the site had concerns about the quality of the architecture and the effect that it might have on them and possibly the value of their property. The logical and efficient site plan which was developed expressed the program for the college and at the same time responded to the surrounding environment and social concerns.

FIGURE 7.12
(a) Foothill College, Zone 5. Photograph by David Arbegast (1966). **(b)** Foothill College, Zone 5. Photograph by Peter Kostrikin (1973).

CASE STUDY 2. VILLAGE HOMES

A growing concern for excessive consumption of energy in the American home and its increasing costs associated with the energy crisis of the 1970s has lead to an appraisal of the role of site planning and architectural design in energy conservation. The site plan of a community can, in a variety of ways, affect energy consumption by (1) reducing the convenience of the automobile and increasing the desirability of cycling or walking or (2) reducing the need for space heating and cooling through insulation and building orientation. Early studies (Davis)[1] showed significant differences in the indoor temperatures of apartments depending on insulation and orientation. The consequence of the difference in summer between 99°F in an upper west-facing apartment and 75°F in a lower south-facing one is self-evident. Similarly in winter, the south-facing room with 55 to 70°F temperature range compared favorably with 48 to 58°F range in rooms facing north, east, or west. These quite simplistic findings, long recognized in "primitive" cultures, if applied seriously, provide a strong organizational framework for community planning and building form.

In addition to orientation and a higher level of insulation in housing construction, other measures to reduce heat loss and gain include the reduction of outside surfaces through common walls and simple building shape, the use of light colors on east- and west-exposed walls, and the outside shading of windows in summer (see page 196). It can be seen that solar considerations of this kind would conflict with traditional building codes and subdivision ordinances requiring setbacks, side yards, and so on. Taken seriously solar orientation results in a new look of asymmetry in community form and a new architecture of solar collection and protection.

Village Homes (Fig. 7.13), a commercial subdivision in Davis, California illustrates not only what happens when you plan for energy conservation through house orientation and design, but also for reduction of automobile use, a strong sense of community, conservation of water, and the use of the land for food production. The rainfall of Davis is approximately 20 inches per year and the temperatures range from a low in winter of 30°F to a high of 100°F in summer.

The 70-acre community, started in 1972, is designed to accommodate approximately 200 dwellings at an average density of 3 houses per acre (slightly less than Radburn, see page 94). North–south orientation is maintained for all the houses, many of which employ solar collectors, but all of which benefit from lower indoor temperatures in summer and higher in winter. Automobile access is in the form of 20- to 24-foot wide culs-de-sac and enclosed courtyards face the street. Pedestrian and bicycle paths

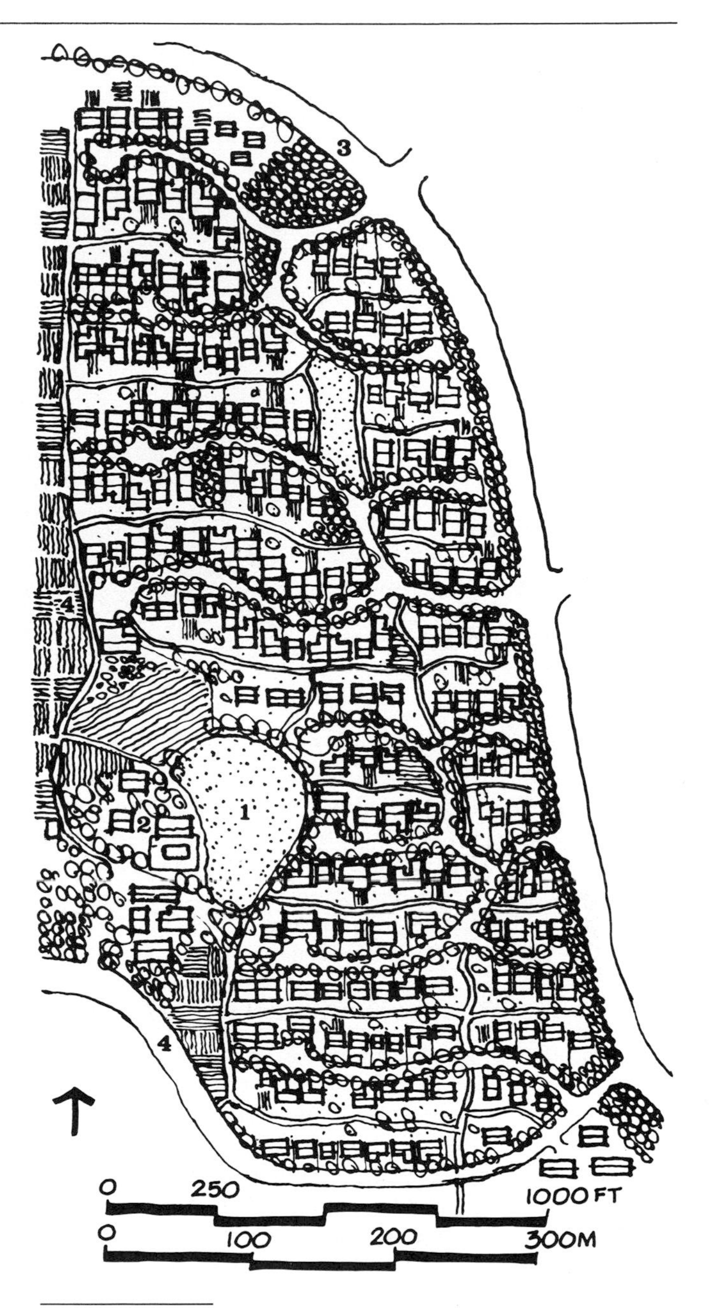

FIGURE 7.13
Plan of Village Homes, Davis, California, designed in 1972 by Michael Corbett. Apricot trees line the eastern edge and other small orchard trees and vineyards are interspersed between houses. Culs-de-sac provide automobile access. Pedestrian and bicycle paths provide convenient access between houses, community center, and gardens and the town of Davis. Key: **(1)** common, **(2)** community center, **(3)** orchard, **(4)** community gardens.

[1] Hammond, John, et al., A Strategy for Energy Conservation and Solar Utilization Ordinance for the City of Davis, California, 1974.

FIGURE 7.14
View of Village Homes showing the common green space and pathway running between the houses with individual vegetable and fruit gardens.

run in a right of way at the back and also at right angles to the roads. Gardening is limited, vegetable and fruit trees predominate (Figs. 7.14 and 1.9). Public plantings are of native or drought tolerant species and the ground is graded in such a way that rainwater collects in seepage ponds and percolates into the water table below (zero run-off) (see page 228). The community owns 12 acres distributed through the development in the form of a common and community center, vineyards, orchards, and pathways. A small commercial center with co-op foodstore, bakery, and other services is served by the convenient pedestrian and cycle routes and helps to reduce automobile use. For this design to be implemented several new city ordinances were required.

CASE STUDY 3. OAK PARK, ILLINOIS

In 1965 the community of Oak Park, an old suburb of Chicago with a population of 62,000 suffered a decline as a regional shopping center. This was induced by traffic congestion and inadequate parking and by the competition of new outlying shopping centers. In 1970 Oak Park commissioned a planning study. After analysis of the population, the history and pattern of retail activity, and the movement of automobile traffic and pedestrians, the report concluded first that there was a need for a better match between the people living around the center and the retail outlets in it. This implied that competition with regional mass markets was inappropriate and that shops should concentrate on proven markets for higher income specialty items and convenience goods specifically related to the status of the community. Second, conflicts were identified between pedestrians, automobiles and trucks, and between through traffic and local traffic. Third, the downtown lacked image and focus.

An urban design concept was proposed, centered on and involving the pedestrianization of two commercial streets, rear service access to the stores and other buildings, and the formation of adequate parking space within easy walking distance. The community adopted this proposal (Fig. 7.15). Landscape architect Joe Karr of Chicago was selected to develop the planning concepts into physical form.

Client's Program

The client's program for the landscape architect was for a pedestrian mall that would provide freedom of movement between stores, places to sit in sun and shade, night lighting, convenient parking and access, and a strong identity that would attract shoppers and revitalize the old center of town. In short, they asked for "a mall," using the term as it had come to be used in cities and towns in the 1960s and 1970s.

Program Development

The basic program concept, "a mall," was developed in more detail by the designer exploring the characteristics of a variety of likely users (active shoppers, children, elderly persons, merchants, staff and office workers) and their anticipated needs and behavior (crossing from one side to the other, pleasant places to sit in sun or shade, bicycle parking, sheltered waiting areas for buses, wide paved areas for ease of movement and activities, tele-

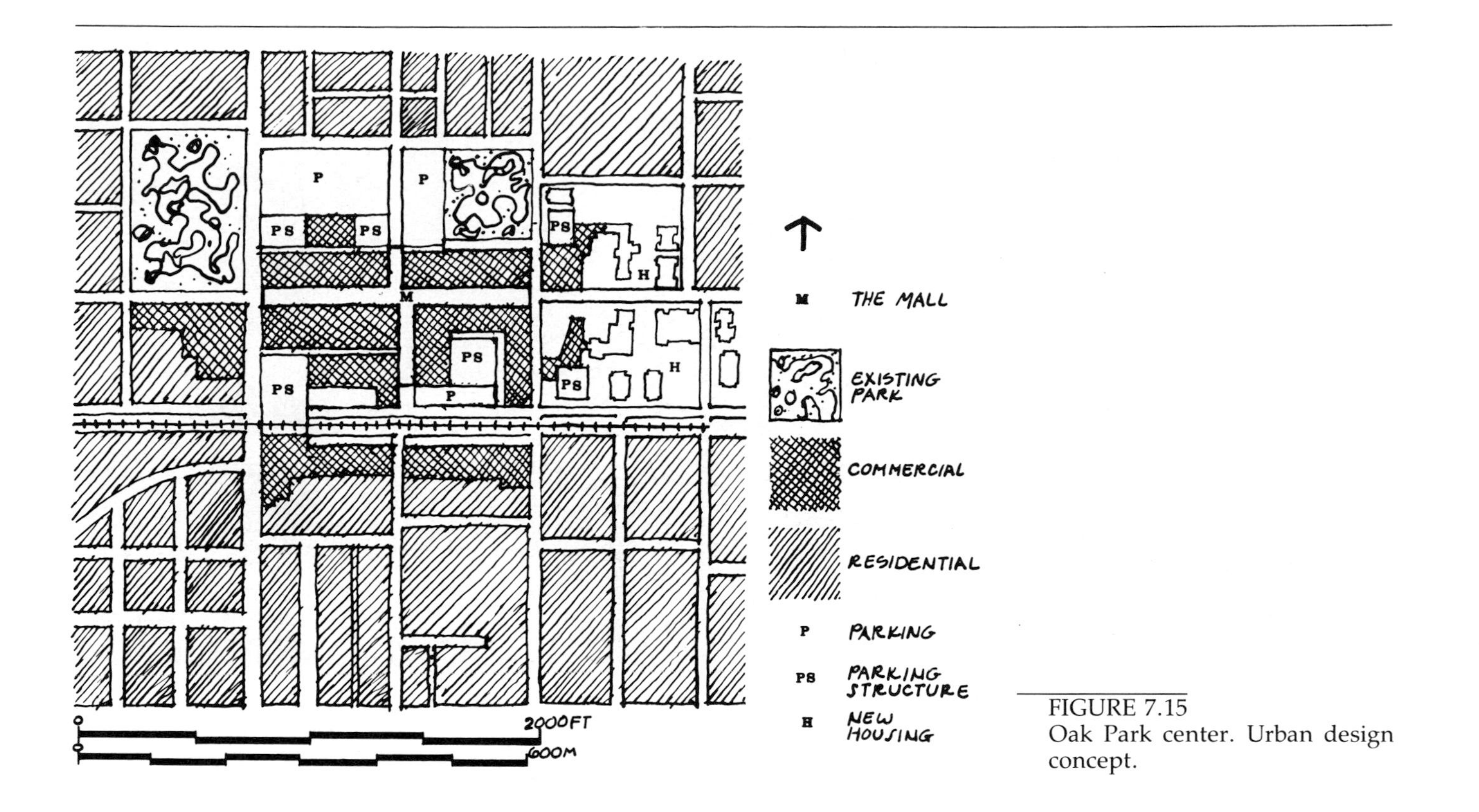

FIGURE 7.15
Oak Park center. Urban design concept.

phones, mailboxes, and unique features to give identity). Other program requirements came from practical issues, the most important being the necessity for fire truck access to the fronts of the buildings. This required a continuous, though not necessarily straight, 24-foot wide clear path from the major streets. Other functional requirements included lighting, trash receptacles, and ease of maintenance and cleaning.

Some less tangible design issues related to the program included a need to unify the mall as an identifiable unit in the town while incorporating considerable variety in architecture and building height, a need to develop a human scale in a space originally designed for traffic and, since the street would no longer be a street, to make it feel like a public square, even a garden. In association with this a need was perceived to counteract the linearity of the space so that it would look less like a strip, suggesting through movement, and more like a market place in which to circulate and spend time enjoying the setting and the people in it.

Site Analysis and Evaluation (Fig. 7.16)

Context

The two intersecting streets designated as the project lay more or less in the center of the downtown commercial area. The north–south street connected to the commuter station; the east–west street led to a major bus route. Adjacent existing and proposed land uses included commercial, housing, automobile parking, and two parks. As an urban site, few typical ecological processes of consequence could be identified. Regional weather statistics indicated hot summers (temperatures up to 100°F) and cold winters (temperatures down to minus 25°F), annual precipitation (30 to 33 inches) spread evenly throughout the year with a potential of 20 to 25 inches of snow at any one time during the months of December to March. The poor condition of the surrounding blocks suggested that the mall project was regarded by the client as a starting point for revitalization of the entire downtown area. The residential area beyond remained in good condition, its streets lined with mature trees. This contextual analysis identified major entry points and destinations for pedestrians. A general picture of the climate as it would effect use and require amelioration also indicated the capacity of drains for surface runoff and the need for snow clearing. It also suggested that a strong image which would influence the quality of the surroundings would be beneficial.

Geology and Soil

The program did not necessitate a study of geology for foundation material. Existing soil was clay with poor drainage. The essential underground information for this project was the location and size of utilities within the rights of way.

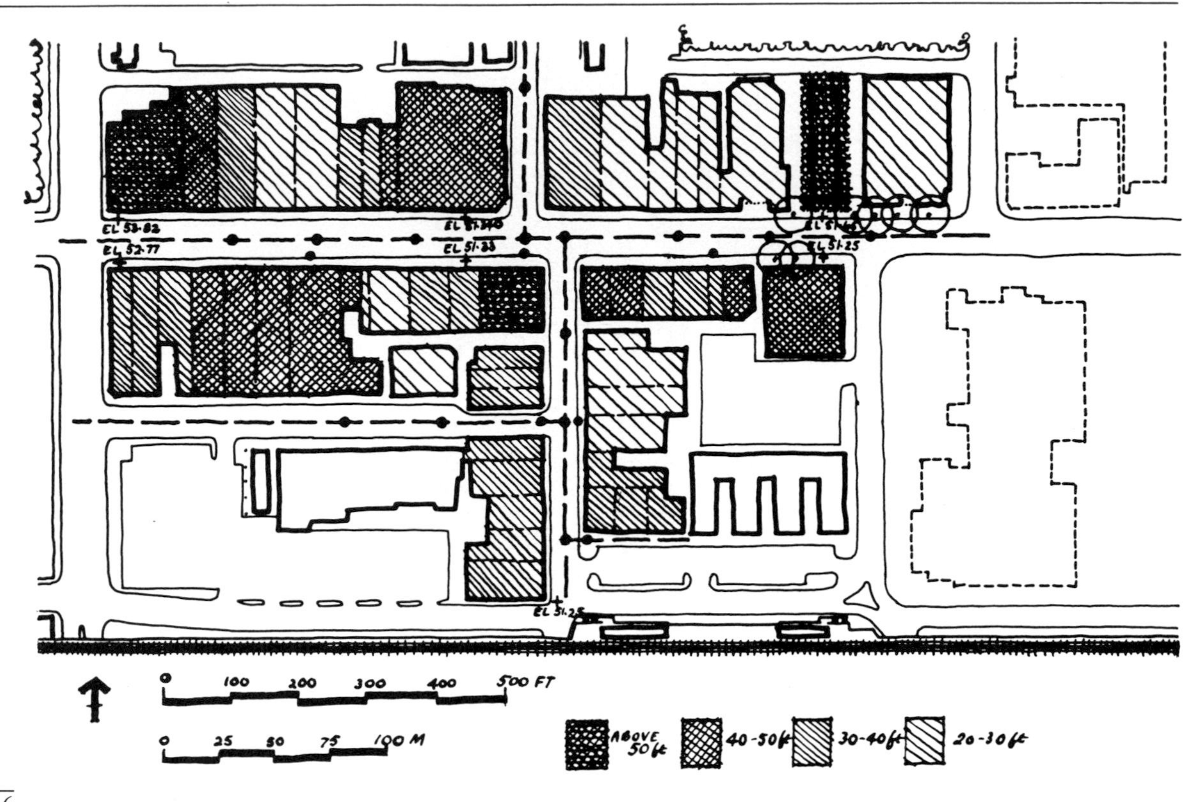

FIGURE 7.16
Oak Park center. Site analysis.

Topography
The site was essentially flat with minor slopes on the streets and their cross sections. With no slopes of any consequence, critical information included precise spot elevations, necessary in the design of surface drainage and where new paved surfaces must meet the thresholds of shops and other structures.

Vegetation
There were only a few existing street trees. Earlier, in the 1920s, the streets were narrower and were lined with trees for shade similar to the rest of town where American elms, maples, lindens, honey locusts, red and pin oaks were commonly planted.

Microclimate
Interpretation of the general data in terms of the site suggested that rain and snow shelter would be desirable for essential outdoor use such as bus stops. Sun angles and shadow patterns indicated that the east–west street would receive the most sun throughout the day and year, the north–south street little midday shade from buildings in summer (Figs. 7.17 and 7.18). The scale and form of the buildings did not result in major eddys or draft situations. In summer, cooling breezes come from the lake in a southeast or southwest direction and in the winter, storms with excessive windchill come from the northwest (windchill down to −83°F). Implications of this analysis include the use of deciduous trees, appropriately placed, to provide shade within the mall during the summer but not block the winter sun. The problem of a low morning and evening sun in summer causing overheating in the shops is negated by the location and heights of buildings.

Visual and Physical Survey
The designer reviewed the history of the town, as it might be expressed by the site or individual buildings. Historical buildings or buildings outstanding in some other way were noted. Dominant construction materials, colors, and the overall quality of the street were assessed. A great variety of architecture and building types were found. Building heights were 2 or 3 stories; the main street was 81 feet wide and 1100 feet long and the cross street 51 feet wide and 700 feet long. Views within and from the site were plotted, the vistas to the ends of the streets being most important.

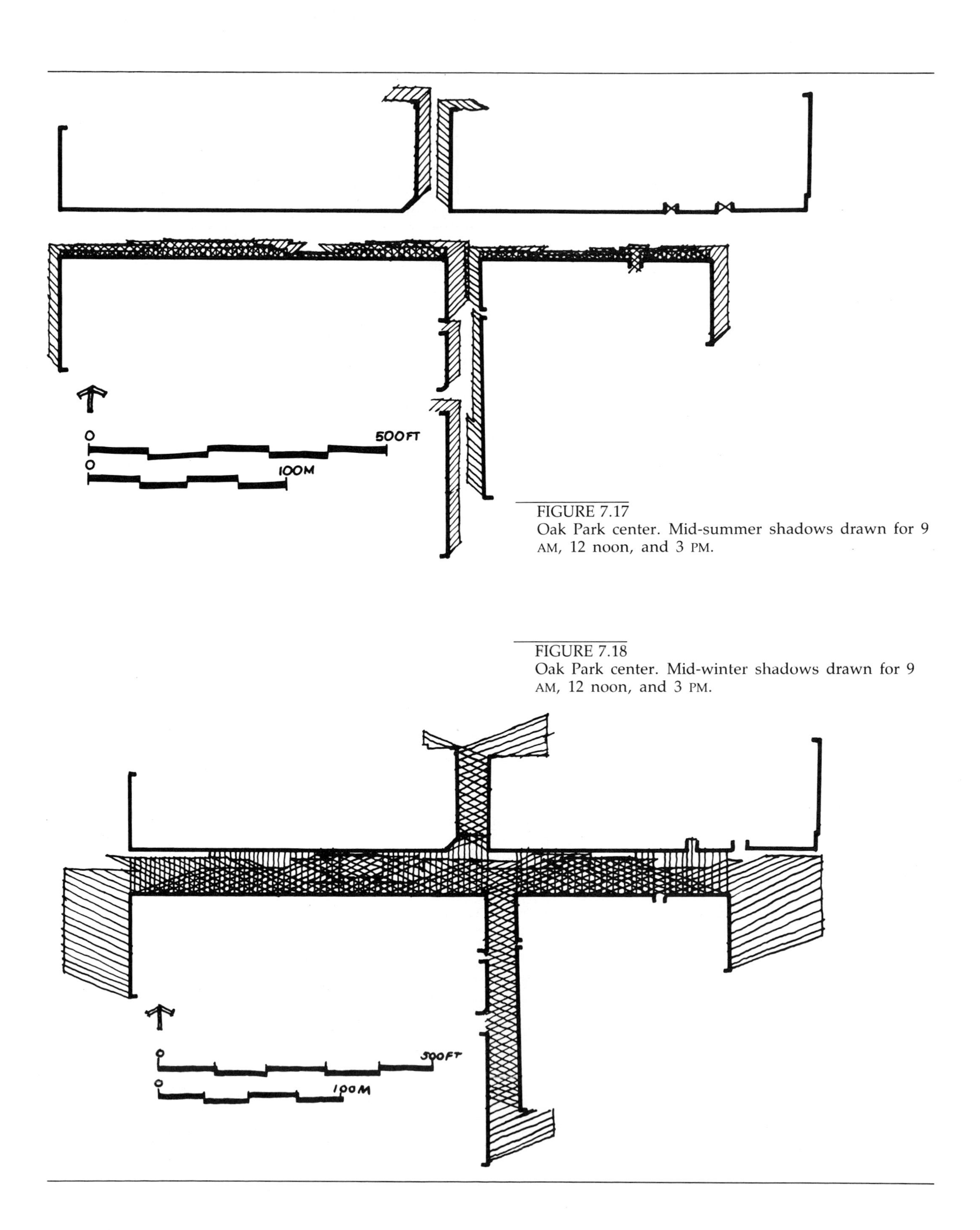

FIGURE 7.17
Oak Park center. Mid-summer shadows drawn for 9 AM, 12 noon, and 3 PM.

FIGURE 7.18
Oak Park center. Mid-winter shadows drawn for 9 AM, 12 noon, and 3 PM.

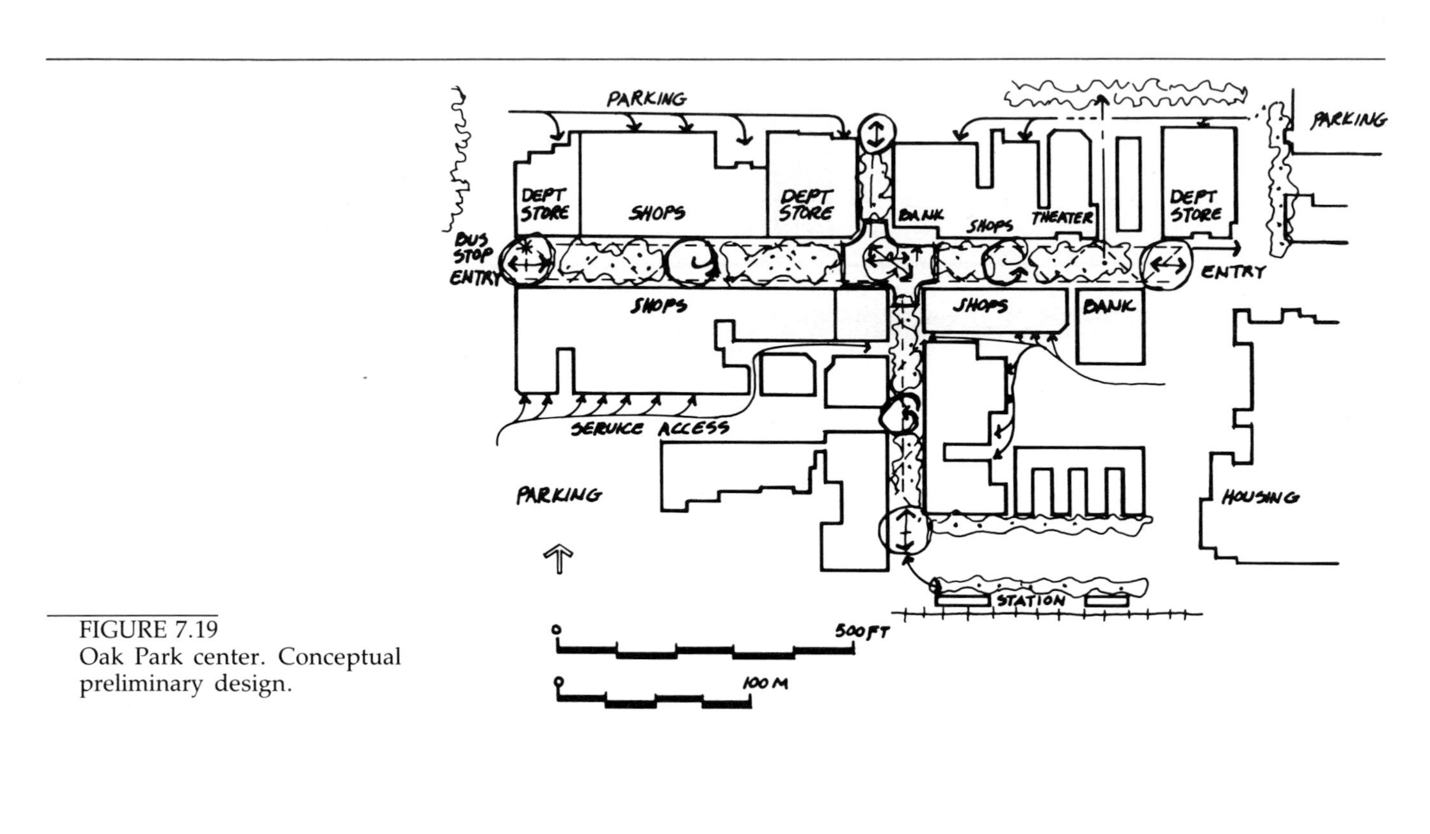

FIGURE 7.19
Oak Park center. Conceptual preliminary design.

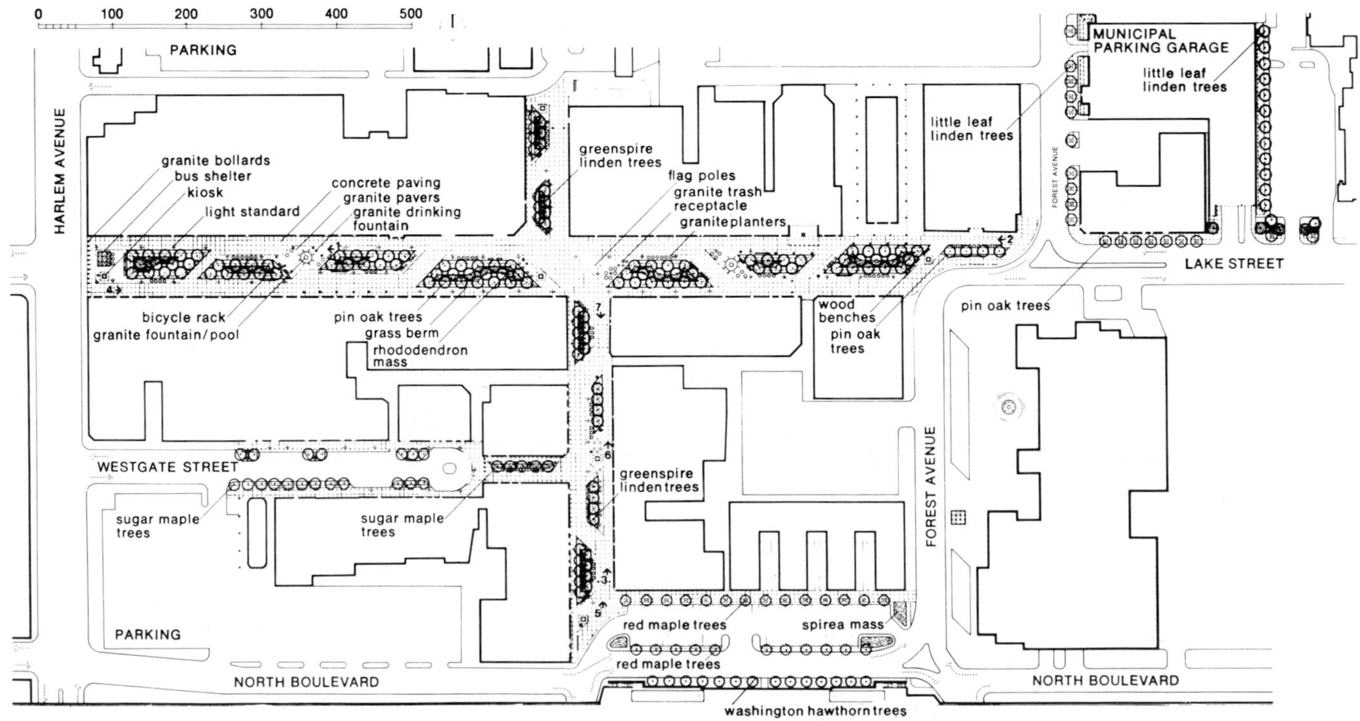

FIGURE 7.20
Final plan of Oak Park center, Illinois, designed by Joe Karr, landscape architect, in 1970. A paving grid provides unity and wide surface for pedestrian flow and emergency vehicle access. The entrances are marked with information kiosks. Tree groupings provide shade in summer and are staggered to break the linearity of the space. Fountains and sitting areas give focus and identity to the center and subcenters of the mall.

Synthesis (Fig. 7.19)

The program and the site were brought together in synthesis, the constraints and opportunities of the site being explored in terms of the program needs. Alternatives, including predominantly soft, predominantly hard and totally enclosed malls, were compared and evaluated in terms of image, use and cost. The opinion of the client was sought on these conceptual alternatives. In the end, an essentially green mall evolved as the most appropriate, with masses of closely planted deciduous shade trees set in green berms and underplanted with rhododendrons (Figs. 7.20 and 7.21). This shade and garden-like image was in keeping with the park-like character of the town. At the same time, by virtue of its architectural enclosure and removal of traffic, the place became unique. In addition to the trees, unity was brought to the area and to the diverse architecture with a 6 by 6 foot paving grid matrix across the ground plane permitting all the necessary circulation. A central area at the intersection of the two pedestrian streets was marked with a special fountain, seats and planters, and other subspaces were created along the mall where people could linger to enjoy a concert, fashion show, or other event (Fig. 7.22). The street furniture, such as benches, bollards, drinking fountains, and trash receptacles were made from granite cylinders, castoffs from a local quarry, and were low-cost but high-style. Lights, flagpoles, and other accessories were of bronze. The consistency and careful design of these details contributed to the image and identity of the project and to the sense of place which was a major goal. The cost of the mall was low due to the high proportion of soft area to paved surface. In 1975 it was $6.50 per square foot, which was approximately 35 percent less than most similar mall projects at the time, and the project came in well under budget. Increased retail sales during the first four years of operation were recorded and it has maintained its popularity as an urban and community center.

FIGURE 7.21
Sketch of the proposal for Oak Park center showing the intimate quality of a subcenter in relation to the main flow of pedestrians.

FIGURE 7.22
Oak Park mall. Completed project (1976). Joe Karr, landscape architect.

SUGGESTED READINGS

Site Planning

Alexander, Christopher, *Notes on the Synthesis of Form.*

Alexander, Christopher, *A Pattern Language.*

Baker, Geoffrey H., and Bruno Funaro, *Parking*, p. 164, "Parking Layout and Dimensions."

Booth, Norman, *Basic Elements of Landscape Design*, Ch. 3, "Buildings," Ch. 7, "Design Process."

Corbett, Michael, *A Better Place to Live; New Designs for Tomorrow's Communities.*

Cullen, Gordon, *Townscape*, pp. 121–127, "Legs and Wheels," pp. 17–55, "Serial Vision."

De Chiara, J., *Site Planning Standards.*

Dober, Richard P., *Campus Planning.*

Eckbo, Garrett, *Landscape for Living*, pp. 71–73, "Approach."

Eckbo, Garrett, *Urban Landscape Design*, pp. 7–33, "Elements of Space Organization."

Halprin, Lawrence, *Notebooks, 1959–71.*

Land Design Research, Inc., *Cost Effective Site Planning.*

Lynch, Kevin, *Site Planning*, 3rd edition.

Mazria, E., *The Passive Solar Energy Book*, Ch. IV, pp. 66–104.

Ritter, Paul, *Planning for Man and Motor.*

Rubenstein, Harvey, *A Guide to Site and Environmental Planning*, 2nd edition.

Rutledge, Albert, *Anatomy of a Park.*

Simonds, John O., *Landscape Architecture*, pp. 44–53, "Site Analysis," pp. 20–77, "Site Structure Unity," pp. 67–69, "Site Structure Plan Development," pp. 173–183, "Structures in the Landscape," pp. 190–193, "Arrangement of Buildings," Ch. 5, p. 145, "Circulation."

Temko, Allen, *Architectural Forum*, "Foothills Campus is a Community in Itself." February 1962.

Untermann, Richard, *Site Planning for Cluster Housing.*

Weddle, A. E., ed., *Techniques of Landscape Architecture*, pp. 1–32, "Site Planning," by Sylvia Crowe; pp. 43–54, "Site Survey and Appreciation," by Norman Clarke.

Urban Design

Appleyard, Donald, *Liveable Streets.*

Bacon, Edmund, *Design of Cities.*

Brainbella, Roberto, and Longo, G. *For Pedestrians Only—Planning, Design and Management of Traffic Free Zones.*

Cutler, Lawrence, and Cutler, S. *Recycling Cities for People—The Urban Design Process.*

Halprin, Lawrence, *Cities.*

Krier, R., *Open Space.*

Laurie, Ian, ed., *Nature in Cities.*

Lynch, Kevin, *A Theory of Good City Form.*

Rubenstein, Harvey M., *Central City Malls.*

Rudofsky, Bernard, *Streets for People.*

Taylor, Lisa, *Urban Open Spaces.*

Wiedenhoft, Ronald, *Cities for People.*

DESIGN

8

Landscape design is an extension of site planning and, as we have seen, is involved in the site planning process. It is concerned with the selection of design components, materials, and plants and their combination as solutions to limited but well-defined problems within the site plan. Whereas the site plan indicates use areas and circulation routes, detailed landscape design deals with surfaces, edges and joints, steps and ramps connecting specific differences in elevation, paving, and drainage, and all the decisions that have to be made before the project can be built and planted (Fig. 8.1).

A knowledge of this level of design is essential in site planning if solutions to the detailed design problems which result are to be realistic. Landscape design is the process through which specific quality is given to the diagrammatic spaces of the site plan and is another level on which landscape architecture may be discussed or criticized. It should be rational but also imaginative. The criterion for success is a sense of inevitability—a look of fitness derived by evolution out of the original environment.

VISUAL RELATIONSHIPS

In addition to the technicalities of the materials, dimensions, and details, landscape design is concerned with visual relationships. The designer has the ability to control and manipulate visual experience as well as tactile and other sensory qualities.

In the final stages of design, it is the development of form and shape, the relative size of elements and their sequential relationship, their color and texture, the play of light and shadow that together produce the ultimate experience of the project. Beyond satisfying functional, human, and ecological criteria, the final qualitative experience depends upon the designer's understanding of aesthetics and perception.

The way the landscape architect deals with the visual organization of design varies according to the environmental context. The spectrum of settings for design ranges from "wilderness" or nature (which may or may not be great distances from cities) through landscapes which are predominantly agricultural and productive, field, farms, and so on, to suburban zones of housing, gardens, streets, parks, and shopping centers, designed and organized as human habitat, and finally to urban centers, paved, built over and up, in which nature is essentially symbolic and introduced.

In the first context and to some extent the second, it is more than likely that the appropriate direction will be to blend things into the environment using indige-

FIGURE 8.1
Pomona College, California. Ralph Cornell, landscape architect.

nous planting, ground forms to screen buildings and facilities. Understanding the nature of the setting, both ecologically and visually, is the key to success in situations where nature has priority or where the pattern, as in agriculture, is so strong that it is a dominant characteristic difficult to disregard.

In the other two major contexts, as the setting becomes more architectural and engineered, and as the visual evidence of nature becomes less and less (as you approach city centers), so the aesthetic relationships—dimensions and proportions of open space and buildings, color, texture, and pattern of planting and hard surfaces, position, size, and type of trees—become the factors which determine the quality of the environment. Here the landscape architect, lacking the imperative to blend with nature, must understand how these variables are related, and how together they constitute an environment whose perception will induce, facilitate, or inhibit human behavior, understanding, and emotions.

Optically, spaces can be made to appear larger. Perceived space can be affected by design. Blue colors, which are visually receding, or small textured plants can be used to increase the sense of distance. Concealing the boundaries of the site and the use of diagonal or curving lines may enhance the sense of space in actually quite limited situations. The small town gardens of Thomas Church show these design devices used expertly and to good effect (Fig. 2.61). Of course it is also possible to do the reverse by manipulating

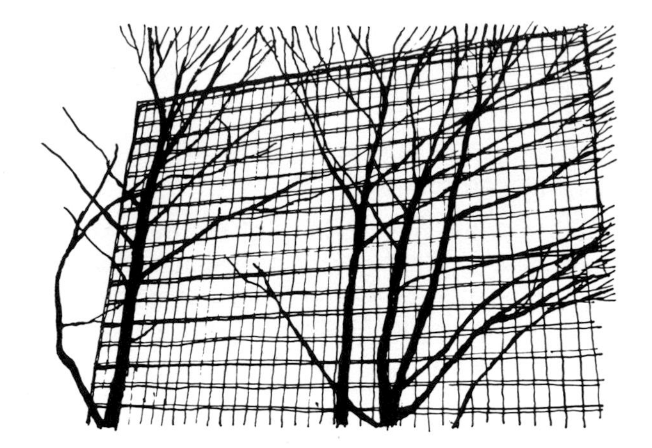

FIGURE 8.2
Trees relate to large scale architecture and the individual on the street.

color, texture, and edge, making large spaces appear smaller.

The most important visual relationship is scale. It is a difficult and much misused term. It is concerned with the relative size of things. The skyline of Manhattan is a pleasing visual composition seen from some distant point like Brooklyn or Staten Island. The buildings are generally "in scale" with each other. When experienced from the sidewalk, however, they are "out of scale" with the human figure. The architecture of a London square is more humanistic (Fig. 5.2). The buildings are not excessively tall in relation to the

FIGURE 8.3
(a) and **(b)** The role of trees in modifying scale relationships.

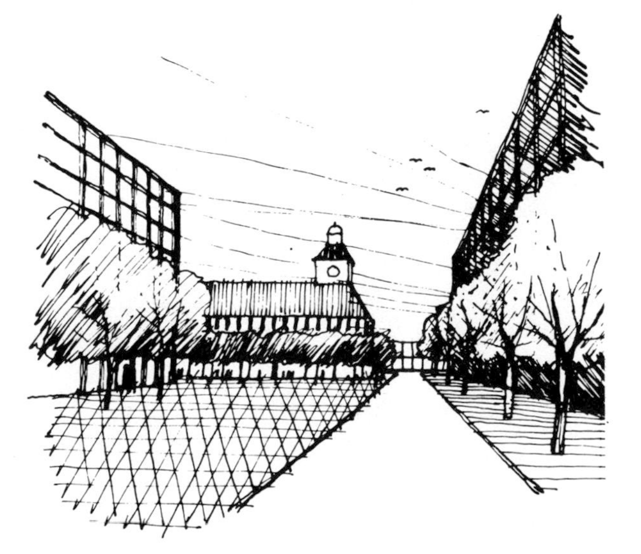

open space they surround, and the doors and windows provide a modulation of the surface which brings it into scale with the human experience and our attraction for detail. The scale of the squatter towns of South America is paradoxically perhaps even more appropriate or comfortable. The houses are more or less built around the family and are almost exactly scaled to the human figure and a human's basic needs. There is no monumentality.

One frequent task in landscape design is creating transitions from the human experience to large elements around us in the environment. This applies to cities and to natural landscape as well, but it is perhaps more important in cities. For this purpose, trees have a unique attribute in that they are relatively large elements when seen at a distance, yet on closer inspection they break down into a connected system of branches, twigs, leaves, and buds. This quality makes trees an excellent scale transition, being in scale with people and with large structures at the same time. Thus trees planted around tall buildings may be thought of as a scale transition from the multiple building to the individual (Figs. 8.2 and 8.3).

At another level, scale relationships may concern the right fit among dimension, space, and people. In a private garden, where the human scale is set by the dwelling, the danger will be to avoid the excessive breaking up of the space, making the garden seem small and the people feel too big for it. In a children's garden, on the other hand, what might appear cluttered to an adult would seem satisfactory to a child. Thus in design for children we might deliberately reduce the size of everything. The child's eye view is extremely important in the design of playgrounds and tot lots. Disneyland is scaled to two-third size and is especially effective for children because of this.

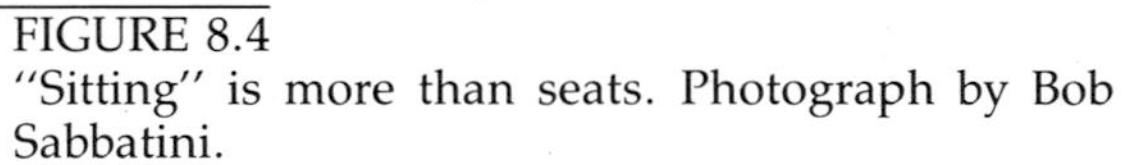

FIGURE 8.4
"Sitting" is more than seats. Photograph by Bob Sabbatini.

SOURCES OF PLAN FORM

Just as in landscape planning and site planning, form and shape in landscape design result from the constraints and potentials of the site and a clear definition of the design problem.

Boundaries

A fundamental source of form in landscape design is the shape of the site itself, as defined by the boundary lines and the topography (Fig. 7.1). There are also form-giving influences on the site from beyond the boundaries and the plan must show and deal with the modification of the site as it responds to those outside forces, especially climate, views, adjoining buildings, and land uses. The edge zone of the site is thus a double design project. It must relate to the outside while at the same time it has an inside edge that must relate to and be part of the features of the site plan. From the point of view of efficient use of space, the alignment and location of playing fields and parking lots, buildings, and roads are likely to be parallel to the site boundaries or major slopes and ridges unless there is a physiographic reason or a strong program requirement, such as optimum orientation, to dictate otherwise (Fig. 7.6).

Use and Function

Within this larger framework, we must design spaces or areas to satisfy the program requirements located and connected according to the site plan.

The second source of form in design, then, is from an appraisal of the function or use to be accommodated. Getting at the meaning of the program requirements calls for research. If we are to design a place for quiet sitting, then we must start by analyzing sitting, not seats (Fig. 8.4). That is to say, we should define and investigate the problem in its unique context. Seats or benches are the solution to a particular interpretation of the need for sitting in a particular situation. It is possible, however, to sit without seats at all. The design of seats and sitting areas is not as simple as it may seem. Steps and the edges of fountains may serve as seats for certain age groups under

FIGURE 8.5
Steps as seats.

FIGURE 8.6
Edge of a fountain as seats.

FIGURE 8.7
Seat with something to look at.

FIGURE 8.8
Game with a box. Photograph by Bob Sabbatini.

FIGURE 8.9
Childrens' playground. Royston, Hanamato, Mayes and Beck (1957).

FIGURE 8.10
Captains of the Seven Seas.

certain circumstances (Figs. 8.5 and 8.6). A bench without a back is uncomfortable for most people for any length of time, but such benches have a multi-directional aspect suited for situations where this is needed (Fig. 8.7). Similarly, if we are to design a playground, then we should start by analyzing play, not only playgrounds, and recognize the variables of age and culture (Figs. 8.8 to 8.11). We must ask ourselves to what extent anything we design for children's play is in fact limiting to the child's imagination. The design of playgrounds must clearly emanate from an understanding of being a child with basic needs for security, muscular development and movement, with possibilities for discovery and challenge. Whatever the use to be provided and facilitated, there must be enough space for it to take place and the three-dimensional forms and two-dimensional shapes should result from an analysis of the use.

Circulation

Circulation, in addition to connecting different places and facilities, may in fact define and separate areas and give shape to some of them. In landscape design pedestrian movement is critical. How do you get from one place to another and under what conditions? When is a straight line best? People in a hurry going between two known fixed points tend to choose the shortest distance. College campuses are one of the best places to see the effect of this (Fig. 8.12).

The width and surface of the circulation routes themselves are determined in terms of the numbers of people who may be expected to move along a particular pathway at any one time. Where many people are expected in a flow of movement between two major attractors such as a football stadium and a parking area, or a bus stop and an office building entrance, the paths should obviously be wide and straight or at most gently curved so that the movement can be easy and fast. Major desire lines of this sort should be satisfied. If, within the same context, it is desirable to divert the direct route to protect an area for some other use as in a city square or park, then some element or "hazard" must be designed into the landscape to give reason and meaning to the diversion as perceived by the hurrying pedestrian (Fig. 8.13). Changes in level, ponds and lakes, and land shaping may be used for this purpose (Fig. 8.14). Apart from directing circulation around use areas, the circulation route may be varied simply for aesthetic reasons or to provide an alternative experience. Thus if the function of the circulation is slow, informal walking and stopping, as in parks or botanic gardens, then the paths can be less

FIGURE 8.11
Basketball hoop and friends turns sideyard into a park.

FIGURE 8.12
Paths worn through planting where important direct route was not provided. Photograph by Peter Kostrikin.

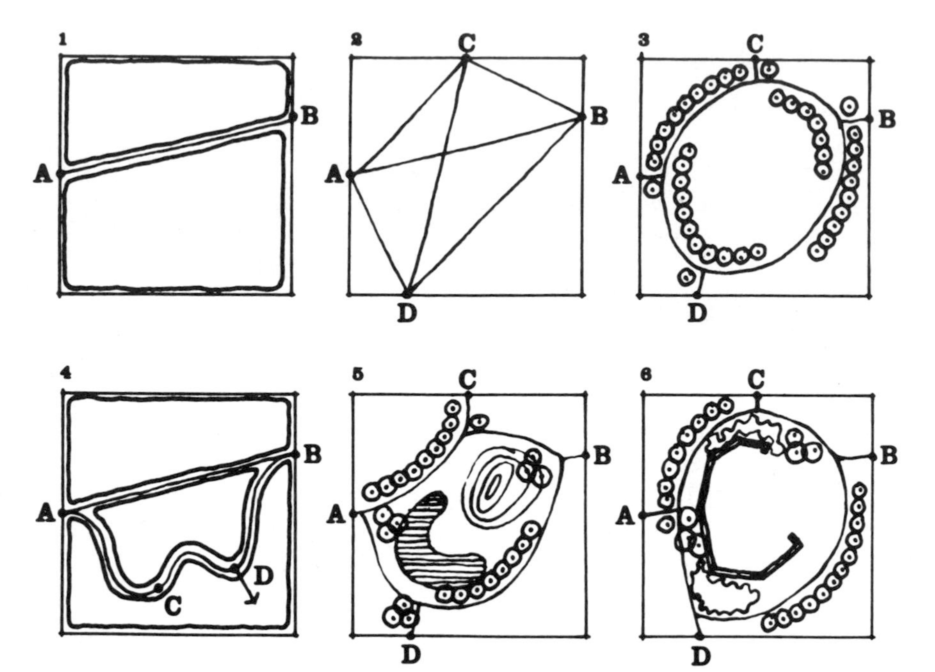

FIGURE 8.13
The most direct route between A and B is a straight line **(1)**. The most obvious solution to pedestrian circulation is to connect up all the doors or access points **(2)**. Circulation which is not purposeful as in a park may be circuitous, connecting up viewpoints and places of interest. Distance is no objection and, in fact, becomes desirable **(4)**. Deviation from the straight line approach may be acceptable as long as the route is not excessively roundabout and is most successful when emphasized by planting **(3)** or made imperative by hazards **(5)**, **(6)**.

direct, less wide, and have expansions in them at places to permit people to pause, sit quietly, or collect in groups.

How wide should a path be? Experiments or observations might be carried out in existing city or campus situations to see at what point paths became inadequate. Beazley suggests that a path 2 feet wide can accommodate a wheelbarrow or baby stroller if the path is unfenced and there are no hazards on either side.[1] But this is very minimal and does not permit two-way traffic. A 7-foot path will allow a baby stroller and a pedestrian side by side. In shopping areas or malls, or where crowds are expected, a minimum of 20 feet is recommended. Shopping street sidewalks should be approximately 12 feet (Figs. 8.15 to 8.17). Automobile circulation should also be dimensioned according to use and frequency consideration and, if possible, separated from pedestrian routes.

FIGURE 8.14
The route of the path is related to the form of the landscape and therefore seems logical.

Circulation, auto, or pedestrian, since it implies movement, is clearly intimately connected with change and the succession of sensual experiences and environments that occur along the route. It is important therefore to recognize the design possibilities in circulation for the sequential experience which can be developed even when the route is straight. We can learn much from the eighteenth-century landscape garden in this respect. The design of a pedestrian route may involve such concepts as place and identity, enclosure, variety, and mystery.

Topography

Land form has intrinsic shape and a logical extent and outline related to that shape and to the angle of repose of the material. Rolling topography at whatever scale logically calls for flowing curves in circulation or the outline of paved areas or use zones (Figs. 7.7 and 7.8). Thus contours of land may indicate appropriate shapes or form.

[1] Elizabeth Beazley, *Design and Detail of the Space between Buildings* (London: Architectural Press, 1960).

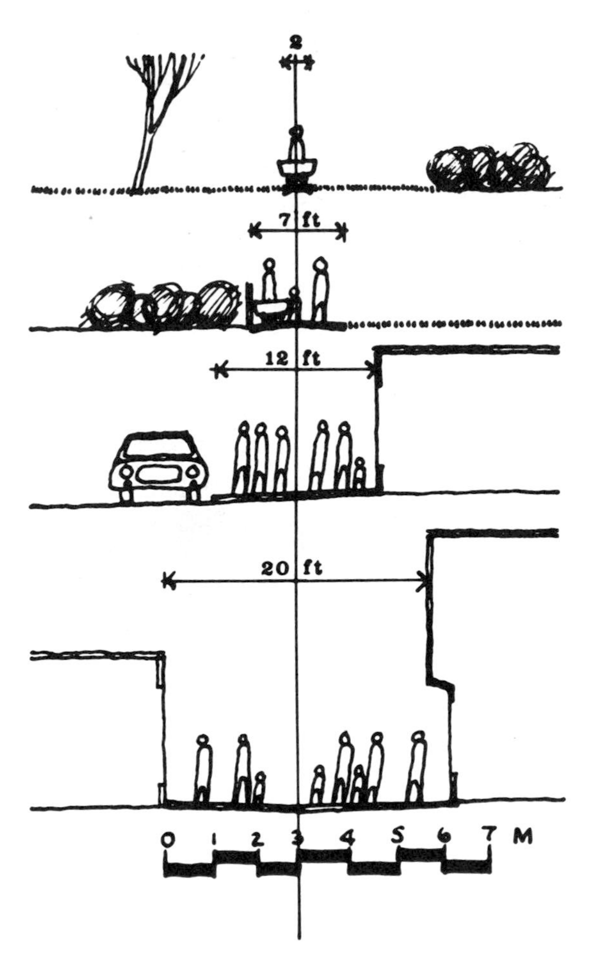

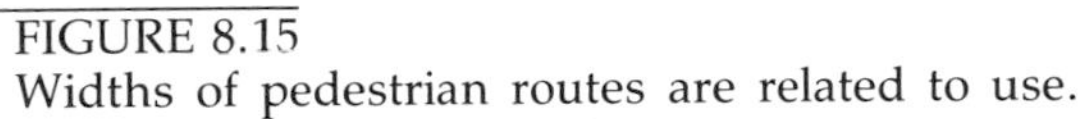

FIGURE 8.15
Widths of pedestrian routes are related to use.

Architecture

Architecture is also an influence on the shape of areas. Buildings project imaginary lines into the landscape. When these relate to other form-giving forces, they should be adopted. These principles apply whether we are dealing with a natural site or one which is to be completely created in an urban setting.

Materials

Another way to define shapes is through the materials they are made of. For example, asphalt, grass, and poured concrete are flowing materials; that is, they can take on any shape they are molded into. The surface is uniform, although in the case of concrete, expansion joints do provide a design pattern; the edges are still arbitrary and are determined by considerations other than the material. By contrast, bricks and paving blocks have a fixed unit shape which cutting violates (although this is often seen). Such precast units differ

FIGURE 8.16
Path approximately six feet wide.

from cut stone, which is cut to any shape required out of a larger stratum or bed of rock. Bricks and concrete pavers are precast and have an integrity as individual units. The outline of paving using these materials should therefore be rectangular, or reflecting the unit shape whatever it is. Curves can be achieved by stepping back with each unit and allowing grass or planting to form the curve.

Maintenance

Finally, maintenance is an important factor in the evolution of specific shapes. Narrow, pointed areas of grass are very difficult to cut with the large scale mowing machinery commonly used in public landscapes. Such narrow strips may simply be trampled out of existence. The edge or shape of grass lawns should therefore be simple. Curvilinear shapes are probably best, but no angular outlines should have points less than about 90 degrees. The narrowest width of grass and the space between tree trunks should be dimensioned to accommodate the mowing machinery to be used.

FIGURE 8.17
Shopping street in Copenhagen.

FIGURE 8.18
Space defined by natural elements. Canyon del Muerto, Arizona. Photograph by R. Burton Litton, Jr.

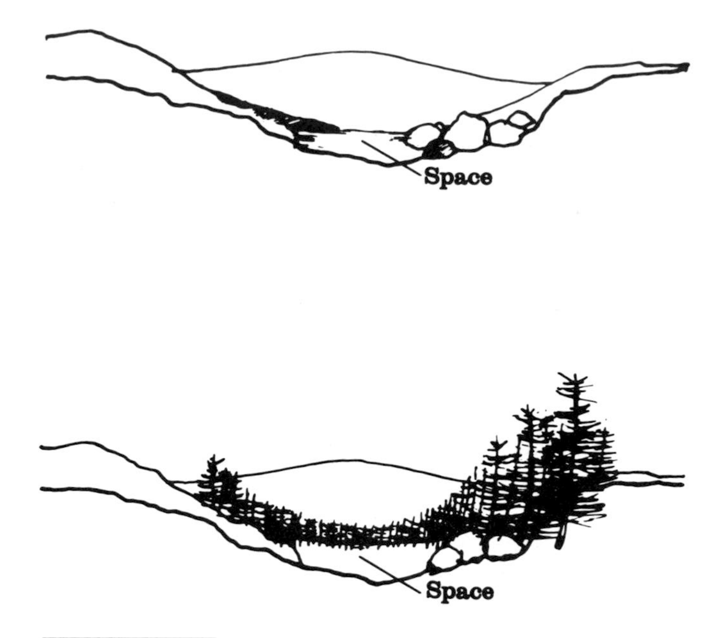

FIGURE 8.19
Two types of natural enclosure of space.

SPATIAL DEFINITION

Landscape design results in three-dimensional space. The way in which that space is defined gives rise to a range of spatial qualities. Space may be defined entirely by natural materials, land form, and plants. A valley or bowl in a treeless landscape has spatial identity, a form that is emphasized by light and shadow and the skyline. Clearings in forests are spaces defined entirely by vegetation. Not only are these spaces defined by nature, they are also the result of natural processes (Figs. 8.18 and 8.19). Similar spatial enclosures can also be man-made out of natural materials in a slightly more self-conscious way by design (Figs. 11.15, 11.25 and 11.26). Space can be formed entirely out of man-made inert materials, buildings, paving, and glass. However, landscape design is most likely to involve spaces made out of a combination of natural materials and man-made structures. The important point to realize is that vegetation and land form are as effective in defining space as are buildings and walls (Fig. 8.20).

SELECTION OF MATERIALS

The way in which the type of paving material may influence the shape of the area to be paved was noted previously. Let us now pursue further the differences in surfaces and some considerations for their selection and combination in design.

Concept of Variation

It seems reasonable that there should be some logic for selecting, combining, and changing paving materials. Why should all hard surfaces not be asphalt? Changing surface provides variety, which may be reason enough, but the variety should relate to some factor of use or communication about use. Traditionally, surfacing materials have been used in such a way that any change in material reflects a change in use, purpose, or function, or a change in level; that is, a change designed to emphasize something. Old cities are full of such traditions. Steps in which the risers are made out of white marble and the treads out of dark granite emphasize their physical form and clear up visual ambiguity (Fig. 8.21). In old European streets paved with rough cobbles, we can still find two tracks of smooth granite set into the streets for cart wheels. The wheels thus ran smoothly on the tracks while the horses' hoofs had good traction on the cobbles.

Differences in paving materials, especially texture and color, can be used where a warning is needed to indicate danger or hazard (as if to a blind person) at the edges of pools and in other situations such as pedestrian crosswalks and at curbs and to separate incompatible uses (Fig. 8.22). By changing materials for such reasons, variety, pattern, and visual interest are introduced. Where the type of traffic changes, we may expect the surface to change. For example, grass and concrete are two surfaces with entirely different traffic

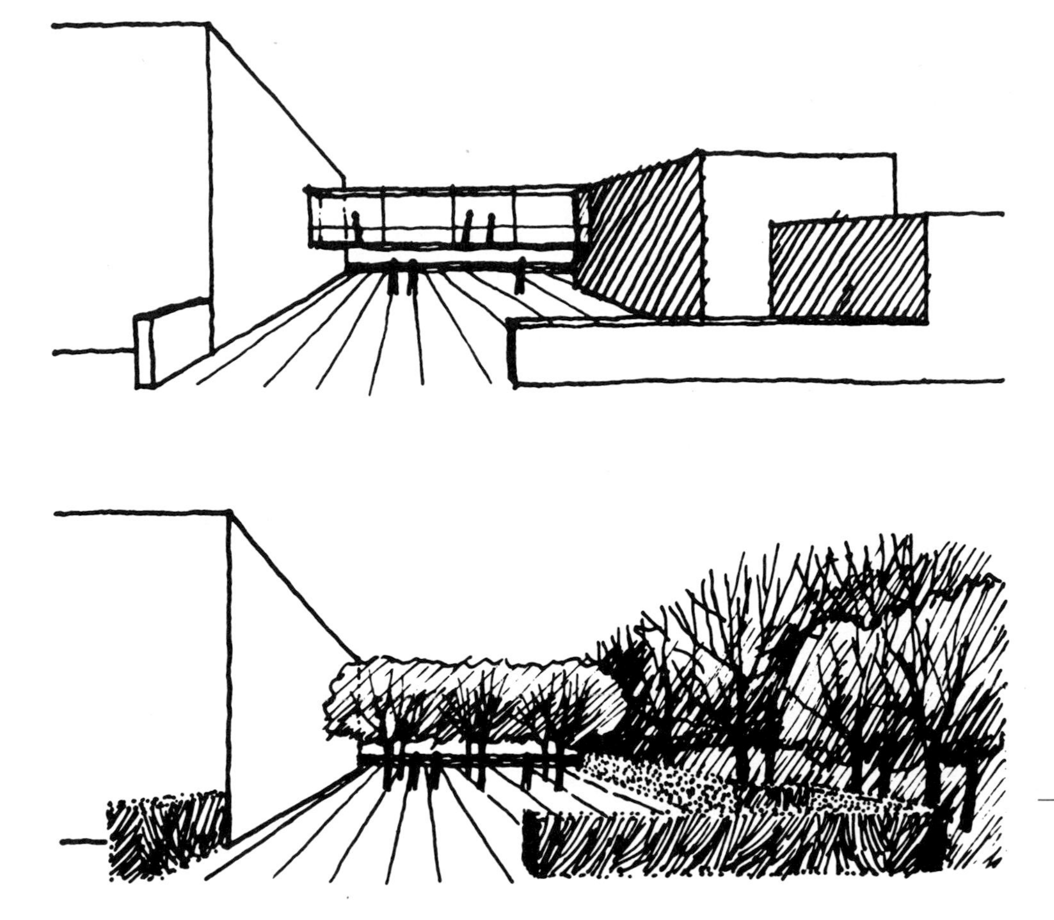

FIGURE 8.20
Space defined alternatively by architecture and plants.

FIGURE 8.21
Variation in structural material to emphasize form.

FIGURE 8.22
Pedestrian crosswalk indicated by a change in surface.

FIGURE 8.23
Paving pattern related to the architectural concept.

FIGURE 8.24
Directional paving pattern for purposeful circulation, gravel surface for casual use.

expectations. Asphalt and concrete paving suggest fast, unimpeded movement, whereas gravel suggests slower, more casual strolling or standing around (Fig. 8.23). The practice of paving the crosswalks at street intersections with bricks emphasizes the use of those areas by pedestrians and identifies territories for automobiles and pedestrians (Fig. 8.22). Changes in surface can also suggest direction of movement, and the texture of the material or the linear arrangement of

FIGURE 8.25
Paving pattern brings unity to diverse architecture. Plazza del Campo, Sienna. Photograph by Charles Rapp.

paving blocks and expansion joints can emphasize direction (Fig. 8.24). Paving patterns can be thought of as information about the environment. Understanding our perception of these clues in the environment is important if the messages we want to communicate are to be clear, yet not overly heavy.

Paving patterns also may be used as a technique of design to link elements or buildings together, to emphasize some sculpture or object; in doing so they may connect and to some extent conceal such mundane things as drain inlets. Successful paving patterns should emanate from and reinforce the inherent character of the place where it is strong and there is a clear relationship between the buildings and the space between them; alternatively, paving can be used to bring unity to a group of varied buildings. At the Campidoglio in Rome the paving is part of a larger concept and is clearly related to the total composition designed at one time by Michelangelo (Fig. 8.23). By contrast, in the Medieval marketplace of Sienna the paving brings unity to an organic collection of buildings of various heights and styles (Fig. 8.25).

It is also possible to affect scale relationships with paving materials. Paving materials that consist of small but identifiable units provide a fine-textured surface (Fig. 8.26). The unit relates easily to the human dimensions. Alternatively, poured concrete, which does not have small identifiable units, takes on the scale of the unit delineated by the expansion joints (Fig. 8.27). The spacing between these is a function of the thickness of the concrete and whether or not it is reinforced. The thicker and the greater the reinforcing, the larger the unit may be. Thus we can have expanses of paving made up of small units like cobblestones or bricks, or we can have concrete surfaces in which the units are 20 by 20 feet, or asphalt in which there is no discernible unit at all. The patterns the eye perceives then may be large or simple or small-scaled and textured. It is possible to combine the two in such a way that the larger perceived shapes relate to the surrounding buildings while smaller units within the pattern relate to the human experience (Fig. 8.28).

The same unit paving materials can present a different quality of surface depending on the way they are laid. Concrete blocks laid with wide joints seeded with grass present a more rustic and informal surface than the same blocks laid flush with cement joints—a surface more suitable for large pedestrian crowds or wheeled toys (Fig. 8.29; see also Fig. 8.17). The use of a very small but tough material, such as granite blocks laid with open joints or a hollow concrete frame, seeded with grass and treated like a lawn can result in one surface looking like another; thus a "lawn" can be used as a parking area or take the weight of a fire truck.

FIGURE 8.26
Granite blocks, hard wearing material providing fine texture.

FIGURE 8.27
Poured concrete can form any shape. Expansion joints give pattern.

FIGURE 8.28
Bricks grouped into larger units (see also Fig. 8.4). Photograph by Trinidad Juarez.

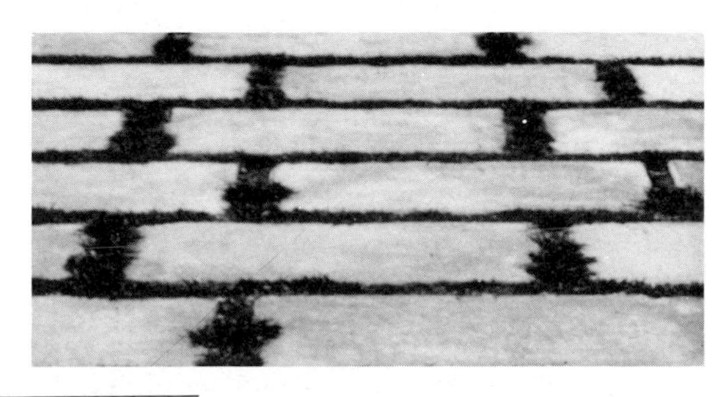

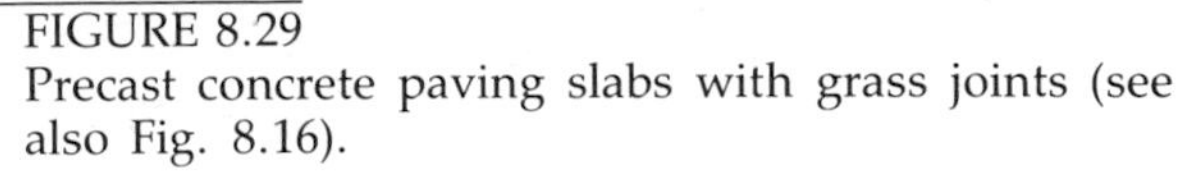

FIGURE 8.29
Precast concrete paving slabs with grass joints (see also Fig. 8.16).

FIGURE 8.30
Concrete paving surface with exposed aggregate. Photograph by Trinidad Juarez.

On the other hand, the reverse is also possible—a surface may look like lawn but actually be plastic! This seems to have some practicality for sports but is one of those modern innovations that are difficult to accept. The plastic lawn is in fact a solution to a problem related more to short-term economics than to human sensibility.

Standard paving surfaces have many variations and applications. The final selection of materials is determined by the intended use, its maintenance needs and durability factor, cost, and visual quality.

Types of Paving Materials

Asphalt is the cheapest hard surface, and one of the most common. It is widely used for roads, paths, playgrounds, courts, and parking lots. It is durable enough to last approximately ten years before resurfacing is needed.[2] Compare this with granite blocks, which essentially last forever but cost a great deal more to obtain and lay in place. Asphalt is a fluid material, which can cover awkward shapes. It is easily laid and can be given a range of supporting capacities for automobiles, trucks, and people.

Gravel is another fluid and relatively cheap material (Fig. 8.23). However, it is not always suitable for general pedestrian movement. This depends on the method of laying and the size of the gravel, which can vary from decomposed granite to pea gravel. The former can be compacted into a smooth, hard surface. Pea gravel is difficult to walk on and impossible to use for bicycles and wheeled toys. As a nonwalking surface, large gravel provides relatively low-maintenance groundcover which permits the direct return of rain water to the soil.

Depending on its thickness and quality and the distance it has to be moved to the job, poured concrete

[2] *Ibid.*

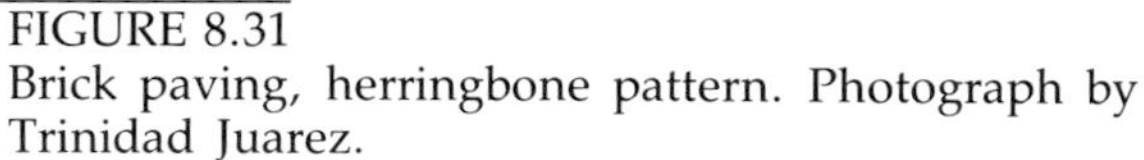

FIGURE 8.31
Brick paving, herringbone pattern. Photograph by Trinidad Juarez.

costs between two and four times as much as asphalt. It is also a fluid material and can be poured into any shape (Fig. 8.27). The location of the expansion joints needed to permit volume changes induced by temperature is also a function of thickness and reinforcement, and is planned to prevent cracking of the surface. As the spacing increases, the concrete's thickness and need for reinforcement increases. The weight the surface has to withstand is also a factor that determines the need for reinforcement. The manipulation of all these variables results in visual patterns on the surface. Expansion joints may be made of wood, bitumin, or steel and may be highly visible or almost invisible. The surface of poured concrete may vary according to its finish and aggregate (Fig. 8.30). Expos-

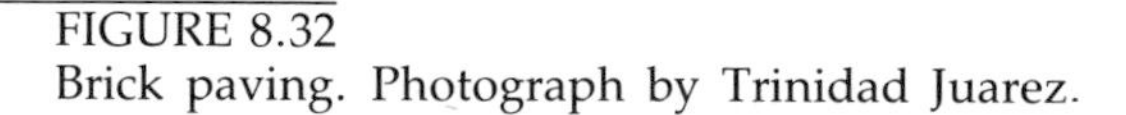

FIGURE 8.32
Brick paving. Photograph by Trinidad Juarez.

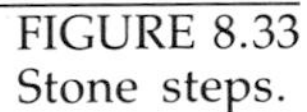

FIGURE 8.33
Stone steps.

ing the aggregate by brushing with acid and washing can reveal texture and color, which are both determined by the nature of the aggregate. On the other hand, the surface may be brush-finished, giving a directional texture. This may be especially suitable in providing a nonslip surface on ramps in cold climates.

Concrete paving blocks are similar in appearance to poured concrete but come precast in specific and relatively small sizes (Fig. 8.17). These may also have texture and color variations and may be laid in a variety of patterns. The joints may be open or closed. They have a unit shape and therefore influence the edge and shape of the areas paved.

Bricks come in a variety of colors depending on their origin and can be laid in several traditional patterns (Figs. 8.31 and 8.32). Their relative cost is between six and eight times the cost of asphalt. They can be laid dry or with cement grouting. If bricks are laid dry, rain water will flow back to the underlying soil and plant roots. If they are laid as a solid surface, the same kind of drainage provision will be needed as for any other hard, impermeable surface. Bricks laid without grouting may even provide ammunition in times of civil disturbance! In cold climates there is a tendency for bricks to "heave" in winter, creating a maintenance problem. Recently a product has become available which is a manufactured, artificial surface that looks like brick paving but is only about an inch thick. This is considerably cheaper than real bricks to purchase and install. At a distance its appearance may be quite satisfactory, but, like plastic grass, on close inspection its true personality is revealed—very synthetic, without variability, and without the ability to age gracefully as bricks do.

Cut stone is very expensive and is used now only in special situations or where tradition demands it (Fig. 8.33). It is likely to cost up to twelve times as much as asphalt. However, its life span is indefinite. It is often thought of as a "gardenesque" material, yet it has paved many an urban plaza and street throughout the world in times when endurance was considered of more importance than short-term economics (although, of course, the men who laid the streets were paid very little for their labor).

Wood has become a gardenesque paving material, popular in California because the relatively dry climate favors it and also because wood is easily available (Fig. 8.34). Its use in gardens derives from its functional nautical origins: decks, piers, boardwalks, and so on. The cost of wood as a walking surface is approximately eight or ten times that of asphalt, depending on construction and quantity. As decking, level areas can be extended out from a hillside; on flat sites the wood may be laid on the ground like a dance floor. The connection between wood and ground, however, is a sensitive one. Although preservatives are used in curing wood, it is proper practice to avoid contact between wood and soil. This can be done in a variety of ways by using concrete piers in the ground and steel clasps to attach the wood to the concrete. Space between boards allows for drainage. Wooden blocks have also been used like bricks but, although the effect is attractive, their life span is limited.

Grass is the cheapest usable surface. Depending on the quantity, the amount of soil preparation, and other operational costs, it is cheaper than asphalt, although it requires more regular maintenance. Its uses are of course determined by the slope of the area, and by maintenance.

Sand is another surface that can be walked on and in which children can play (Fig. 8.9). Its uses are informal and recreational, and it needs containment since it has no capacity to bind together. The edge of sand areas is thus a special design problem.

Connections

The edge or joint between materials and surfaces is a very important aspect of design. Joints, which "read" as lines, are usually highly visible and so should complement the design and connect rather than divide; they should integrate the pieces and surfaces of the overall design. The meeting of soft and hard surfaces is especially important from a maintenance point of view. The classic solution to the meeting of grass and planting is to separate (or join) them

FIGURE 8.34
Wooden deck provides extension of level surface on sloping ground and allows existing trees to be retained. Donnell Garden, California. Thomas D. Church, landscape architect. Photograph by Rondal Partridge.

FIGURE 8.35
The joints between surfaces and elements is one of the major aspects of detailed design. Planting and grass.

FIGURE 8.36
Building and grass.

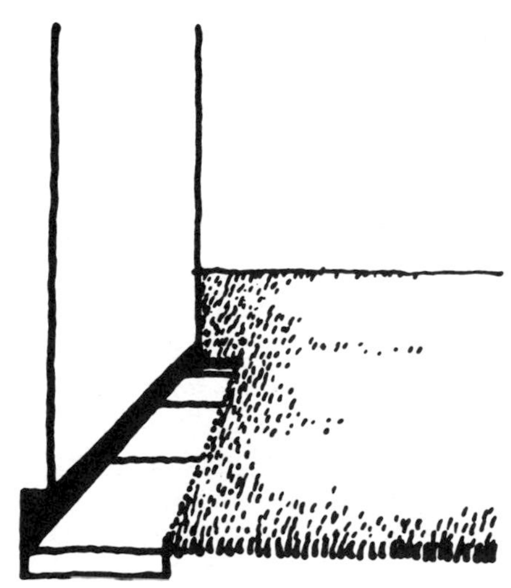

by a paving strip at least 1 foot wide. The grass should be 1 to 2 inches above this mowing strip (Fig. 8.35). These provisions allow for easy cutting of the grass without the destruction of the plants or shrubs, which may branch forward naturally, concealing the edge of the soil. Another critical situation is where grass meets a wall or building. Here again the grass must be separated from the wall by 1 to 2 feet so that the mowing machinery can cut to its edge (Fig. 8.36). If this is not done, a ragged fringe of uncut grass frequently will surround the building. The space between the grass and the building may be paved, providing a solid plane on which the building rests, or else it may be filled with gravel 2 inches below the grass level. If planting is used to make this transition between building and grass, space should be left between the planting and the building to allow for maintenance, window cleaning, and so forth.

Walls

The horizontal surfaces make up only one facet of landscape space. In addition to their use in the walls of buildings, which may have a variety of characteristics—glass, brick, concrete, wood—the same architectural materials can be extended or used to make free-standing and retaining walls and fences to form outdoor space. The selection of materials for these should relate to the uses they enclose or enhance.

WATER

One other important landscape material remains to be mentioned: water. This element, combined with paving and plants, provides detail and quality to the spaces of the site plan. It is a basic component of nature and landscape architecture. In nature we see it in mountain streams, tumbling and gushing and traveling at a speed depending on the gradient of the land and the "newness" of the river (Fig. 8.37). It forms waterfalls and is made white with the interjection of air into it. Its color also varies according to the sky above, its depth, and the nature of the surface

FIGURE 8.37
Mountain stream. Photograph by R. Burton Litton, Jr.

FIGURE 8.38
Still dark water provides perfect reflections of objects in sunlight.

FIGURE 8.39
Reflections are affected by light and wind. Photograph by Peter Kostrikin.

below. In lower lands the water runs smoothly, often without sound, sometimes giving ephemeral, but momentarily exact reflections of the surroundings. Instinctively we know water is not solid except when it may be frozen. As a lake, water defines a very exact edge related to the topography and, if the surface is still, it reflects the sky (Fig. 11.6). Wind and tidal forces create waves and ripples in the oceans. Gravity and light result in the numerous forms in which water is found in nature.

Add human ingenuity to the natural phenomena. First by natural pressure and later by artificial means, water has been forced into the air in foaming jets and allowed to return to the ground in a variety of ways, all pleasing to the viewer. This remains a constant human preoccupation. Historically, water has had symbolic significance and various cultures have appreciated the cooling qualities of water in hot climates. Moorish, Indian, and Persian gardens are examples of this understanding. The reflective quality of water is especially interesting. The water surface must be very still and the bottom of the pool very dark or very deep (Figs. 8.38 and 8.39). The reflection to be seen from any point can be calculated geometrically. Since water

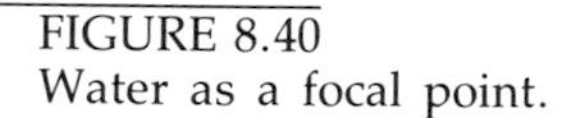

FIGURE 8.40
Water as a focal point.

FIGURE 8.41
Cascade in Portland, Oregon. Lawrence Halprin and Associates, landscape architects. Photograph by Paul Ryan.

reflects the sky, a small pond in a dark, enclosed courtyard may serve to add light. Water is also useful as a cooling agent in hot climates. Water can be jetted into the air to reduce temperatures. Fountains may also be programmed so that the water performance changes, making different sound effects as well as visual variation. The sound of falling or running water (like Muzak) may also be relied on to blot out unwanted sounds and create an additional environmental attribute by design as most elegantly illustrated at Paley Park in New York City. Water for drinking appears in the city and in parks, and there are many ways in which water may be made available to adults and children.

Water has, of course, many recreational uses which can only be touched upon here. Boating and fishing need extensive areas of water (Figs. 4.13 and 8.10). Swimming and skating have special requirements. Swimming pools are painted or paved in light colors so that the bottom and not a reflection can be seen. As we have noted already, to most people—at least when they are dressed—water is something not to get into. It is therefore a "hazard" and can be a controller of circulation (Fig. 8.14). Visual continuity can be maintained between two points while access is prevented. A restaurant may be separated from the sidewalk by a pond (see page 230). Water by its uniqueness, at least in cities, tends to act as a focal point. The fountain in a square becomes a rendezvous (Fig. 8.40). Thus in Portland, Oregon, Halprin's cascades, symbolic of mountain streams yet stylized and urban, attract hundreds of people in the summer. This is a focal point for all segments of the population. It is a landmark and gives distinct quality to part of the city (Figs. 8.41 and 8.42).

Perhaps one of the most critical aspects of designing with water is the edge of the container. In nature water seeks the lowest level and is uncompromisingly horizontal. Thus the edges of an artificial container must be exactly level unless a specific optical illusion is desired, in which water may be made to appear as though it is flowing uphill. But who would want to trifle with that? The edge of the water is always very precise and therefore is visually dominant. The con-

FIGURE 8.42
A cascade in the High Sierras, California.
Photograph by R. Burton Litton, Jr.

FIGURE 8.43
The meeting of land and water may take various forms depending on the nature of the water and the intended relationship between it and people.

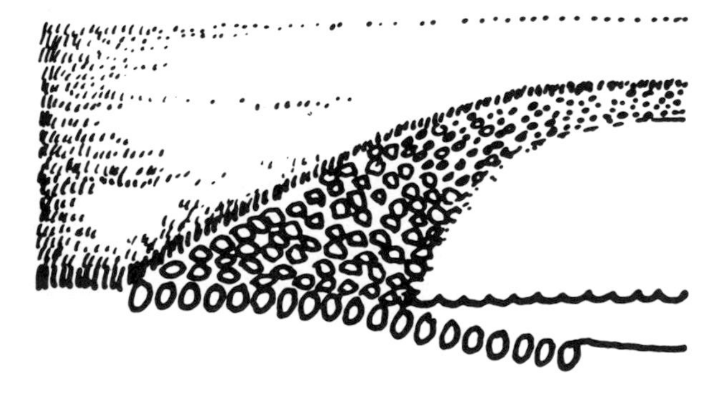

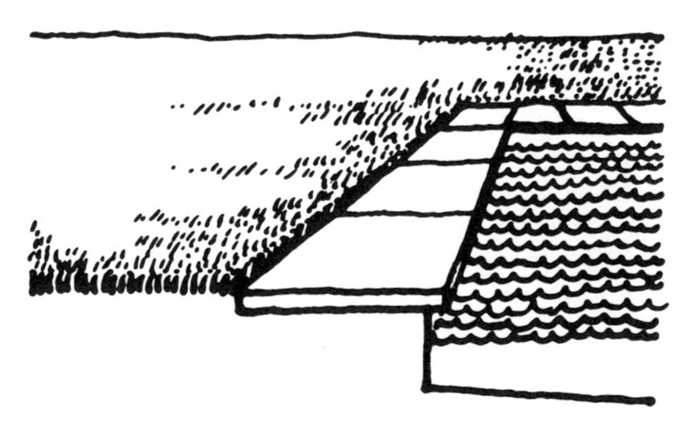

nection of water to land, a very magic zone significant in evolution, attracts us. The nature of our participation with the water at this edge is crucial to the form it should take and the materials it should be made with (Fig. 8.43).

SUMMARY

In summary, landscape design is a very complicated process with many alternatives. It is the solution of a series of problems defined in site planning: the circulation or movement, the surfacing, the location and form of seating, the form and space for any purpose or multiple purposes. It is the giving of form to water and land and the selection of materials. Landscape design is a rational procedure that depends on an experience of life and social behavior. It also depends on an understanding of materials, their technology, and their maintenance. It demands an imaginative design ability to devise new and creative form out of the analysis of the problem and the determinants of form. A design that can be built only on its particular site may be judged successful when affinity with the site and the particular program is evident. Design in these terms is a growth or an evolutionary adaptation of environment. Successful design will express sympathy for the people who will use it, and it will express a feeling and understanding of use. It will exhibit a relationship to all else around, before, and in the future, visually and historically.

SUGGESTED READINGS

Ashihara, Y., *Exterior Design in Architecture.*

Beazley, Elizabeth, *Design and Detail of the Space between Buildings.*

Beazley, Elizabeth, *Designed for Recreation.*

Booth, Norman, *Basic Elements of Landscape Design*, Ch. 4, "Pavement," Ch. 5, "Site Structures," Ch. 6, "Water."

Brookes, John, *Room Outside.*

Ching, F., *Architecture, Form, Space and Order.*

Church, Thomas D., *Gardens are for People.*

Clay, Grady, ed., *Water and the Landscape.*

Crowe, Sylvia, *Garden Design, Part II*, "Principles of Design," Part III, "Materials of Design."

Downing, Michael, *Landscape Construction*, Ch. 4, "Surfacing," Ch. 5, "Simple Structures," Ch. 6; "Water Features."

Eckbo, Garrett, *Landscape for Living*, Ch. XIII, "Structural Elements Out of Doors."

Halprin, Lawrence, *Cities.*

Hannebaum, Leroy, *Landscape Design.*

Jellicoe, Susan, and Geoffrey Jellicoe, *Water.*

Kassler, Elizabeth B., *Modern Gardens and the Landscape.*

Marlow, O. C., *Outdoor Design—Handbook for the Architect and Planner.*

Pile, John, *Design.*

Shepheard, Peter, *Gardens.*

Shepheard, Peter, *Modern Gardens.*

Tandy, Clifford, *Handbook of Urban Landscape.*

Tunnard, Christopher, *Gardens in the Modern Landscape.*

Weddle, A. E., ed., *Techniques of Landscape Architecture*, Ch. 5, "Hard Surfaces," by T. Cochrane; Ch. 7, "Outdoor Fittings and Furniture."

HUMAN FACTORS IN LANDSCAPE ARCHITECTURE

9

Elizabeth Kassler suggests that good planning and design will be the product of a process which respects both the nature of man and the nature of nature.[1] Thus far we have emphasized the natural constraints and opportunities in regional landscape planning and site planning. The criteria for housing, recreation facilities, and use areas have assumed a great deal about human needs. In this chapter we consider how social and psychological theory, behavioral studies, and community participation may contribute to viable decision making and to the development of appropriate form for human use at all scales of landscape architecture.

The movement, which is now characterized by community participation and other efforts to achieve a better fit between design form and the users, started,

[1] Elizabeth B. Kassler, *Modern Gardens and the Landscape* (New York: Doubleday, 1964).

probably, in the 1960s. In *The Death and Life of Great American Cities* (1961), Jane Jacobs criticized large, high-rise New York housing developments which eliminated the street as part of the environment. She attributed lack of personal safety and neighborliness and the non-use of open spaces to the design. By contrast, she argued that the form, scale, and street life of Greenwich Village contributed to a healthier social situation. In other words, she related certain of the ills of society to the physical form of the environment. In addition, she hinted that the perceptions and values of designers (usually white middle class) were often different from those for whom they designed.

Also in the 1960s, the self-help concept was originated. A community group would get together and with the help of public-spirited professionals and often students, would make physical changes to their neighborhood: clear a vacant lot, build a playground, plant trees, and the like (Fig. 9.1). Although not in itself a solution to major problems, the process in one way or another revealed to the participants the variety of concerns, likes and dislikes, priorities and needs of a particular section of the population.

Thus, the development of a stronger link between physical design and the consumer was initiated, based on an understanding of human needs, environmental perception, and behavioral science. Since that time, important research has been done and a flood of literature published dealing with environment and behavior.

In this chapter, we consider how social and psychological theory, behavioral studies, and community participation contribute to responsible decision making and the development of appropriate form for human use in landscape architecture.

Two critical areas of concern in the design process are affected by this approach. They are programming and geometry. In Chapter 7, the program in site planning was described as a set of uses with generic form. In the same chapter, site planning was seen as a process of arranging these uses in relation to each other with reference to the constraints and opportunities revealed in site and regional analyses (page 137). In Chapter 8, it was suggested that the genesis of shape and form (within major constraints of boundaries and topography) lay in the uses of the program (page 155). Strictly from a social perspective, program and geometry are the basic input and product. The objective is to get the right thing in the right place with the right form.

The program then must be concerned with appropriate content as a reflection of user needs and attitudes. The geometry must not only provide what is wanted, but must arrange and orient it in such a way that the resulting relationships are supportive of the intended uses as well as of community involvement and development. Certain aspects of program and geometry are standard or universal. Sports fields and facilities and fundamental criteria of health and safety are not subject to local or cultural variation. Other forms of behavior relating to age particularly, recur in most societies and cultures, as for example to find a cool place when it is hot, to be entertained, to play games, to go out in a boat, to gossip, and so on. Other aspects of content and form, generated by history, social, and cultural traditions, excessive climate, and so on are unique to each situation.

FIGURE 9.1
Direct relationship between the users and the design in a "self-help" project.

The major question for the designer is "who is the client or user?" and knowing that, to what extent can or should this influence form and content of design? Thomas Church (page 56) regarded his clients as major sources of form and content (together with technology and art). The one to one relationship that a garden designer has with a client is potentially an optimum relationship. Perhaps the only better situation would be to design something for oneself. But the real puzzle is the anonymous public; office workers and others who come to but do not live in a place. Even identifiable groups such as a homeowners association, a board of directors, neighborhood improvement groups, Friends of such and such a park, and so forth, often boil down to one spokesperson or represent a special interest, and as such may not really represent a constituency. The question is, for whom do we design?

Generally there are two basic ways to answer the question. One is to learn from observation of peoples' behavior and/or direct consultation with members of a community or a specific group in society. The other way is to become familiar with the general principles or "universals" of behavior and perception.

SOCIAL ANALYSIS

Questionnaires

Various methods have been developed to help designers know more about the needs and attitudes of the public client. One method of gathering attitudinal information is the questionnaire or attitude survey. The success of these forms depends on the selection and wording of the questions. Questions such as "what do you think of so and so?" or "what kind of environment would you like?" are inhibiting. Since most members of the public do not know what all the possibilities are, their answers are limited by their past experiences and imaginations, or loaded by the choices they are given in the questions. Although attitude surveys are becoming increasingly sophisticated, there are so many variables and difficulties that they may only be useful as a way to substantiate the hypothesis or intuitive guess of an intelligent designer or planner who is familiar with the situation (Fig. 9.2).

Factual questionnaire surveys which provide an indication of the actual use of facilities, parks, and playgrounds are probably more valuable. Studies of this nature at least tell us how the existing facilities are used and the distance people of various ages are prepared, if not content, to travel for various recreational activities and experiences. The extent to which particular features of landscape or city have significance or what Lynch[2] calls "imageability" to the majority of the people can also be measured through interview techniques.

Questionnaires may also be employed in post-construction evaluation or user studies. This analysis provides useful information and opinion about a specific environment. In this case questions are answered about an environment in which the respondents live or which they use and about which they are more interested and able and qualified to answer. Several studies have been made of reactions and use patterns of tenants in housing developments in which the findings are contrasted with the original expectations of the architects, which are sometimes at odds with the actual use. It is not possible to make generalizations from these specific studies, but a series of user feedback studies may reveal patterns and recurring problems helpful in designing similar subsequent projects. One of Alexander's techniques of generating form is based on the same concept, that of improving the

FIGURE 9.2
Child's drawing of an ideal park includes swimming pool, boating lake, baseball diamond, swings, trees, grass, and parking.

design by critical analysis of previous solutions to the same problem.[3]

Observation

Direct observation of behavior in particular use or activity areas reveals another level of information. For example, Vere Hole's study of children's playgrounds in London,[4] measuring the child's attention time and the variety of environment needed by children, those occupations and features receiving most attention, and so forth, provides valuable general information for future design work. Its use is limited to some extent, however, by the specifics of the particular case study, since findings related to children's play behavior in London would not necessarily apply in Los Angeles except in the very basic physical needs inherent in maturation and body building. By observing people in parks and public open spaces in a systematic way, it is possible to get an impression of the way in which the environment is used or misused and the way in which the design and arrangement of elements such as fountains and benches result in particular behavioral patterns. Post-construction evaluation may record behavior in map form (Fig. 9.3). The candid camera film of William H. Whyte not only illustrates the variety of activity which takes place in urban open spaces, but also demonstrates successful and unsuccessful design. His findings are articulated in amendments to open-space zoning provisions of New York

[2] Kevin Lynch, *The Image of the City* (Cambridge: MIT Press, 1960).
[3] Christopher Alexander, *A Pattern Language*.
[4] W. Vere Hole, *Children's Play on Housing Estates* (London: H. M. S. O., 1966).
[5] William H. Whyte, *The Social Life of Small Open Spaces*.

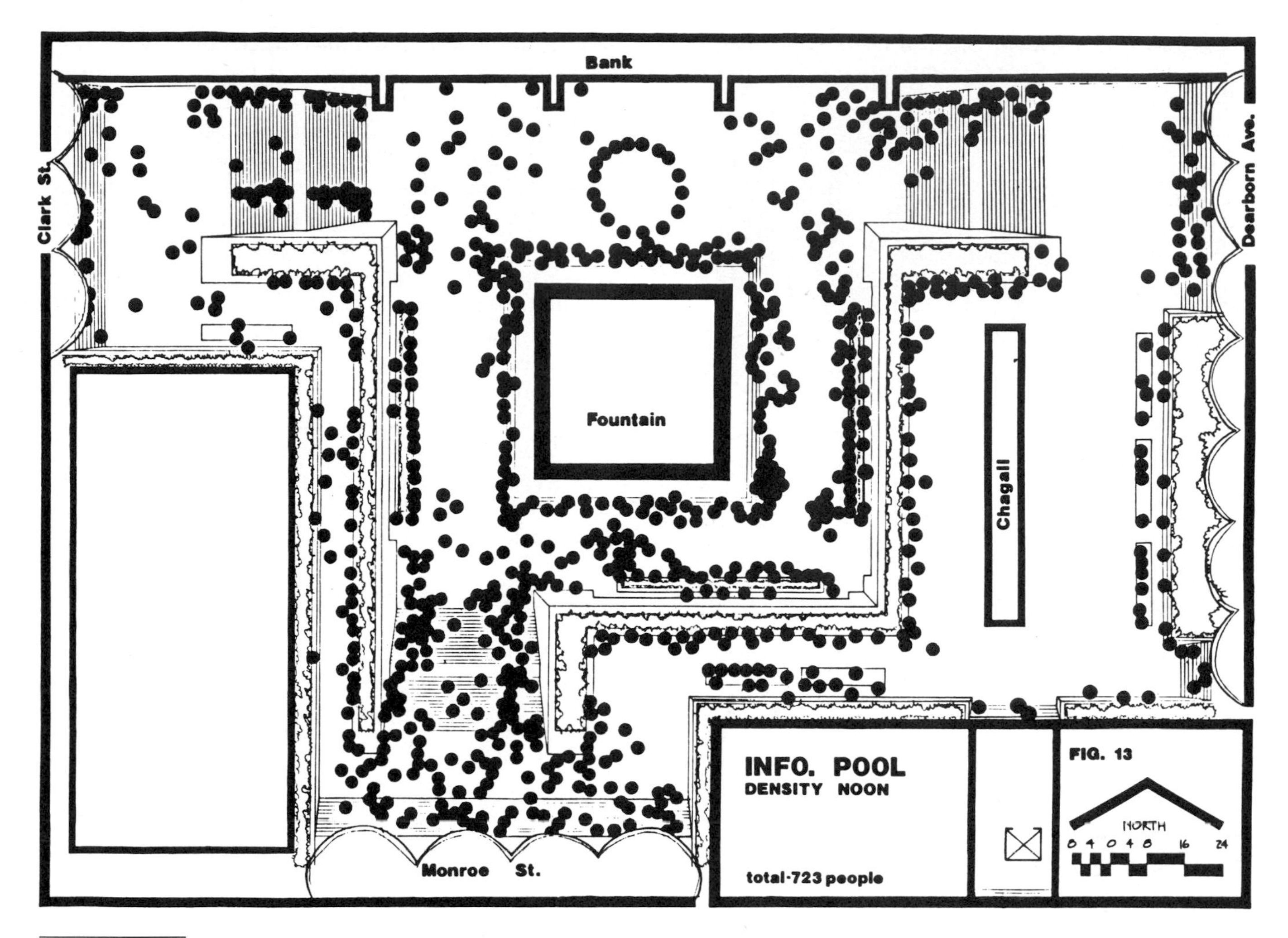

FIGURE 9.3
Map showing the number of people in an urban plaza and their location at a particular time of day. One of many maps prepared from observations of social behavior in a pilot study in the post-construction evaluation of the First National Bank Plaza, Chicago, Illinois. The study was prepared by the Department of Landscape Architecture, University of Illinois, and directed by Professor Albert J. Rutledge in 1975.

City and are important guidelines for anyone designing in a downtown sector. The provisions specify amount and dimensions of seating, tree planting, retail space, lighting, access,and maintenance.[5]

Even without the presence of people to observe, "tell-tale" traces such as litter and worn paths, graffiti, and other marks can give an indication of use patterns or dissatisfaction with the environment.

Community Participation and Workshops

There is one other way by which we can attempt to match design form with the needs and desires of the people who will use it. In recent years, community participation in the design and planning process has become a characteristic of urban renewal and neighborhood development and is often required by law. The roots of cooperative effort go back a long way to tasks that required more than one person or family to complete, such as the harvesting of a crop or raising a barn. The earliest forms of community participation, already mentioned, often did involve building and physical involvement, with specific benefits, but this is not essential (Fig. 9.4). Participation is now more typically confined to the programming phase and frequently involves workshops. Workshops have been described as modern versions of the New England town meeting.

FIGURE 9.4
Community project facilitates group social interaction and group affiliation.

> Participation processes are new experiences, novel situations; sometimes enjoyable, sometimes hard work . . . leading to . . . serious results such as deciding on how and whether your community should have its own planning council; deciding on how your neighborhood should look; deciding on how you would like City Hall to plan for you; deciding on solutions for problems that exist in your community; deciding what physical changes are necessary to make your community better; and many other community decisions and solutions to problems.[6]

The objective is to involve members of a community in reaching mutually agreed upon directions for its future. The issues may be minor or major and the workshops may last a day or a year. The number of participants may range from 12 to an entire community. The duration and degree of participation depends on the issues, the objectives, and the time available. One day is enough for an environmental awareness workshop. A year may be needed to deal with a town's future, problem definition, program development, and generation of alternatives.

The structure of a workshop may vary according to circumstances. Halprin suggests, however, that two important goals should be achieved at the outset. These are that the participants should become aware of the environment they live in as it really is. This leads and contributes to the second goal which is the development of a common language which makes the definition of problems and solutions easier. People have to learn the art of communication which involves active listening and true expression of feelings.[7]

[6] Lawrence Halprin and Jim Burns, *Taking Part.*
[7] *Ibid.*

It is recommended that the place where a workshop is held be large and convenient, a public place like an empty store, not in someone's home, a club or church which may inhibit attendance or freedom of expression. The size is important so that numbers involved are not limited, so that there is space for the use of various media, and so that proposals and ideas can be exhibited and shared with others.

Once the process is started by public announcement, a facilitator or process leader is needed to plan the activities starting with environmental awareness. Thereafter, sessions will be organized around the issues and involve whatever media are thought most suitable to enable participants to express and share their ideas. Media such as colored pens and newsprint, models and video are frequently used. In discussions, it is helpful to have a recorder who graphically portrays the flow and interaction of participants' ideas. A steering committee selected by consensus may be necessary, but in any event decisions should be reached by consensus and not by vote.

Workshops are sometimes criticized because there is no assurance that a cross section of the community is involved. Getting people there is perhaps the most difficult aspect of workshops. Most important is the involvement of elected officers, local government officials, and professionals with a role in the workshop topic. Finally, the decisions and conclusions of a workshop need publicity and communication to City Hall or wherever authority lies. Theoretically, the end result is a strong statement of a community's needs and priorities to which politicians, planners, and designers can respond.

A version of the workshop concept results in people building their own environments, parks, playgrounds, and even housing or at least participating in it as in so-called self-help projects (Figs. 9.1 and 9.4). The designer's role in such situations is clearly to present alternatives, and ultimately to facilitate the implementation of the plan agreed on. This process, although unique in each case, can also contribute to a better understanding of environmental preferences and suitabilities. That is, the experience of working with the potential users is in itself educational for the designer as well as the participants. In addition, the project is more likely to reflect the expressed needs and interests of the users as they then are defined. Flexibility in the solution will presumably take care of future users whose needs and preferences may be different.

All these methods to get closer to the consumer risk the production of misinformation. The questionnaires may be very parochial, inasmuch as data gathered at one time and under certain circumstances may have little relevance a few years later. In observation studies and workshops, we must be cautious of the tremendous adaptability of people to given environmental situations, which can, in fact, lead us to find satisfactory—and even favor—environments that previously or objectively would have been considered unsatisfactory or hostile. Attitudes change, people move, life is ongoing, and there is always the dilemma that what the people seem to want or need at one moment may be in conflict with long-term goals or the needs of others. Thus, although the several techniques described here are potentially valuable sources of information in design, they must be used with caution and the conclusions examined with enlightened skepticism.

BEHAVIOR AND ENVIRONMENT

Studies and research into the relationship of social factors and design require a familiarity with general scientific work in behavior and perception. It is necessary to develop an intellectual framework through which design and planning decisions will be related to the basic principles of sociology and human psychology. In attempting to illustrate this relationship we may be able to answer questions of a general nature serving as a common base, or a set of minimum standards and requirements, with which to relate the specifics and variables of site planning and environmental problems.

The interaction between human behavior and the nonhuman environment is a two-way process. On the one hand, the environment has a definite impact on the individual, and our response may be to adapt to the imposed conditions. On the other hand, we are continually manipulating or choosing our physical surroundings in an attempt to make life physically and psychologically more comfortable (Fig. 9.5).

Behavior is the result of a complex interaction between two main sets of variables. The first is the environment that surrounds and affects the individual. The second is the inner condition of the individual, which has two parts: physiological, related to the body's biological mechanisms; and psychological, related to the cultural background, motives, and experiences of the individual and his or her basic needs. Thus in design we are concerned with three interrelated categories of human factors: physical, physiological, and psychological.

FIGURE 9.5
The impact of the environment may at times be counteracted by strong social needs and traditional

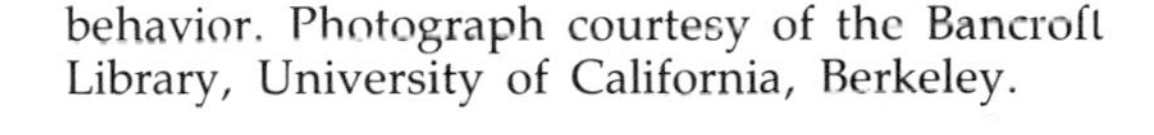
behavior. Photograph courtesy of the Bancroft Library, University of California, Berkeley.

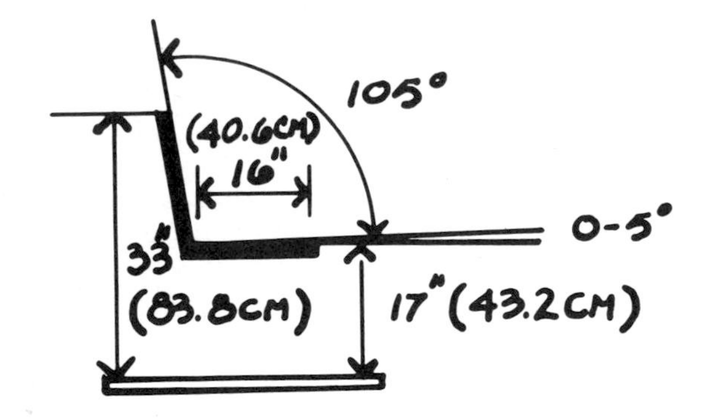

FIGURE 9.6
Best average dimensions for a bench, based on "The Measure of Man," by Henry Dreyfuss (1967).

Physical Factors

The first group is concerned with the rather obvious relationship between human shape and size and the detailed form of the environment. Analysis of average measurements and postures, movement, and growth results in a set of dimensions for parts of buildings and detailed landscape design. A door must be high enough to allow people to pass through without stooping, seats must be at the right level and inclination to be comfortable, steps must have dimensions evolved from basic movement patterns of the human body (Fig. 9.6). The gradients of ramps and the height of hand rails are further examples of form derived from the physical shape and movement characteristics of the users. Design details derived from purely visual considerations may or may not fulfill the condition of fit for the user. Le Corbusier's modular system derived a set of visually pleasing proportions and dimensions from the human body, thereby theoretically relating beauty and functional satisfaction in his design (Fig. 9.7).[8] Special situations may logically result in deviations from usual dimensions and standards. For example, where young children are involved, the environment must facilitate growth and development of the physical form—muscle development and motor ability—and dimensions of playground features, drinking fountains, and so on, must be appropriate for children. Other variations from the norm can be anticipated for the elderly and the handicapped. Obviously, then, we can achieve buildings and an outdoor environment for work and leisure which are designed in relation to the form and shape of the users.

Physiological Factors

Human physiological needs are also relatively easy to specify. They result from the interaction of the inner biological condition of an individual with the surrounding environment. People need food, air, water, exercise, and protection from the excesses of heat and cold. A state of health or disease may be regarded as an expression of the success or failure of an organism to respond adaptively to environmental challenges.[9] The process by which the individual maintains the internal environment in an approximately permanent state is called homeostasis. This process is essentially innate and automatic, resulting in the operation of body mechanisms and glands. Perspiring, shivering, and sleeping are examples of the body's response to environmental conditions.

The homeostatic process is facilitated by modifications to the environment. In the evolution of society, the building of shelters, and the use and control of fire permitted settlement in areas where homeostasis would otherwise have been difficult or impossible to maintain. Homeostasis also may result in migration to places where the conditions are more comfortable.

Thus in theory human physiological needs, like human physical form, can be easily specified. Needs can be fulfilled through the provision of nutritious foods, clean air, adequate and pure water, in addition to the elimination of disease within an effective physical environment which allows for control of cold and heat, provides shelter from weather, and at the same time affords the opportunity for exercise in fresh air and sunlight. A human comfort zone in which maximum and minimum temperatures and humidity are

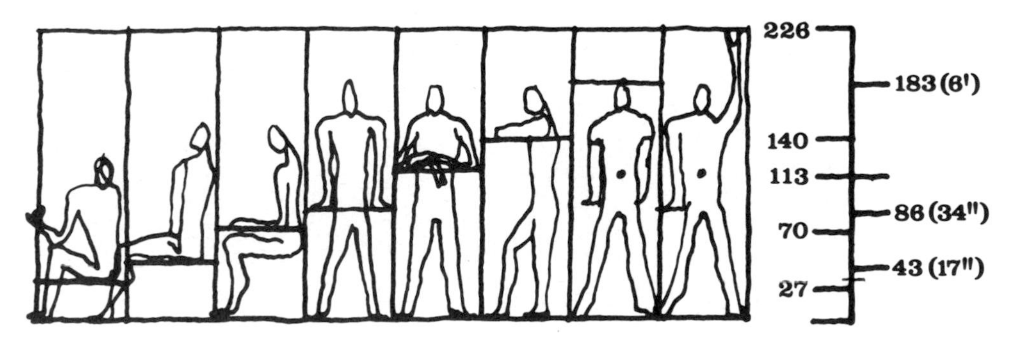

FIGURE 9.7
A series of modular dimensions, in centimeters, developed by Le Corbusier (1948). The measurements, derived from the human body, are interrelated with the golden rule system of proportions.

specified has been developed by Olgay, suggesting an optimum environment in terms of the homeostatic process, human comfort, and ease of living.[10] Some implications for design are discussed in the next chapter.

A semiphysiological need is the need for self-preservation and avoidance of pain. It is a self-protecting device against physical injury and death. The behavioral manifestation is to a large extent instinctive in the sense that we automatically withdraw from excessive heat and take precautionary measures against physical danger. Obviously an environment that is threatening and ambiguous could induce a state of apprehension and ultimately emotional stress harmful to the individual. We therefore seek out and demand a certain level of physical security in the environment. The responsibility of city agencies to provide conditions of safety for citizens has resulted in a series of regulations and design specifications. Fences around swimming pools, and hand rails on bridges and along flights of steps are often legal requirements resulting from safety regulations related to our need for security and fear of injury from falling.

Psychological Factors

Health is not merely the absence of disease or infirmity. The definition adopted by the World Health Organization describes health as a state of physical, mental, and social well-being. Thus we come to the third human component in environmental design: human psychological and social needs, behavioral patterns, and tendencies. It is the most difficult of the three sets of human factors to define and relate to the form of the environment. Yet are we not aware of environments that are not pleasing or useful and do we not desire to modify the environment for the fulfillment of some need? If we hope to plan and design environments that will be sensitive and responsive to the human condition, we must find a way to interpret and take into account our own psychological and emotional needs.

Human psychological needs and perception of the environment differ according to a multitude of variables including age, social class, cultural background, past experience, motives, and daily routine of the individual. These factors influence and differentiate the need structures of individuals and groups. Thus the needs of a child are obviously different from those of an adolescent or an adult. Even if the same needs can be identified, the overt behavior is likely to be different. Despite the complexity of the variables and difficulties in the definition of many needs, it is possible to suggest certain broad categories of inner needs defined on the basis of observed behavior and empirical evidence and social analysis. In reality we have some psychological needs some of the time and other needs at other times; we do not have all needs all of the time. Sometimes some needs are stronger than others, and our need structure changes according to the particular situation.[11]

The basic human inner condition may be classified into five generalized groupings of motivational forces and psychological needs: (1) social, (2) stabilizing, (3) individual, (4) self-expression, and (5) enrichment. There is inevitably overlap and potential conflict among the categories.

Social Needs. The first group, social needs, includes the need of the individual for social interaction, for group affiliation, for companionship, and for love. Together with these go the more subtle need to be needed and to be sustained by others and by implication the need for the protection of other people. The family group and the peer group are obvious manifestations of these needs. The whole of society is organized to a large extent around these basic social needs and the behavioral evidence can be seen in the public dance hall, the beach, senior citizens' clubs, veterans' societies, and so on. It is clear, then, that wherever the environment is meant for people or where the purpose of the design is not contrary to the fulfillment of these social needs, it should characteristically have a sociopetal form designed to draw people together, to engender social relationships or at least to make this possible. The Portland cascades attract people and therefore contribute to the fulfillment of this need (Fig. 8.41). So too the self-help or community project, by its very nature, draws people together in participation (Figs. 9.1 and 9.4). At a detailed level, the design and grouping of park benches can engender or inhibit social interaction (Fig. 9.8).

Stabilizing Needs. The second set of needs have been called stabilizing needs. We have a need to be free from fear, anxiety, and danger. And we have a need for a clear orientation, a need to develop and to hold a clear philosophy of life, a need to order and to organize the environment, a hope to have a say in its form and content through the democratic process. We have an inherent need to manipulate our environ-

---

[8] Charles Edouard Jeanneret-Gris, *The Modular*, 2nd edition (Cambridge: Harvard University Press, 1954).

[9] René Dubos, *Man Adapting* (New Haven: Yale University Press, 1965).

[10] Victor Olgay, *Design with Climate* (Princeton, N.J.: Princeton University Press, 1963).

[11] Peggy Long Peterson, "The Id and the Image," *Landmark '66* (Berkeley: University of California, Department of Landscape Architecture, 1966).

FIGURE 9.8
A grouping of benches in shade facilitates social interaction in Fresno, California. Eckbo, Dean, Austin and Williams, landscape architects.

ment, not only from the point of view of developing physical conditions responsive to our physiological needs, already mentioned, but also to satisfy some more deeply rooted need to make a mark, to form and shape the environment according to a symbolic, metaphysical urge. The concept of advocacy planning (self-help and self-determination) is to an extent related to this desire for stability through participation in decisions concerning one's own local environment. The concept of self-help projects where derelict, unused land is transformed through the energies, initiative, and artistic expression of local people, who will be the users of the land, gives rise to a form of design activity that not only satisfies the human need for a sense of stability and involvement basic to security but also leads to a completely new type of design process. Other design implications are imageability, the ordering of space so that it is free from ambiguity, and the selection of paving surfaces to provide information about a place and its use. There are many other ways in which design can give a sense of familiarity and security and provide opportunity for participation.

Individual Needs. The third group is described as individual needs. Some of these overlap or are similar to needs of self-expression. Here we recognize the need of people at certain moments in their experience and development of self-awareness to be utterly alone for a period of time, that is, the need for privacy. Further, there is a strong need for a certain amount of self-determination, for an identity and sense of personal uniqueness in the environment, and related to this a need to be able to choose or make individual decisions about one's life.

The possibility of privacy in today's urban environment becomes more remote and may be responsible for the influx of campers and backpackers to wilderness or distant landscape areas in search of isolation and a spiritual connection between themselves and nature. The designed environment should make privacy a real possibility. This is most easily achieved within a dwelling itself, although as building economics shrink the size of the house and as other misguided and fashionable concepts lead to more open plans, it becomes a more ephemeral possibility. Privacy also may be attainable by designing the outdoor environment to create areas less accessible to direct use by the urban population yet within minutes of it. Small sitting areas can be located off the beaten path or separated from circulation routes by grade changes (Fig. 12.13). The provision of choice in any environmental situation clearly allows a person to express individuality and identity. Circulation should offer choices. Within reason, we should be able to do what we want. But we must be careful that personal expression will not adversely affect the lives and privacy and equal needs for uniqueness and identity of others in society. It can be seen that there is a potential conflict between need for self-expression and social needs.

Self-expression. There is a variety of component needs making up the self-expression group. They include the need for self-assertion and exhibition, for dominance and power. Some of these needs have been made more specific to the environment in the concept of territory. There is also a need for accomplishment and achievement, for prestige, and to be held in esteem by others. Ardrey calls this the need for status, which is related to the need for territory.[12] The process of "keeping up with the Joneses," so evident in suburbia, is a clear expression of these needs, which, if better understood, could be satisfied in a less wasteful manner (Fig. 9.9).

[12] Robert Ardrey, *The Territorial Imperative* (New York: Atheneum, 1966).

FIGURE 9.9
Sacramento, California (1965). Photograph by William A. Garnett.

FIGURE 9.10
Barbed wire and warnings, physical manifestations of territoriality.

It has been suggested that the aggressive defense of territory is a form of self-expression fundamental to all animals, including humans. Territoriality can be seen not only in the walls and fences we erect around our houses and gardens (Fig. 9.10), but also in the areas we stake out for ourselves on the public beach or in the camping ground, which indicate territorial rights to be infringed at peril (Fig. 9.11). Much evidence related to human territorial instincts derives from studies of animal behavior.[13] The extent and location of territory tend to vary with the species, mating activity, seasonal change, and availability of food in the environment. Territoriality ensures proper spacing and thus prevents the overexploitation of the environment the family depends on for sustenance. Thus, by regulating density, territoriality ensures propagation of the species.

Territoriality has been identified as one of the three fundamental human drives, the other two being status and sex.[14] Laying claim to a territory and maintaining a certain distance from one's fellow may be considered a real human biological need, as it appears to be in other animals, although its human expression may be different and culturally conditioned.[15] Trespass laws and the legal status of private property are clear manifestations of a territorial urge.[16] We are also only too well aware of the concept of "turf," an area where members of a gang feel safe and where intruders will be regarded with hostility.[17]

There is a clear relationship between space or territory and animal survival. Since we are not highly dependent on our immediate environment, this is not a human concern. However, we must be interested in the relationship between space and behavior. Observations indicate that space limitations or crowding can

FIGURE 9.11
Territoriality in Yosemite National Park. Photograph by Bruce Davidson.

FIGURE 9.12
(a) Beach scene in Venezuela. People possibly spaced closer than they might be in Scandinavia.
(b) Desolate beach on which to be alone.
Photograph **(a)** by Francis Violich.

force people into stressful situations; on the other hand, in certain cases there can be too much space or distance between people, inhibiting conversation and use.[18] A second aspect of importance is the evidence of pronounced variations in spacing mechanisms and personal space exhibited by people of different cultural background and nationality. Sensitivity to this fact may lead to different design criteria for ostensibly the same facility or use area, depending upon regional variation. The crowding limit of a popular public place or beach is subject to a culturally imbued sense of territory and personal space. The carrying capacity of a recreational area is both a function of the landscape's ability to withstand wear and tear and the tolerance of the users for crowding (Fig. 9.12).[19]

Is there a point at which too little personal space may result in psychological breakdown or antisocial behavior? Experiments with rats in an artificial environment in which food was not a territorial factor have shown that severe conditions of overcrowding result in serious physiological effects and unnatural behavior.[20] The virtual impossibility of solitude leads to the disorganization of the society of rats and ultimately to population collapse. Although there are strong arguments that overcrowding in urban slum conditions is equally detrimental to the mental and physical health of its inhabitants, the human population is so profoundly conditioned by cultural and social factors that the question of human overcrowding in cities is more complicated than is the case with animal populations. Thus it is still not conclusive that high densities in cities are undesirable and that we are unable to design urban forms that would emphasize benefits of large city life and high concentrations of people, at the same time reducing the ill effects.[21] In other words, it does not follow that suburban form and low densities are best. The studies suggesting the prevalence of mental ill health in New York City have not been paralleled by similar studies in suburbia or a midwestern farm community where we may find similar or other problems.

Another form of self-expression is play (Fig. 9.13). We must thus ensure that the environment will provide possibilities for play as a general concept more than simply through the provision of "playgrounds" for organized games and sports. A city should have built-in variety and possibilities for imaginative response. The pedestrian circulation system at Cumbernauld was augmented with boulders and other features that could be perceived in any way a child or adult wished—as a mountain, a bench, or a hideout.

Enrichment. The last group of human needs is called enrichment needs. People (and especially children) have a thirst for knowledge. Related to this is a need for self-realization and personal creativity, and, it seems, a strong need for beauty and aesthetic experience. People have very definite creativity urges, although their strength and relative fulfillment take various forms and result in artifacts of various degrees of quality. Thus, although we are all artists, some are greater than others. The popularity of scenic and beautiful landscapes such as the Grand Canyon of

[13] Konrad Lorenz, *Studies in Animal and Human Behavior*, translated by Robert Martin (Cambridge: Harvard University Press, 1970).
[14] Ardrey, *op. cit.*
[15] Dubos, *op. cit.*
[16] Edward T. Hall, *The Hidden Dimension* (New York: Doubleday, 1966).
[17] Robert Sommer, *Personal Space* (Englewood Cliffs, N.J.: Prentice-Hall, 1969).
[18] E.g., "West Side Story."
[19] Hall, *op. cit.*
[20] John B. Calhoun, "The Role of Space in Animal Sociology," *Journal of Social Issues*, XXII (4) (October 1966).
[21] Christopher Alexander, *The City as a Mechanism for Sustaining Human Contact* (Berkeley: University of California, Center for Planning and Development Research, 1966).

FIGURE 9.13
(a) (b) Two contrasting forms of play fulfilling the same need for self-expression. Photograph **(b)** by Robert Sabbatini.

Arizona (Fig. 1.13), Yosemite (Fig. 3.10), and Yellowstone, the lake district and western highlands of the United Kingdom, all of the great natural wonders of the world, leads one to think that we do indeed have a very strong need for visual beauty, although obviously the basis of trips to such landscapes is also a response to some of the other needs already discussed. Human enrichment needs, then, seem to require the provision of information about the environment so that our understanding of what we see may be increased in detail. Moreover, the environment should not only be intrinsically beautiful itself, since this seems to be a basic human need, but it also should provide the possibility for creativity in the form of environmental manipulation or simply in the provision of opportunities within some kind of open space or recreation program for personal involvement in the arts, in sculpture, in gardening, or in play and theater.

In design, enrichment may be equated with complexity. The instinctive and continuing human need to decorate the environment can be seen in primitive cave drawings, in the supergraphics of the 1970s, and in all that lies in between. Modern architectural theory of the 1930s and subsequent economic constraints have tended to work against our desire for ornament. The "lean-to" architecture of the 1960s and 1970s, the renewed interest in the decoration of earlier eras, and the revival of the traditionally complex cottage garden, in which fruit, vegetables, and flowers are combined, indicate a fresh and intuitive understanding of this need. Here, in parallel with arguments favoring complexity in the natural environment for ecological purposes, are arguments for complexity and variety in the human or built environment also.

Having reviewed the generalities of human needs, we must be aware of the danger of becoming oversensitive and self-conscious about these needs, which are part of our general awareness. There is a danger in the development of specific design forms to satisfy or fulfill some of these needs which would lead in all probability to disappointment and conflict. It is not the intention here to suggest that design should be, or indeed can be, specifically oriented toward the fulfillment of any specific aspect of this spectrum of human emotional needs. On the contrary, it is simply suggested that the design process should identify some of the basic demands or needs which a particular component of the environment may reasonably be expected to satisfy and then should ensure that the geometric arrangement of the design does not prevent the fulfillment of those stated needs and desires. And, if possible, the design of any piece of environment—be it building, open space, park, or street—should be formed through an understanding of and sensitivity to the complexity of the human personality. In addition, it should be remembered that the physical environment is only one part of a larger process. It is the setting in which we interact with other human beings or the social environment.

A theoretical example of residential neighborhood form by Christopher Alexander illustrates the unexpected possibilities that may result when preconceived spatial designations are abandoned and emphasis is given to behavioral factors (Fig. 9.14).[22] This incom-

[22] *Ibid.*

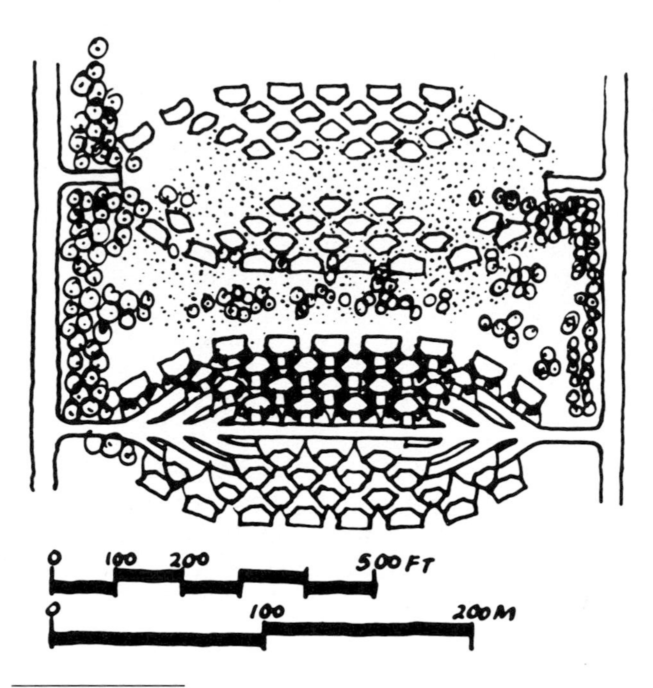

FIGURE 9.14
Two plan views of Christopher Alexander's theoretical neighborhood. **(a)** The private patios as they would relate to the hillside park. **(b)** The internal road system and houses.

plete study, essentially a diagram, concentrates on the human need for frequent intimate social contact, which, according to Alexander, contemporary society tends to inhibit. Its form is designed to allow ease of access by freeway networks for potential visitors in an automobile-oriented suburb. The number of homes in the cluster is based on probability studies which will ensure the presence of enough children of the same age to form play groups. The surface of the hill is a park in which the children can play but are insulated from the roads. Each house maintains its privacy and the idea is to emphasize the advantages of suburban living and counteract the undesirable qualities. The solution may be debatable, but nonetheless it is a good example of a form resulting from a process emphasizing certain social factors, a concept that can be applied with other and more precise data to all aspects of the environment.

Environmental Perception and Behavior

Behavior, then, results from the interaction of the individual with other individuals (the social environment) and with the surrounding (the physical environment). Consequently, the environmental designer must be interested in the structure of the environment and its effect on the individual. Second, and very much related to this, we must understand the way in which the environment is perceived by the individual; and third, we must be interested in general behavioral reaction to situations, social and physical.

Experiments show that variation in physical environmental stimulation is necessary for normal orientation and even for mental balance in the human being. Our sensitivity to the environment and our adaptability or response to environmental conditions can result in specific behavior, although we are actually unconscious of the effect of the environment on us. This possibility underscores the power that is in the hands of the environmental designer. It has been demonstrated that behavior and social interaction can be influenced by the arrangement of furniture in a room.[23] It has also been suggested that architectural arrangements can result in conditions alien to man, for example, where there is no opportunity for privacy (the open plan house) or little physical contact with the ground (a high-rise apartment).[24] The judgments in this case are made not on the basis of human survival, which is not in doubt, but in terms of probable mental stress and discomfort to which such environments may contribute. Environments can thus be specifically designed to bring people together agreeably for some purpose, as in an amphitheater, or to engender a social relationship, as in the arrangement of seats in a park. Alternatively, design can prevent or discourage such possibilities.

Another way in which the influence of environment on behavior can be seen is in the way places assume meaning. A church, a cemetery, a library produce specific behavior conforming to the understood rules and meaning or symbolism of such buildings and places. Various types of landscape may also result in specific behavioral response. This was in fact an important aspect of the eighteenth-century landscape gardens. Here the configuration of the landscape and the development of a sequence of changing views and experiences, including the introduction of allegorical and mythological allusions in the form of statuary, temples, grottoes, and other buildings, was intended to induce specific responses of sublimity, joy, amusement, sorrow, beauty, fear, awe—not all at once, but in sequence. The fullest response to these

[23] Sommer, *op. cit.*

[24] Humphry Osmond, "Function as the Basis of Psychiatric Ward Design" (sociopetal and sociofugal buildings), in *Environmental Psychology: Man and His Physical Setting*, edited by Harold M. Proshansky, William H. Ittelson, and Leanne G. Rivlin (New York: Holt, Rinehart & Winston, 1970).

FIGURE 9.15
The artist selects and emphasizes whatever he is attracted to.

eighteenth-century situations demanded a high level of intellectual understanding and literary knowledge (Fig. 2.43).

The value of understanding the mechanics of visual sensation is, of course, obvious. Knowing how the eye works and transforms retinal images of constantly shifting light patterns into the visual world makes it possible for the designer to eliminate distracting situations which make life difficult. For example, our 180 degree peripheral vision exaggerates the sense of movement, and the closer the walls of a tunnel or passageway are, the greater is our sense of movement. Drivers tend to slow down on roadways lined with regularly spaced trees or when going under a bridge whose supports are close to the road. Perception of color and contrast can be manipulated to clarify territory and information about the environment. The painted crosswalk indicates a zone of relative safety. Finally, through the manipulation of perspective, as in trompe l'oeil, the use of color and proportion, illusions can be created making areas seem larger, smaller, and wider than they really are.

But perception is a more complex process than just seeing. Through it, people select, organize, and interpret sensory stimulation into meaningful and coherent images of the world. Sensation shades into perception as experience goes from the isolated and simple to the complex interactions characteristic of an ongoing awareness of the environment. The perceived environment normally contains so many objects and sensory stimuli that behavior is frequently less the result of a response to the total environmental influence than to specific elements selected through perception. Immediate experience then results from the interaction between sensory impulses from the environment and certain predispositions and states of mind in the individual which influence the selection and organization processes, and then give meaning to the result.[25]

The processes of selection and attribution of meaning or symbolism to the environment, or the development of an emotional response to aspects of the environment, clearly vary according to the individual. This fact is what makes the subjects of perception and behavior so complicated and so unlikely to produce universal rules. Although general patterns and principles are identifiable, what is seen by an individual is what he or she wants to see, or is looking for. Thus we can compare drawings and paintings of landscape or

[25] Bernard Berelson, *Human Behavior* (New York: Harcourt, Brace and World, 1966).

FIGURE 9.16
Mural, Venice, California.

FIGURE 9.17
Venice, California

city views with photographs of the same scenes and realize the artist's selectivity and concern for emphasis (Fig. 9.15). A good example is a mural on a building along the boardwalk of Venice, California. The artist has painted the view to be seen from that spot, but the scene is covered with snow, which has in fact never happened and is never likely to. It is an artist's fantasy (Figs. 9.16 and 9.17). Another case is the Thomas Hill painting of Yosemite Valley in the nineteenth century. The sides of the valley and the jaggedness of the peaks are exaggerated, reflecting Hill's sensation rather than what he really saw (Figs. 9.18 and 9.19).

Previous experience and learning condition what we see and how we interpret it. The motive of the individual or the particular needs which seek fulfillment, or the interests, wishes, or desires of the individual, clearly influence perception at any particular time. In a *New Yorker* cartoon, a couple in a furniture salesroom looking at a rather exotic lamp in the shape of a bird ask the salesman whether he has anything more ornate because, they explain, they are "nouveaux riches." That is to say, they see the lamp only in terms of what they believe to be fitting for a style of life they wish to adopt in the belief that it is in fact desirable, although the term *nouveau riche*, to those who coined it, was regarded as something to be avoided and distasteful. In another situation, mid-twentieth-century youth may describe the Taj Mahal as ticky-tacky. The significance of it, historically and architecturally, is merely incidental from the point of view from which they see it. For them it may be a materialistic manifestation of a form of society for which they have no sympathy, or it may merely be an incident on their journey in search of meditation and spiritual fulfillment with a guru in the foothills of the Himalayas. Alternatively, we may regard their attitude as simply a piece of antiestablishmentarianism. The two examples, however, show the extent to which perception, or at least the meaning given to objects and environments, is conditioned by variables in past experience, knowledge, age, socioeconomic class, and the personal motive of the individuals involved. The recognition of symbols, such as a cross, or a red traffic light, also depends on preknowledge.

FIGURE 9.18
Yosemite. Painting by Thomas Hill (circa. 1885). Courtesy Oakland Museum.

FIGURE 9.19
Yosemite. Photograph by R. Burton Litton, Jr.

Another factor determining perception, or what is selected out of a great bombardment of stimulation, is the intensity or quality of a stimulus. An element or object in the environment can be so dominant because of its shape, color, contrast, or symbolism, that it cannot fail to be identified and selected by almost everyone, although its meaning and induced behavioral response will vary according to the individual.

The house is regarded in a variety of ways by different social and economic groups of society in certain Western cultures.[26] The perception of the home by the lower economic groups of society is frequently as a shell into which to withdraw for security. The middle-income professional member of society tends to regard the house as a piece of property to be looked after and improved. High-income groups tend to regard the home as a sort of hotel.

One other example of variable perceptions and behavior can be seen in the case of a tree. In history, trees were regarded as symbols of fertility around which a form of religion and worship developed. Today the child will perceive the tree as a challenging object and his subsequent behavior will be to climb it and to use it as an element of play (Fig. 9.20). A teenager, on the other hand, depending upon the circumstances, may view the tree simply as a form that provides shade and gives uniqueness to a spot, resulting in an attraction to it as a place to hang out with friends of the peer group. He may carve his initials on it. A passing adult will view the tree simply as

[26] Clare Cooper, *The House as a Symbol of Self* (Berkeley: University of California Center for Planning and Development Research, Working Paper No. 120).

a pleasing neighborhood feature and will associate it casually with environmental quality and possibly property values. The developer will view trees on his land in all probability as a good selling point, and he will therefore make efforts to protect them from damage and may even name the subdivision after the trees. Older people, on the other hand, may see the tree in terms of the possibility of falling limbs and the slipperiness of autumn leaves. Their impulse will be to have the tree severely pruned or cut down. A schizophrenic who has made a friend of this tree in an anthropomorphic way will respond appropriately to this event. And a street sweeper will have his own opinion on the leaf question.

AESTHETIC SATISFACTION

For landscape architecture, another interesting theory about the interaction of people with the physical surroundings concerns aesthetic satisfaction. It has been suggested that the requirements for aesthetic enjoyment are simply the requirements for visual perception itself, raised to a higher degree. The essential thing in each case is to have a pattern which contains the unexpected. This seems to be the heart of what we call "beauty."[27] This is explained as follows. Our grasp and enjoyment of the world rest on two complementary neurophysical principles: the principle of response to novelty, change, and stimulation; and the principle of response to repetition or pattern. Our perceptual system thus paradoxically demands variety and new information while at the same time seeking regularity or pattern.

FIGURE 9.20
To the youngster, a tree is a playground and a challenge. Photograph by R. Burton Litton, Jr.

The brain, which is a pattern-selecting or pattern-perceiving system, can be thought of as consuming and requiring information as a stomach consumes food. It is argued that since this process of perception was vital in the evolution and survival of the human species, it will still have a strong influence in our lives today. It is further suggested that a major aspect in feeling pleasure in aesthetic satisfaction may be related to the brain doing its job efficiently, that is, selecting patterns and seeking novelties within it. Thus if fluctuations and patterns are basic to perception, these must also play a large part in aesthetic enjoyment. Aesthetic satisfaction, and therefore visual beauty, may be regarded either as a flux in which we can find a pattern or a pattern that contains unexpected fluctuations. A brick wall with its repetition of similar units provides a pattern. Changes and fluctuations occur, however, at different scales. At the scale of the bricks, the texture may vary or fluctuate. At the scale of the wall, a window becomes a fluctuation (Fig. 9.21). The same can apply to a fern frond which has a repetitive, identifiable structure with minor variations. Both are visually attractive because of these contrasts between a strong pattern and unexpected fluctuation within it.

SUMMARY

In this chapter I have attempted to show the range of human characteristics, needs, and motives intrinsic to the people for whom we design. Second, I have attempted to indicate the way in which the environment may be regarded as a source of stimulus and a determinant of behavior. Third, I have tried to show the mechanisms of perception and the variables that affect it and the relationship between perception and behavior. One of the major objectives of environmental design must be the development of a framework that facilitates rather than inhibits the fulfillment of individual needs without social conflict.

[27] S. R. Maddi and D. W. Fiske, *Functions of Varied Experience* (Homewood, Ill.: Dorsey Press, 1961).

FIGURE 9.21
The essence of beauty is a pattern that contains fluctuations. Photograph by Peter Kostrikin.

The evidence and concepts discussed here indicate the potential power of designers, whether they realize it or not, to influence human behavior. In the past there seems to have been a tendency to rely on personal experience for design concepts rather than on research into behavioral patterns, recognizing that all people—their perceptions, behavior, and satisfactions—are not alike and are quite unlikely to have taste similar to that of the designer. We seem to have slipped into a situation in which we preconceive environmental form in terms of a designation such as a house, a park, a town square, which is already a solution, rather than a statement of a problem.[28] This prevents the examination of alternative solutions more in keeping with the specific people for whom the environment is to be designed. This does not mean that everything has to be new. Valid universal concepts need to be separated from stylistic panaceas.

Sommer has suggested that design should be seen as the development or enclosure of space in which certain activities can take place comfortably and efficiently, in which form must not only follow function but must assist it in every way, and in which the personal expression of the architect or landscape architect must yield to the function the building or landscape serves.[29] Design and the arrangement of space and environmental elements should then, when possible, fit the user's needs if these are clearly understood. If the needs are not understood or are ambiguous, the design should allow flexibility and choice.

[28] Raymond G. Studer and David Stea, "Architectural Programming, Environmental Design and Human Behavior," *Journal of Social Issues*, XXII(4) (October 1966).

[29] Sommer, *op. cit.*

SUGGESTED READINGS

Recreation

American Academy of Political and Social Science, *Recreation in the Age of Automation.*

De Grazia, Sebastian, *Of Time, Work and Leisure.*

Friedberg, M. Paul, *Play and Interplay.*

U. S. Outdoor Recreation Resources Review Commission, *Reports*, 1962.

Ward, C., *The Child in the City.*

Williams, Wayne, *Recreation Places*, pp. 235–247, "Planning for Recreation."

Wurman, R. S., and Katz, J., *The Nature of Recreation.*

The Physical Environment and Social Behavior

Alexander, Christopher, *The City as a Mechanism for Sustaining Human Contact.*

Alexander, Christopher, Sara Ishikawa, and Murray Silverstein, *A Pattern Language.*

Ardrey, Robert, *African Genesis.*

Ardrey, Robert, *The Territorial Imperative.*

Chermayeff, Sergius, and Christopher Alexander, *Community and Privacy.*

Cooper, Clare C., *Easter Hill Village: Some Social Implications of Design.*

Craik, Kenneth, "Environmental Psychology," in *New Directions in Psychology*, Vol. IV.

Department of the Environment, *The Estate Outside the Dwelling—Reactions of Residents to Aspects of Housing Layout.*

Dubos, René, *Man Adapting.*

Dubos, René, *So Human An Animal.*

Gans, Herbert J., *The Levittowners.*

Goffman, Erving, *Behavior in Public Places.*

Hall, Edward T., *The Hidden Dimension.*

Hall, Edward T., *The Silent Language.*

Halprin, L., and Burns J., *Taking Part.*

Hester, R., *Neighborhood Space*, 2nd edition.

Ittleson, W. H., et al., *An Introduction to Environmental Psychology.*

Jacobs, Jane, *Death and Life of Great American Cities.*

Kaplan, S., and Kaplan, R., *Humanscape: Environments for People.*

Landmark 71, "User Feedback Studies."

Lang, J., et al., *Designing with Human Behavior: The Behavioral Basis for Design.*

Lynch, Kevin, *What Time is This Place?*

Maddi, S. R., and D. W. Fiske, *Functions of Varied Experience.*

Newman, Oscar, *Defensible Space.*

Perin, Constance, *With Man in Mind.*

Peterson, Peggy Long, "The Id and the Image," *Landmark '66.*

Porteous, J. D., *Environment and Behavior: Planning and Everyday Life.*

Proshansky, H. M., ed., *Environmental Psychology.*

Rapoport, Amos, *House Form and Culture.*

Shepard, Paul, *Man in the Landscape.*

Skinner, B. F., *Science and Human Behavior.*

Sommer, Robert, *Design Awareness.*

Sommer, Robert, *Personal Space.*

Taylor, (Lord) Steven J. L., and Sidney Chave, *Mental Health and the Environment.*

Tuan, Yi-Fu, *Topophilia.*

Whyte, William H., *The Organization Man.*

Whyte, William, H., *The Social Life of Small Urban Spaces.*

CLIMATE AND MICROCLIMATE

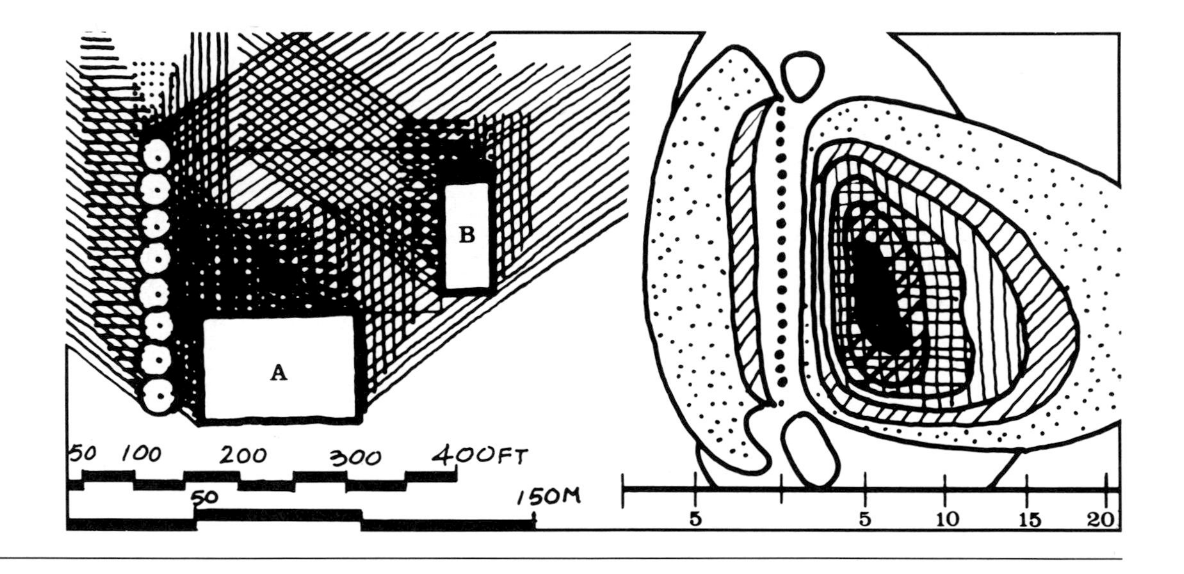

10

This chapter deals with climate and microclimate as factors of design in landscape architecture. We will look at them in terms of the way in which they can become determinants of form, as at Sea Ranch. In addition, we will investigate ways in which microclimate can be specifically created by design and how the use of open space may be affected by it.

CLIMATE

Climate is the net result of several interacting variables, including temperature, water vapor, wind, solar radiation, and precipitation. Like topography, vegetation, and water, climate is a major component of the environment. The ideal climate for human comfort has been defined as follows: clean air, temperature in the 50 to 80°F range, humidity between 40 and 75 percent, air which is neither stagnant nor subject to severe prevailing winds, and protection from precipitation.[1]

As discussed in Chapter 9, people seek the human comfort zone, and it has been a major concern of architecture and landscape design, for centuries, to provide it.

In recent years technology has made it possible to counteract adverse climates by engineering devices. Adequate heating and cooling can be provided for any structure in the desert or in the arctic, but at a considerable cost, which may be prohibitive for large sections of society. Moreover, the increasing demand for power is in itself a drain on resources and a potential threat to the environment. In many places the creation of a completely artificial climate would seem to be a desirable goal, and many shopping centers show that this is possible. But an entirely artificial environment can be maintained only in a limited area. The smog and air pollution of urban centers would still remain a problem. The ecological repercussions of large-scale climate modification by enormous domes or through the seeding of clouds to induce rainfall in the deserts are as yet undetermined. Besides all this, we cannot be certain that a completely controlled climate without the stimulus of change is in itself good for our health or psychological well-being. It seems more reasonable to design with climate rather than against it, to build and plant in such a way that the favorable aspects of a climate are taken advantage of and the unfavorable aspects are anticipated and ameliorated if possible. Temperature and air flow inside and outside a building can be modified significantly by orientation and siting, construction techniques, and tree planting.

Architectural Response

In the past, dwellings were designed to counteract at least some of the disadvantages of climates in which they were situated, in order to achieve an environment of health and comfort. In the hot, moist areas of the world, ventilation is vital. The veranda hut raised on piles in the humid tropics provides protection from the rain and at the same time allows air to circulate freely under and through the structure (Fig. 10.1). In Charleston, South Carolina, verandas or shaded porches were faced in the direction of the prevailing wind. The front porch in many instances became a side porch for this reason. In hot and sunny areas such as Italy, the Mediterranean, and Southern California insulation and the need for shade are the important factors. In North African towns we find narrow streets which prevent the sun from shining down into them (Fig. 10.2). The houses of ancient Rome were essentially windowless, thick-walled structures with inner courtyards and arcades providing shaded access to the rooms (Fig. 2.10). The marketplace of the Greek and Roman cities had colonnaded covered walks to provide public areas shaded from the heat of the sun. The thick adobe walls and covered arcades of the California missions did the same. All tourists in Italy know that temperatures inside the thick stone-walled churches are refreshingly cool in the heat of summer. In cold regions as in hot the key to comfort is insulation. The walls of traditional houses in central Europe become thicker in relation to their distance from the

FIGURE 10.1
The veranda hut of the humid tropic combines ventilation with shelter.

FIGURE 10.2
Aerial view of North African town; narrow streets create shade.

[1] Helmut Landsberg, "The Weather in the Streets," *Landscape*, 9 (1) (Autumn 1959).

FIGURE 10.3
Stone house with sod roof provides insulation in cold climate.

FIGURE 10.4
Parking lots contribute to higher temperatures in urban areas.

FIGURE 10.5
Light-reflecting, desertlike characteristics of parking lots raise temperatures in cities.

warming influence of the Atlantic Ocean, to compensate for the colder temperatures. In Norway and elsewhere thick stone or timber walls were frequently topped with sod roofs for further insulation from a cold and wet winter climate (Fig. 10.3). The 3,000-year-old cave dwellings in Pantalica, in Sicily, and the underground villages of Northern China illustrate the role of insulation in temperature modification.[2]

Climate and the City

The record of modern city building and house design has tended to ignore climates. The deep canyons of central city areas are frequently sunless and draughty. The free flow of natural air movements also has at times been disrupted in places where it would bring welcome relief. It is claimed that the average wind velocity in Detroit has been reduced by about half due to the placement of large buildings. Trees are cut down where shade would be welcome. Parking lots bring light-reflecting, temperature-raising desertlike characteristics to our cities (Fig. 10.4). Just as wind velocities tend to be decreased as cities are built up, so the temperatures tend to increase. This results from the high percentage of heat-absorbing surfaces and inadequate ventilation (Fig. 10.5).

Climate and the Landscape

Natural landscape, on the other hand, tends to stabilize temperatures and reduce the extremes. Plants act as an absorbent material in the landscape, "blotting up" heat and light, and also, as we will see, sound. The moisture dispelled into the atmosphere through transpiration contributes to the lowering or stabilizing of temperatures. Organic surfaces reradiate less heat than do inorganic materials such as concrete. In the summer the city may be as much as 10 degrees warmer than the countryside.

To what extent should green areas be considered the "lungs of the city"? Most statistics seem to indicate that the oxygen-replenishing characteristics of green vegetation to dispose of the carbon dioxide produced in cities by heating installations, exhausts, and so on is significant only in terms of vast urban parks, and is scarcely worth calculating.[3] Eric Kuhn cites the opinion of Camillo Sitte that a wooded area of three acres could absorb only as much carbon dioxide as four human beings would produce in the course of breathing, cooking, and heating. Martin Wagner has stated

[2] Bernard Rudofsky, *Architecture Without Architects*, 1965.
[3] Eric Kuhn, "Planning the City's Climate," *Landscape*, 8 (3) (Spring 1959).
[4] *Ibid.*

that to improve the air of Berlin to any marked degree, a green area of 3 million acres would be needed.[4] (Golden Gate Park in San Francisco is 1,000 acres.) If trees in cities are too few in number to photosynthetically improve the oxygen supply, they do serve many other important microclimatological functions, such as dust and sound absorption, wind shelter or ventilation channels, and temperature modification.

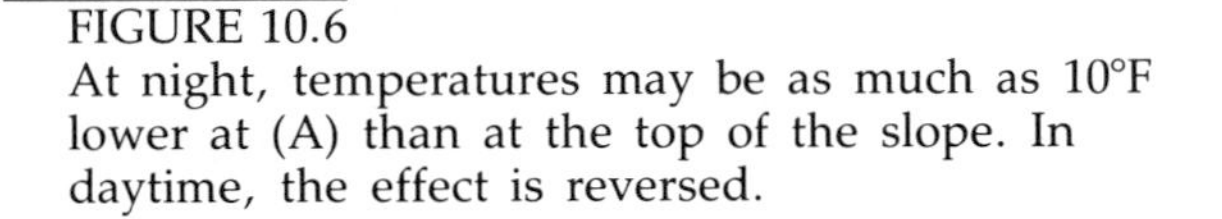

FIGURE 10.6
At night, temperatures may be as much as 10°F lower at (A) than at the top of the slope. In daytime, the effect is reversed.

Climatic Data

General climatic data describing the weather patterns in states and counties are usually easily obtainable. As planners and designers rather than meteorologists, our concern is with minimums and maximums of temperature, rainfall and the distribution of precipitation, the direction, force, and frequency of prevailing winds, days of sunshine, fog, snow, and frost, and so forth. In addition, extreme weather conditions resulting in flooding or other climate-caused disasters have been recorded in most places for a fairly long period of time. Thus by using recorded local occurrences and the overall general data, a fairly accurate image of the climate of a region can be compiled.

The maximum snowfall to be expected and the maximum wind speeds are important in the design of roofs and in building construction. In landscape, the greatest amount of rainfall that can be expected over any given number of years will be a critical factor in the design of drainage systems and culverts. The cooling power of the air and the degree of discomfort caused by heat and humidity will be influential in indoor and outdoor design, indicating the need for shade, covered walkways, wind shelter planting, and so on. The selection of plant material in landscape design must take into account the climatic conditions of temperature and wind, rain and sunshine.

MICROCLIMATE

Within the general climate patterns that make Detroit different from Los Angeles, London different from Rome, and so forth, there are detailed variations or microclimates. The term microclimate refers to the scope of the area studied and not necessarily to the size of the climatic differences, which may be great within close proximity. Unlike regional climate data, microclimatic information is not readily available. Local weather bureau statistics may be useful, but these are taken for the purpose of forecasting weather and tend to be taken in relatively undisturbed areas such as airports. Measurements of wind speed and direction, temperature variation, precipitation, fog, and sunshine may have to be specially taken (as at Sea Ranch) or, with luck, a local resident may already have such records for several previous years. Depending on the importance of the judgments to be made, intuitive conclusions can be drawn from an understanding of how microclimates arise, both in nature and in the man-made environment of buildings, paving, walls, and planting.

Determinants of Microclimate

In the landscape, topography is the major determinant of microclimate. At night cold air falls down to the lowest points, and nighttime temperatures may be as much as 10 degrees lower and the humidity 20 percent higher in a valley than on the slopes. In addition, fog may form in the valleys by morning; not a good place for siting a major highway. When the free flow of cold air is prevented by tree plantations or buildings, "frost pockets" may be formed at higher levels. In the daytime the conditions are reversed: the valley bottom will tend to be warmer than at the ridges swept by winds, and the humidity will be lower. Thus the ridge and valley topography accentuates extremes of temperatures. And thus valley bottoms and frost pockets would be relatively unsuited for habitation. This may be interpreted in terms of indoor heating costs and outdoor comfort. The best place to site a house would be halfway up the south-facing slopes. This location would provide the best all-round living environment for many geographic regions in the northern hemisphere (Fig. 10.6).

Water also has a warming and cooling effect. Land on the lee side of a lake or ocean will be warmer in winter and cooler in summer. It may also contribute to the humidity, depending on the general temperature pattern. The larger the body of water, the larger its impact will be on the microclimate. In warm seasons the shores of lakes and oceans benefit from a daytime breeze blowing from the water to the land as part of a larger pattern of cold–warm air exchange. This has a cooling effect (Fig. 10.7).

In Chicago the offshore breeze from Lake Michigan on the hottest days of summer will tend to lower the maximum temperature by about 10 degrees on

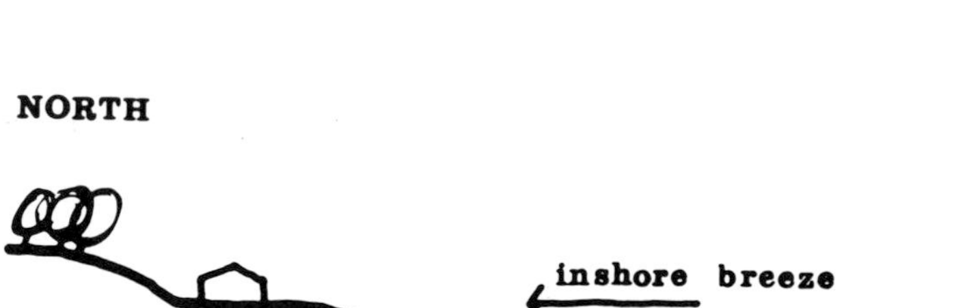

FIGURE 10.7
Land at water's edge benefits from a cooling breeze in summer and warmth in winter.

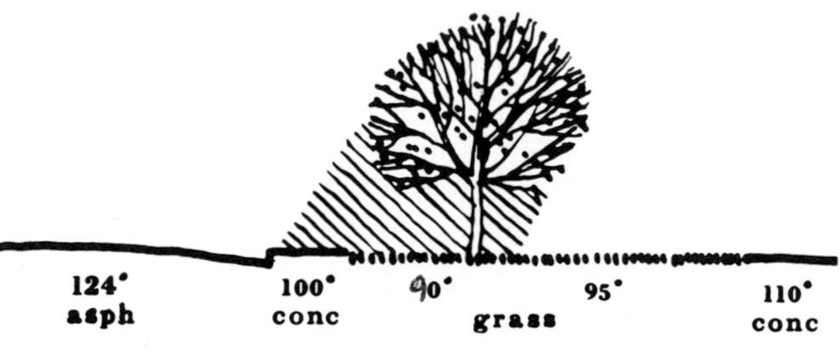

FIGURE 10.8
Surface temperatures vary according to the surface and exposure.

the edge of the so-called Gold Coast, but the cooling effect of this is rarely felt more than ½ mile inland. Apart from the views of the lake, there is good reason therefore for the Gold Coast to be where it is (Fig. 10.7).[5]

In Toronto measurements taken on a clear winter night showed that the temperatures gradually decreased as one moved away from the lake to a point 200 feet higher in elevation and 7 miles away, with intervening high ground. The temperature difference was 30 degrees (+15 at the lake and −15 at the inland point). Thus, even within one city, very large variations can occur. If cities were planned in terms of climate alone, they would no doubt be different from those laid out according to transportation networks or real estate operations, which, in the case of Toronto, seem to have been completely at odds with the climatic environment.[6]

Temperature can also be affected to a small degree by variations in soil. A dry soil (sand, gravel, and the like) tends to result in higher temperatures and lower humidity; wet soils, loams, and predominantly clay soils in poorly drained marshy areas tend to cause lower temperatures and higher humidities. Although they are small in magnitude, in certain situations, such as siting a house, the differences might be significant.

Plants and natural vegetation are good indicators of microclimate. For example, the day on which similar flowering trees come into bloom in a city frequently varies according to their location. This is due to differences in shelter and sunshine. The wind-clipped characteristics of trees in certain locations indicate the relative exposure of these areas to strong winds and their prevailing direction. The temperatures inside forests are usually higher at night and cooler during the day than in adjoining open land. Plants that thrive best in moist, cool situations will be found in areas of higher precipitation or north-facing slopes. It may be deduced that such areas are more moist and cooler (Fig. 11.4).

Sun and Shade

The sun is perhaps the most constant climatic factor. It is always there and, except for clouding over, its effect and seasonal change are predictable. The effect of the sun varies according to the latitude and the season, which causes changes in its intensity and the angle at which its rays strike the earth. The surface of the land or its vegetative cover and shade patterns also affect surface temperatures.

Data from Arizona indicate the temperature variations that can occur. With an air temperature of 108°F (160°F on the roof of a house), the ground temperatures varied depending on the surfaces and whether they were in the shade of a tree or not. Thus it was found that the temperature in full sun on concrete was 110°F, on asphalt 124°F, and on grass 95°F. In the shade the surface temperature of the concrete was 100°F and that of the grass 90°F. At 4 feet above the ground in full sun the temperature over concrete was 96°F and that over asphalt 102°F. The extremes were grass in shade, 90°F, and asphalt on its surface, 124°F. Even in the shade the difference between concrete and grass was 10 degrees (Fig. 10.8).[7]

As the sun appears to move during the day, so the area of shadow changes in position and extent. These dimensions can be calculated and shade patterns projected for different times of day and year (Fig. 10.9). The use of outdoor spaces is related to these shade patterns. Siting a tall building on the south side of an urban square in a cool summer climate puts the whole area into shade at the lunch hour, which will ensure that it is not used for eating or any other social purpose. In a hot climate a park without shade will be unusable. Natural daylighting can be modified by shade patterns cast by trees and buildings. Glare can also be reduced in this way.

[5] *Architectural Forum*, 86 (March 1947).
[6] *Ibid.*
[7] *Ibid.*

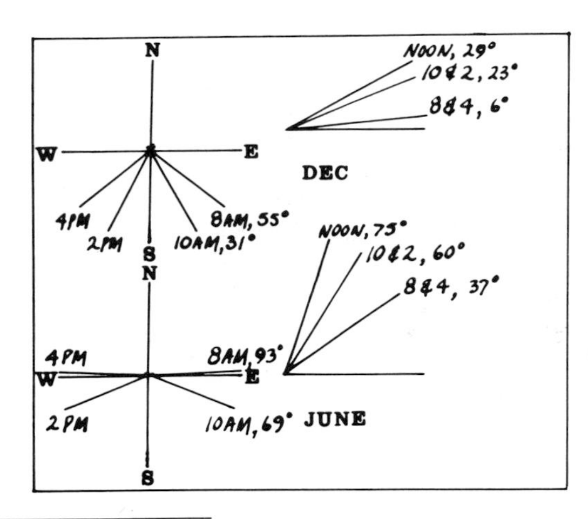

FIGURE 10.9(a)
Azimuth angles of the sun for December and June at 38 degrees latitude, and the degrees of altitude of the sun for the same months. Source: Graphic Standards.

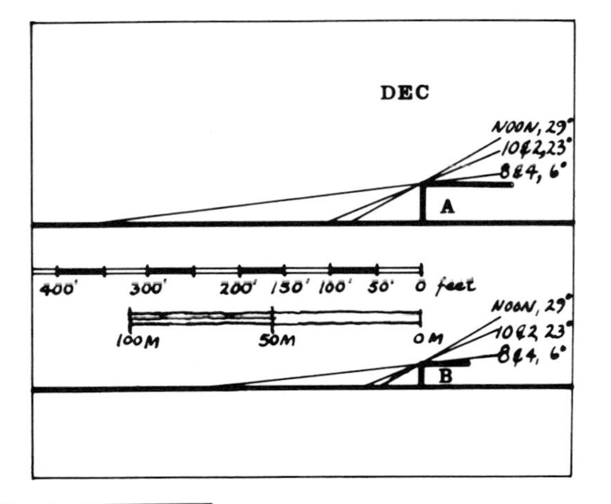

FIGURE 10.9(b)
Extent of shadow cast by building A (50 feet high) and building B (30 feet high) in December.

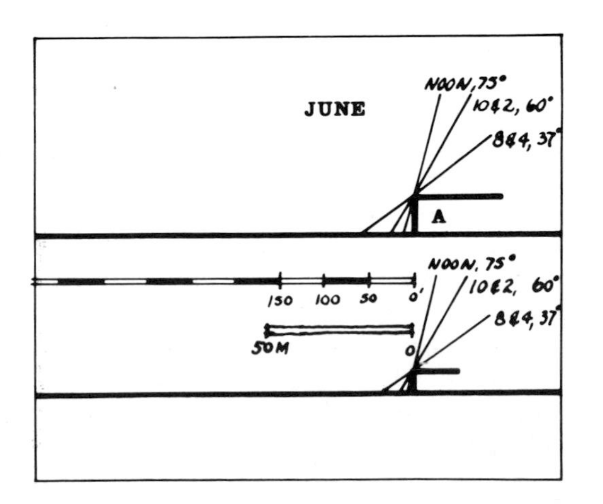

FIGURE 10.9(c)
Extent of shadow cast by building A (50 feet high) and building B (30 feet high) in June.

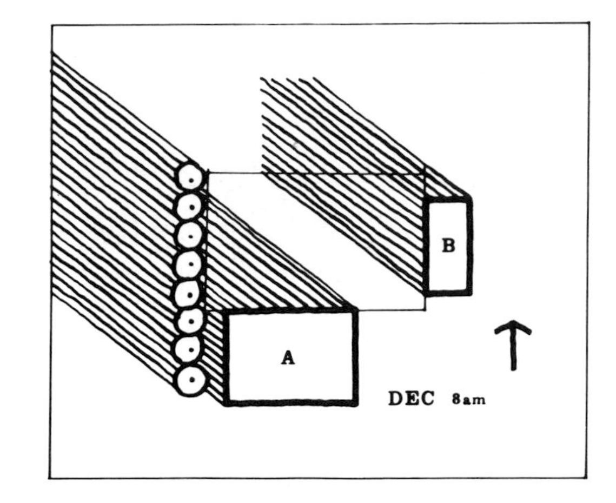

FIGURE 10.9(d)
Plan of shadows cast in December, 8 AM.

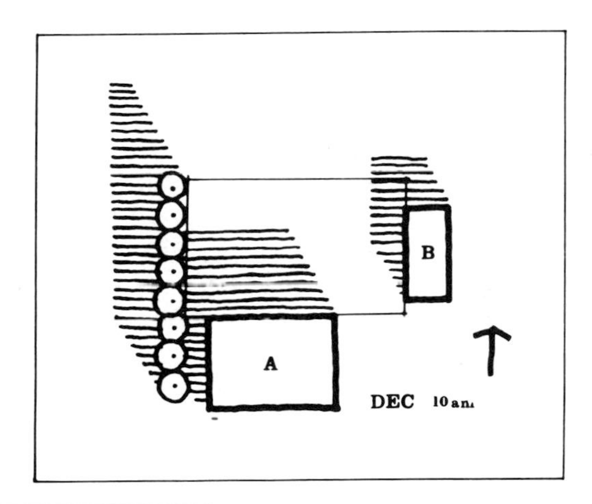

FIGURE 10.9(e)
Plan of shadows cast in December, 10 AM.

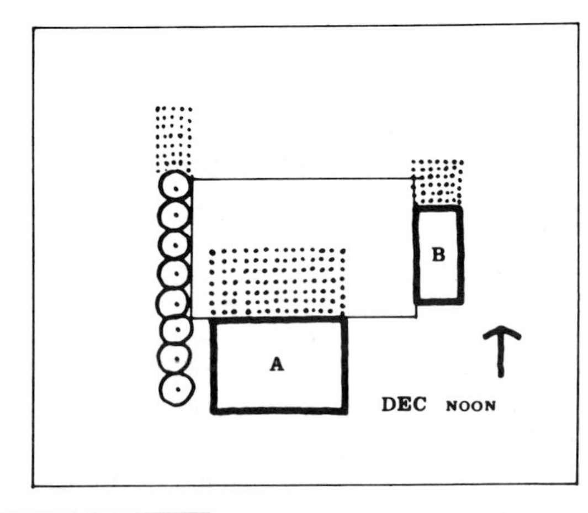

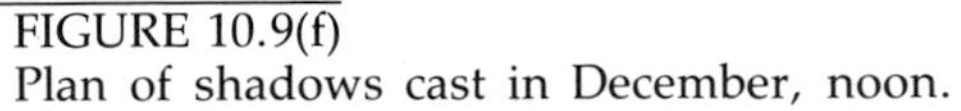

FIGURE 10.9(f)
Plan of shadows cast in December, noon.

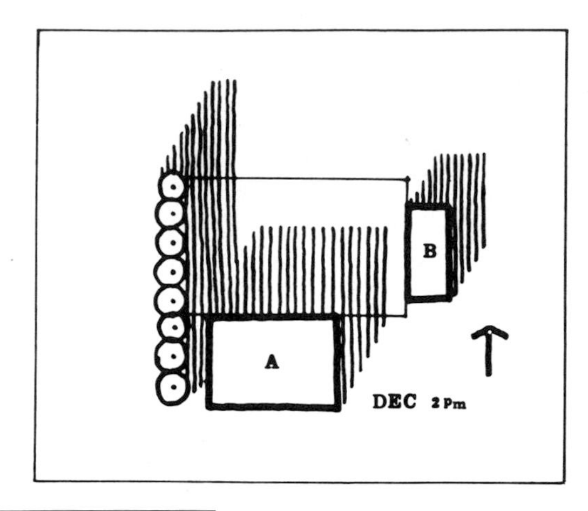

FIGURE 10.9(g)
Plan of shadows cast in December, 2 PM.

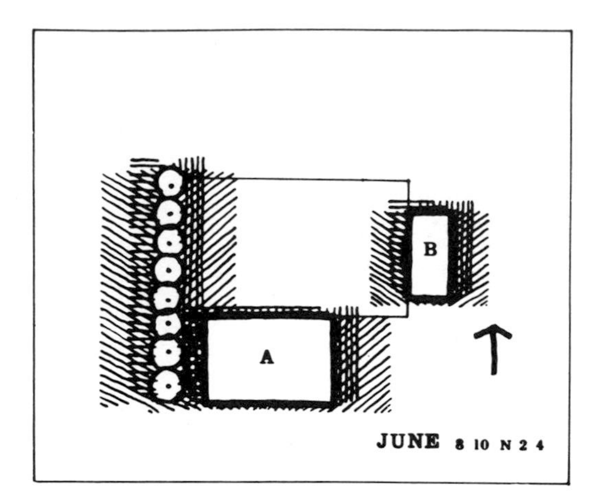

FIGURE 10.9(j)
Composite of June shadows shows that much of the open space is in full sun, all day.

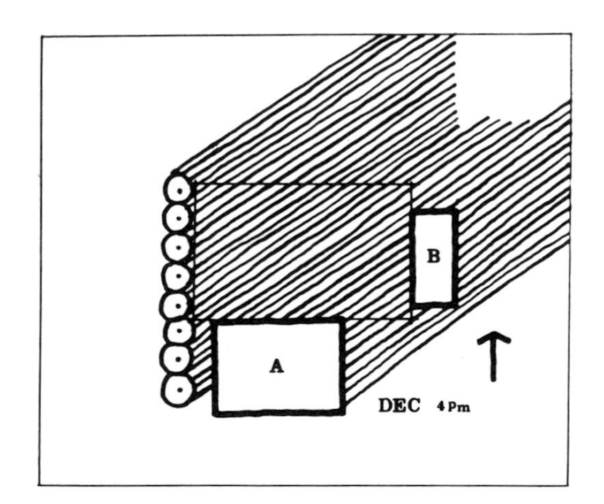

FIGURE 10.9(h)
Plan of shadows cast in December, 4 PM.

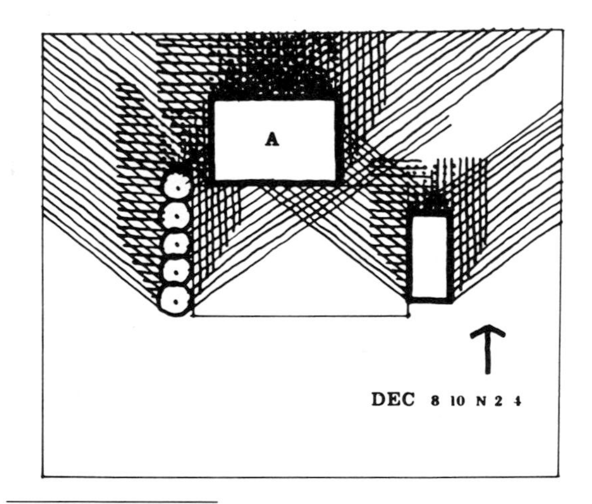

FIGURE 10.9(k)
With building (A) moved to the north side of the open space, even in December, a considerable portion of it is in full sun all day.

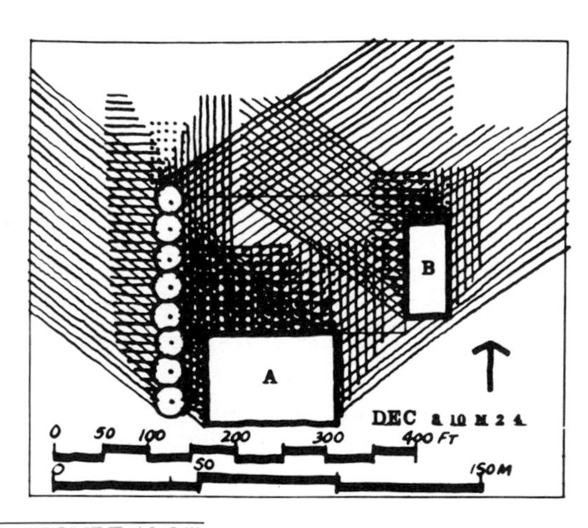

FIGURE 10.9(i)
Composite of December shadows for the day shows no part of open space in full sun, all day.

Energy Conservation

Concern for energy conservation of all kinds, stimulated by the oil embargo of 1978 and the subsequent escalation of fuel costs, has reminded us of those early forms of architecture which provided livable temperatures without the benefits of technology. At Village Homes (described on page 143), houses are oriented north and south, are solar tempered, and have solar collection devices for heating air and water. In addition to insulation, the south-facing orientation of all main windows with an overhanging shading device maintains the most beneficial sun control for summer and winter. The horizontal and vertical angles of the sun throughout the day and year are basic data in calculation of shadows (Figs. 10.9a to 10.9i). Latitude is a major variable and is a key to specific design features such as window overhangs on south facing windows. The minimum dimension for these is determined by multiplying the height of the window by the latitude and dividing by 50.[8] The optimum horizontal orientation for rooftop solar collection is a fraction to the west of due south and the angle of the roof is calculated by adding 15 degrees to the latitude. Thus, for latitude 38, the angle should be 53 degrees.[9] Since 50 percent of the heat loss and gain is through the windows, those which must face east or west should be shaded with trees or some outside screening device such as a trellis or hedge. Curtains inside the house are not as effective in shading the windows as they would be from the outside.

Wind

After temperature and precipitation, perhaps the next most important aspect of weather is wind. We are mainly, but not always, concerned with creating shelter from wind. There is a difference between the shelter offered by windbreaks composed of plants and that offered by solid screens, fences, or buildings. Solid screens tend to create a turbulence on the lee side, which reduces the extent of the shelter. By contrast, the permeability of plant material, which permits certain amounts of air to move through the screen, results in less turbulence and a greater total area of shelter. The extent of shelter from a natural windbreak depends on the degree of permeability and its height. In general, the totally sheltered zone to the leeward will probably be about thirty times the height of the shelter belt. Small reductions in wind speed may be important in erosion control and agriculture, but for human purposes it may be desirable to be more specific about the reduction in wind velocity, which is significant. If a 20 percent reduction of wind speed is taken as the criterion, then the protected zone will be between 15 and 20 times the height of the planting. A 50 to 60 percent reduction in the original wind speed might be even more realistic in areas where strong winds prevail. In this case the area of protection would extend to only six to nine times the height of the shelter belt. If the trees were 50 feet high, then the zone of shelter would lie between 200 and 500 feet (Fig. 10.10). The greatest shelter begins in fact a distance of four or five times the height from the belt, and the wind speed tends to be increased at the ends. There is also an area of reduced velocity on the windward side. The movement of air through and around natural windbreaks is a science. It is of extreme importance in the development of microclimates and in understanding the microclimates that may already

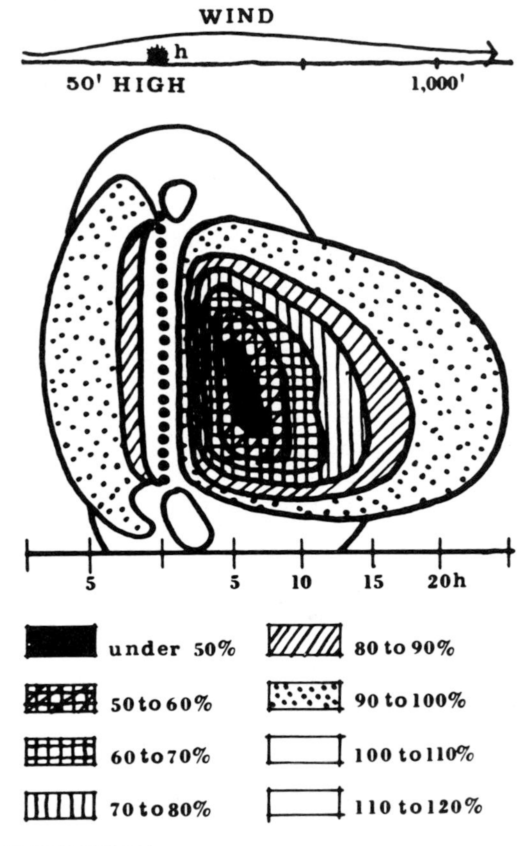

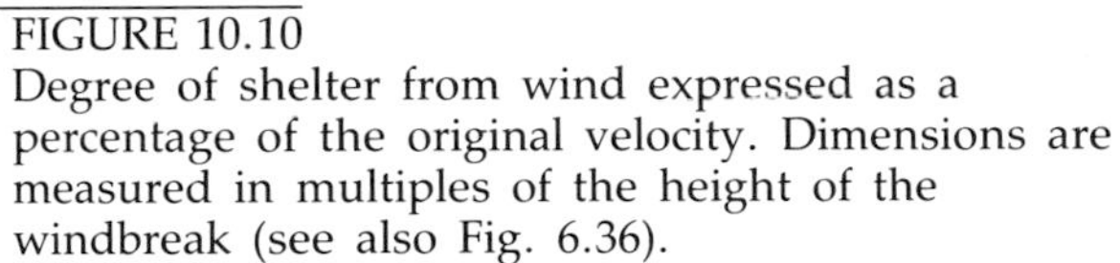

FIGURE 10.10
Degree of shelter from wind expressed as a percentage of the original velocity. Dimensions are measured in multiples of the height of the windbreak (see also Fig. 6.36).

exist on a site. The width of a shelter belt is not necessarily a variable in the amount of shelter it will provide from wind.

Air movement or winds are equally affected by buildings. Wind tunnels are important devices by which to predict the flow of air around and over buildings. Models can be tested in this way. Predicting the effects of large new buildings in the landscape and especially in cities is important if a livable street-level environment is to be maintained. Draughty corridors and wind-swept corners can be inadvertently created or, as in Detroit, the free flow of cool air as a ventilation system may be prevented by the placement of buildings and the relationships of one building to another. In cities air flow between buildings is more important than air movement around any building considered in isolation.

8. John Hammond, et al., *A Strategy for Energy Conservation.*
9. *Ibid.*

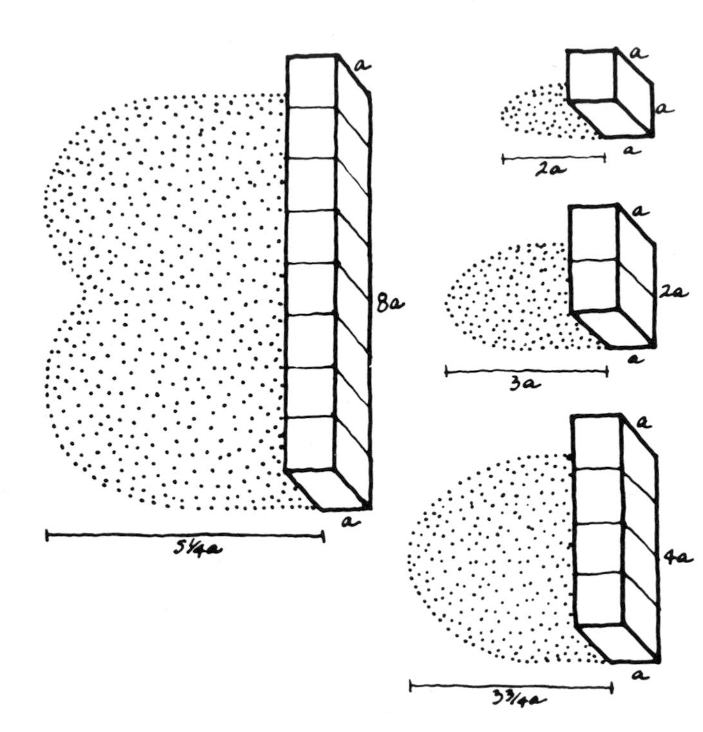

FIGURE 10.11(a)
Extent of shelter from wind provided by a building increases in proportion to its length. Based on "Natural Air Flow Around Buildings," by Benjamin Evans (1957).

FIGURE 10.11(b)
Extent of shelter from wind provided by a building increases in proportion to its height.

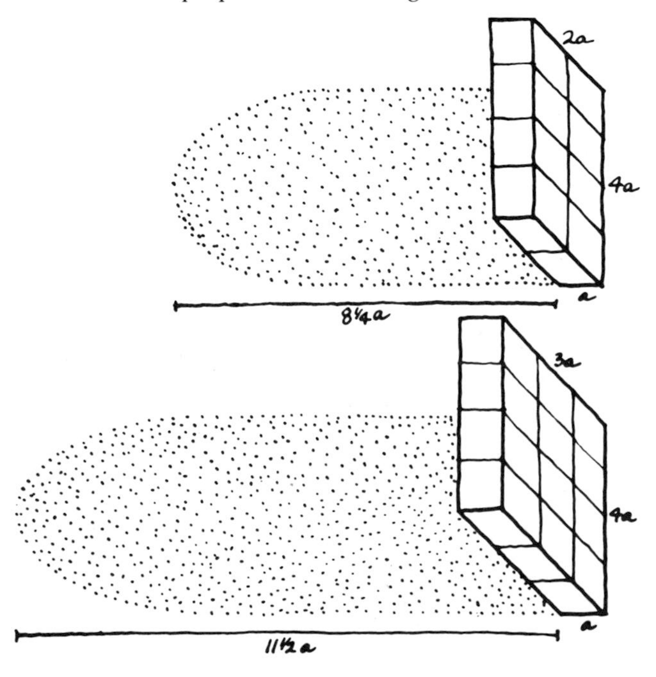

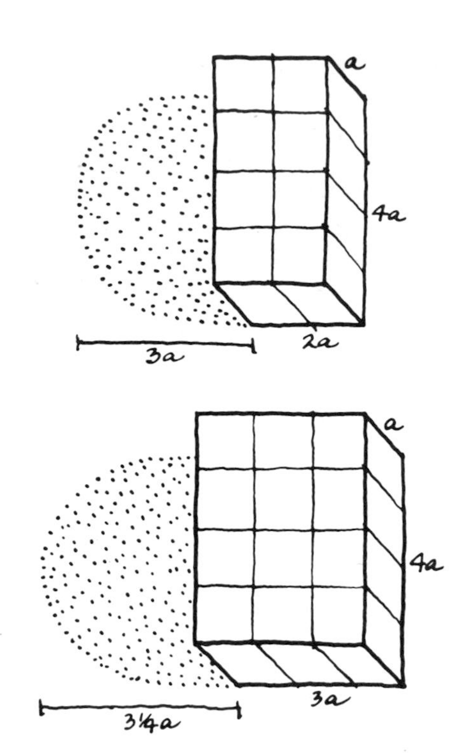

FIGURE 10.11(c)
Extent of shelter from wind provided by a building is hardly affected by its width.

FIGURE 10.11(d)
The roof pitch of a building affects the extent of shelter from wind.

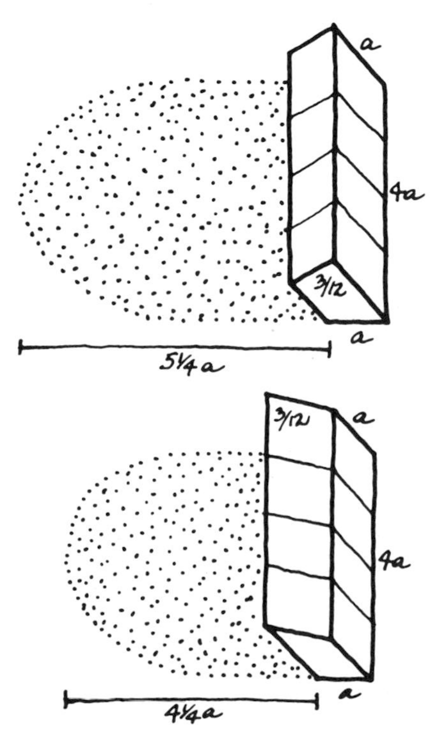

A series of wind tunnel experiments at the Agricultural and Mechanical College of Texas offers some generalities about the flow of wind in relation to single buildings and the degree of shelter they provide (Fig. 10.11).[10] They show that as the building gets wider, the area of shelter in fact decreases. However, as the length of the building is varied, keeping the width and height constant, the area of protection does increase. Thus the longer the building, the greater will be the eddy space or shelter zone. But the degree to which the wind is reduced is not calculated in these studies. The height is also a significant variable. The higher the building, the greater the zone of protection. The pitch of the roof can also have an effect on the shelter caused by a building. Thus the shape and form of buildings can have a distinct impact on the surrounding microclimate factor of wind, and therefore on temperature and comfort, and this, in turn, affects the way in which adjacent spaces may be used and should be designed and planted.

The cooling effect of breezes is sometimes desirable and of value in reducing indoor temperatures in hot climates by either channeling breezes through windows or, if this is undesirable on account of humidity, then over the roof. A knowledge of the direction of prevailing summer winds and a skillful planting design are essential to the success of this idea.

Wind is also a source of energy and, in areas of relatively constant wind, windmills have been used with considerable success to generate electricity. The visual impact of large-scale wind and solar power generation may become a new and unfamiliar feature of future landscapes.

Noise

Noise pollution has become a significant environmental problem. Noise may be considered a factor of microclimate. It has been believed for some time that tree planting could reduce sound levels, but without any evidence to prove it or on which to base guidelines. Recently research has been done in Germany, where the sound-absorbent quality of specific plants has been found to vary according to leaf size and density of foliage. Other experiments have been conducted in Nebraska. Shelter belts planted as a soil conservation measure in the 1930s have been used in tests to evaluate their effectiveness in reducing sound. Many were very wide, frequently consisting of five or six rows of different tree types, often several miles in length. Studies made on the shelter belts placed noise sources on one side, and scientific measurements were taken on the other.[11]

The results showed that trees and shrubs have a high potential for absorbing sound. Reductions of sound levels (attenuations) on the order of 5 to 8 decibels were common and attenuations of 10 decibels (approximately half as loud) were not unusual for wide belts of tall, dense trees. The relative placement of noise screens between sound source and protected area is of great importance: a screen placed relatively close to a noise source is more effective than one placed close to an area to be protected. Thus plantings to screen noise from a freeway should be alongside the road. The study states that urban residential property was effectively screened from passenger car noise with a single row of dense shrubs backed by a row of taller trees totaling a depth of 20 feet. However, screening of rural areas from freeways where large

FIGURE 10.12
Sound modification with physical form. Based on "Designing Against Noise from Road Traffic," Building Research Station Current Paper 20/71.

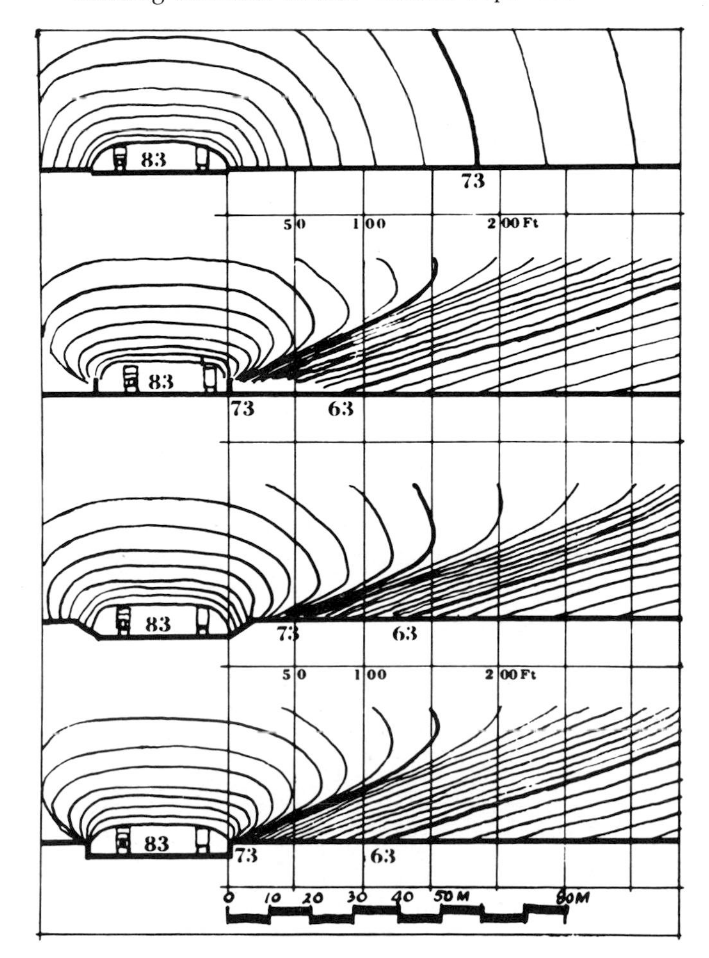

[10] Benjamin Evans, *Natural Air Flow Around Buildings* (College Station: Texas A & M College System, 1957).

[11] David Cook and David Haerbeke, *Trees and Shrubs for Noise Abatement* (U.S. Forest Service and University of Nebraska, 1971).

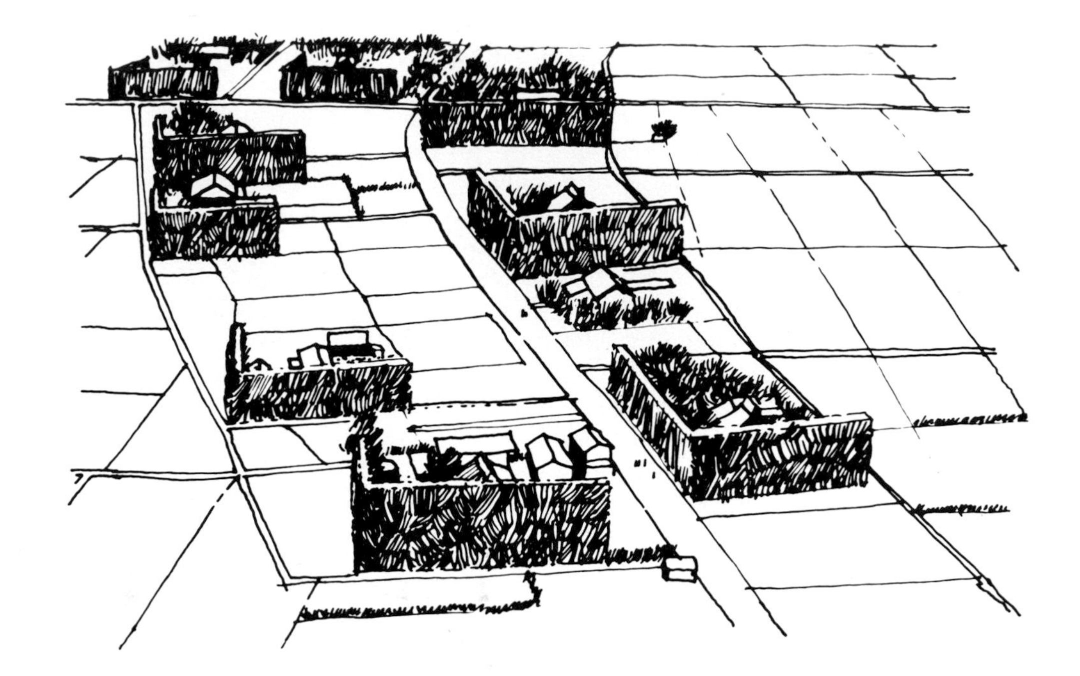

FIGURE 10.13
50-foot hedges of pine shelter farmstead against winter winds and snowstorms in Shimani prefecture, western Japan.

trucks account for much of the noise requires wider belts consisting of several rows of tall trees in dense plantings. The sound-reducing planting belts would have to be a minimum of 100 feet in width.

Some other work has been done on the reduction of noise emanating from high-speed motorways or freeways in England. It is not concerned with the use of planting but rather with solid vertical barriers and grading. The results, summarized in Fig. 10.12, show that considerable reductions can be achieved.

SUMMARY

Although the general climate is essentially unalterable, the climate of a specific portion of the land can be influenced easily and altered by design (Fig. 10.13). Put another way, advantage can be taken of existing microclimatic variations if they are recognized. The siting of buildings to take advantage of warm conditions in winter and cool in summer is clearly an advantage, providing a more pleasant environment, permitting extended use of the outdoors, and cutting heating and cooling costs indoors. Landscape design and planting, careful siting, and architectural design combine in the development of a livable microclimate.

The use of outdoor areas is affected by wind and shade, noise and temperature. These are critical indices of environmental quality.

SUGGESTED READINGS

Architectural Forum, "Microclimatology," March 1947, pp. 116–119.

Building Research Station, Current Paper 20/71, "Designing Against Noise from Road Traffic."

Caborn, James, M., *Shelterbelts and Windbreaks*.

Cook, David, and David F. Haerbeke, *Trees and Shrubs for Noise Abatement*.

Dickinson, Jim, *New Housing and Traffic Noise*.

Eckbo, Garrett, *Art of Home Landscaping*, pp. 18–23.

Geiger, Rudolf, *The Climate Near the Ground*.

Givoni, B., *Man, Climate and Architecture*.

Hammond, John, et al., *A Strategy for Energy Conservation*.

MacDougall, E. Bruce, *Microcomputers in Landscape Architecture*, Ch. 9, "Sun and Shadow Calculations."

Mather, J. R., *Climatology Fundamentals and Applications*.

Mazria, E., *The Passive Solar Energy Book*, Ch. IV.

Moffat, Anne, *Landscape Design that Saves Energy*.

Olgay, Victor, *Design with Climate*, pp. 1–23, "General Introduction," pp. 44–53, "Site Selection," pp. 74–77, "Shading Effects of Trees and Vegetation."

PLANTS AND PLANTING DESIGN

11

Why should plants have such symbolic and aesthetic importance in our lives, in parks and gardens, window boxes and pots? It is not surprising that primitive man and early civilizations held plants in esteem. One manifestation of this is the use of plant forms in architectural decoration since ancient times (Fig. 11.1). Beyond their obvious value as food, fiber, and building materials, plants were the very essence of life, exhibiting growth and reproduction. The major religious faiths described paradise gardens at the beginning of time or at the end of life. Specific plants assumed symbolic significance in various cultures. Certain trees were sacred, and tree worship was perhaps the first form of religion. Trees were thus symbols of fertility, long life, knowledge, and temptation. The lotus was the symbol of upper Egypt, and the fig tree was honored and worshiped by the peasants for its wood, fruit, and shade. The olive, vine, date palm, acacia, and avocado similarly were imbued with

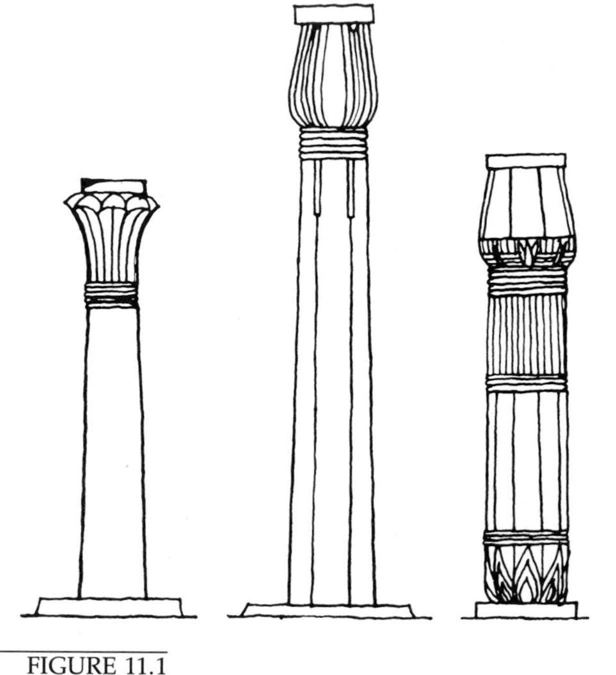

FIGURE 11.1
Ancient Egyptian columns. Capital detailing derived from **(a)** palm leaf, **(b)** lotus bud, and **(c)** papyrus bud.

symbolic significance. A more recent example is the rowan or mountain ash, which is found in almost every old Scottish garden and gardens of Scots overseas. It was believed to be capable of warding off evil spirits. Similarly, the lilac seems to have a traditional and symbolic place in American gardens.

The evolution of more sophisticated religions, the urbanization of society, and the development of an agricultural industry has changed the intimate relationship between plants and people which existed up to the nineteenth century. We are now unlikely to eat the food we see growing in the local fields, and we are even less likely to be treated for illness with potions made from medicinal herbs grown in our gardens. Today we are left with a somewhat inexplicable and apparently irrational love for plants and trees, which seems to have grown out of our heritage and belongs perhaps to our animal origins and instincts. Thus we legislate the preservation of trees, protest the removal of ancient oaks and chestnuts, and allocate public funds to preserve the last virgin stands of redwoods. In Britain the second most popular adult leisure occupation, according to a recent study, is gardening. In recent years the popularity of indoor plants indicates even more the intensity of our need to nurture and cultivate plants and to watch growth. We are also fascinated with plants in composition with topography and have designated landscapes as areas of outstanding natural beauty, and we go and admire these as though they were paintings. In recent times some scientists, although notably not biologists, have imbued plants with feelings similar to, but of a lower order, than animals'. Other people feel anthropomorphically about plants and would take to criminal court those responsible for the deaths of large trees due to careless construction.

As landscape architects, we come heir to this traditional and changing involvement with plants. We are preceded by a long line of distinguished planters for profit and pleasure; and these have not always been mutually exclusive objectives. In the seventeenth century John Evelyn recommended that English gentlemen should replant their estates to replenish the diminishing supply of oak for shipbuilding.[1] In the eighteenth century the English landscape garden structured the entire agricultural scene with belts of woodland and clumps of trees (Fig. 2.45). In both cases the adornment of the landscape with coppices and hedgerows of oak and beech provided a source of valuable timber at a later date. More recently there have been conflicts between profit and pleasure. In England some consider the use of faster growing coniferous species suitable for shorter term forestry alien to the character of the English landscape. Another potential conflict in agriculture lies in the trend toward larger fields suited for modern machinery and more efficient production, which will alter the characteristic and loved pattern of small irregular enclosures, hedgerows, and woods in Europe and on the East coast of the United States. Lumbering practices in the forests of the United States have also begun to conflict with federal agencies' interest in their use for recreation.

The nineteenth-century planters J. C. Loudon, William Robinson, and Gertrude Jekyll developed the art of planting design using the wide variety of trees, shrubs, and herbaceous plants which became available as a result of world-wide botanical expeditions and plant breeding. Planting for aesthetic effect, education, and pleasure thus reached its zenith in the late nineteenth and early twentieth centuries, being supported and maintained by numerous trained and skilled gardeners. Horticultural societies, flower shows, and the horticultural industry grew and thrived on the intense interest and zeal of plant enthusiasts from all walks of life.

Before discussing specific uses of plants in design, we must deal with the problem of classifying the

[1] John Evelyn, *Sylva* (London: J. Martyn, 1664).

enormous amount of material available for use. To do this plants are considered in terms of six classifications: (1) ecology; (2) botany; (3) horticulture; (4) growth and management needs; (5) design potential; and (6) aesthetics.

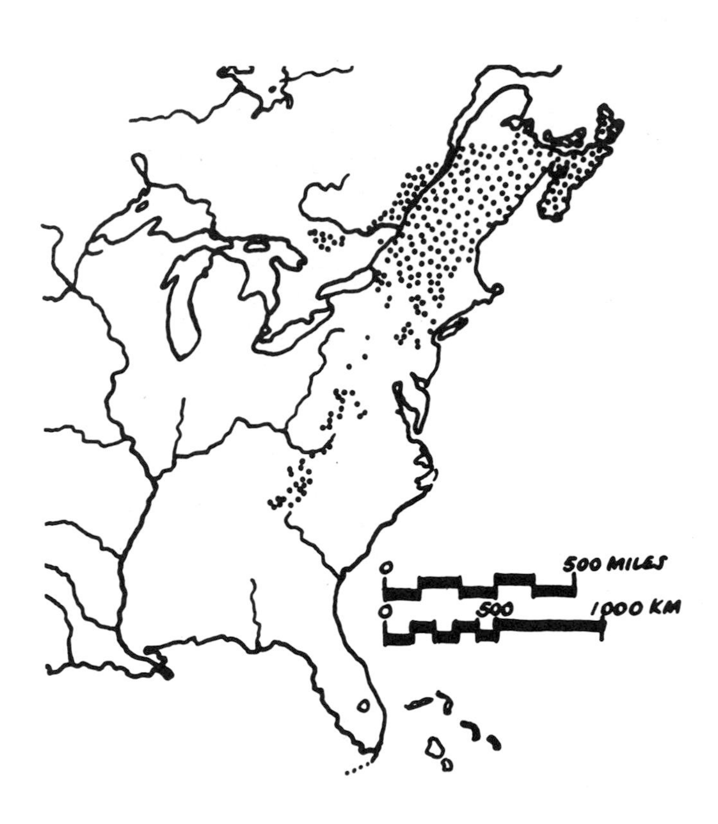

FIGURE 11.2
The geographical range of red spruce *(Picea rubens)* (at left). (Based on Silvics of Forest Trees of the United States Agricultural Handbook No. 271, U.S. Department of Agriculture, Forest Service, 1965.) Distribution is related to temperature range, soil type, rainfall, and elevation above sea level. Red spruce attains maximum development in the higher parts of the Southern Appalachian Mountains, where the atmosphere is more humid and the rainfall heavier during the growing season than in other parts of its range.

The largest existing forested area lies in the Great Smokey Mountains National Park where all sites about 4,500 feet (1600 m) which are not occupied by beech or heath are occupied by forests of red spruce and Fraser fir. (Shelford, Victor E., "The Ecology of North America," 1965).

ECOLOGICAL COMMUNITIES

The distribution of species—that is, where plants are found naturally—is a function of their genetically established tolerance range. This corresponds with the range of environmental conditions which allows the growth and reproduction of a given species if the seeds or spores are present. Temperature, water, and soil are the major limiting factors to plant distribution. The mosaic of vegetation which results is a response to worldwide limiting factors, such as latitude, and, at a smaller scale, to local variations in growing conditions: river banks, hot dry slopes, moist woodlands, and so on. Each plant has a natural range (Figs. 11.2 to 11.7; see also Fig. 6.10).

In nature we find a range of plant types, minute alpine plants and enormous trees, creeping plants, herbaceous perennials and annuals, those with long life spans and short, those which can withstand drought and desert conditions and those which thrive best in marshland or rain forest, those which can tolerate frost and those which cannot. The greatest variety exists in the tropics; the least in the arctic.

Native or indigenous plants are those associated

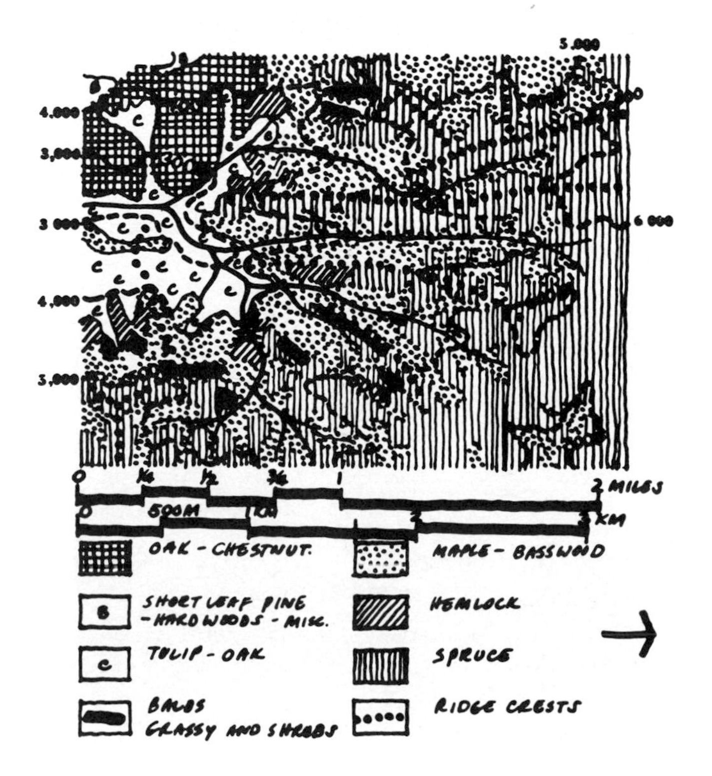

FIGURE 11.3
Local variations in soil, temperature, and moisture result in a mosaic of vegetation within the generalized range of a particular species. Thus, we find in the headwaters of the Little Pigeon River in the Great Smokey Mountains National Park that there is a tendency for tulip/oak to be in the deep valleys and on north-facing slopes, whereas red spruce is found on south-facing slopes and at a higher altitude. Oak/chestnut occurs on south-facing slopes of broad valleys (Shelford). (Map based on F. H. Miller, 1941, U.S. National Park Service.)

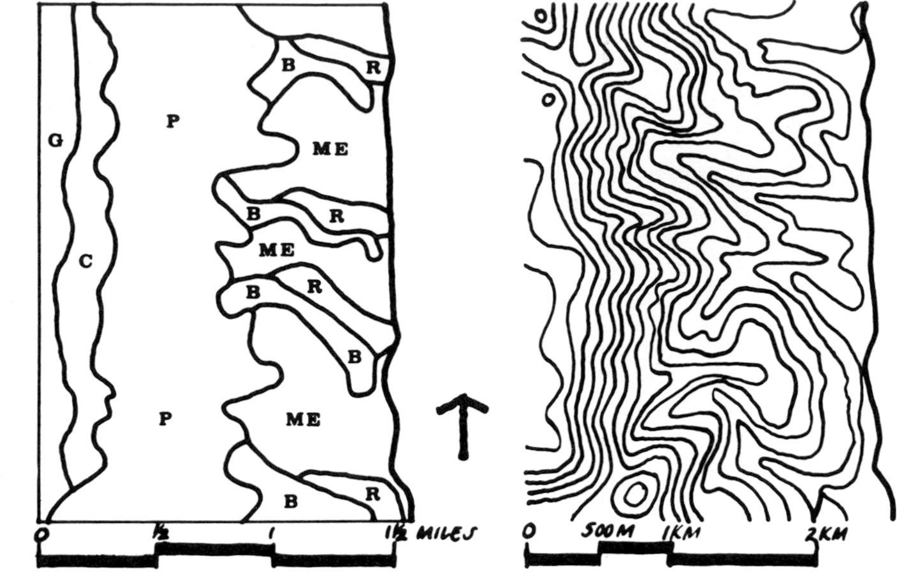

FIGURE 11.4
Distribution of vegetation at Inverness, California. The windswept ridge is covered with grassland **(G)** and chaparral **(C)**. The higher slopes with shallow sandy soil are covered with Pine **(P)**. The north-facing, moisture-retaining slopes favor California Bay **(B)** and riparian vegetation including alder and willow that occupy the valleys. Introduced planting dominates the built-up residential areas **(M.E.)**

with specific regions. In general, they are likely to have the closest fit in their own regions and should be selected for use there whenever possible and desirable. Plants can be classified by natural communities, which usually include the whole range of plant types from trees to herbaceous. Thus we talk of the oak-maple community, the redwood forest community, and so on. Each consists of a characteristic series of plants in tree, shrub, and groundcover layers (Fig. 11.8).

The plants we use are not new, but their use in design requires them to be located, propagated, and made available in commercial quantities. Plant selection and breeding have produced some genetic variations not found in nature. These cultivars and varieties have been developed in greatest profusion in flowering plants such as roses, chrysanthemums, and dahlias. It is possible also to "design" street trees according to an ideal specification of size, durability, leaves, and so forth. The Modesto ash and the thornless honey locust are examples of specially bred improved varieties for street tree planting.

FIGURE 11.5
Vaca Mountains, California. A low rainfall area (15 inches). Soil and moisture must be exactly right for tree growth. Warm south slopes are bare. Heavier vegetation of blue oak and digger pine clothe the cooler northern slopes. Photography by R. Burton Litton, Jr.

FIGURE 11.6
Grand Teton Range, Jackson Lake, Wyoming. Vegetation mosaic related to soil type. Lodgepole pines prefer the coarse, highly drained soils of glacial moraines. Sagebrush grows on the finer soil of the alluvial flats. Photograph by R. Burton Litton, Jr.

FIGURE 11.7
Desert conditions of climate and soil are extremely restrictive and support a specialized flora. Photograph by R. Burton Litton, Jr.

BOTANICAL NOMENCLATURE

The botanical classification orders the mass of plant material into families, genera, species, and varieties according to similarities in flower, fruit, leaf, and so on. Thus the Fagacea family includes the genera oak *(Quercus)*, beech *(Fagus)*, and alder *(Alnus)*. This taxonomy is useful in identifying unknown species with a flora. It also gives plants universal Latin names which are the same the world over and therefore essential in specifications. They are more reliable than common names, which vary from place to place. For example, the genus *Liriodendron tulipifera*, of the Magnoliaceae family, is known in some places as the tulip tree and in others as the yellow poplar.

FIGURE 11.8
Despite deep shade cast by a redwood forest, it contains other species in a "community": California laurels, Pacific madrone, and alders may be found mixed with the redwoods. The forest understory might include vine maple, rhododendron, and *Vaccinium*. A low growing broad-leafed shrub layer might include seedlings of understory trees, bigleaf maple, hazel, and California blackberry and bracken. An herb layer frequently includes redwood sorrel. Photograph by R. Burton Litton, Jr.

HORTICULTURAL TYPES AND VALUES

The horticulturist uses botanical nomenclature but classifies plants essentially by form into trees, shrubs, herbaceous and annual plants, groundcovers, and vines. This is a useful breakdown of the plant kingdom for landscape architecture and design. In briefly reviewing each type, mention of certain design implications will be inevitable.

Groundcover Plants

Groundcovers are defined as low-growing, prostrate, surface-covering plants which can be used for erosion control on slopes or to make a pattern to be seen from above, as in a parterre. As a surface, such plants—provided they have low maintenance needs—are cheaper than concrete or paving. They absorb heat, moisture, and dust, and control erosion. Groundcovers vary in form, leaf size, color, and texture. Low, creeping plants like fragaria or ajuga spread close to the ground. Prostrate plants like juniper grow taller and spread farther to shade out and cover the ground with dense foliage (Fig. 11.9). Low-growing dense shrubs like hypericum do the same job, but with a different visual effect (Fig. 11.10).

Shrubs

Shrubs range from approximately 3 to 10 feet in height, are defined as woody plants, and are often multistemmed and low branching (Figs. 12.2 and 12.3). Low-growing shrubs can be arranged to divide

FIGURE 11.9
Juniper used as a ground cover.

FIGURE 11.10
Hypericum used as a ground cover.

FIGURE 11.12
Privet hedges at Radburn.

space at ground level, a physical separation rather than a visual one (Fig. 11.11). Larger shrubs growing above eye level will define space more strongly. Plants with thorns can increase the physical effect of shrubs planted as barriers to separate areas. In addition to growing shrubs in their natural form for flowers and fruit, they may be clipped or pruned into hedges, achieving strict divisions of various heights and textures within a limited space (like a fence) (Figs. 11.12 and 11.13) Some plants are more adaptable to making hedges than others. Dense branching and foliage such as those of cupressus, privet, and pittosporum are excellent. The potential height of the hedge depends on the plant selected.

FIGURE 11.11
Shrubs forming a visual and physical separation.

Trees

Trees are defined as having a single stem and growing to a height greater than 10 feet (Figs. 11.14 to 11.16). They are subdivided into deciduous (for example, liquidambar, London plane), broad-leaved evergreen (southern magnolia, camphor), and coniferous (Scots pine, cedar). Broad-leaved evergreens tend to cast year-round and denser shade than deciduous trees. They are therefore most suitable for hotter climates. Trees allowed to grow to maturity will occupy a considerable amount of space, the actual height and spread depending on the species. The rate of growth varies according to the species and the environmental conditions. It is especially true of conifers that as they grow, so their form may change. Since

FIGURE 11.13
Yew hedges at Sissinghurst define space as precisely as the walls of a room.

FIGURE 11.14
Strong planting of elms in Chicago. Being deciduous, their form changes seasonally.

even the fastest growing tree will take some time to reach full size, tree planting may be done in two stages. Close planting to encourage upward growth may be specified first with the intention of thinning to one or two specimens at a later date. This concept is expressive of the dynamic nature of landscape architecture.

In recent years moving large, established trees to achieve a more mature effect quickly has become popular (Fig. 11.17). This is not a new idea; there were tree-moving machines in the nineteenth century. The technique is widely used today with a high rate of success. Small- to medium-sized trees can be dug up on a site, boxed for a few years, and returned after a project has been completed. Soil preparation is extremely important, as are various techniques for preventing transpiration during the moving procedure. It should be recognized, however, that the growth and life span of such moved trees will probably never equal that of a young tree planted in place. The tree will take a few years to adapt. In areas where growth is fast, it may be just as effective to plant vigorous young trees in the first place. This will also allow us to watch the early rapid growth of the tree, which in itself is peculiarly satisfying and educational.

FIGURE 11.15
Camphor trees, a medium-sized broad-leafed evergreen.

FIGURE 11.16
Canary pines make a strong vertical statement.

Vines

Some vines need support, others twine or cling. Combined with an overhead structure, vines can provide delightful shaded areas (Fig. 11.18). The walls of buildings can be covered for insulation and to reduce glare. Wire fences can be transformed into green fences. Many vines, like clematis, have conspicuous flowers, others are leafy evergreen or deciduous types. Grapes may be grown in suitable climates.

Herbaceous Plants

Herbaceous plants and bulbs, herbs, and annuals are usually grown for their flowers, although many also have attractive foliage. Almost everybody likes

FIGURE 11.17
Mature tree being replaced.

FIGURE 11.19
(a) Classic English mixed flower border at Sissinghurst. **(b)** The same border in spring.

flowers, and they are planted for pleasure. The work and labor involved in planting and properly maintaining the herbaceous border of the nineteenth and early twentieth centuries have made this form of gardening and use of herbaceous plants increasingly rare (Fig. 11.19). In addition, the modern designer's obsession with sculptured foliage plants has relegated herbaceous flowers to the enthusiast's private yard. Annuals and other bedding plants bring welcome relief to shopping areas and places of civic importance (Fig. 11.20).

Flowers should be seen close up and with simple backgrounds. Seats should be placed close to raised flower beds or boxes (Figs. 11.21 and 11.22). Containers are popular in Northern Europe where the winters are long and flowers are an especially welcome relief in the summer. In Stockholm planting in the public places is replaced overnight from municipal greenhouses, so that there is no time when the containers are empty. Window boxes are standard elements of every apartment (Fig. 5.17).

FIGURE 11.18
Vines provide a shaded roof terrace in Italy.

GROWTH AND MANAGEMENT

The fourth consideration used in the selection of plants concerns conditions and requirements for their growth and survival, and the fulfillment of the design intent.

To ensure their survival, plants must be chosen with an understanding of their growth requirements, tolerances, or preferences of soil and climate and, of course, an understanding of the principles of vegetative growth in general. The real world compared with

FIGURE 11.20
Flowers in containers can be restocked or removed when out of bloom.

FIGURE 11.21
Seating placed in relation to flowers and both set off the beaten track in the foreground. Copenhagen.

FIGURE 11.22
Seats and flowers. Copenhagen.

the nursery environment from which new plants come is a hard place with varied conditions of light, water supply, soils, and bugs. Once planted in a project, the plant must adapt to the new conditions. The soil provides support for the plant and a reservoir of water and nutrients. Excessive compaction of the soil makes root growth difficult, and lack of certain minerals in impoverished soils of urban areas restricts growth. Waterlogged conditions and badly drained soils will kill most plants or impair normal growth. Water is extremely important and must be available naturally or by regular and deep irrigation.

Wind is an environmental factor most plants are sensitive to although some are more tolerant than others. For example, liquidambar is vulnerable to wind, whereas Monterey cypress can tolerate not only wind but also the salt spray of the sea. Evergreens are typically susceptible to soot and dust which clog the pores through which the plant transpires. Deciduous trees, which produce new leaves each season, can survive better. Light is also, obviously, a critical factor, since photosynthesis takes place only in the presence of sunlight. Some plants, however, are better adapted to shade conditions than others, due to their evolution in the understory of a natural forest. Temperature is also critical and freezing is a clear cut-off point. From freezing up to 80°F (27°C) is the most favorable temperature range, but some plants require lower and higher temperatures. Altitude, latitude, and geomorphology delineate natural growth zones. Reflected heat or glare from walls and pavement can also cause leaf burn.

Maintenance after planting is extremely important and has a strong bearing on plant selection. There are four main considerations. The first is water. Plants must have it to grow and in dry regions there must be periodic irrigation of nonnative plants. Drainage is also important and soil must not be allowed to become waterlogged. The second need is a program of fertilization that will provide nutrients in poor soils to stimulate growth and the establishment of plants. Third, weed control is essential to avoid competition for the moisture and nutrients intended for the selected plants. Control is effected by hoeing or by preemergent weed killers. Finally, pruning is important in terms of the ultimate form of trees and shrubs, the quality and development of hedges, grass and lawns, and so on. Pruning is a skill which helps to maintain the form of the tree or shrub but reduces the amount of foliage and shade. In fruit trees, of course, it is essential to productivity, and in flowering plants it is critical in the production of blossom (e.g., roses).

Some plants need less maintenance than others. Watering can be reduced for native plants once estab-

FIGURE 11.23
Plastic plants.

FIGURE 11.24
Ivy planted to control erosion on a highway embankment.

lished. Pruning is not needed for some plants. Grass needs regular cutting, whereas most groundcovers do not. Quick growing, spreading plants will reduce the amount of weeding necessary. Thus the maintenance factor and associated costs should be carefully evaluated in the selection of plants for functional or aesthetic reasons. Plastic plants may seem to be the ideal answer to the maintenance problem; no water, no fertilizer, no pruning, only an occasional light dusting (Fig. 11.23). Yet the public outrage in Los Angeles over the installation of plastic trees and shrubs on a highway median strip demonstrates that people are not yet as insensitive as some bureaucrats seem to think.

DESIGN POTENTIAL

Our fifth concern is selecting plants to perform some design purpose or function as indicated in the site planning diagrams. The process is complex, combining all the objective preferences of soil, water, temperature, and other factors, with a clear understanding of the purpose of the planting (Fig. 11.24). This must be clearly defined. Plants should never be used simply to fill leftover spaces; their positioning and selection should result from and be part of the solution to a design problem. Plants are structural just as paving is and can be used according to much the same principles. And, as with paving, maintenance and replacement costs are additional considerations.

Plants can be used to give form to a project. Carefully massed they can structure space as effectively as architecture. Shrub plantings and hedges can enclose areas and screen out unwanted views. Spreading trees or vines on trellises can give a canopy or ceiling effect (Fig. 11.25). Both provide a delightful tracery of cast shadows. At Villandry, plants are clipped into "architectural" forms and arranged to enclose large open spaces (Fig. 11.26). Hedges of yew at Sissinghurst are as precise as the walls of a room and create background textured surfaces for flowering plants (Fig. 11.13). Hawthorns in Chicago's Lakeside Park, planted close together, form an "architectural" tunnel from within and strong linear form seen from outside (Fig. 11.27). The elms in the same park enclose or define the larger spaces of the design, separating roadways from the green lawns (Fig. 11.14). The classic avenue is another example of the use of plant-

FIGURE 11.25
A large single tree defines space.

FIGURE 11.26
Villandry. Clipped limes provide strong architectural definition.

ing to structure space and direct attention and movement through the landscape. Depending on the scale, the sense of division or enclosure of space with trees is inferred rather than actual, whereas hedges and shrubberies tend to produce physical and visual barriers (Fig. 8.20). In the regional landscape, forest clearings are spatially defined by the trees (Fig. 8.19.)

Circulation is another aspect of design which can be emphasized by planting. Shrubs can be strategically placed to indicate edges, to accent junctions, to emphasize directional lines, or to act as a physical barrier. At the city scale, street tree planting can give identity to areas or to major streets or routes. The boulevards of Paris or any of the Beaux Arts civic developments elsewhere demonstrate the use of trees to emphasize city form. The changes in natural vegetation around a pond provide an excellent ecological model. This variation in plantings provides information about the place.

FIGURE 11.27
Gothic tunnel of Hawthorn, Chicago.

Erosion control is an extremely important function of plants. They hold together soil with their root structure, thus preventing it from being washed away down banks or causing landslides. Another function of the plant is to prevent the rain from falling with its full force on bare ground. By reducing the rate of runoff, planting contributes to the conservation of moisture and the replenishment of groundwater resources. Turf, ivy, and native vegetation are excellent for this purpose (Fig. 11.24).

Another important functional use of plants is in microclimate control. At Sea Ranch, we have seen the importance of tree belts to break the wind and provide areas of shelter, originally for crops and livestock, later for houses and schools. Fine-leaved trees help to diffuse the wind. Conifers are especially suitable (but they must also be wind tolerant) and mixtures of small and large trees in multiple rows are especially effective (Fig. 10.10).[2] Temperatures can be affected also by the shade cast by trees in warm climates (Fig. 10.8). In addition, the transpiration of water vapor from plants may, at the scale of a forest, have an additional cooling effect. The seasonal shading characteristic of deciduous trees is particularly important in places with hot summers and cold winters. Plants are also beneficial to some degree in keeping the air fresh and the level of pollution down. Certain types of plants are well suited to catch dust by virtue of their texture and form. As we have seen, noise can be controlled by planting if the scale is large enough. To all these "air conditioning" effects may be added the possibility of providing agreeable scents, albeit as a temporary effect. Nicotiana and other plants such as *Viburnum fragrans* can be selected especially for this attribute. The smell of orange blossom on a hot night in the Imperial Valley of California is memorable.

AESTHETICS

So far our discussion has been concentrated on the use of plants for structuring the landscape in relation to practical aspects of design such as space division, movement, visual relationships, microclimate, and erosion control. Although there is a sculptural quality in the geometric arrangement of planting for these purposes, which in itself has an aesthetic appeal, a further level of design quality involving color, texture, and form has yet to be achieved.

[2] J. M. Caborn, *Shelter Belts and Windbreaks* (London: Faber and Faber, 1965).

In order to achieve this level of refinement in landscape design, it is necessary to define the units of the medium (i.e., plants) in terms of their shape or form, their texture (as produced by their leaves and branches), and color (as produced by leaves and flowers). These characteristics are found in plants of all types in the horticultural classification. Just as plants can be ordered into lists on the basis of their usefulness for practical purposes, so they can be ordered in terms of these characteristics.

Form: Size, Shape, Habit, Density

A critical aspect of shrubs and trees in design is their ultimate size: height and spread (often referred to as stature). Where plants are to provide horizontal and vertical definition of space, alone or in combination with architecture, knowledge of size is essential if the desired ultimate scale and proportion relationships are to be achieved. Next comes the question of shape. It is tempting to think of shape as silhouette, to say that a young pine tree is triangular or that the form of an oak is round. They are, of course, conical and globular, i.e., three dimensional, with substantial depth, casting shadows which reinforce the reality of their volume. These volumes, which consist chiefly of branches, twigs, and leaves, vary from one another according to their growth pattern, i.e., how the branches originate from the ground, and how they divide and bear the leaves, flowers, and fruits. This is often described as the habit of a plant, the third variable within the category of form. To some extent trees and shrubs with sparse or open foliage, or because the foliage is close to the branches, reveal their branching habits more than those densely clothed. Deciduous trees automatically reveal their structure in winter when the growth pattern becomes clearly visible. In any event, plants that have easily identifiable growth pattern, e.g., a horizontally, a drooping, or an ascending quality, can be selected accordingly for a design purpose (contrast, drama, focus, and so on). With time and cultivation, the habit of a tree may change.

The organization of the branches, the twigs, and the size of the leaves gives plants yet another quality—relative density. This is a measure of the extent to which light can filter through the structure. This affects the intensity of shade (from dappled to deep) and the degree of visual screen and wind shelter. This quality also varies with time, and (particularly with deciduous plants) with season.

Within the attribute of form, the four characteristics of size, shape, habit, and density are relatively definable (Figs. 11.15, 11.16 and 11.28).

FIGURE 11.28
The willow tree is large, reaching a height of 50 or 60 feet and a spread of 40 feet. It is globular shaped, drooping in habit, and casts light shade due to its widely distributed small leaves.

Color

Color is an attribute of plants provided by all of their parts—leaves, flowers, fruits, twigs, branches, and bark. Frequently the effects are seasonal and therefore, subject to change. These characteristics are further complicated by other variables from the outdoors, weather, light, and shade. These variables modify and constantly change the color of plants and other objects in the landscape. Thus, absolute color theory, which is a quantifiable science for the artist or interior designer, becomes for the landscape architect the basis of a relatively unpredictable phenomena due to environmental conditions.

Green (and the range of greens from yellow to blue) is essentially a restful color. As a contrast to architecture, it is soothing to the eye. In the landscape the many shades of green, yellow, and brown provide an harmonious matrix for incidents such as buildings,

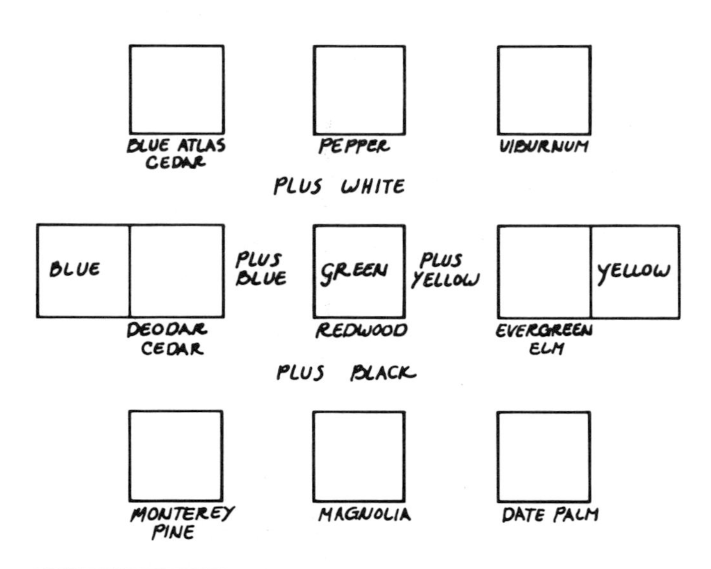

FIGURE 11.29
The green color of the foliage of any particular plant can be allocated one of nine values produced by preparing this chart. The central hue is a plant selected as a middle green to which the other eight can be compared and therefore to each other.

patches of bright color and water, which create focus and contrast, vitalizing the view. Since it is so fundamental a color in the appearance of plants, it is important to have some way of describing the various shades of green. Bracken suggests the selection of a plant with middle green color (*Acer saccharum* is his choice) as a point of reference against which the green of other plants is compared on two scales, dark to light and yellow to blue.[3] Thus, the foliage of any given plant would be described as either darker or lighter, yellower or bluer than the green of the sugar maple (or any other tree chosen as the median). But it is not that easy, since the foliage of deciduous plants frequently changes as the season progresses from spring to fall. The yellow green of newly opened leaves turns to the darker green of summer and before falling may turn bright red or yellow (Fig. 11.29).

In addition to green and the seasonally induced changes, the foliage of some plants is, in fact, a color other than green, or may be green combined with another color on the reverse side of the leaf, or in a variegated form. Thus purple and gray and combinations of white and green must be added to the already complex set of foliage colors and seasonal changes.

Even though we cannot be very scientific in our expectations from the use and combination of colors in the landscape, a basic knowledge of color theory and color phenomena helps to explain the striking and successful effects identified in the field. But for landscape purposes, and with the uncontrollable variables already discussed, we need to derive color principles that have a realistic chance of noticeable impact in the three dimensional dynamic outdoor environment. It is my judgment that only the crudest theory of harmony and contrast in the use of color (and texture) is worth consideration in landscape design. In more detailed situations, flower borders and particular areas subject to close scrutiny, it may be possible to be more sophisticated in the organization of color combinations.

In the same way that green varies according to its lightness or darkness, blueness or yellowness, other colors, found in flowers and building materials, can be described in terms of their relationship to the basic hue (whiter or blacker) and to the adjoining hue in the color spectrum (the tendency of blue to yellow through green or of red to yellow through orange, and so forth). The problem for the landscape architect is to what extent color distinction observed scientifically in the laboratory can be made meaningful for design in the outdoors. It seems possible to identify eight variations of any of the six basic hues and this makes a workable system (Fig. 11.29).

Texture

The practical difficulties of consistency, which we have described in dealing with plant color in the landscape, apply equally to the attribute of texture. Variables in the environment such as light and distance, and in the plants themselves, due to seasons and specific growing conditions, make it difficult to produce a reliable and uniform categorization of plant textures in which minute differences are taken into account. Our interest lies in the broadest differences on a relative scale. As with color, a middle value plant may be selected and the textures of others compared to it on a scale of coarser to finer, with perhaps two major categories in each direction from the median.

Variations between two plants, such as size and form of the leaves, how they are attached to the twigs, and how the twigs are subtended by the branches, are responsible, with light, for differences in texture (Figs. 11.30 and 11.31). Seen close, at a distance of two or three feet, as we see shrubs and flowers, even the surface quality of the leaf or bark (e.g., shiny or matte), is important. The overall effect may be assessed through half-closed eyes or some other device which will subjugate detail for pattern (Fig. 11.31). We must

[3]John Bracken, *Planting Design*.

FIGURE 11.30
Gunera Manicata.

then assign it a value. Fine and coarse are the terms traditionally used. Perhaps the addition of "grain" is helpful, giving us fine grain, and coarse grain. A middle value and perhaps "very fine" and "very coarse" for clearly identifiable extremes, may also be established on a relative scale. But the textural grain of a plant varies with distance. Colvin has suggested three critical distances[4], other landscape architects, two. The bunching of leaves on shrubs and trees may provide a different pattern of shadows when seen at 50 to 100 feet than it does at close hand. At a still greater distance, say 100 yards to ¼ mile, plant texture values in relation to others may change again. These greater distance variations apply only to large trees, since shrubs tend to lose their apparent texture at such distances, retaining form to some extent and color (Figs. 11.9 and 11.10). At the most, therefore, we could have a scale of three distances and five values of textural grain. The seasonal variable of greatest importance for texture is the winter appearance of deciduous plants. Thus, branches and twigs give yet another set of texture values to plants differentiating it from its summer appearance (Figs. 11.32 and 11.33).

FIGURE 11.31
Plants with obviously different textural effect at close distance, fine on top, coarse below.

The clipping of shrubs and trees into hedges or forms (topiary), of course, changes their visual texture. However, hedges made from different plants also vary, but most successful hedges are in the "fine" or "finest" category with possible winter variations if deciduous plants are used.

SUMMARY

Although it is customary to classify plants in terms of their design attributes of form, texture, and color, this is a very abstract way of dealing with a complex subject. In fact, it is the combinations of all the visual characteristics of any plant which give it identity. Beyond that, it is the organization of a set of plants by design which reinforces that identity through contrast.

In addition, it should be remembered that architecture and other structural elements in the landscape, walls, paving, and so on, each with their own attributes of form, color, and texture, are frequently involved in landscape design and must be considered equally with the plantings in the evolution of environmental quality.

Finally, although plants are usually discussed horticulturally as individuals, from a design point of view, it is more typical to use them in groups in which the individual form becomes secondary to the effect of mass (Figs. 11.11 and 11.27).

In the process of distributing and arranging plants in accordance with the site plan, we are automatically, among other things, organizing and opposing different forms, colors, and textures. This should support the design intent, e.g., by providing backgrounds for flowering plants, sculptures, or people, emphasizing direction, giving focus and spatial identity, and so forth. In other words, plant forms, colors, and textures should reinforce the plan.

Coarse texture and bright colors are strong and can be used to give emphasis. Fine textures, blue hues, and light tones visually recede and may be used to suggest distance. In relation to architecture, plant texture, color, and form may contrast or they may play a role in setting scale relationships. Unity, variety, and

[4] Brenda Colvin, *Land and Landscape*.

[5] E. Bruce MacDougall, *Computers in Landscape Architecture*, Ch. 4, "Plant Selection."

	VERY FINE		FINE		MEDIUM		COURSE		VERY COURSE	
	W	S	W	S	W	S	W	S	W	S
CLOSE-UP										
50'-100'										
DISTANT										

W WINTER
S SUMMER

FIGURE 11.32
The texture of plants can be categorized according to a five-stage range, modified by distance and, in some cases, season.

FIGURE 11.33
Photograph by William A. Garnett.

visual balance are clearly influenced by the organization of form, color, and texture in planting. Coarse texture has the same weight as bright and dark colors. A little goes a long way in composition. Because every plant has color and texture, the conscious use of both can reinforce the plan and its inherent specification for design quality and continuity with the surroundings.

Form, color, and texture of plants are the unique medium of landscape architecture, which together with growth and change, make success in the field so ephemeral and difficult to evaluate.

The selection of plants to fulfill the goals of site planning and landscape design requires knowledge of the six systems of classification described here. The range of plants available is immense, but the plants available commercially have been restricted by a process of simplification, inspired by economic agriculture, and a misinterpretation of the modern movement in architecture. Computer programs[5] or any other system, which objectively interrelate the criteria for the suitability of plants for any particular purpose and situation with the range of material available, are likely to contribute to a much needed diversity in landscape planting which has become highly standardized under the influence of garden magazines and the nursery industry.

SUGGESTED READINGS

Arnold, Henry, *Trees in Urban Design*.

Booth, Norman, *Basic Elements of Landscape Architectural Design*, Ch. 2, "Plant Materials."

Bracken, John, *Planting Design*.

Butz, Richard, *The Edible City—Resource Manual*.

Brooks, John, *Room Outside*, Ch. 10, "Skeleton Planting," Ch. 11, "Planting Design."

Buckman, Harry O. and Nyle C. Brady, *The Nature and Properties of Soils*, pp. 1–15, "The Soil in Perspective."

Carpenter, Philip, et al., *Plants in the Landscape*.

Clauston, Brian, ed., *Design with Plants*.

Colvin, Brenda and Jacqueline Tyrwhitt, *Trees for Town and Country*.

Crowe, Sylvia, *Garden Design*, 2nd edition, Ch. 10, "Plant Material."

Diekelmann, Jahn and R. Schuster; *Natural Landscaping—Designing with Native Plant Communities*.

Gaines, Richard, *Interior Plantscaping*.

Gardner, Victor R., *Basic Horticulture*, pp. 13–23, 81–150.

Hackett, Brian, *Planting Design*.

Hudack, Joseph, *Trees for Every Purpose*.

Hunter, Margaret, *The Indoor Garden*.

MacDougall, E. Bruce, *Microcomputers in Landscape Architecture*, Ch. 11, "Plant Selection."

Perry, Frances, *The Water Garden*.

Robbins, Wilson W., T. Eliot Weier, and C. Ralph Stocking, *Botany, An Introduction to Plant Science*, pp. 9–12, "Subdivisions of Botany," pp. 61–71, "Physiology of the Cells," pp. 172–183, "Soil and Mineral Nutrition," pp. 202–214, "Photosynthesis and Respiration," pp. 303–322, "The Plant as a Living Mechanism."

Robinette, Gary O., *Plants, People and Environmental Quality*.

Robinson, Florence Bell, *Palette of Plants*.

Robinson, Florence Bell, *Planting Design*.

Scrivens, Stephen, *Interior Planting in Large Buildings*.

Weddle, A. E., ed., *Techniques of Landscape Architecture*, pp. 176–193, "Tree Planting," by Brenda Colvin.

Zion, Robert, *Trees for the Architecture and the Landscape*.

LANDSCAPE ENGINEERING

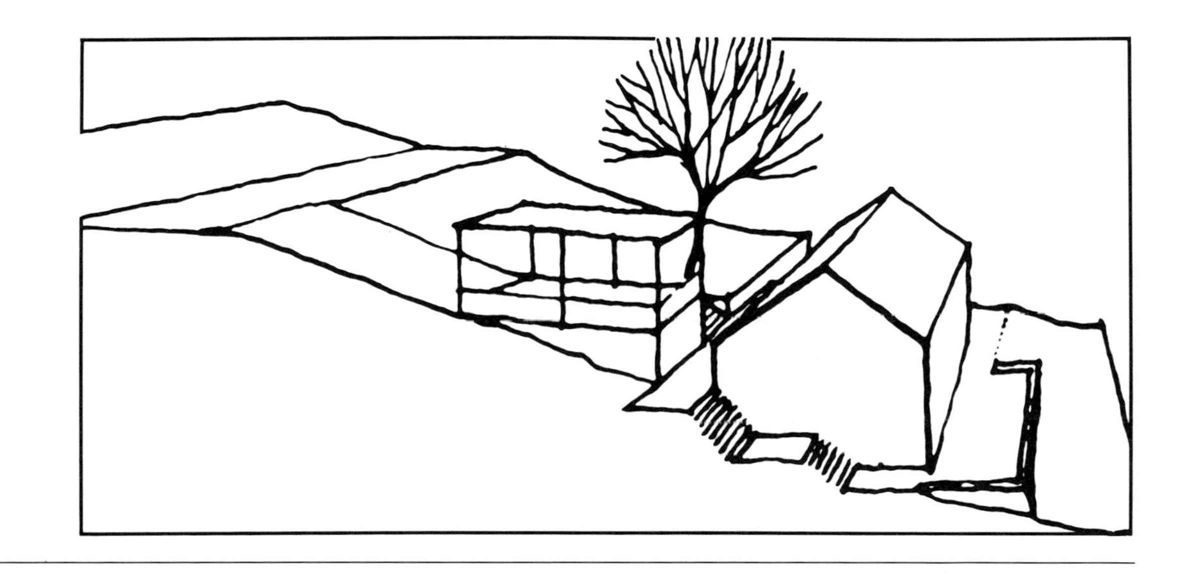

12

Landscape engineering or grading is a fundamental technical aspect of landscape architecture. It involves the remodeling of existing land form to facilitate the functions and circulation of the site plan and to ensure adequate drainage. Thus a knowledge of grading technology is useful in the site planning process. Detailed leveling is needed to make connections between architecture and landscape, between indoors and out (Figs. 12.1 to 12.3). Psychologically there is perhaps more satisfaction in a house or building being directly on and related to solid land. Being on the earth, dug into it, is probably a positive psychological urge and need.

The site-to-structure relationship is a visual as well as a functional matter. The floor levels of buildings should be higher than the surrounding ground. Surfaces adjacent to and outside buildings should also slope away from the building so that rain water will not easily enter the structures or undermine foundations.

FIGURE 12.1
Grading is the connection of given or required levels. A house with two floor levels with indoor/outdoor relationships from each.

FIGURE 12.2
The change in level is hidden by planting.

FIGURE 12.3
Steps connect the two levels.

At Foothill College (Chapter 7), the original landscape was extensively reshaped to fit the buildings and open space into buildable and usable land. The sensitivity with which this was done resulted in a landscape that did not look as though it had been remodeled. Buildings were set well back from the edge of the hill, permitting them to sit comfortably on level ground (Fig. 7.10).

There are two principal relationships between buildings and land. The land may be graded or adjusted to suit the architectural or engineering requirements, or the architecture may be adapted to meet variations in ground level so that the original surface is disturbed less (Fig. 12.4). Buildings that stand on pilotti and do not touch the ground at all require little grading except to provide access. The land will be disturbed to some extent during construction and will result in changed light and moisture conditions under the structure. On the other hand, construction that assumes conventional foundations results in a building-to-ground relationship all around the structure. Single-level houses on steep hillsides require extensive cut and fill grading, eliminating the original soil relationship which may lead to unstable conditions resulting in erosion, landslides, floods, and a complete destruction of the ecosystem (Fig 6.6 and 12.5). The appropriate way to site buildings depends on a careful analysis of the land, its slope, soil, geology, and so on. In addition, the initial decision to build in any area should result from land suitability studies (Chapter 6), so that truly destructive processes can be prevented or special construction techniques instituted to match the conditions.

THE PRINCIPLES AND TECHNOLOGY OF GRADING

Let us now proceed to the more conventional problems in which buildings and use areas are sited on suitable land and in which the site plan essentially creates a new and working landscape to replace the existing ''natural'' condition. The technology of grading represents a unique skill of landscape architecture and is connected with the process of placing the diagram of the site plan onto a given topographical landscape. Our concern is not only with fitting or connecting buildings to the land but also with sitting use areas such as playing fields, parking lots, and circulation routes. All of these have specific criteria for slope, foundation depth, and drainage.

Landscape engineering is concerned with economical development and with sensitivity to the existing conditions. The basic principles and goals of grading may be summarized as follows.

1. The ground surface must be suitable for the intended purpose or use.
2. The visual result should be pleasing; indeed the purpose of the grading may be purely aesthetic, to screen views or create symbolic land form.
3. The resulting ground surface must have positive drainage.
4. The grading plan should attempt to keep the new levels as close as possible to the original state of the land. In nonurban areas especially, existing landscape represents an ecological balance, a natural drainage system, and a developed soil profile.
5. When ground is reshaped it should be done positively and at the scale of the machinery. Grading machinery is by definition gross in nature and subtle details are difficult to achieve except by hand labor.
6. Topsoil should be conserved wherever possible. It may be stripped, stockpiled, and reused after heavy grading.
7. In the grading operation, the quantity of cut should approximately equal the amount of fill. This eliminates the need to import soil or to find a place to dump unwanted material.

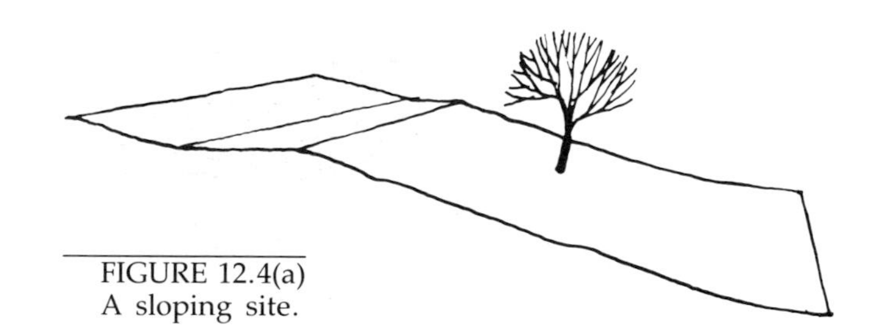

FIGURE 12.4(a)
A sloping site.

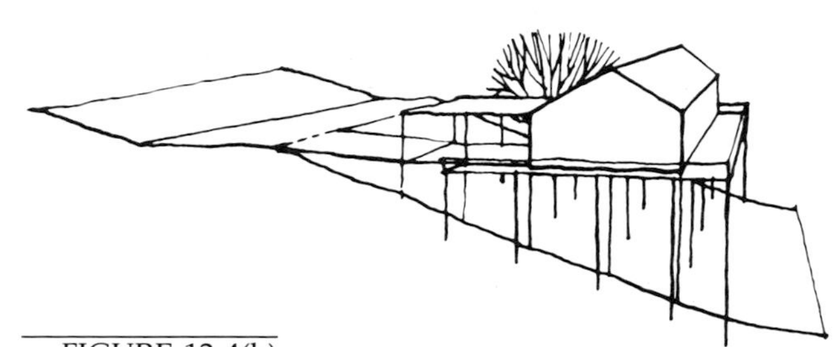

FIGURE 12.4(b)
A single story house set on stilts leaves the ground relatively undisturbed. The tree can be saved.

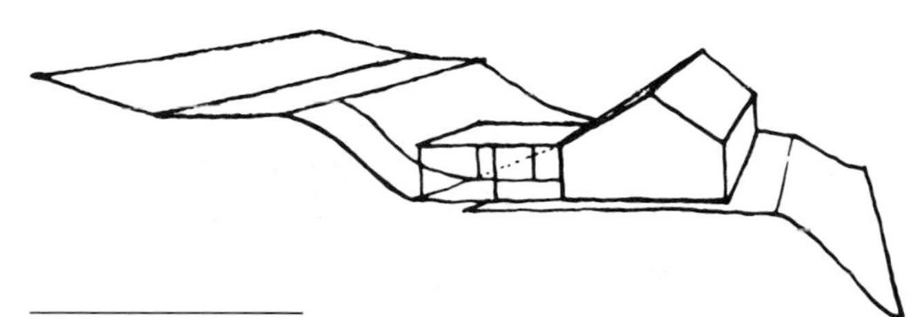

FIGURE 12.4(c)
A single story house set on conventional foundations requires considerable cut and fill resulting in steeper slopes at each side of the lot.

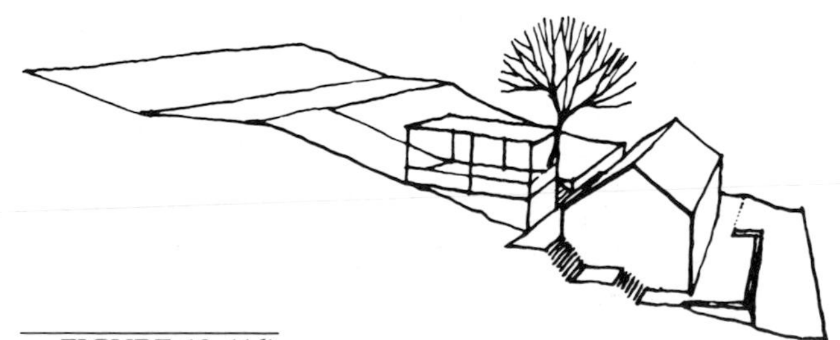

FIGURE 12.4(d)
A split-level house with retaining walls maintains shallow slopes at each side of the lot and the tree can be saved. The house is closely related to the form of the landscape.

Grading Plans

Grading plans are technical documents and are instruments by which we show and calculate changes to the three-dimensional surface of the land (Fig. 12.6). Contour lines are used to indicate the extent of that change. Depending on the scale, contours show relative elevation at intervals of 1 foot, 5 feet, or more. Existing contours are shown as dashed lines. The proposed new land form is shown by solid lines drawn where this varies from the existing form. The difference between these lines shows where land is to be cut and where filled and, in general, the extent and nature of the change. Such drawings, showing two sets of contour lines, express the difference between the existing condition and the design intent. From these drawings quantities of cut and fill can be calculated. The plans must be accurate if calculations and therefore cost estimates are to be reliable.

Site planning and grading take care of the adjustment necessary between fixed levels, structures, and use areas within the boundaries of the site. Fixed levels or control elevations include the levels of exist-

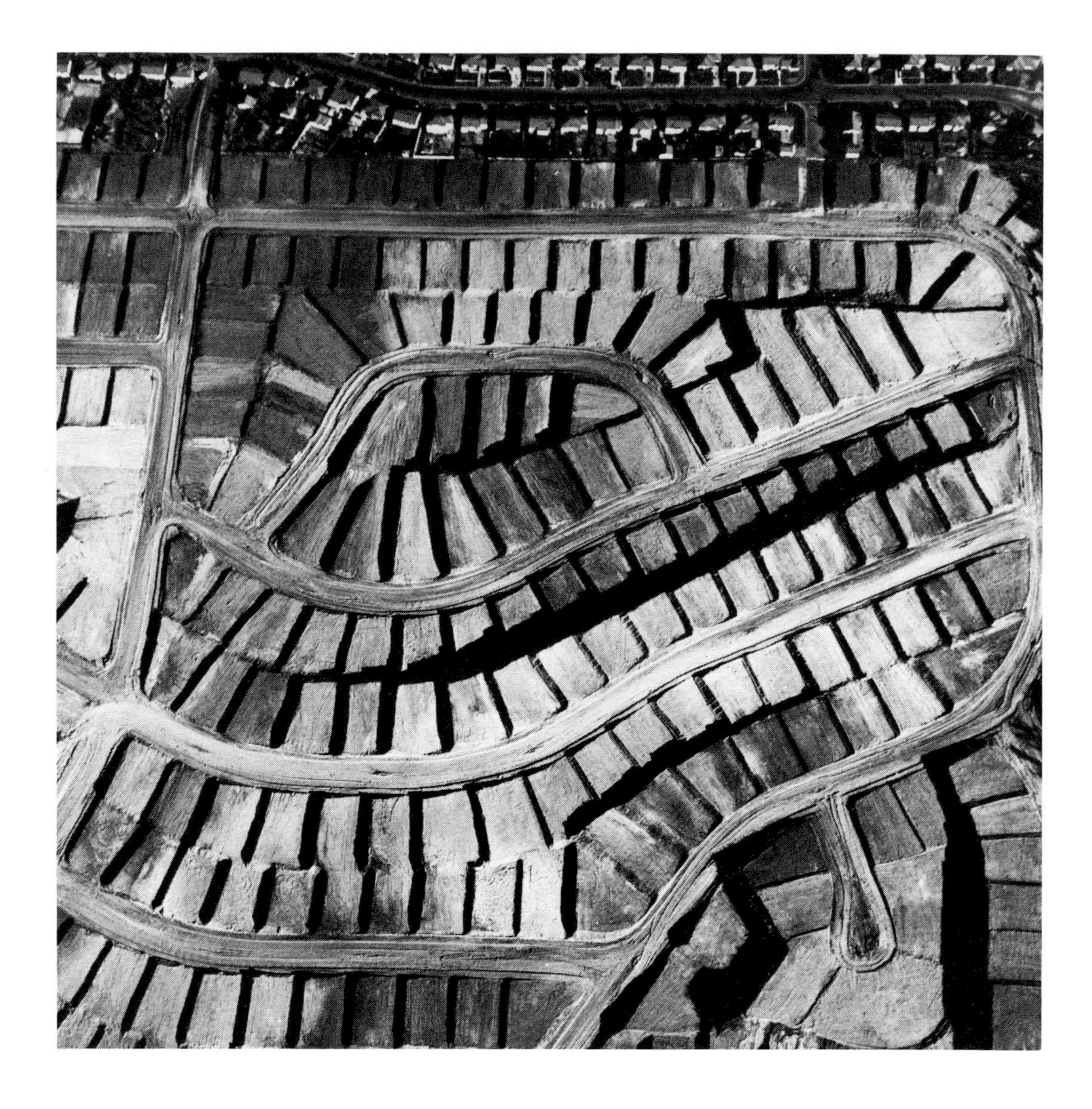

FIGURE 12.5
Graded and leveled building sites on hilly terrain, Los Angeles (1955). Photograph by William A. Garnett.

ing trees or vegetation to be retained, existing and proposed buildings and roads, the levels at the boundary of the site, existing land forms to be included in the design, lakes and natural swales, existing and proposed underground utilities. Such levels constrain the reshaping possibilities.

The terminology of the grading plan is simple. *Contour lines* are abstractions which join all points of the same elevation above a fixed datum. *Spot elevations* provide additional information beyond that given by the contour lines. They indicate micrograding; that is, specific levels that lie between the intervals of the contour lines. They show level differences needed to ensure drainage on "flat" surfaces and to indicate specific levels at important points in the plan. Typical locations at which spot elevations are shown are at tops and bottoms of steps, tops of retaining walls, outside entrances to buildings and their inside floor levels.

Another term frequently used is *grade* or *gradient*. This refers to the rate of slope between two points, expressed as a percentage, or as a ratio of horizontal distance to vertical change in elevation, or as an angle. Thus a 1 percent slope is the same as 100-1. A 10 percent slope is the same as 10-1 or a 6° angle. A 50 percent slope is the same as 2-1 or a 26°30′ angle, and

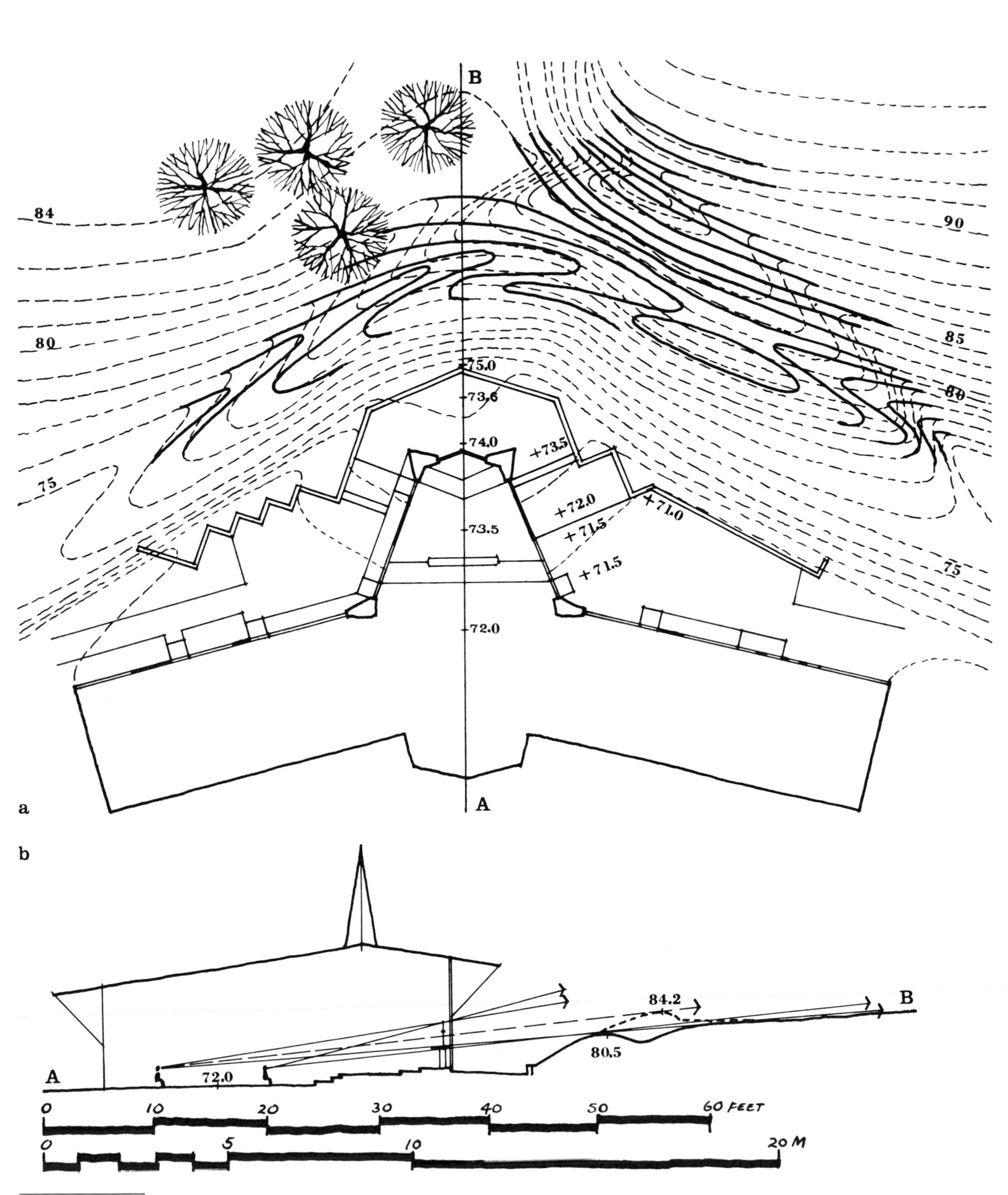

FIGURE 12.6
(a) Grading plan deals with drainage on the hillside and on the paved surfaces. Usable space is provided around the church and the steepness of the original slope is reduced. **(b)** Section.

a 100 percent slope is 1-1 or a 45° angle. Key variables in figuring gradients are the horizontal distance between two points and the vertical change in elevation.

Frequently the surface has to be changed to provide some specific gradient or to fit into some maximum or minimum slope criteria. The process of developing a grading plan involves the manipulation of the three factors: *gradient (G), horizontal distance (L),* and *difference in elevation* between two points *(D).* If, for example, the existing *G* between two points 100 feet apart is too great for an entrance road (say 15 percent), then either the vertical difference must be made less (10 feet) or the horizontal distance must be increased (to 150 feet). The variables interact as follows.

$$G = \frac{D}{L}; \qquad L = \frac{D}{G}; \qquad D = L \times G$$

Altering these variables produces solutions with different economic and aesthetic implications (Fig. 12.7).

In landscape design there are generally accepted maximum grades. These figures have been developed by engineers, architects, and landscape architects from experience and practice. They become determinants of form in site planning, and they are also economic factors. For example, walks and paths usually have a crowned cross section and if possible should not have a longitudinal gradient of more than 6 percent in areas of cold winters, or 8 percent in milder climates where frost is not persistent. These are preferred slopes for long distances of path. For shorter distance, ramps with a gradient of up to 12 percent can be used; over 12 percent, steps become the most reasonable way to overcome changes in level, but they should be avoided wherever possible. For wheelchairs and bicycles, steps are an obstacle and a hazard. Flights of three or fewer steps become an irritation for movement, although they can serve as informal seating, especially on school grounds and college campuses (Fig. 8.5).

Steps are purely functional in changing elevation in the shortest possible space and are subject to preferred dimensions derived from the physical act of walking developed over centuries of building in both vernacular and Renaissance modes (Figs. 8.21 and 8.33). For example, one "rule" states that the riser multiplied by the tread should equal approximately 74 inches. This allows alternative dimensions, for example, 6-inch

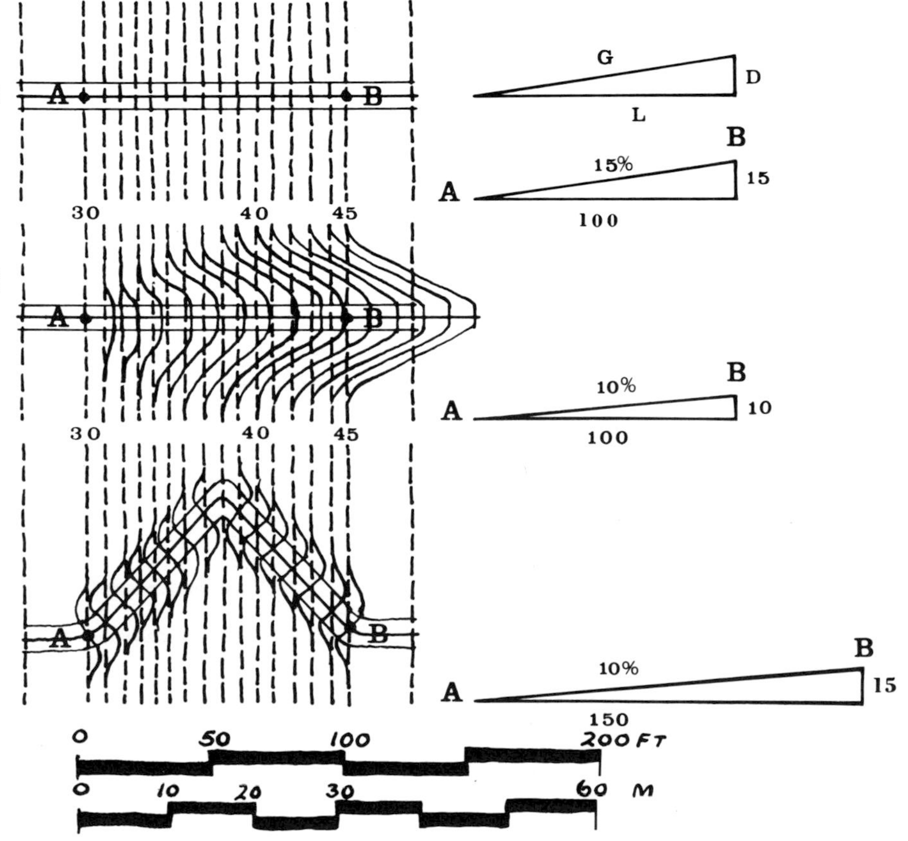

FIGURE 12.7
A road from A to B in plan 1 would have a gradient of 15 percent. By cutting into the hillside and extending the road length beyond the plan area, the gradient between A and B can be reduced to 10 percent (plan 2). Alternatively, a gradient of 10 percent can be achieved within the plan area and without extreme changes to the land as shown in plan 3. The length of road is increased, however.

riser and 12-inch tread, 5-inch riser and 15-inch tread, 4-inch riser and 18-inch tread. As the riser is reduced, the tread becomes wider. However, when the tread becomes excessively wide, the rhythm of walking and the dimensions of a stride must enter into the calculations. Designers should measure and record steps they find comfortable.

Roads and driveways also have preferred maximum gradients. Although 6 percent is considered desirable, 8 to 10 percent is permissible for short distances. In exceptional cases (in San Francisco, for example, where fortunately the weather is mild) streets are found at 15 percent and more. These standards and rules of thumb must be viewed in terms of the specific problem to be solved and its context of geography, custom, and use.

In the cut and fill process necessary to fit use elements with criteria of flatness onto land of variable slope, the procedure is as elementary as it sounds. However, depending on the type of material and the compaction process, the quantity of cut should be calculated to be about 5 percent more than would appear to be theoretically necessary for the fill. This is due to the fact that when loose material from a cut is filled, the compaction makes it take up less volume. This is important in large scale grading where 5 percent may be a considerable quantity. Cross sections, which are an essential technique in developing a grading plan, are used in the calculations of cut and fill quantities. Computing is done most accurately with a planimeter, which measures the cross sections of a cut and fill area. The average of the cross section is multiplied by its length to give the volume (Fig. 12.8). Computer programs are now available to do these calculations and contribute to better design by quickly generating alternatives which can be compared before a final decision is made.[1]

Existing trees in a landscape which is to be altered require special care if they are to survive (Fig. 12.9). The vulnerable area around a tree trunk varies according to its rooting characteristics. In general, however, it is possible to develop some principles which, with the foregoing proviso, apply to most situations. The vulnerable area on the ground equals the spread of the tree plus an additional one-third of that on each side. Trees tend to extend their feeder roots, which take up nutrients in solution, beyond the drip line. This zone is therefore particularly important for the health of the tree, and the inner zone is important for its physical support. To be absolutely certain of the tree's survival, no grading, cut, or fill should take place in the total vulnerable area. The levels or elevations of this surface then become control elevations as discussed earlier.

Sometimes, however, total conservation is impossible. If it is necessary to cut to a depth more than 6 inches in the vicinity of the tree, no more than one-third of the vulnerable area should be cut. In this case, since some structural and feeder roots may be lost, the tree should be pruned to reduce the weight to be supported and the demand for nutrients and water. If, on the other hand, the levels around the tree have to be raised in excess of 4 inches, it may be saved by taking measures to keep air and water in the same relationship to the roots as in the existing condition. Twelve inches of coarse gravel should be laid over the entire vulnerable area under the fill as shown in Figure 12.9. Drainpipes laid vertically to the top of the fill will allow air to circulate freely. With this technique, the relationship of the roots to air will remain essentially the same and the adjustment the tree will have to make will be relatively gentle. Further, horizontal drains may be needed to maintain the water table at the original level. None of these techniques can be considered particularly satisfactory. Even if the trees do survive, their growth may be affected. In addition, the way in which trees grow naturally out of the ground is an important aspect of their aesthetic quality.

The machinery that will do the grading can be an economic constraint and a determinant of form. Several factors influence the cost of the grading operation, and under tight budget situations these factors should indicate the most suitable methods. For example, in the cut and fill process it is best and most economical that the cut area be as close to the fill area as possible. If the cut is 2 miles away from the fill area, the length of haul will increase the cost of the operation. Sometimes the nature of the material being excavated can affect the time involved. Clay and silt and loam are easy to load, spread, and compact, whereas sand is harder to handle, as are shale and hard pan. Thus the nature of the material may extend the time or incur excessive wear and tear on machinery, both increasing costs.[2] Soil analysis can thus be seen to relate to grading. Machinery of different types and sizes has specific minimum turning circles. Therefore in terms of the ease and speed with which the work can be done, the type of machinery available is an important factor that may influence certain aspects of the grading plan. Curved grades with gentle shapes are easier to create than are specific angular grades. Finally, there are certain maximum slopes beyond which some machinery cannot operate.

---

[1] E. Bruce MacDougall, *Microcomputers in Landscape Architecture*. Ch. 10, "Earthwork Calculations."

[2] Brian Hackett, "Land Form and Cost Factors," *Landscape Architecture* 56 (6) (July 1964).

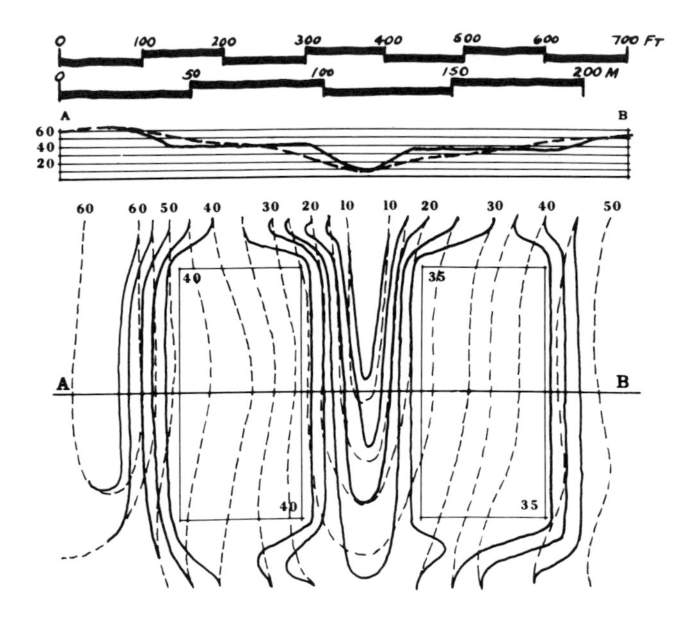

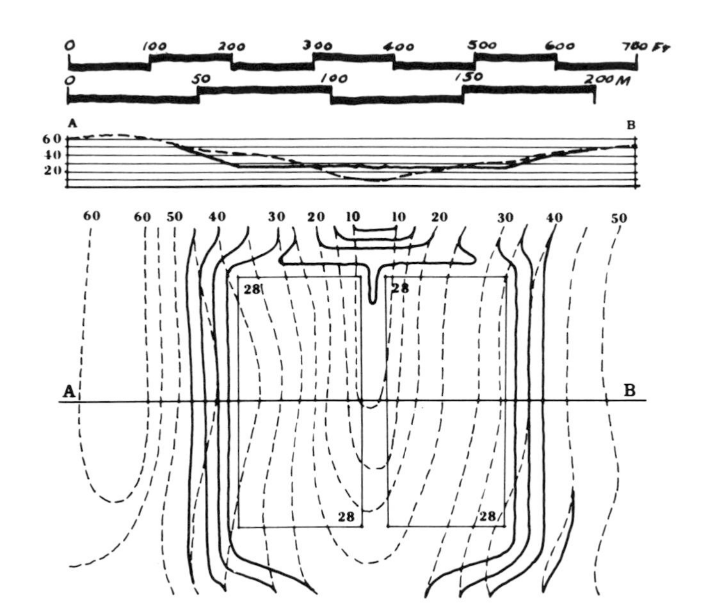

FIGURE 12.8
(a) and **(b)** Two grading solutions fitting playing fields into uneven terrain (above). In both cases the cut balances the fill. Solution **(a)** is perhaps the most sensitive of the two, but might have some disadvantages.

In grading we should be sure that the surfaces which result are stable. As the banks or graded slopes increase in steepness, so the amount of surface water that runs off will increase and with it the greater possibility of soil erosion (depending on the vegetative cover). The less steep the banks are, the better. Basically the type of material forming the banks dictates the maximum slopes that are possible by virtue of its natural angle of repose. Thus solid rock may be cut almost vertical at, say, ¼-1; this will be safe for banks no greater than 20 feet high. On the other hand, fill with broken rock will have an angle of repose of approximately 1-1 (a 100 percent slope, or 45°). Average soil has an angle of repose of about 55° for cut and 17° for fill. What is safe, in equilibrium or in balance, depends on the nature of the soil or material being excavated and compacted for fill. In certain situations of geology and soil, slopes of greater than 25 percent are considered unsafe.

Another reason to keep slopes as gentle as possible is maintenance. Grass cutting machinery is not practi-

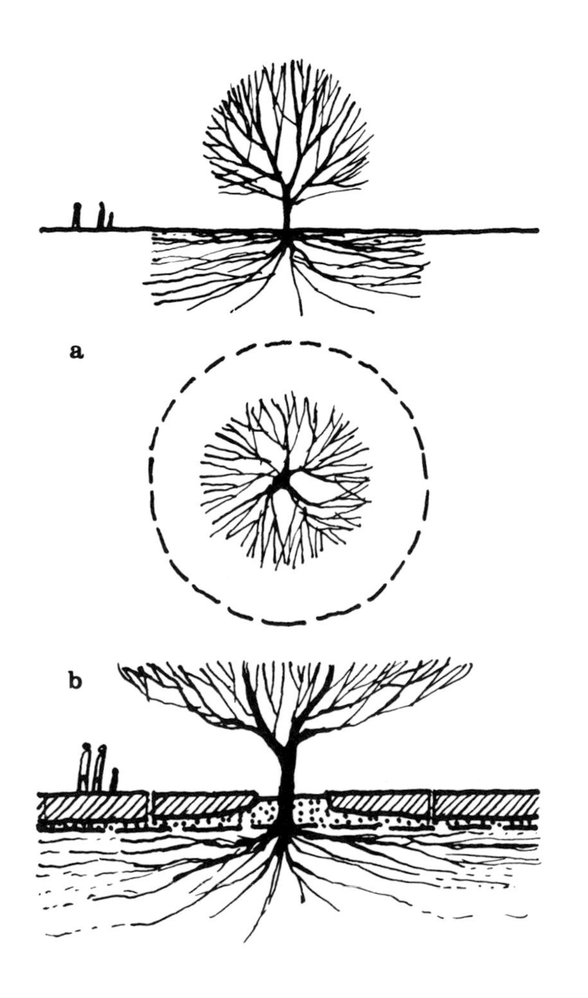

FIGURE 12.9
(a) The vulnerable area around a tree is equal to its spread plus one-third. **(b)** A system of filling land over the vulnerable area that attempts to maintain the original relationship of air and water to the tree's roots.

cal at slopes greater than 30 percent. Thus the permissible slope will depend on a number of factors, including the nature of the original material, whether the surface of the slopes is planted, paved, or grassed, and what kind of drainage provisions are made at the top and bottom of banks. It is generally best to stay away from the maximums represented by the angles of repose. Retaining walls should be considered in situations where changes in elevation cannot be accommodated with acceptable slopes. Retaining walls are devices that can take up differences in elevation abruptly; they are expensive, requiring reinforcing if they are over 3 feet in height. Gravel backfill and "weep holes" at the base of the wall are needed to relieve the pressure and weight of rain water behind the wall (Fig. 12.10). Being architectural elements, retaining walls of any material can be used as an effective design technique to link buildings or structures to the landscape. Where land is excessively steep, flat areas can be achieved only with retaining walls or decks.

Since grading by definition involves disturbance of the land surface, the maintenance of soil conditions which will permit plant growth is an important concern. Good soil is a valuable resource, the product of thousands of years' evolution; it should not be disposed of lightly. The less disturbance to the surface topsoil, the better. If big changes are needed, the topsoil should be stripped, stored, and reused. Even so, the structure and its relation to the soil profile will be altered. In urban situations where the soil has already been disturbed or built on, the problem may be the development of fertile soil suitable as a growing medium. This is a matter of fertilization and cultivation and possibly importation of topsoil.

SURFACE DRAINAGE

Rainfall is the usual source of surface water. When it falls, a proportion of it percolates into the soil, the amount depending on the soil type and vegetative cover. Another proportion of it drains or runs over the surface of the land to some low point on the site. Another proportion may flow off the site, and some will evaporate. That portion of the rain which does not enter the soil or evaporate is called runoff. Grading and construction provisions must be made for this runoff, so that flooding will be avoided and valuable topsoil will not be lost by erosion. One of the functions of the grading plan is to shape the ground in such a way that rain water will flow through the site to collecting points without causing washouts (Figs. 12.6 and 12.8). It is therefore economical and usual to grade the land in such a way that water is collected in channels, grass swales, or gutters (depending on the nature of the project) and directed around buildings and away from major use areas into either natural channels or, in urban areas, into drain inlets connected to a storm sewer system.

FIGURE 12.10
Brick retaining wall with "weep holes."

Predictions of water runoff quantities are necessary in order that the size of the pipes or swale dimensions can be calculated and provided adequately so that they can cope with the worst possible conditions. Historical climate data are used to provide 100-, 50-, 25-, or 10-year storm expectancies. The frequency selected depends on whether occasional flooding would be acceptable, as on playing fields and recreation areas. An agricultural engineering formula is frequently used in which the quantity of water (Q) arriving at any point in a watershed is derived from a combination of several variables.

$$Q = ACi$$

The variables are the area of the watershed in acres (A), a coefficient of runoff (C), and a quantity derived from the amount of rain that can be expected for a selected storm frequency combined with the farthest distance that a drop of water will have to run before reaching the collecting point (i).

The coefficient of runoff is the most interesting variable. It varies according to two site factors: the condition of the surface and the topography or slope. The coefficient represents the percentage of rain which is not absorbed or delayed before reaching a specified point or drain inlet. Tables have been prepared to give values for a variety of conditions. For example, in urban areas where 30 percent of the surface is estimated to be impervious (roofs, roads, and so on) in a generally flat landscape, 40 percent of falling rain will become runoff for drainage purposes. With a similar percentage of impervious surface in a situation of rolling terrain, the runoff may rise to

FIGURE 12.11(a)
At Village Homes, Davis, California, the concept of zero runoff is employed. The surface of the open space between houses is shaped to collect rainfall. In dry weather, the grassy areas provide informal areas for children's play. Photographs courtesy of Lisa Caronna-Perley.

FIGURE 12.11(b)
During storms, rain collects in ponds and slowly percolates into the ground, thus directly replenishing the groundwater.

50 percent. As the amount of impervious surface increases, the quantity of runoff increases. With building roofs and roads that have runoff coefficients between 85 and 100 percent, it can be seen that urban conditions in areas of heavy rainfall either throughout the year or at selected times within the year pose very serious drainage problems in the design of open space and paved plazas. By contrast, in more natural situations the runoff is considerably less.

To the variables of surface cover and topography is added soil, which can have a considerable impact on the quantity of water that becomes runoff. Thus in a wooded landscape on flat ground with open sandy loam soil the runoff will be about 10 percent. In the same situation but with a heavy clay soil the runoff may be as much as 40 percent. As the topography becomes steeper, the rate of runoff increases. The coefficient of runoff on hilly land with slopes of between 10 and 30 percent with sandy soil will be about 30 percent, which will double if the soil has a high clay content.

These figures are significant not only for drainage purposes but also for water conservation. Paul Sears argues that the longer water can be kept on or in the land, the better for mankind.[3] Delay of the water cycle in its land phase is desirable, and in certain circumstances spreading water over the land and allowing it to percolate into the soil, replenishing groundwater, is preferable to immediate removal by storm sewers. The zero runoff design at Village Homes, Davis, California, illustrates how this may be done in a favorable situation and climate (Figs. 12.11(a) and (b)).

For drainage purposes there are some minimum gradients for surfaces. Drainage, especially around buildings or use areas such as playing fields, must be positive. Water must flow if ponds and puddles are to be avoided. It is therefore undesirable to have dead level surfaces. The minimum gradients vary according to the nature of the surface and/or its permeability. For example, the minimum gradient for asphalt is between 1.5 and 2 percent. For smooth finished concrete the minimum is 1 percent, whereas on coarser, exposed aggregate the minimum would be 2 percent since water will not flow as easily over the rougher surface. Bricks laid in sand need a minimum of 1 percent, whereas brick paving laid with grouted joints needs 2 percent. Lawns and grass areas should have a minimum of 1 percent in the open and 2 percent adjacent to buildings and in grass swales.

The design of a storm sewer system is properly the work of an engineer. However, drain inlets are surface manifestations of the hidden underground system. Their position and elevation are related to economics and the constraints of water flow technology. They are the places where landscape design meets engineering, requiring collaboration between the two. They must be designed as part of the surface treatment or pattern rather than incorporated as afterthoughts, as so often seems to happen.

Just as there are minimum gradients to facilitate positive drainage, so there are maximums. These are important in erosion control. Groundcover or grass planting on banks of 25 percent or more is absolutely necessary to prevent erosion and excessive runoff. In solving drainage problems without a storm sewer system, that is, in natural swales or streams, it is important to know what the effect of the runoff will be downstream. Silting up of streams and channels may occur, thus reducing their capacity to remove water from the area at a subsequent time (Figs. 6.5 and 6.6).

Roof gardens require very rapid drainage since the weight of water added to soil, paving, and plants places stresses on the structure. The slopes on paved surfaces in such situations should be greater than slopes normally required. Special lightweight and porous soil at least 12 inches in depth should be used in planting beds with subsurface drains to remove excess water.

VISUAL CONSIDERATIONS

In addition to all the functional considerations discussed so far, grading also has visual implications. The created land form can have an aesthetic appearance in its own right, as at the Stockholm Cemetery (Fig. 12.12) or at Foothill College (Fig. 7.8). In addition, land form can help to screen out undesirable views such as parking lots and freeways (Fig. 12.13). With the addition of planting, earth mounds can provide a quick and effective visual barrier and also wind shelter (Fig. 6.40). The sunken fence or Ha Ha, product of the eighteenth-century landscape garden, is a grading technique devised to conceal the boundary fence, the

[3] Paul B. Sears, *The Living Landscape* (New York: Basic Books, 1962).

FIGURE 12.12
Crematorium, Stockholm (1937–1940). Gunar Asplund, Architect.

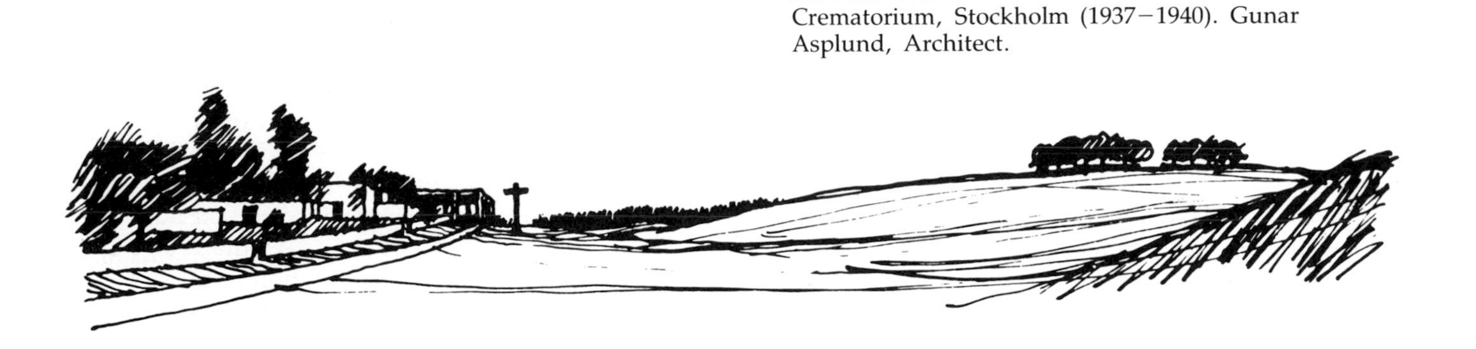

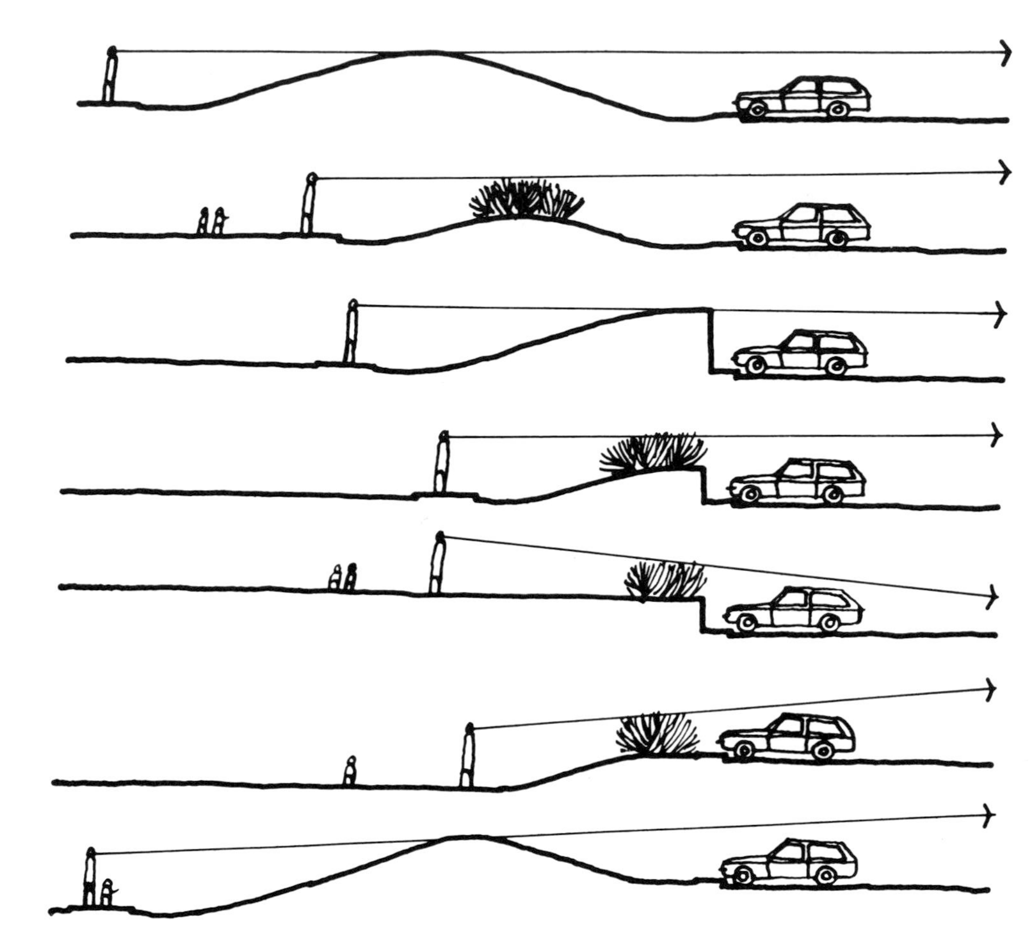

FIGURE 12.13
Land form combined with retaining walls and/or planting, and differences in relative levels can be used in design to conceal and separate.

FIGURE 12.14
Articulation of levels to separate circulation and use areas.

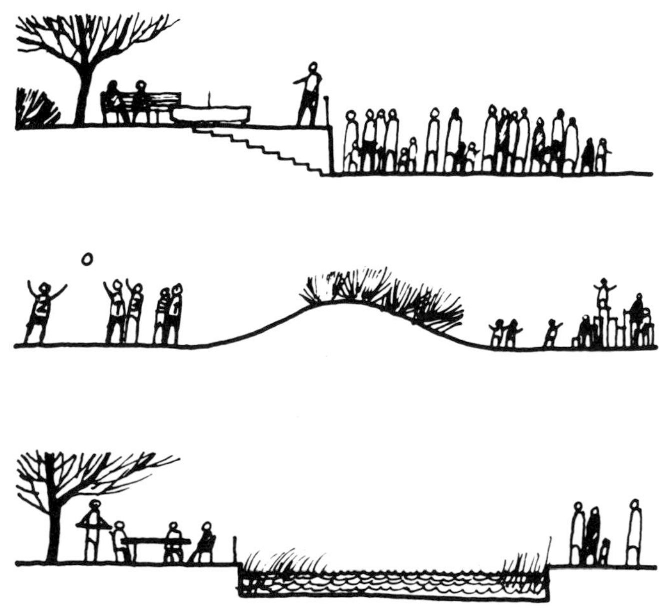

division between pastureland and garden (Fig. 2.42). Changes in level may also be devised to separate circulation and social uses in site planning and detailed design (Fig. 12.14). Geometric land shaping as opposed to natural form can produce interesting and exciting results, as the wind protection earthworks at Sea Ranch show with bold angular forms (Fig. 6.40). Land forms that are not imitations of nature are especially appropriate where new landscapes are being made in the restoration of derelict land or in the disposal of excess fill. Open-air theaters provide other opportunities for creative land shaping.

CASE STUDY

Discussion of a small and simple case study may help to show the interrelationship of the grading principles and goals outlined here. The success of the Church project seen in Fig. 12.6 depended on a careful assessment of regrading possibilities. There were three requirements. First, the provision of level paved open areas for outdoor meetings and for after church social hours. Second, the grading had to produce a stable slope out of one that was too steep and subject to slides and provide a drainage swale half-way up. Third, the view from the window behind the altar was involved in the regrading. From the church the visual line caused by the top of the existing bank seen from the window cut across a very beautiful but delicate cross on the altar. Visually, whatever line resulted from the regrading should therefore be either above or below its present location to eliminate this aesthetic conflict.

Cross sections drawn through the site suggested the dimensions for the paved areas, the acceptable slopes, and the location, depth, and gradient of the drainage channel. Levels obtained from the cross sections were transferred to the contour plan, and proposed contours were drawn, which when implemented would result in the desired cross section. The quantities of cut and fill could be calculated from these lines, and since more cut was needed than fill a suitable area nearby was located to dispose of the excess. The paved courtyards also had to be graded so that the paved surface would drain away from the building and into an open drain (removing the water from the immediate area but not off the site).

This simple example illustrates how various problems were solved. The existing unstable bank was graded to a more acceptable slope and a drainage swale was provided at the top, both contributing to its greater stability. Retaining walls were also used to reduce the slope, and level areas were provided outside the doors of the church. The visual background to the altar was also made more simple, eliminating the visual conflict.

SUMMARY

In summary, grading is the means by which we modify the surface of the land to meet the requirements of a design and program. The extent to which surface changes can normally be made depends on the control elevations of the site and fixed elements on its surface. Further determinants of form are maximum gradient criteria for roads, paths, and slopes, the balance of cut and fill, bank stability, erosion control, and surface drainage. Economics, soil conservation, and the characteristics of earth-moving machinery are further variables in the specific transformation of site plans into three-dimensional reality. In addition to these functional matters, the shaping of the land in relation to use for visual impact is also fundamental to the process of surface articulation in landscape architecture.

The translation of the grading plan and its elevational details into reality is in itself a creative process. Surveys are never totally accurate and the bulldozer can be only roughly specific. Supervision demands creativity in connecting up disparate levels in the spirit of the original design and with regard to the basic concepts of drainage, erosion control, visual effect, and maintenance. Thus minor adjustments are always needed on site, and the design process continues into the execution or implementation of the work.

SUGGESTED READINGS

American Association of State Highway Officials, *A Policy of Geometric Design of Rural Highways.*

Ayres, Quincy Claude, *Soil Erosion and Its Control,* pp. 83–99, "Rainfall and Runoff," pp. 20–38, "Factors Affecting Rate of Erosion."

Beazley, Elizabeth, *Design and Detail of the Space Between Buildings.*

Booth, Norman, *Basic Elements of Landscape Design,* Ch. 1, "Landform."

Crowe, Sylvia, *Garden Design,* pp. 101–105, "Land Form."

Cullen, Gordon, *Townscape,* pp. 175–181, "Change in Level."

Downing, Michael, *Landscape Construction,* Ch. 2, "Earthworks," Ch. 3, "Drainage."

Eckbo, Garrett, *Landscape for Living,* pp. 79–85, "Earth, Earthwork."

Hackett, Brian, "Land Form Design and Cost Factors," *Landscape Architecture,* July 1964, p. 273.

Halprin, Lawrence, *Cities,* pp. 116–127, "The Third Dimension."

Landphair, Harlow, and F. Klatt, *Landscape Architecture Construction.*

Lynch, Kevin, *Site Planning,* pp. 125–128, "The Grading Plan."

MacDougall, E. Bruce, *Microcomputers in Landscape Architecture,* Ch. 6, "Slope, Solar Potential and Runoff," Ch. 5, "Digital Terraine Models," Ch. 10, "Earthwork Calculations."

Marlow, Owen, *Outdoor Design—A Handbook for the Architect and Planner.*

Munson, A. E., *Construction Design for Landscape Architects.*

Nichols, Herbert Lownds, *Moving the Earth.*

Parker, Harry, and John W. McGuire, *Simplified Site Engineering for Engineers and Architects,* pp. 124–129, "Contours," pp. 133–153, "Use of Contours," pp. 155–165, "Cut and Fill."

Simonds, John O., *Landscape Architecture,* pp. 25–35, "Nature Forms, Forces, and Features."

Untermann, Richard, *Principles and Practices of Grading, Drainage and Road Alignment: An Ecological Approach.*

Walker, Theodore, *Site Design and Construction Detailing.*

Weddle, A. E., ed., *Techniques of Landscape Architecture,* pp. 55–72, "Earthworks and Ground Modeling," by Brian Hackett, pp. 73–89, "Hard Surfaces," by T. Cochrane.

POSTSCRIPT

In Chapters 1 and 6 I reviewed some of the factors and changes that indicate the need for a reorganization of our environment. The needs of an expanding population have to be fulfilled without destroying natural resources. I have tried to develop an environmental theory responsive to this concept which can contribute to the location and building of new communities and the revitalization of established but decaying cities. In it, natural and ecological factors interact with social needs and behavioral analysis in a creative process called landscape architecture, which includes as indispensable ingredients aesthetic sensitivity and a concern for visual quality. The theory assumes a technology for construction and implementation, and implies methodologies for evaluating resource data and environmental quality.

FIGURE P.1
The interaction of subject areas is illustrated by the matrix. Each number represents a potential discussion topic.

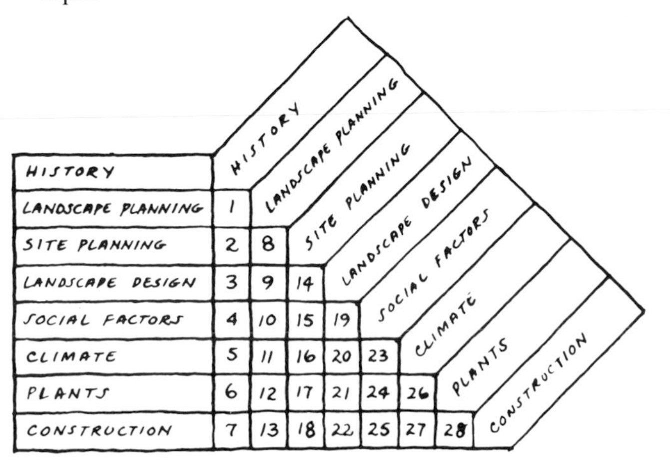

I have tried to stress the interrelationship of the scales of operation from regional planning to detailed design, and I emphasize further by means of the matrix (Fig. P.1) how the subject areas of the various chapters interact. Thus history and climate (5) can be discussed in terms of early solutions to the problems of counteracting the adverse effects of weather. The social implications of regional landscape planning (10) is a subject dealing with perception and evaluation of landscape, its "imageability," and the socioeconomic pressures of the recreation industry. The relationships between site planning and regional policy (8) are represented by the concept of the environmental impact statement in which the effect of a project is measured in terms of regional impact. The use of social analysis in the development of a site plan (15) deals with development of a program that will provide those facilities most desired by the users in a form which can be used. The influence of climate and microclimate on the use of open space (23) is a subject concerned with behavioral analysis and the technology of microclimate. There are innumerable ways in which each specialized area of knowledge relates to others.

By now it must be clear that landscape architecture is a very complex profession involving a wide range of possible tasks with many scientific and technical inputs (Fig. P.2). It is a profession involving interdisciplinary relationships on the basis of which decisions about the planning and design of the environment are made. At the same time, it is a profession of judgment—value judgments requiring an attitude of stewardship and responsibility to alternative futures and a commit-

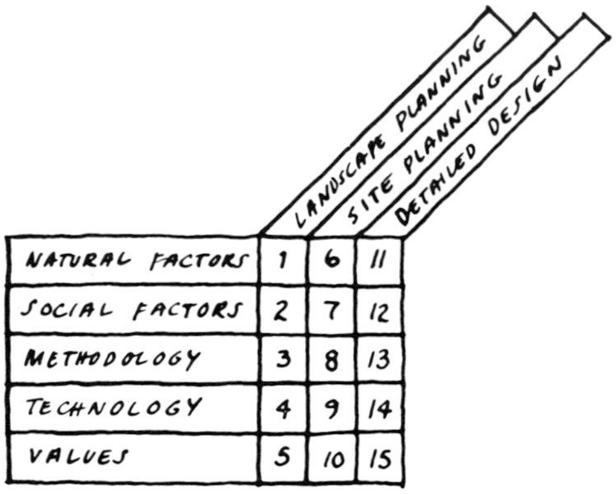

	LANDSCAPE PLANNING	SITE PLANNING	DETAILED DESIGN
NATURAL FACTORS	1	6	11
SOCIAL FACTORS	2	7	12
METHODOLOGY	3	8	13
TECHNOLOGY	4	9	14
VALUES	5	10	15

FIGURE P.2
The five basic components of landscape architecture apply at all scales. Each number represents a possible synthetic phase in the process of landscape design and planning.

ment to environmental health and fitness for human use. The landscape architect may be seen as a bridge between the natural scientist and the land developer and economist, and as an advocate for society attempting to secure the wise use of resources and the prevention of catastrophic consequences resulting from ill-considered social intervention in the ecosystem.

We must remember that theory without implementation has little use. It is necessary therefore to develop a political ability at various levels so that good design will be understood and built by the client and planning policies will be approved by the community, then legislated, and enforced. Finally, we must be equipped to study the effects and results of our work so that improvements can be effected from experience and, as a consequence, the theory improved through practice.

BIBLIOGRAPHY

Adams, William H. *The French Garden 1500–1800*. New York: George Braziller, 1964.

Alexander, Christopher. *Pattern Language*. New York: Oxford University Press, 1977.

Alexander, Christopher. *The City as a Mechanism for Sustaining Human Contact*. Berkeley, Calif.: State University Center for Planning and Development Research, Working Paper No. 50.

Alexander, Christopher. *Notes on the Synthesis of Form*. Cambridge, Mass.: Harvard University Press, 1964.

American Academy of Political and Social Science. *Recreation in the Age of Automation*, Paul F. Douglas, et al., eds. Philadelphia, 1957.

American Association of State Highway Officials. *A Policy of Geometric Design of Rural Highways*, rev. ed., Washington, D.C., 1966.

American Society of Landscape Architects. *Colonial Gardens: The Landscape Architecture of George Washington's Time*. George Washington Bicentennial Commission, Washington, D.C., 1932.

Anderson, Paul F. *Regional Landscape Analysis*. Reston, Va.: Environmental Design Press, 1980.

Appleyard, Donald. *Liveable Streets*. Berkeley: University of California Press, 1981.

Ardrey, Robert. *African Genesis*. New York: Atheneum, 1963.

Ardrey, Robert. *The Territorial Imperative*. New York: Atheneum, 1966.

Arnold, Henry F. *Trees in Urban Design*. New York: Van Nostrand Reinhold, 1980.

Ashihara, Yoshimoto. *Exterior Design in Architecture*. New York: Van Nostrand Reinhold, 1981.

Ayres, Quincy Claude. *Soil Erosion and Its Control*. New York, London: McGraw Hill Book, 1936.

Bacon, Edmond H. *Design of Cities*, rev. ed., New York: Penguin Books, 1976.

Baker, Geoffrey H., and Bruno Funaro. *Parking*. New York: Reinhold, 1958.

Bates, Marston. *The Forest and the Sea: A Look at the Economy of Nature and the Ecology of Man*. New York: Random House, 1960.

Bates, Marston. *Man in Nature*. Englewood Cliffs, N.J.: Prentice-Hall, 1961.

Beazley, Elizabeth. *Design and Detail of the Space Between Buildings*. London: Architectural Press, 1960.

Beazley, Elizabeth. *Designed for Recreation: A Practical Handbook for All Concerned with Providing Leisure Facilities in the Countryside*. London: Faber and Faber, 1969.

Belknap, Raymond, and John Furtado. *Three Approaches to Environmental Resource Analysis*. Washington, D.C.: Conservation Foundation, 1967.

Berral, Julia S. *The Garden: An Illustrated History*. New York: Viking Press, 1966.

Blake, Peter. *God's Own Junkyard: The Planned Deterioration of America's Landscape*. New York: Holt, Rinehart and Winston, 1964.

Blomfield, Reginald. *The Formal Garden in England*. London: Macmillan, 1892.

Booth, Norman. *Basic Elements of Landscape Architectural Design*. New York: Elsevier, 1983.

Bracken, John. *Planting Design*. Pennsylvania State College, Pa., 1957.

Brambilla, Roberto, and Gianni Longo. *For Pedestrians Only—Planning, Design and Management of Traffic-free Zones*. New York: Whitney Library of Design, 1977.

Bring, Mitchell. *Japanese Gardens*. New York: McGraw-Hill, 1981.

Britz, Richard. *The Edible City—Resource Manual*. Los Altos, Calif.: William Kaufman, 1981.

Brooks, John. *Room Outside, A Plan for the Garden*. London: Thames and Hudson, 1969.

Brown, Jane. *Gardens of a Golden Afternoon*. New York: Van Nostrand Reinhold, 1982.

Buckman, Harry O., and Nyle C. Brady. *The Nature and Properties of Soils: A College Text of Edaphology*, 6th rev. ed. New York: Macmillan, 1960.

Building Research Station. *Current Papers*, No. 20. "Designing Against Noise from Road Traffic." London: H.M.S.O., 1971.

Butler, George D. *Introduction to Community Recreation*, 3rd ed. Prepared for the National Recreation Association, New York: McGraw-Hill Book Co., 1959.

Caborn, James M. *Shelterbelts and Micro-Climate*. Great Britain Forestry Commission Bulletin No. 29. Edinburgh, 1960.

Caborn, James M. *Shelterbelts and Windbreaks*. London: Faber and Faber, 1965.

Callenbach, Ernest. *Ecotopia*. Berkeley: Banyan Tree Books, 1975.

Canter, Larry. *Environmental Impact Assessment*. New York: McGraw-Hill, 1977.

Carpenter, Philip L., Theodore D. Walker and Frederck O. Landphair. *Plants in the Landscape*. San Francisco: W. H. Freeman, 1975.

Chadwick, George F. *The Park and Town: Public Landscape in the 19th and 20th Centuries*. London: Architectural Press, 1966.

Chadwick, George F. *The Works of Sir Joseph Paxton, 1803–1865*. London: Architectural Press, 1961.

Chermayeff, Serge, and Christopher Alexander. *Community and Privacy*. Garden City, N.Y.: Doubleday, 1963.

Ching, Francis. *Architecture, Form, Space and Order*. New York: Van Nostrand Reinhold, 1979.

Church, Thomas. *Gardens are for People*. 2nd ed. New York: McGraw-Hill, 1983.

Clark, H. F. *The English Landscape Garden*. London: Pleiasdes Books, 1948.

Clauston, Brian, ed. *Landscape Design with Plants*. New York: Van Nostrand Reinhold, 1979.

Clay, Grady, ed. *Water and the Landscape*. New York: McGraw-Hill, 1979.

Cleveland, Horace W. S. *Landscape Architecture: As Applied to the Wants of the West*. Pittsburgh: University of Pittsburgh Press, 1965.

Clifford, Derek. *A History of Garden Design*. London: Faber and Faber, 1962.

Coffin, David, ed. *The Italian Gardcn*. Washington: Dumbarton Oaks, 1972.

Colvin, Brenda. *Land and Landscape: Evolution, Design, and Control*, 2nd ed. London: J. Murray, 1970.

———, and Jacqueline Trywhitt. *Trees for Town and Country: A Selection of Sixty Trees Suitable for General Cultivation in England*, 3rd rev. ed. London: Lund, Humphried, 1961.

Cook, David, and David F. Haerbede. *Trees and Shrubs for Noise Abatement*. Research Bulletin 246, The Forest Service in cooperation with the University of Nebraska College of Agriculture, 1971.

Cooper, Clare C. *Easter Hill Village; Some Social Implications of Design*. New York: Free Press, 1975.

Corbett, Michael N. *A Better Place to Live—New Designs for Tomorrow's Communities*. Emmaus, Pa.: Rodale Press, 1981.

Coyle, Davis C. *Conservation, An American Story of Conflict and Accomplishment*. New Brunswick, N.J.: Rutgers University Press, 1957.

Craik, Kenneth H. "Environmental Psychology," in *New Directions in Psychology*, Vol IV. New York: Holt, Rinehart and Winston, 1971.

Cranz, Galen. *The Politics of Park Design*. Cambridge, Mass.: M.I.T. Press, 1982.

Creese, Walter. *The Search for Environment: The Garden City Before and After*. New Haven, Conn.: Yale University Press, 1966.

Crisp, (Sir) Frank. *Medieval Gardens*, limited ed. London: John Land the Bodley Head Ltd., 1924.

Crowe, Sylvia. *Garden Design*. Chicister: Packard Publishing, 1981.

———. *The Landscape of Power*. London: Architectural Press, 1958.

———. *The Landscape of Roads*. London: Architectural Press, 1960.

———. *Tomorrow's Landscape*. London: Architectural Press, 1956.

Crowe, Sylvia, et al. *The Gardens of Moghul India*. London: Thames and Hudson, 1972.

Cullen, Gordon. *Townscape*. New York: Reinhold, 1961.

———. *The Concise Townscape*, new ed. London: Architectural Press, 1971.

Cutler, Laurence Stephan, and Sherrie Stephens Cutler. *Recycling Cities for People—The Urban Design Process*. 2nd ed. Boston, Mass.: CBI Publishing, 1982.

Darling, F. Fraser. *Wilderness and Plenty*. New York: Ballantine Books, 1971.

———, and John P. Milton, eds. *Future Environments for North America*. (Record of the 1965 Conservation Foundation Conference, Warrenton, Va.) Garden City, N.Y.: Natural History Press, 1966.

Dasmann, Raymond F. *Environmental Conservation*, 2nd ed. New York: John Wiley & Sons, 1968.

———. *The Destruction of California*. New York: Macmillan, 1965.

De Chiara, Joseph, and Lee E. Koppelman. *Site Planning Standards*. New York: McGraw-Hill, 1978.

DeGrazia, Sebastian. *Of Time, Work and Leisure*. New York: Twentieth Century Fund, 1962.

Department of the Environment. *The Estate of Outside the DWELLING* (Reactions of Residents to Aspects of Housing Layout). London: H.M.S.O., 1972.

Dickert, Thomas, ed. *Environmental Impact Assessment: Improving the Process*. Berkeley, Calif.: University of California Extension, 1973.

Diekelmann, John, and Robert Schuster. *Natural Landscaping— Designing with Native Plant Communities*. New York: McGraw-Hill, 1982.

Dober, Richard P. *Campus Planning*. New York: Reinhold, 1963.

Downing, Andres Jackson. *Landscape Gardening and Rural Architecture*, 10th ed., rev. by Frank A. Waugh. New York: John Wiley & Sons, 1921.

Downing, Michael. *Landscape Construction*. London: E and F N Spon, 1977.

Dubos, René. *Man Adapting*. New Haven, Conn.: Yale University Press, 1965.

———. *So Human an Animal*. New York: Charles Scribner's Sons, 1968.

Dutton, Ralph. *The English Garden*. London: B. T. Batsford, 1937.

Eaton, Leonard K. *Landscape Artist in America: The Life and Work of Jens Jensen*. Chicago: University of Chicago Press, 1964.

Eckbo, Garrett. *Home Landscape*, revised and enlarged ed. New York: McGraw-Hill, 1978.

———. *Landscape for Living*. New York: Architectural Record, with Duell, Sloan & Pearce, 1950.

———. *Urban Landscape Design*. New York: McGraw-Hill, 1964.

Elsner, Gary, and Richard Smardon. *Our National Landscape*. Berkeley: USDA Forest Service, 1979.

Fabos, Julius G., Gordon T. Milde, and V. Michael Weinmayr. *Frederick Law Olmsted, S.R., Founder of Landscape Architecture in America*. Amherst: University of Massachusetts Press, 1968.

———, with Richard Careaga, Christopher Greene, and

Stephanie Williston. *Model for Landscape Resource Assessment*. Amherst, Mass.: Department of Landscape Architecture and Regional Planning, 1973.

Fairbrother, Nan. *Men and Gardens*. London: Hogarth Press, 1956.

Favretti, Rudy J., and J. P. Favretti. *Landscape and Gardens for Historic Buildings*. Nashville: American Association for State and Local History, 1978.

———. *New Lives, New Landscape: Planning for the 21st Century*. New York: Alfred A. Knopf, 1970.

Fein, Albert. *Frederick Law Olmsted and the American Environmental Tradition*. New York: G. Braziller, 1972.

———. *Landscape into Cityscape: Frederick Law Olmsted's Plans for a Greater New York City*. Ithaca, N.Y.: Cornell University Press, 1968.

Fox, Helen. *Andre le Notre, Garden Architect to Kings*. New York: Crown, 1962.

Freidberg, M. Paul. *Play and Interplay*. New York: Mcamillan, 1970.

Gaines, Richard L. *Interior Plantscaping—Building Design for Interior Foliage Plants*. New York: Architectural Record Books, 1977.

Gans, Herbert J. *The Levittowners: Ways of Life and Politics in a New Suburban Community*. New York: Pantheon Books, 1967.

Gardner, Victor R. *Basic Horticulture*, rev. ed. New York: Macmillan, 1951.

Geiger, Rudolf. *The Climate Near the Ground*. Coupta Technica, Inc., trans. Cambridge, Mass.: Harvard University Press, 1963.

Giedion, Sigfried. *Space, Time and Architecture: The Growth of a New Tradition*, 5th ed. Cambridge, Mass.: Harvard University Press, 1967.

Givoni, B. *Man, Climate and Architecture*, 2nd ed. London: Applied Science Publishers, 1976.

Goffman, Erving. *Behavior in Public Places: Notes on the Social Organization of Gatherings*. New York: Free Press of Glencoe, 1963.

Gothein, M. Louis. *The History of Garden Art*. Walter P. Wright, ed; Laura Archer-Hind, trans. London and Toronto: J. M. Dent & Sons; New York: E. P. Dutton & Co., 1928.

Graham, Dorothy. *Chinese Gardens: Gardens of the Contemporary Scene*. New York: Dodd, Mead & Co., 1938.

Green, David. *Gardener to Queen Anne, Henry Wise and the Formal Garden*. London, New York: Oxford University Press, 1956.

Gutkind, Erwin A. *Our World From the Air: An International Survey of Man and His Environment*. Garden City, N.Y.: Doubleday, 1952.

———. "Our World from the Air: Conflict and Adaptation," in *Man's Role in Changing the Face of the Earth*, William L. Thomas, ed. Chicago: University of Chicago Press, 1956.

Hackett, Brian. *Landscape Planning: An Introduction to Theory and Practice*. Newcastle-upon-Tyne: Oriel Press, 1971.

———. *Planting Design*. New York: McGraw-Hill, 1979.

Hadfield, Miles. *Gardens*. New York: Putnam, 1962.

Hall, Edward T. *The Hidden Dimension*. Garden City, N.Y.: Doubleday, 1966.

———. *The Silent Language*. Greenwich, Conn.: Fawcett Press, 1967.

Halprin, Lawrence. *Cities*. New York: Reinhold, 1963.

———. *Notebooks, 1959–71*. Cambridge, Mass.: MIT Press, 1972.

———, and Jim Burns. *Taking Part—A Workshop Approach to Collective Creativity*. Cambridge, Mass.: MIT Press, 1974.

Hammond, John, et al. *A Strategy for Energy Conservation*. Davis, California, 1974.

Hannebaum, Leroy. *Landscape Design*. Reston, Va.: Reston, 1981.

Harvey, John. *Medieval Gardens*. Beaverton, Oregon: Timber Press, 1981.

Hazlehurst, F. Hamilton. *Garden of Illusion—The Genius of Andre le Notre*. Nashville, Tenn.: Vanderbilt University Press, 1981.

———. *Jacques Boyceau and the French Formal Garden*. Athens: University of Georgia Press, 1966.

Hecksher, August. *Open Spaces: The Life of American Cities*. New York: Harper and Row, 1977.

Hester, Randolph. *Neighborhood Space—Planning Neighborhood Space with People*, 2nd ed. New York: Van Nostrand Reinhold, 1984.

———, and Frank Smith. *Community Goal Setting*. Stroudsburg, Pa.: Hutchinson Ross, 1982.

Holborn, Mark. *The Ocean in the Sand. Japan: From Landscape to Garden*. Boulder, Colorado: Shambala Publications, 1978.

Horiguchi, Sutami. *Tradition of Japanese Gardens*. Tokyo: Kokusai Bunka Shinkokai, 1962.

Howard, (Sir) Ebenezer. *Garden Cities of Tomorrow*. F. S. Osborn, ed. London: Faber and Faber, 1951.

Hudak, Joseph. *Trees for Every Purpose*. New York: McGraw-Hill, 1980.

Hunt, John Dixon, and Peter Willis, eds. *The Genius of the Place—The English Landscape Garden 1620–1820*. New York: Harper & Row, 1975.

Hunter, Margaret K., and Edgar H. *The Indoor Garden*. New York: John Wiley & Sons, 1978.

Hussey, Christopher. *The Picturesque: Studies in a Point of View*. London and New York: Putnam, 1962.

Huth, Hans. *Nature and the American: Three Centuries of Changing Attitudes*. Berkeley: University of California Press, 1957.

Hyams, Edward S. *The English Garden*. London: Thames and Hudson, 1971.

———. *A History of Gardens and Gardening*. New York: Praeger, 1971.

International Union for Conservation of Nature and Natural Resources. *Towards a New Relationship between Man and Nature in Temperate Lands*. Morges, Switzerland: IUCN, 1967.

Ittleson, W. H., et al. *An Introduction to Environmental Psychology*. New York: Holt, Reinhart and Winston, 1974.

Jackson, John B. *American Space*. New York: W. W. Norton and Company, 1972.

Jacobs, Jane. *Death and Life of Great American Cities*. New York: Random House, 1961.

Jellicoe, Geoffrey A. *Studies in Landscape Design*. London and New York: Oxford University Press, 1960.

Jellicoe, Geoffrey, and Susan Jellicoe. *Landscape of Man*. London: Thames and Hudson, 1975.

Jellicoe, Susan, and Geoffrey Jellicoe. *Water*. London: A & C Black, 1971.

Jones, H. *John Muir and the Sierra Club*. San Francisco: Sierra Club, 1965.

Jourdain, Margaret. *The Work of William Kent: Artist, Painter, Designer and Landscape Gardener*. London: Country Life; New York: Charles Scribners & Sons, 1948.

Kahn, Herman. *The Year 2000*. New York: Macmillan, 1967.

Kaplan, S., and R. Kaplan, eds. *Humanscape: Environments for People*. N. Scituate, Mass.: Duxbury Press, 1978.
Kassler, Elizabeth B. *Modern Gardens and the Landscape*. New York: Museum of Modern Art, Doubleday, 1964.
Kelley, Bruce. *The Art of the Olmsted Landscape*. New York: The Arts Publisher, 1981.
Keswick, Maggie. *The Chinese Garden*. New York: Rizzoli, 1978.
Krier, Rob. *Urban Space*. New York: Rizzoli International Publications, 1979.
Krutilla, John, ed. *Natural Environments*. Baltimore: Johns Hopkins University Press, 1972.
Land Design/Research Inc. *Cost Effective Site Planning—Single Family Development*. Washington, D.C.: NAHB, 1976 (2nd printing).
Landmark '71. Berkeley: Department of Landscape Architecture, University of California, 1971.
Landphair, Harlow C., and Fred Klatt, Jr. *Landscape Architecture Construction*. New York: Elsevier North Holland, 1979.
Lang, Jon, et al. *Designing for Human Behavior*. Stroudsburg, Pa.: Community Development Series, 1974.
Lassey, William. *Planning in Rural Environments*. New York: McGraw-Hill, 1977.
Laurie, Ian C., ed. *Nature in Cities*. Chichester, John Wiley and Sons, 1979.
Laurie, Michael. "A History of Aesthetic Conservation in California," in *Landscape Planning*, Vol. 6, 1979. Amsterdam: Elsevier Science.
Lehram, Jonas. *Earthly Paradise—Garden and Courtyard in Islam*. Berkeley: University of California Press, 1980.
Leighton, Anne. *Early American Gardens*. Boston: Houghton Mifflin, 1970.
Leopold, Aldo S. *A Sand County Almanac, and Sketches Here and There*. New York: Oxford University Press, 1950.
Lewis, Philip H. *Regional Design for Human Impact*. Kaukauna, Wis.: Thomas, 1969.
Litton, R. Burton. *Forest Landscape Description and Inventories—A Basis for Land Planning and Design*. U.S. Department of Agriculture, Forest Research Paper PSW49, Berkeley: U.S. Department of Agriculture, 1968.
———. "Landscape and Aesthetic Quality," in *America's Changing Environment*, R. Revelle and H. H. Landsberg, eds. Boston: Beacon Press, 1970.
Lockwood, Alice G. B. *Gardens of Colony and State: Gardens and Gardeners of the American Colonies and of the Republic before 1840*. New York: Charles Scribners & Sons, 1931–1934.
Lovejoy, Derek, ed. *Land Use and Landscape Planning*, 2nd ed. Glasgow: Leonard Blackie Publishing Group, 1979.
Lynch, Kevin. *Site Planning*. Cambridge, Mass.: MIT Press, 1962.
———. *What Time Is This Place*. Cambridge, Mass.: MIT Press, 1972.
———. *A Theory of Good City Form*. Cambridge Mass.: MIT Press, 1981.
———. *Site Planning*, 3rd ed. Cambridge, Mass.: MIT Press, 1984.
MacDougall, E. Bruce. *Microcomputers in Landscape Architecture*. New York: Elsevier, 1983.
McHarg, Ian L. *Design with Nature*. Garden City, N.Y.: Natural History Press, 1969.
———. "Ecological Determinism," in *Future Environments for North America*, Frank Darling, ed. Garden City, N.Y.: Natural History Press, 1966.
McLean, Teresa. *Medieval English Gardens*. New York: Viking Press, 1980.
Maddi, S. R., and D. W. Fiske. *Functions of Varied Experience*. Homewood, Ill.: Dorsey Press, 1961.
Marlowe, Olwen C. *Outdoor Design—Handbook for the Architect and Planner*. New York: Watson-Guptill, 1977.
Marsh, George Perkins. *Man and Nature*, David Lowenthal, ed. Cambridge, Mass.: Harvard University Press, 1963.
Marsh, William M. *Environmental Analysis—For Land Use and Site Planning*. New York: McGraw-Hill, 1978.
Massingham, Betty. *Miss Jekyll: Portrait of a Great Gardener*. London: Country Life, 1966.
Masson, Georgina. *Italian Gardens*. London: Thames and Hudson, 1961.
Mather, J. R. *Climatology: Fundamentals and Applications*. New York: McGraw-Hill, 1974.
Mazria, Edward. *The Passive Solar Energy Book*. Emmaus, Pa.: Rodale Books, 1979.
Meyerson, Martin. *Face of the Metropolis*. Prepared for the National Council of Good Cities. New York: Random House, 1963.
Moffat, Anne Simon, and Marc Schiler. *Landscape Design that Saves Energy*. New York: William Morrow, 1981.
Morse, Edward S. *Japanese Homes and Their Surroundings*. New York: Dover, 1961.
Moynihan, Elizabeth B. *Paradise as a Garden in Persia and Moghul India*. New York: George Braziller, 1979.
Muir, John. *Yosemite and the Sierra Nevada*. Charlotte C. Mauk, ed. Boston: Houghton, Mifflin, 1948.
Mumford, Lewis. *The Brown Decades: A Study of the Arts in America*, 2nd rev. ed. New York: Dover, 1955.
Munson, Albe E. *Construction Design for Landscape Architects*. New York: McGraw-Hill, 1974.
Nash, Roderick. *Wilderness and the American Mind*. New Haven, Conn.: Yale University Press, 1967.
Newman, Oscar. *Defensible Space: Crime Prevention through Urban Design*. New York: Macmillan, 1972.
Newsom, Samuel. *A Thousand Years of Japanese Gardens*, 3rd ed. Tokyo: Tokyo News Service, 1957.
Newton, Norman T. *Design on the Land: The Development of Landscape Architecture*. Cambridge, Mass.: Belknap Press of the Harvard University Press, 1971.
Nichols, Herbert Lownds. *Moving the Earth: The Workbook of Excavation*. Greenwich, Conn.: North Castle Books, 1955.
Odum, Eugene P. *Fundamentals of Ecology*, 2nd ed. Philadelphia: Saunders, 1959.
Olgay, Victor. *Design with Climate*. Princeton, N.J.: Princeton University Press, 1963.
Ortolano, Leonard. *Environmental Planning and Decision Making*. New York: John Wiley and Sons, 1984.
Parker, Harry, and John W. McGuire. *Simplified Site Engineering for Architects and Builders*. New York: John Wiley and Sons, 1954.
Patri, Tito, David C. Streatfield, and Thomas J. Ingmire. *Early Warning System*. Berkeley: University of California, Department of Landscape Architecture, 1970.
Perin, Constance. *With Man in Mind: An Interdisciplinary Prospectus for Environmental Change*. Cambridge, Mass.: MIT Press, 1970.
Perry, Francis. *The Water Garden*. New York: Van Nostrand Reinhold, 1981.
Peterson, Peggy Long. "The ID and the Image," *Landmark '66*. Berkeley: Department of Landscape Architecture, University of California, 1966.

Pevsner, Nikolaus. "The Genesis of the Picturesque," *Architectural Review*, Vol. 96, November, 1944, pp. 139–166.
Pile, John. *Design*. New York: W. W. Norton, 1979.
Platt, Charles. *Italian Gardens*. New York: Harper and Brothers, 1894.
Porteous, J. D. *Environment and Behavior: Planning and Everyday Urban Life*. Reading, Mass.: Addison-Wesley, 1977.
Proshansky, H. M., ed. *Environmental Psychology*. New York: Holt, Rinehart & Winston, 1970.
Rapoport, Amos. *House Form and Culture*. Englewood Cliffs, N.J.: Prentice-Hall, 1969.
Rau, John G., and David C. Wooten, eds. *Environmental Impact Analysis Handbook*. New York: McGraw-Hill, 1980.
Reps, John W. *The Making of Urban America: A History of City Planning in the United States*. Princeton, N.J.: Princeton University Press, 1965.
Ritter, Paul. *Planning for Man and Motor*. Elmsford, New York: Pergamon, 1964.
Robbins, Wilfred W., T. Elliot Weier, and Ralph Stocking. *Botany: An Introduction to Plant Science*, 2nd ed. New York: John Wiley & Sons, 1957.
Robinette, Gary O. *Plants, People and Environmental Quality*. U.S. Department of the Interior. Washington, D.C.: G.P.O., 1973.
Robinson, Florence Bell. *Palette of Plants*. Champaign, Ill.: Garrard Press, 1950.
———. *Planting Design*. New York: McGraw-Hill Book Co.: London, Wittlesey House, 1940.
Robinson, William. *The English Flower Garden*. London: J. Murray, 1909.
Rubenstein, Harvey. *A Guide to Site and Environmental Planning*. New York and London: John Wiley & Sons, 1969.
Rubenstein, Harvey M. *Central City Malls*. New York: John Wiley & Sons, 1978.
Rudofsky, Bernard. *Architecture without Architects*. New York: Museum of Modern Art, 1965.
———. *Streets for People*. New York: Van Nostrand Reinhold, 1982.
Rutledge, Albert J. *Anatomy of a Park*. New York: McGraw-Hill, 1971.
Scientific American. *Cities*. New York, 1965.
Scott, Mel. *American City Planning Since 1890*. Berkeley, University of California Press, 1969.
Scrivens, Stephen. *Interior Planting in Large Buildings - A Handbook for Architects, Interior Designers and Horticulturists*. London: Architectural Press, Ltd., 1980.
Sears, Paul B. *Life and Environment*. New York: Teachers' College, Columbia University, 1939.
———. *Where There is Life*. New York: Dell, 1962.
Shepard, Paul. *Man in the Landscape: A Historical View of the Aesthetics of Nature*. New York: Alfred A. Knopf, 1968.
Shepheard, Peter. *Gardens*. London: MacDonald and Company, in association with Council of Industrial Design, 1969.
———. *Modern Gardens*. London: Architectural Press, 1953.
Shepherd, John C., and Geoffrey A. Jellicoe. *Italian Gardens of the Renaissance*. New York: Charles Scribners & Sons, 1925.
Simonds, John O. *Earthscape—A Manual of Environmental Planning*. New York: McGraw-Hill, 1978.
———. *Landscape Architecture*. New York: F. W. Dodge, 1961.
Siren, Osvald. *Gardens of China*. New York: Ronald Press, 1949.
Skinner, B. F. *Science and Human Behavior*. London and New York: Macmillan, 1953.
Sommer, Robert. *Personal Space: The Behavioral Basis of Design*. Englewood Cliffs, N.J.: Prentice-Hall, 1969.
Sommer, Robert. *Design Awareness*. San Francisco: Rinehart Press, 1971.
Sorenson, Carl Theodore. *The Origin of Garden Art*. Kobenhavn: Danish Architectural Press, Arkitektens Forlag, 1963.
Sprin, Ann Whiston. *The Granite Garden*. New York: Basic Books, 1984.
Strong, Roy. *The Renaissance Garden in England*. London: Thames and Hudson, 1979.
Stroud, Dorothy. *Humphry Repton*. London: Country Life, 1962.
———. *Capability Brown*. London: Country Life, 1950.
Tamura, Tsuyoshi. *Art of Landscape Gardens in Japan*. Tokyo: Kokusai Bunka Shinkokai (The Society for International Cultural Relations), 1935.
Tandy, Clifford, consultant ed. *Handbook of Urban Landscape*. London: Architectural Press, 1972.
Taylor, Geoffrey. *The Victorian Flower Garden*. London, New York: Skeffington, 1952.
Taylor, Lisa, ed. *Urban Open Spaces*. New York: Rizzoli, 1981.
Taylor, (Lord) Stephen J. L., and Sidney Chave. *Mental Health and the Environment*. Sidney: Longma Green, 1964.
Tetlow, R. J., and S. Sheppard. *Visual Resources of the North East Coal Study Area*. Province of British Columbia, Ministry of the Environment, 1977.
Thacker, Christopher. *The History of Gardens*. London: Croom Helm, 1979.
Thomas, William L., ed. *Man's Role in Changing the Face of the Earth*. (From the 1955 International Symposium on Man's Role in Changing the Face of the Earth.) Chicago: University of Chicago Press, 1956.
Treib, Marc, and Ron Herman. *A Guide to the Gardens of Kyoto*. Tokyo: Shufunotomo Co., 1980.
Tuan, Yi-Fu. *Topophilia—A Study of Environmental Perception, Attitudes and Values*. Englewood Cliffs, N. J.: Prentice-Hall, 1974.
Tunnard, Christopher. *American Skyline: The Growth and Forms of Our Cities and Towns*. Boston: Houghton Mifflin, 1955.
———. *Gardens in the Modern Landscape*, 2nd rev. ed. London: Architectural Press; New York: Charles Scribners & Sons, 1948.
———, and Boris Pushkarev. *Man-Made America—Chaos or Control*? New Haven, Conn.: Yale University Press, 1963.
Twiss, Robert, David Streatfield, and Marin County Planning Department. *Nicassio: Hidden Valley in Transition*. San Rafael, Calif., 1969.
Udall, Stewart. *The Quiet Crisis*. New York: Holt, Rinehart and Winston, 1963.
Untermann, Richard. *Site Planning for Cluster Housing*. New York: Van Nostrand Reinhold, 1977.
———. *Principles and Practices of Grading, Drainage and Road Alignment: An Ecological Approach*. Englewood Cliffs, N.J.: Reston, 1978.
U.S. Outdoor Recreation Resources Review Commission. *Outdoor Recreation for America: A Report to the President and to the Congress*. Washington, D.C., 1962.
Villiers-Stuart, Constance M. *Gardens of the Great Moghals*. London: A. and C. Black, 1913.
———. *Spanish Gardens, Their History, Types and Features*. London: B. T. Batsford, 1929.

Walker, Theodore D. *Site Design and Construction Detailing*. Mesa, Arizona: PDA Publishers, 1978.

Ward, Colin. *The Child in the City*. London: Architectural Press, 1977.

Way, Douglas S. *Terrain Analysis: A Guide to Site Selection Using Aerial Photographic Interpretation*. Stroudsburg, Pa.: Dowden, Hutchinson and Ross, 1973.

Weddle, A. E., ed. *Techniques of Landscape Architecture*. New York: American Elsevier, 1967.

Whyte, William H. *The Last Landscape*. Garden City, N.Y.: Doubleday, 1968.

Wiedenhoft, Ronald. *Cities for People—Practical Measures for Improving Urban Environments*. New York: Van Nostrand Reinhold, 1981.

———. *The Organization Man*. New York: Simon and Schuster, 1956.

———. *The Social Life of Small Urban Spaces*. Washington, D.C.: Conservation Foundation, 1980.

Williams, Wayne. *Recreation Places*. New York: Rheinhold, 1958.

Wright, Richardson Little. *The Story of Gardening: From the Hanging Gardens of Babylon to the Hanging Gardens of New York*. New York: Dodd, Mead, 1934.

Wurman, R. S. and J. Katz. *The Nature of Recreation*. Cambridge, Mass.: M.I.T. Press, 1972.

Zaitzevsky, Cynthia. *F. L. Olmsted and the Boston Park System*. Cambridge, Mass.: Harvard University Press, 1982.

Zion, Robert L. *Trees for Architecture and the Landscape*. New York: Reinhold, 1968.

Zube, Ervin, ed. *An Inventory and Interpretation of Selected Resources of the Island of Nantucket*. Cambridge: University of Massachusetts, Cooperative Extension Service, 1966.

———. *The Islands: Selected Resources of the United States Virgin Islands and Their Relationship to Recreation, Tourism, and Open Space*. Prepared for U.S. Department of Agriculture by the Department of Landscape Architecture, University of Massachusetts, 1968.

———, et al. *Landscape Assessment*. Stroudsburg, Pa.: Dowden, Hutchinson and Ross, 1975.

INDEX